Innovative Research and Practices
in Second Language Acquisition and Bilingualism

Language Learning & Language Teaching (LL&LT)

The LL&LT monograph series publishes monographs, edited volumes and text books on applied and methodological issues in the field of language pedagogy. The focus of the series is on subjects such as classroom discourse and interaction; language diversity in educational settings; bilingual education; language testing and language assessment; teaching methods and teaching performance; learning trajectories in second language acquisition; and written language learning in educational settings.

For an overview of all books published in this series, please see
http://benjamins.com/catalog/lllt

Editors

Nina Spada
Ontario Institute for Studies in Education
University of Toronto

Nelleke Van Deusen-Scholl
Center for Language Study
Yale University

Volume 38

Innovative Research and Practices in Second Language Acquisition and Bilingualism
Edited by John W. Schwieter

Innovative Research and Practices in Second Language Acquisition and Bilingualism

Edited by

John W. Schwieter
Wilfrid Laurier University

John Benjamins Publishing Company
Amsterdam / Philadelphia

The paper used in this publication meets the minimum requirements of
the American National Standard for Information Sciences – Permanence
of Paper for Printed Library Materials, ANSI z39.48-1984.

Library of Congress Cataloging-in-Publication Data

Innovative Research and Practices in Second Language Acquisition and Bilingualism /
    Edited by John W. Schwieter.
    p. cm. (Language Learning & Language Teaching, ISSN 1569-9471 ; v. 38)
Includes bibliographical references and index.
    1. Second language acquisition--Study and teaching. 2. Second language acquisition-
        -Research. 3. Language and languages--Study and teaching. 4. Language
        and languages--Research. 5. Education, Bilingual. 6. Language acquisition.
        I. Schwieter, John W., 1979- editor of compilation.

P118.2.I54   2013
418.0071--dc23   2013020754
ISBN 978 90 272 1317 4   (Hb ; alk. paper)
ISBN 978 90 272 1318 1   (Pb ; alk. paper)
ISBN 978 90 272 7166 2   (Eb)

© 2013 – John Benjamins B.V.
No part of this book may be reproduced in any form, by print, photoprint, microfilm, or any
other means, without written permission from the publisher.

John Benjamins Publishing Co. · P.O. Box 36224 · 1020 ME Amsterdam · The Netherlands
John Benjamins North America · P.O. Box 27519 · Philadelphia PA 19118-0519 · USA

Table of contents

Acknowledgments

In addition to the internal review process by the editor, each of the chapters presented in this book were anonymously reviewed and evaluated by at least two international scholars. It is without a doubt that the expertise and guidance of these peer-reviewers has helped to diversify and strengthen the contents of this book. As such, I would like to extend my sincere gratitude to the following researchers for helping in this important process:

Panos Athanasopoulos, Newcastle University
Joe Barcroft, Washington University
Sara Beaudrie, University of Arizona
Jennifer Behney, Youngstown State University
Alessandro Benati, University of Greenwich
Joyce Bruhn de Garavito, Western University
Alejandro Cuza, Purdue University
Annette de Groot, University of Amsterdam
Eileen Fancher, Florida State University
Aline Ferreira, Wilfrid Laurier University
Fanny Forsberg Lundell, Stockholm University
Deanna Friesen, York University
Susan Gass, Michigan State University
Gregory Keating, San Diego State University
Oksana Laleko, State University of New York at New Paltz
James Lee, University of New South Wales
Juana Liceras, University of Ottawa
Jared Linck, Center for Advanced Study of Language, University of Maryland
Shawn Loewen, Michigan State University
Drew Long, University of Florida
Kim McDonough, Concordia University
Lourdes Ortega, University of Hawai'i at Mānoa
Silvia Perpiñán, Western University
Anat Prior, University of Haifa
Leila Ranta, University of Alberta
Jason Rothman, University of Reading

Gretchen Sunderman, Florida State University
Natasha Tokowicz, University of Pittsburgh
Danielle Thomas, University of Illinois at Urbana-Champaign
Alba Tuninetti, University of Pittsburgh
Bill VanPatten, Michigan State University
Melinda Whong, University of Leeds
Jessica Williams, University of Illinois at Chicago
Wynne Wong, Ohio State University

Preface

John W. Schwieter and Gabrielle Klassen
Wilfrid Laurier University and University of Toronto

This volume brings together theoretical perspectives and empirical studies in second language acquisition (SLA) and bilingualism and discusses their implications for L2 pedagogy. The book has been organized into two main sections that focus on prominent linguistic (i.e., generative) and cognitive theories and together provide a compelling set of state-of-the-art works. Part I consists of studies that give rise to innovative applications for second language teaching and learning and Part II discusses how findings from cognitive research can inform practices for L2 teaching and learning.

Part I, begins with a contribution that is intended to introduce a new way of theoretically contemplating SLA and bilingualism by examining the often overlooked idea that language is multi-faceted. In Chapter 1, VanPatten puts forth the notion that language consists of two primary domains including mental representation and language use. Within each of these are separable sub-domains, some of which are argued to be amenable to L2 instruction and practice while others are resistant. With these ideas in mind, Wong's Chapter 2 applies these theories of mental representation and skill to the L2 classroom. The author reviews the multifaceted nature of language in terms of classroom teaching and acquisition, and offers a melange of practical applications. The author provides specific examples of each type of learning, and explains how to use the complexity of language to the advantage of pedagogical design and execution.

Chapter 3 by Behney and Gass presents the first empirical study to date in which the differential effects of priming are compared when the prime is either a subject or a direct object relative clause. The results of their study are discussed in the context of learning complex L2 structures, contrasting the effects of priming to the Accessibility Hierarchy. Implications are outlined of syntactic priming research on pedagogical approaches. In Chapter 4, Long and Rothman elaborate on sociocultural theoretical principles to explore how researchers may deepen their commitment to unify theoretical/practical concerns and L2 research agendas. They argue that a redefinition of basic implicit categories in L2 teaching and learning is an essential element in validating the relevance of scholars as practitioners. By examining evidence from a previous study that incomplete pedagogy prohibits native-like development in tutored L2 learners because of the repercussions of the Competing Systems Hypothesis (CSH), this chapter emphasizes the importance of linguistically-informed pedagogical resources and instruction. In Chapter 5, Bruhn de Garavito examines the concept of grammatical mood selection in L2 learners. The results of previous research give direction for how to teach this difficult area of language. The author compares intermediate, advanced, and native speakers to show where textbooks should adapt to meet the gap in acquisition.

Barcroft provides an overview of methods of teaching L2 vocabulary in Chapter 6. The author posits the input-based incremental (IBI) model as a culmination of what to teach, how to teach it, and when to teach it. Several resources are included in this chapter, from a checklist of components necessary for an effective vocabulary lesson to a series of principles to guide lesson preparation. This chapter uses research on vocabulary acquisition to form models of acquisition, providing L2 professionals, teachers, and researchers alike, with an effective guideline for teaching and investigating L2 vocabulary acquisition. Chapter 7 authored by Presson, Davy, and MacWhinney, discusses advances in language learning technology. The author explores how these advances benefit language learners and what areas still need improvement. In Chapter 8 by Perpiñán, the researcher discusses modality and linguistic structure in experimental testing. These variables may have an impact on interpretation of analyses by comparing results of oral (implicit) and written (explicit) tasks of the same nature, as well as direct object and oblique syntactic structures in relative clauses. This chapter explores these two sets of contrasting variables in native and L2 speakers (of English and Arabic) and shows how natural development and level of difficulty can inform pedagogical organisation and research task design. Chapter 9 by Cuza and colleagues addresses variation in L2, bilingual, and monolingual speakers of Spanish across age groups. It considers the extent to which child heritage speakers compared to adult heritage speakers have knowledge of a particular grammatical structure in their less-dominant language. By exploring their competence on aspectual morphology, the chapter puts forth important implications between current psycholinguistic theories and heritage language instruction.

Part II consists of several chapters that present cognitive perspectives on SLA and bilingualism and discuss their implications for pedagogy. Chapter 10 by Friesen and Bialystok reviews studies that investigate the interaction between language control and representation during bilingual language processing tasks and discusses how this relationship can inform L2 pedagogy. The chapter compares bilingual and monolingual children's executive control and language abilities, and compares the strengths and weaknesses of each. The authors go on to suggest how immersion of the bilingual language learner can practically apply to the strengthening of both areas of language: representational and executive control. In Chapter 11, Schwieter and Ferreira review recent developments in bilingual research exploring the specific cognitive underpinnings of bilingual speech production. In particular, the chapter explores how the bilingual mind selects the language in which to speak and overcomes cross-linguistic lexical interference in order to support and execute lexical access. Sunderman & Fancher in Chapter 12 take the reader from bilingual speech production to comprehension by describing a theoretical account of selectivity effects in word recognition with a particular focus on the L2 learner. Theoretical models of bilingual speech comprehension are reviewed and pedagogical techniques are discussed that could facilitate lexical access among L2 learners. Chapter 13 by Jarvis and colleagues reviews current research exploring a variety of types of linguistic transfer in bilingualism, namely: conceptual knowledge; patterns of conceptualization and event construal; attention and recall; and working memory capacity. Results of this study outline how these areas of research can be applied to L2 teaching and learning.

Chapter 14 concludes the book with a summative commentary by Lee, which synthesizes and ties together many issues raised in the volume. It provides summative remarks, based on the book contributions, on where the field is headed in the context of some of the most innovative and thought-provoking issues in SLA and bilingualism. This final chapter is meant to provide an enriching commentary that takes a direct standpoint based on the common ground of the contributions and point to future research. Lee's chapter also concludes the book by reflecting on each chapter's contribution to current and future research in SLA and bilingualism.

In all, this volume focuses on linguistic and cognitive research and their relationships to and implications for second language teaching and learning. With the vast number of questions still to be answered and the huge gap for improvement in teaching, this volume sets the stage towards a better understanding of linguistic and cognitive perspectives in SLA and bilingualism and their implications for L2 pedagogy. In all, the studies represented in this volume put forth ways in which L2 pedagogy can best reflect the complex process of L2 acquisition.

PART I

Linguistic perspectives and implications for L2 pedagogy

CHAPTER 1

Mental representation and skill
in instructed SLA*

Bill VanPatten
Michigan State University

In this chapter, I argue something that ought to be self-evident but is often overlooked in instructed SLA research: language is multifaceted and not reducible to a single concept. In simplest terms, this means that language consists of two broad domains: (1) mental representation, and (2) skill (language use). Within each domain there are separable sub-domains (e.g., syntax, phonology, lexicon, semantics, and so on in mental representation; and reading, writing, speaking, and so on, in the domain of skill). The implications of such a view are that the development of different parts of language may respond to different stimuli in the environment. What is more, some domains may be more or less amenable to instruction and practice while others are stubborn or resistant to external influences. I also discuss and argue against a commonly held notion in language teaching: that grammar is a skill. As I argue, grammar is part of the mental representation, and is not something that can be internalized "via practice." What is more, the kind of grammar that instructors use in classrooms (e.g., pedagogical grammar) is not how language is represented in the mind/brain of a human being, and thus is not something with which one "develops skill."

1. Introduction

One of the fundamental questions in instructed SLA is whether or not instruction makes a difference (e.g., Long 1983; Norris & Ortega, 2000; Spada & Tomita, 2010). Two critical issues underlie this question. The first is what is meant by instruction. The second is what is meant by language. In this essay, I will address the second

* This paper is a revised version of a paper originally published by the *International Journal of English Studies* in 2010 (*IJES* 10 (1): 2010, pp. 1–18). We are grateful to the journal and to the editor, Aquilino Sánchez, for the permission to publish this version here.

question,[1] discussing something that ought to be self-evident (and not necessarily a new idea) but is often overlooked in instructed SLA research: language is multifaceted and not reducible to a single concept. In simplest terms, this means that language consists of two broad domains: (1) mental representation, and (2) skill (use), although within each domain there are separable sub-domains (e.g., syntax, phonology, lexicon, semantics, and so on in mental representation; and reading, writing, speaking, and so on, in skill). The implications of such a view are that the development of different parts of language may respond to different stimuli in the environment. What is more, some domains may be more or less amenable to explicit instruction and practice while others are stubborn or resistant to external influences.

2.   Language as mental representation

2.1   What is mental representation of language?

I take mental representation to mean the abstract, implicit, and underlying linguistic system in a speaker's mind/brain (VanPatten & Benati 2010: 107). By *abstract* I mean that the linguistic system is not something akin to a set of textbook or prescriptive rules, but instead is a collection of abstract properties from which rule-like behavior is derived (e.g., Harley & Noyer 1999; Jackendoff 2002; Radford 2001; Rothman 2010; White 2003). From a Minimalist Perspective (Chomsky 1995; Herschensohn 2000; Radford 1997) these abstract properties include universal constraints on language (e.g., Structure Dependency, Extended Projection Principle, Overt Pronoun Constraint, Binding) as well functional categories and features (e.g., Tense, Agreement, Aspect, Number) that can vary across languages (parametric variation). As an example, let's look at auxiliary *do* in yes-no questions in English. Typical yes/no question are formed using *do*, while other options, such as subject-verb inversion, are prohibited as in (1) and (2) below. The reverse is true in a language like Spanish that has subject-verb inversion and lacks an auxiliary like *do* as in (3).

(1)   Does John live near the university?
(2)   *Lives John near the university?
(3)   ¿Vive Juan cerca de la universidad?

While we can describe the use of *do* in questions with a statement like "insert *do* for yes-no questions and invert with the subject," in a mental grammar of English

---

1.   I have addressed the nature of instruction in other publications (e.g., VanPatten, 1996, 2009). The reader is also referred to Doughty (2003).

do is the result of a series of interactions between abstract features of the grammar. Comp, which is the head of the Complementizer Phrase (CP), contains the feature + STRONG. Strong Comp forces the movement of *do* out of the Inflectional Phrase (Infl) where it is generated to carry Tense features given that English is +STRONG for Tense as well. These kinds of syntactic operations occur when features are +STRONG in a language, requiring lexical insertion or movement of a constituent into a phrase to get that feature checked. Thus, our textbook type rule of "insert do and invert subject and auxiliary verb" is not what actually exists in the grammar or in people's minds; it is a specific short hand way to describe a particular consequence of more abstract principles of the grammar.

By *implicit* I mean that the content of the mental representation exists outside of awareness: speakers may know they have mental representation for language but they generally do not know the content of that representation. In the example just given, speakers of English (except linguists) do not consciously know about CPs, Comp and the concept of ±STRONG as a parametric variation of features across languages. They can accept sentences such as *Do you know the way to San Jose?* as possible English sentences while rejecting **Know you the way to San Jose?* as possible English sentences. However, they cannot articulate why based on the abstract principles of grammar that underlie their judgments. This knowledge exists outside of their awareness.

Finally, by *underlying*, I mean that the linguistic system underlies all surface manifestations of language. What is produced by a speaker must conform to the content of this mental representation, be it the utterances of two-year old or the utterances of a 30-year old. Each has an underlying grammar that cannot be violated by the output mechanisms responsible for speech. At the same time, the parsing mechanism used by listeners and readers to comprehend sentences must ensure that all requirements of the mental representation are met during real-time comprehension. Otherwise, the listener/reader experiences the double-take (e.g., "Huh?" when hearing or reading something). In the grammar of English for native speakers, as one example, the verb *put* has an underlying representation that includes semantic information (e.g., an agent projects into the subject position, a theme projects into the object position, a goal projects into a prepositional phrase). If any one of these elements is absent in a stretch of speech (e.g., *John put the cake*), the parser stops and says "Whoa! Isn't something missing in what I just heard?" Because English is not a null subject language, the parser would also stop and do a double-take when processing a sentence like *Is raining today*.

The contents of the mental representation include all formal features of language (e.g., syntax, phonology, lexicon-morphology) as well as the semantics that relate to structure. As such, one of the main functions of the mental representation is not just to ensure that speakers know what is possible in a language but also what is impossible. In the phonological domain, for example, the speaker of English "knows" that schwaing vowels is possible in unstressed syllables but impossible in stressed syllables. In the syntactic domain, the speaker of English "knows" that complementizers such as *that* can be omitted in sentences like *John thinks (that) Bill is a nifty linguist* but can't be omitted in others, such as **John complains Bill is too nice*. In the lexicon-morphology domain, a speaker of English "knows" that adjectives like *honest* take *dis-* to form opposite meanings (*honest/dishonest*) but adjectives like *faithful* can't (*faithful/*disfaithful*), and that verbs like *submit* and *do* can take *re* (*resubmit, redo*) but verbs like *sleep* and *drink* can't (**resleep, *redrink*). Within the lexico-semantic domain of language, a speaker has an abstract underlying meaning for *roundedness* that may be almost impossible to articulate, but that speaker knows the meaning of *round* when he or she sees or hears it. In a similar vein, the speaker of Spanish "knows" only one of the following can refer to a specific event while the other refers to a generic event: *El café es servido* and *El café está servido* '(The) coffee is served.'

To summarize, the mental representation of language in a speaker's mind/brain consists of abstract properties of language that exist outside of the speaker's ability to describe, unless that person is trained in linguistics and/or how to analyze language. These properties include all of the formal domains of language including syntactic, lexical, phonological, morphological properties, as well as certain properties of semantics and interfaces between these various domains.

2.2   How does mental representation develop?

The development of a mental representation is deceptively simple to describe. It is the result of three different factors working together: (1) input, (2) Universal Grammar, and (3) the parsing/processing mechanisms that mediate between the other two.

Input is the language to which everyone is exposed in communicative settings, be it in or out of classrooms. By communicative I mean that the sample speech stream the person is exposed to exists to communicate some kind of meaning; it is not a sample of language to illustrate how language works.

Universal Grammar (UG) is the uniquely human knowledge system that is genetically determined. It consists of abstract principles to which all language must adhere, as well as variations regarding certain principles (e.g., parameters). We can see both principles and parameters at work in question formation. UG allows for *wh*-elements to move when forming questions, giving rise to both *John knows what?* and *What does John know?* (the *wh*-element moves from its object-of-verb position to occupy a "higher" position in the sentence). But not all languages allow *wh*-movement. Chinese, for example, only allows the equivalent of *John knows what?* Thus, parametrically, languages can be ± WH- MOVEMENT. However, UG stipulates that there are restrictions on *wh-* movement; languages are not free to move *wh-* elements from just any position and to any position. So, although English is +WH- MOVEMENT, it disallows the extraction of *wh-* elements from what are traditionally called "islands," as in **What does John wonder who bought?* The *what* cannot be moved from its object-of-verb position in the embedded clause (e.g., *John wonders who bought what*). Where the element moves to is also under the constraints of UG, ruling out something like **John wonders what who bought.*

Parsing and processing refer to the syntactic computations made during real-time comprehension. When listening to (or reading) a stretch of language, we automatically assign it structure in that we must identify the verb, determine what the relationships of any nouns are to that verb, which phrases modify which parts of the utterance, and so on. We also identify and tag particular words to mean particular things, including any inflections or grammatical markers that indicate meaning or function (e.g., *-ed* on a verb indicates pastness, *the* in front of a noun phrase indicates a particular entity presumably known to the speaker and listener). These processes happen unconsciously and in real-time. (I am ignoring here phonological processing for ease of illustration.)

Acquisition proceeds in the following manner: Learners process and parse input they hear or read, and the processed data are used by Universal Grammar to determine appropriate values (parameters) of the language and to ensure that the language obeys the properties of all human languages. Again, this is deceptively simple. A number of questions arise.

– How do learners parse and process incoming data if they have no grammar of the language being learned? The basic question here is what the starting point for processing input in the L2 context is. Learners can rely on universal aspects of processing and parsing or they may rely on an L1 parser and set of processors. There might even be some combination of universal and L1-based processing involved (see, for example, Carroll 2001, as well as VanPatten 2007, 2009).

– What is the role of the L1 in the interaction of input, processing/parsing, and UG? Some scholars believe that learners begin acquisition by transferring all the properties of the L1 (i.e., all of its parametric values), and that the job of acquisition is to write over these values (i.e., reset parameters). Others believe the L1 operates at the level of processing as per the first question in this list. It could be that the L1 operates at all levels – in processing and in initial parametric values (see White 2003).

– What elements trigger what within the context of UG? For example, does morphological development trigger syntactic development or is it the other way around? In the context of languages with rich verbal inflection (e.g., Spanish,

Italian, Russian) some scholars claim that the acquisition of verbal inflections precedes and thus drives related syntactic operations (e.g., verb movement, null subject parameter). Others believe the opposite, although evidence is beginning to accumulate that abstract properties of syntax and their operations are in place before acquisition of morphological inflections is complete (VanPatten, Keating & Leeser 2012).

–   What about elements of language that are not governed by UG or are not necessarily part of a parametric variation? These may well be acquired in the same way as any other part of language. For example, research on lexical acquisition suggests that vocabulary is acquired incidentally through reading and interaction (i.e., as a byproduct of comprehension – see Coady & Huckin, 1997). The same is true of morphological inflections, which – under many accounts – reside within the lexicon.

–   What role, if any, does speaking play in this scenario? The question here refers to Swain's well known Output Hypothesis as well as the research on interaction (Swain 1985; Gass 2003). Simply put, does speaking somehow trigger the development of grammar? The jury is out on this debate, but I have argued elsewhere that the role of speaking in the development of a mental representation is limited and surely cannot play a role on par with input (VanPatten 2004c).

–   Why does adult SLA look different from child L1A in terms of ultimate attainment and, in some cases, developmental paths? This particular question has invited a plethora of responses that cannot be summarized here. One major aspect of divergence between L1A and adult SLA seems to be the presence of an L1 in the adult SLA context, something that either affects the processing of input data or the actual hypotheses that learners make about language (see, for example, Herschensohn 2009 for an excellent overview).

The above list is partial – and we are of course ignoring for illustrative purposes issues surrounding the social context of language learning and use. Nonetheless, while three ingredients are required for acquisition (input, parsers/processors, UG), what remains to be worked out are the details of how these work together (e.g., Carroll 2001; Truscott & Sharwood Smith 2004), as well as how other factors work (or do not work) with them (e.g., Gass 2003). In addition, while the three ingredients may be present, complete acquisition is not guaranteed. Non-native-likeness seems to be the norm among L2 speakers/learners (e.g., Herschensohn 2008; Sorace 2003; White 2003). Just because a piece of data appears in the input does not mean it gets processed or gets processed correctly (e.g., VanPatten 2004b, 2007). What is more, that a piece of data is processed does not mean that UG makes use of it immediately (e.g., Hawkins 2001). The reasons for these situations are not clear, although evidence is converging on the role of the L1 in complicating

SLA, in both processing and in how UG works (e.g., Herschensohn 2008; Sorace 2003; White 2003), as well as other factors.

2.3   Is the development of mental representation amenable to instruction?

As defined here, mental representation is not amenable to manipulation from the outside. What this means is that instruction cannot directly cause mental representation to develop. It cannot be directly or explicitly taught. However this does not mean that instruction cannot make a difference in *some* way (albeit indirectly). To clarify, UG – as part of the language faculty – operates only on processed data from the input; it cannot operate on information *about* the language (Schwartz 1993; White 1989, 2007). Thus, UG-related aspects of acquisition are not susceptible to external influences such as explicit information, drilling, correction, and other means by which many instructional formats attempt to induce learning. Parsers and processors, too, operate only on input data. They are designed to tag language, and like UG they do not operate on information about the language, nor do they operate on explicit error correction or output. This scenario is akin to the systems that read bar codes in a grocery store. The scanner reads the striped bar codes – ignoring surrounding print, pictures, labels, and other visual information the scanner is not designed to read. This is what parsers and processors do with input; they read only what they are designed to read and ignore everything else. The bar code scanner then sends the data to a computation device that converts it into information that can be used by the register. This is what UG does with processed input data. The important point here is that the scanning system is designed for one and one purpose only, and each of its components responds to only certain kinds of data. The language faculty of the human mind is also designed for one purpose only and it responds to only certain kinds of data (see Schwartz 1993 and also the discussion in VanPatten 2011). In the case of *do*-support in English, teachers can and do teach *do*, and learners can and do take tests on what they learn. What we are saying is that although you can teach *do*, what you can't teach are the abstract underlying features such as ±STRONG in CP, Tense, or any other syntactic phrase, as well as why English questions behave the way they do. This knowledge is derived implicitly from interaction with the language. Instruction on *do* may draw learners' overt attention to this little word, but it clearly cannot affect how *do* is incorporated and organized into the grammar. That is the job of the language specific processors and UG.

This scenario leaves us with the question of input. If the language processors can only operate on input data, and if UG only operates on the data delivered to it by the processors, can we manipulate the input in some way in order to push acquisition along? Theoretically this is possible, and some promising avenues have been explored, such as processing instruction (Benati & Lee 2008; VanPatten 2004a, 2009; VanPatten & Cadierno 1993; among many others). Processing instruction provides manipulated input (called *structured input*) such that the processors are forced to process data in ways they might not under naturalistic conditions. The result of processing instruction is richer "intake"; that is, data useable by UG. Although processing instruction typically provides explicit information as part of the treatment, research on processing instruction has repeatedly shown that this information is not needed. Structured input alone is sufficient to cause changes in learner knowledge – which is predicted by the very nature of acquisition (i.e., input + processors + UG) (see, for example, Fernández 2008; Henry, Culman & VanPatten 2009; VanPatten & Oikennon 1996, and various papers in VanPatten 2004a).

To be sure, the point of any input manipulation – be it processing instruction or any other kind – is not to promote the development of communicative ability. The point of manipulating input is to alter the data used by the processors and by UG in the development of a mental representation. The development of communicative ability falls outside of the realm of mental representation, although presumably language use requires some kind of underlying mental representation. We turn our attention to language as skill.

3.   Language as skill

3.1   What is skill?

I use skill as it is normally used in the literature on cognitive psychology; that is, the speed and accuracy with which people can perform certain actions or behaviors (Anderson 2000; Schmidt 1992; Segalowitz 2003). Skills can be general (e.g., problem solving, learning) or they can be domain- or context-specific (e.g., cooking omelets at a restaurant, mixing margaritas in a bar, delivering a speech). Regardless of generality or specificity of domain, that skill involves both speed and accuracy is important – and how skill is measured considers both how quickly someone can do something and how well (the "how well" being contextually defined). A person very skilled in making omelets is not only accurate but generally speedy (i.e., the omelet comes out just right and the person doesn't take long to produce it). A person not skilled in making omelets may be accurate but exceedingly slow, or may be quick but inaccurate, or may be both slow and inaccurate, and these variations may be classified as "more or less skilled" depending on the needs of the person making the classification (e.g., someone who is slow but makes a good omelet may be classified as "more skilled" than someone who is fast but makes a lousy omelet).

In the case of language, skill refers to communication in all of its manifestations: interpretation (reading, listening), expression (writing, speaking), and negotiation (conversational interaction, turn taking). Note that some of these can be context specific. For example, writing in a chat room is not the same thing as writing this essay. Reading clues for a cross-word puzzle is not the same thing as reading Chomky's writings on minimalist syntax as background research for an article. Speaking while ordering a meal is not the same thing as speaking during an interview with a commentator of a national news broadcast. Thus, when we speak of language skills we must ask ourselves, "Language as skill for what purpose and in what context?" And just like cooking omelets, language as skill involves both speed and accuracy. A skilled reader of Chomsky reads quicker than an unskilled or novice reader and makes few(er) mistakes in interpreting the text. A skilled essay writer produces text faster than the unskilled writer and makes few(er) mistakes (in style, punctuation, word choice, collocation, ambiguity, and so on).

What is interesting about language skill with native speakers and also makes it different from, say, beginning learners of an L2 is that the native speaker has a relatively mature mental representation of language in place prior to skill onset (with the exception of basic conversational skills). Whether a native speaker is skilled at reading cross-word clues or at reading about minimalist syntax, the mental representation for language (e.g., syntax, morphology, phonology) was in place before the skill was developed. As established in first language research, most of the mental representation for the formal properties of language exists by the time a child begins school. This is not the case for the beginning L2 learner, especially the classroom learner. Long before a mental representation is in place, learners are asked to read, write, listen, and speak using language that is far beyond their underlying representation.

3.2   How does skill develop?

Assuming skill refers to an intersection of speed and accuracy, how skill develops in any domain depends on tasks in which people are engaged. What is understood from the literature is that skill develops with task- and context-appropriate behavior. A person learns to make omelets by making omelets. A person learns to write essays by writing essays (although it also seems that there is relationship between writing and reading; reading lots of essays may instill in the mind/brain of the writer an implicit template for essay writing). In short, people become skilled at doing something not by mechanistic activity, but by engaging in the very activity they would like to become skilled in – or at least by engaging in behaviors that have some kind of "transfer appropriateness" (Segalowitz 2003).

To be sure, one hears of "drilling", which is a kind of mechanistic activity in which a piece of the skill is isolated and practiced apart from the context in which it is used. In tennis, for example, a player in training might hit repeated backhands against a ball machine in order to work on the backhand technique. What makes this different from drills that occur in classrooms is that the tennis player in training already has backhand knowledge; that player is perfecting something. No tennis player in training *at the beginning* spends the first day drilling a backhand. Tennis players begin training by playing tennis. The perfection of technique comes later. This is different from what often happens in classrooms, in which learners engage in low-level mechanistic activities devoid of communicative purpose or goal from the get go, where accuracy supposedly precedes communication, a questionable practice (see, for example, DeKeyser 1998, and Segalowitz 2003, who question the role of mechanical practice in skill development).

3.3   Is skill development amenable to instruction?

It is difficult to determine to what extent instruction has an effect on skill development (again, in all of its manifestations – expression, interpretation, negotiation). If skills develop because of engagement with the very behaviors that people would like to develop, then skills cannot be taught per se; teachers and materials can only provide opportunities for their development. If one defines instruction very loosely as "providing opportunities" then, yes, instruction can facilitate skill development. However, if one defines instruction in more traditional terms (e.g., as explicit intervention), then instruction probably can't impact skill development. For example, how does one explicitly "teach" comprehension to language students? What normally occurs is that comprehension *happens* to learners as they try to ascertain what someone else is saying. It is true that teachers can teach strategies for comprehension (e.g., gisting, going for key words, repeated listening/reading), but teaching strategies for coping with language that is above one's level is not the same thing as teaching comprehension itself. What is more, there is no definitive research that the teaching of isolated strategies actually leads to comprehension overall (*pace* Vandergrift & Tafaghodtari 2010, who argue for the effect of metacognitive process teaching on listening comprehension abilities, not particular skills within listening). The same can be said for speaking and writing.

In a native language, skill development happens not because of explicit teaching and intervention, but by providing appropriate opportunities. When children begin school, they learn to read by being given opportunities to read. To be sure, they may start with Dick and Jane in the earliest grades, making their way to Melville by secondary school (with a Harry Potter or Twilight romp in-between), but the point is they learn to read by reading. By reading I don't mean learning to make word-grapheme correspondences; by reading I mean weaving words into idea units and then weaving these smaller idea units into larger idea units to construct a meaning that is intended in the passage. This process is something much bigger than knowing that *cat* stands for /kæt/. Likewise, learning to write essays happens not because one is taught how to write essays but because one engages in writing essays. Again, to be sure, people might receive explicit feedback ("this was good", "this point isn't clear", "you don't have a main idea in this paragraph") which one can construe as some type of explicit intervention. What is not clear from the research, however, is to what extent this feedback actually impacts development (Williams 2005). As alluded to earlier, there is a relationship between reading and writing in the L1 and it is not clear to what extent skilled adult writers are skilled writers because they received feedback on their writing or because they've read so much along the way or because of some complex interaction between the two. (It's worth pointing out that even skilled writers get their work copyedited.)

In addition, with or without instruction, research is fairly clear that L2 learners never develop skill that is quite native-like. If we take reading, for example, as one type of skill, do L2 learners ever read like native speakers? The answer is "not really." Although on some tests of comprehension, the performance of non-native readers is not significantly different from that of native readers, other research suggests something different. Sentence level interpretation research suggests that very advanced (i.e., long-time speakers/learners of a second language) may not process anaphoric reference the same way natives do. In Spanish and Italian, for example, there are null and overt subject pronouns. When these have multiple antecedents, Spanish speakers seem to demonstrate a preference: null subjects tend to be interpreted as co-referential with a previous subject (no topic shift) while overt subject pronouns tend to be interpreted as co-referential with non-subjects (topic shift). Thus, in *Juan vio a Roberto después que (él) regresó de Francia* ('John saw Robert after [he] returned from France'), the tendency of native readers/comprehension is to have the null subject refer to Juan and the overt pronoun (*él*) refer to Roberto (e.g., Alonso-Ovalle et al. 2002; Carminati 2002). Very advanced learners of Spanish and Italian tend not to make this distinction when reading or listening; both null and overt subject pronouns tend to be linked to the subject of the previous clause or sentence (e.g., Jegerski, VanPatten & Keating 2011; Sorace & Filiaci 2006). Thus, a very subtle aspect of comprehension is missed.

And – just to be sure it is mentioned here – research using on-line measures such as eye-tracking and self-paced reading has repeatedly demonstrated that even though native speakers and non-native speakers might arrive at the same comprehension of sentences, non-native readers are generally slower than natives in reading sentences no matter how advanced the former are (e.g., Frenck-Mestre 2005).

Finally, as stated earlier, L1 learners arrive at formal schooling with a mental representation for the formal aspects of language pretty much in place. A few peripheral features of language may be missing (e.g., passive structures in English, certain morphological inflections in Russian, anaphoric interpretation of pronouns in Spanish) but the underlying representation that allows for these things to be incorporated into language are already there. What happens to L1 speakers after the onset of formal education is not so much the development of the formal properties of language, but the continued development of skills that involve discourse, vocabulary, pragmatics, interaction, reading, writing, and other things. These domains of language use and knowledge *assume* an underlying formal system. In the L2 context, this scenario is not the same. Whereas the sequence in L1 is generally mental representation precedes skill (e.g., even babies can distinguish sounds and function words before they begin speaking), in L2 circles there is no sequence; mental representation and skills are pushed at the same time (at least for literate learners).

So far, we have been talking about skill in its broadest sense. In the next section, I touch upon an aspect of language instruction that I think represents a confusion or conflation of concepts in language teaching. That confusion involves applying the concept of skill to formal properties of language.

4. A confusion in the profession

As defined earlier, the formal properties of language are not skill; they exist as mental representation. However, it is not clear to me that teachers, textbooks, and many researchers in instructed SLA see the formal properties of language in this manner. I begin with a discussion of teaching.

4.1   Grammar as skill in teaching

For many language-teaching professionals, there is the belief that textbook rules are somehow representative of what winds up in learners' minds/brains. This idea dates back to the concept of "skill-getting", as espoused by teaching methodologists in the 1970s and 1980s (e.g., Omaggio 1986; Rivers 1981). The concept still permeates most of language instruction practices today when one examines typical foreign language textbooks for adults. Let's return to our earlier example from English. When teachers teach something like *do*-support in English, many believe that the rules they provide are the rules that underlie both representation and production. Thus, by teaching and practicing the rule, learners acquire the rule. The idea here is that the grammar is the skill to be acquired. But is it the case that the pedagogical rules for *do*-support are what exists in the mental representation for language? The answer is "they cannot." *Do*-support is a syntactic reflex of several aspects of abstract syntax: that English has strong Tense features (that is, tense must always be represented somehow in a finite clause), but also has weak Agreement features (that is, there is no clear mapping of person-number features in English onto verbs except for the irregular verb *be* in the present tense). These two underlying features of English force *do* insertion in emphatic statements as well as *yes-no* questions. The reason for this is that some kind of finite verb must carry tense features (the strong Tense issue) and lexical verbs (as opposed to auxiliaries and modals) in English cannot move to create subject-verb inversion in questions as is the case with languages like Spanish (the weak Agreement issue). In short, learners must create (and do create) abstract underlying syntactic representations that have little to do with textbook rules (e.g., Herschensohn 2000; Rothman, Judy, Guijarro-Fuentes & Pires 2010).

This simplified description of *do*-support is one example that begs the question: then what "skill" is it that learners are getting when they are practicing pedagogical grammar rules? If pedagogical rules don't exist in the head, then what are learners learning to do as part of their skill? My point here is that by moving grammar into the realm of skill acquisition (as opposed to real skill acquisition – production skills and comprehension skills as part of communication), teachers and theorists conflate two constructs that really aren't supposed to be conflated. In short, grammar as the formal properties of language is not a "skill" to be acquired; it is knowledge (as abstract and implicit mental representation) that is tapped during linguistic performance (see the discussion above in 3.3).

This leads me to a discussion about speaking as skill. The usual conceptualization of speaking as skill conflates grammar acquisition with skill development (e.g., DeKeyser 1997; Rivers 1990). That is, the classic paradigm for the ability to speak involves grammar as declarative knowledge, that then gets proceduralized, that then gets automated. It is in the proceduralization to automatization stage that this paradigm marks as the beginning of skill development with grammar, with automatization suggesting some kind of fluency (DeKeyser 1997). There are two observations I would like to make here. The first is that it is not clear to me that this particular scenario is the correct one for how grammatical "stuff" gets used in real time. As mentioned above, the mental representation that people carry around in their heads for language does not look like any rules at all, so rules per se aren't even internalized under current thinking about both language and language acquisition. Yet, most skill theory research uses rules that are a-theoretical in content; sometimes these are pedagogically-oriented rules, sometimes rules from a structural description, but they are never derived from linguistic theory. For example, in DeKeyser (1997), participants explicitly learned and then practiced four isolated grammar rules for an artificial miniature language. Training and practice lasted for 22 sessions of one hour or less (over 11 weeks). His results clearly showed the typical learning curves observed in skill research and his conclusion was that "the learning of second language grammar rules can proceed very much in the same way that learning in other cognitive domains, from geometry to computer programming, has been shown to take place" (Dekeyser 1997: 214). Although this conclusion is indisputable for his particular study, there is a larger problem here when interpreting this kind of research in the real world of language acquisition. The first is that, again, learners don't have rules in their heads like textbook rules or the rules that were used in DeKeyser's study. These rules are artificial, mere shorthand ways for us to talk about language that is too complex to talk about to students. The second problem is that language acquisition does not proceed by learning isolated rules. At any given time, learners are working on a variety of things in language, from phonology (including prosody), to morphology, to underlying syntax, and so on. The learner's mind/brain does not stop and say "Let's just work on this one thing until we get it right." In the domain of morphology, for example, it is not clear that learners "get the present tense" before moving on to the past. In Spanish, with a complex system of verbal inflections unique to each person-number, learners do not "master" these in one fell swoop. Indeed, there is some evidence that they first learn 3rd person singular and use it as a default verb form. From there on, acquisition (and errors made during speaking) is constrained by what is called feature geometry, such that singular forms precede the acquisition of plural forms (see McCarthy 2006, for some discussion). And to be sure, there is sufficient evidence about the acquisition of formal properties of language over time such that stages of acquisition exist along side linear and curve-like learning. That is, changes may be abrupt, with new structures created unrelated to the target language structure. Thus, there is not necessarily a smooth progression indicative of "practice makes perfect." (I will touch upon this again later when I discuss processability.) So, while the results of skill research are suggestive about what happens in laboratory settings, it's not clear that they speak to issues related to both what language is and how such a complex thing is acquired outside the laboratory.

The perspective taken in skill theory in which isolated bits of language are learned and practiced stands in stark contrast to research from a generative perspective, for example, in which the relationship between surface features of language (e.g., tense markers on verbs, person-number markers on verbs, pronoun case) is linked to underlying functional features (e.g., finiteness, strong versus weak tense, strong versus weak agreement). For example, Lardiere (2007) argues that her subject – who appears to be a fossilized speaker of English L2 with Chinese L1 – shows clear underlying mental representation for the functional features, but that the interface between the mental representation and spell out (e.g., the phonetic and acoustic realization of underlying phonological representations) is compromised in some way. In our recent research (VanPatten, Keating & Leeser 2012), we use on-line processing as a measure of grammatical sensitivity, comparing native and mid-level non-native speakers of Spanish on syntactic and morphological features related to strong agreement. Our results were very clear: native speakers showed sensitivity to violations in all domains (three features of syntax plus subject-verb agreement); the non-natives showed the same sensitivities to syntactic violations but not to the subject-verb agreement violations. What makes the results of this experiment interesting is this: the learners never practiced or explicitly learned the syntactic aspects we tested yet they had explicitly learned and had practiced (including feedback) on subject-verb agreement since the beginning of their language studies. In short, they acquired that which they weren't taught and yet were unable to show sensitivity to the things they had been taught and they had practiced. A skill theory approach to the acquisition of grammar has difficulty accounting for something like Lardiere's research as well that of VanPatten, Keating, and Leeser's study, unless of course, one sweeps linguistic theory under the rug.

At the same time, a skill theory perspective ignores some important research that has emerged on speech (output) processing in SLA, namely Processability Theory (e.g., Pienemann 1998, 2005). Within Processability Theory, the emergence of grammatical operations in learner output (e.g., agreement of an adjective with a noun, agreement of a verb with its subject) is constrained by a universal implicational hierarchy. The complex interaction of this hierarchy with a learner's mental representation yields staged development, and staged development is not predicted by skill theory as applied to grammatical features of language. To be sure, Processability Theory is concerned with the emergence of grammatical operations in learner output and not with the development of skill per se, but it seems that some kind of reconciliation of the two perspectives on how learners learn to speak is in order. Currently, I don't see such a reconciliation happening in the near future.

The second observation I would like to make about the application of skill theory to grammar acquisition and use is perhaps more important than the previous observation: Is the correct use of surface features of language in real-time speaking a simple matter of automatization of grammatical operations? Schmidt (1992) suggested that fluency may indeed involve such automatization, but speaking (output) in general – especially by native speakers, and one would presume this would apply to non-native speakers as well – can't be a simple application of grammatical rules in real time. That is, a good deal of fluency must involve the use of chunks and phrases of language that are stored as such; not all language production must or can involve word-by-word sentence formulation. What is more,

Schmidt cautioned the field against the importation of constructs from psychology that may not have relevance to language and language teaching:

> ...it is unsettling to realize that the mechanisms made available by psychological theorizing for understanding L2 fluency derive primarily from the study of skill in such tasks as typing, the detection of target letters in fields of distractors, judgments about digital logic gates, alphabet arithmetic, and computer simulations of the same tasks, tasks that cannot be assumed to rely necessarily on the same learning mechanisms as speaking a second language (p. 378–379).

Some twenty years later, Schmidt's concern is still valid. There are but a handful of studies that actually address skill development from a second language perspective, and – as noted above – their focus on discrete points of language gives pause in terms of their applicability to actual skill development as described at the outset of this section. We are still importing ideas and paradigms from psychology that may not be valid for the complexity (and subtlety) that is language acquisition.

5.   Conclusion and pedagogical implications

In this chapter I have argued that there are two distinct aspects of acquisition. One involves the acquisition of an abstract and implicit mental representation – what linguists traditionally call competence. The other is skill – the ability to use language fluently (measured by speed and accuracy) in both production and comprehension. I have also posited that mental representation evolves one way (input + processors + UG) while skill evolves in another (use of language in particular contexts). I have also argued that mental representation is not amenable to instruction as normally conceived. I have also argued that skill itself is not teachable in a direct sense, although classroom activities can be provided that facilitate its development. Finally, I have suggested that many teachers and some scholars mistakenly (in my view) attempt to apply skill theory to the acquisition of grammar, when grammar is not a skill but a mental representation.

The implications for research on instructed SLA are clear: researchers need to be sharper in their claims about what instruction is affecting. Is the point of a study to affect mental representation? If so, how? And how is this effect measured without inviting a performance factor obscuring underlying knowledge? If the point of a study is to affect skill, how is the skill affected? And what relationship is the researcher assuming between underlying representation and skill? In short, the field of instructed SLA needs to be much clearer about what it believes instruction is doing, how it's doing it, and how that thing is measured.

For those who are looking for implications for language instruction or curriculum development, I offer some general and broad suggestions for implications from the arguments. The first is that mental representation – which is dependent on universal internal factors/mechanisms interacting with processed input data – cannot be explicitly and directly taught. Whether the representation we are referring to is syntactic, lexico-morphological, phonological or belonging to some other formal component, that representation only builds up over time through exposure to input. Thus, any so-called pedagogical interventions must be (1) input oriented and (2) couched in some communicative/meaningful context. Such types of interventions include text enhancement, processing instruction (see Wong, this volume), and other interventions that work at the interface between input and internal mechanisms. Not all are equally useful as a review of research would clearly indicate, but at the same time no intervention is a guarantee of or a direct intervention for the development of mental representation. At best, such interventions speed up acquisition, but we should be clear not to suggest that such interventions cause any immediate and/or long-term changes. The outcomes of such interventions are, rightly so, the domain of research on instructed SLA.

As for skill development, it should be clear that the only kinds of pedagogical interventions worthy of consideration are those that involve behavioral transferability. That is, pedagogical selections must be made based on the extent to which the behaviors learners engage somehow resemble behaviors in language use. Minimally, this means that "speaking practice" must involve making meaning, for example, or that reading must be reading for meaning (as opposed to, say, reading aloud for some other kind of practice). In short, without "meaningfulness," practice that targets skill development is, at best, a waste of time. Thus, practices such as structured output and information-exchange tasks (see Lee & VanPatten 2003, for example) would be the most compatible with skill development. However, teachers also need to have realistic expectations, something that is often missing in many curricula around the world. It is not uncommon for teachers to think that what they teach and what they practice is immediately available for skill. This is simply not the case.

To close, I underscore that understanding how language and acquisition work allows teachers and curriculum developers to be (better) informed consumers of the latest trends in language teaching. Different pedagogical techniques and interventions may be better suited to the development of mental representation as opposed to skill development, and some techniques may be better suited to skill development.

References

Alonso-Ovalle, L., Fernández-Solera, S., Frazier, L., & Clifton Jr., C. (2002). Null vs. overt pronouns and the topic-focus articulation in Spanish. *Rivista di Linguistica, 14*(2), 151–169.

Anderson, J. (2000). *Learning and memory* [2nd edition]. New York, NY: John Wiley & Sons.

Benati, A., & Lee, J.F. (2008). *Grammar acquisition and processing instruction: Secondary and cumulative effects*. Bristol: Multilingual Matters.

Carminati, M.N. (2002). *The processing of Italian subject pronouns*. Unpublished PhD dissertation, University of Massachusetts at Amherst.

Carroll, S. (2001). *Input and evidence: The raw material of second language acquisition*. Amsterdam: John Benjamins.

Chomsky, N. (1995). *The minimalist program*. Cambridge, MA: The MIT Press.

Coady, J., & Huckin, T. (Eds.). (1997). *Second language vocabulary acquisition*. Cambridge: CUP.

DeKeyser, R. (1997). Beyond explicit rule learning: Automatizing second language morphosyntax. *Studies in Second Language Acquisition, 19*(2), 195–222.

DeKeyser, R. (1998). Beyond focus on form: Cognitive perspectives on learning and practicing second language grammar. In C. Doughty & J. Williams (Eds.), *Focus on form in classroom second language acquisition* (pp. 42–63). Cambridge: CUP.

Doughty, C. J. (2003). In C.J. Doughty & M.H. Long (Eds.), Instructed SLA: Constraints, Compensation, and Enhancement. *The handbook of second language acquisition* (pp. 256–310). Oxford: Blackwell.

Fernández, C. (2008). Re-examining the role of explicit information in processing instruction. *Studies in Second Language Acquisition, 30*(3), 277–305.

Frenck-Mestre, C. (2005). Eye-movement recording as a tool for studying syntactic processing in a second language: A review of methodologies and experimental findings. *Second Language Research, 21*(2), 175–198.

Gass, S.M. (2003). Input and interaction. In C. Doughty & M.H. Long (Eds.), *The handbook of second language acquisition* (pp. 224–255). Oxford: Blackwell.

Harley, H., & Noyer, R. (1999). Distributed morphology. *Glot International, 4*(4), 3–9.

Hawkins, R. (2001). *Second language syntax: A generative introduction*. Oxford: Blackwell.

Henry, N, Culman, H., & VanPatten, B. (2009). More on the effects of explicit information in instructed SLA: A partial replication and response to Fernández (2008). *Studies in Second Language Acquisition, 31*(4), 559–576.

Herschensohn, J. (2000). *The second time around: Minimalism and L2 acquisition*. Amsterdam: John Benjamins.

Herschensohn, J. (2008). *Language development and age*. Cambridge: CUP.

Herschensohn, J. (2009). Fundamental and gradient differences in language development. *Studies in Second Language Acquisition, 31*(2), 259–289.

Jackendoff, R. (2002). *Foundations of Language*. Oxford: OUP.

Jegerski, J., VanPatten, B. & Keating, G. (2011). L2 processing of anaphoric pronouns: L1 transfer at the syntax-discourse interface. *Second Language Research, 27*(4), 481–507.

Lardiere, D. (2007). *Ultimate attainment in second language acquisition*. Mahwah, NJ: Lawrence Erlbaum Associates.

Lee, J.F. & VanPatten, B. (2003). *Making communicative language teaching happen* [2nd edition]. New York, NY: McGraw-Hill.

Long, M.H. (1983). Does second language instruction make a difference? A review of research. *TESOL Quarterly, 17*(3), 359–382.

McCarthy, C. (2006). Default morphology in second language Spanish: Missing inflection or underspecified inflection? In J.-P. Montreuil & C. Nishida (Eds.), *New perspectives on Romance linguistics: Selected papers from the 35th Linguistic Symposium on Romance Languages* (pp. 201–212). Amsterdam: John Benjamins.

Norris, J.M., & Ortega, L. (2000). Effectiveness of L2 instruction: A research synthesis and quantitative meta-analysis. *Language Learning, 50*(3), 417–528.

Omaggio, A.M. (1986). *Teaching language in context*. Boston, MA: Heinle & Heinle.

Pienemann, M. (1998). *Language processing and second language development: Processability theory*. Amsterdam: John Benjamins.

Pienemann, M. (Ed.). (2005). *Cross-linguistic aspects of processability theory*. Amsterdam: John Benjamins.

Radford, A. (1997). *Syntactic theory and the structure of English*. Cambridge: CUP.

Radford, A. (2001). *Syntax: A minimalist introduction*. Cambridge: CUP.

Rivers. W. (1981). *Teaching foreign language skills*. Chicago, IL: University of Chicago Press.

Rivers. W. (1990). Psychological validation of methodological approaches and foreign language classroom practices. In B. Freed (Ed.), *Foreign language acquisition research and the classroom* (pp. 283–294). Lexington, MA: D.C. Heath.

Rothman, J. (2010). Theoretical linguistics meets pedagogical practice: Pronominal subject use in Spanish as a second language. *Hispania, 93*(1), 52–65.

Rothman, J., Judy, T., Guijarro-Fuentes, P., & Pires, A. (2010). On the (un)ambiguity of adjectival modifications in Spanish determiner phrases: Informing debates on the mental representation of syntax. *Studies in Second Language Acquisition, 32*(1), 47–77.

Schmidt, R.W. (1992). Psychological mechanisms underlying second language fluency. *Studies in Second Language Acquisition, 14*(4), 357–385.

Schwartz, B. (1993). On explicit and negative evidence effecting and affecting competence and linguistic behavior. *Studies in Second Language acquisition, 15*, 147–163.

Segalowitz, N. (2003). Automaticity and second languages. In C. Doughty & M.H. Long (Eds.), *The handbook of second language acquisition* (pp. 382–408). Oxford: Blackwell.

Sorace, A. (2003). Near-nativeness. In C. Doughty & M. Long (Eds.), *The handbook of second language acquisition* (pp. 130–151). Oxford: Blackwell.

Sorace, A., & Filiaci, F. (2006). Anaphora resolution in near-native speakers of Italian. *Second Language Research, 22*(3), 339–368.

Spada, N., & Tomita, Y. (2010). Interactions between type of instruction and type of language feature: A meta-analysis. *Language Learning, 60*(2), 263–308.

Swain, M. (1985). Communicative competence: Some roles of comprehensible input and comprehensible output in its development. In S. Gass & C. Madden (Eds.), *Input in second language acquisition* (pp. 235–253). Rowley, MA: Newbury House.

Truscott, J., & Sharwood Smith, M. (2004). Acquisition by processing: A modular perspective on language development. *Bilingualism: Language and Cognition, 7*(1), 1–20.

Vandergrift, L. & Tafaghodtari, M. (2010). Teaching L2 learners how to listen does make a difference: An empirical study. *Language Learning, 60*(2), 470–497.

VanPatten, B. (1996). *Input processing and grammar instruction*. Norwood, NJ: Ablex.

VanPatten, B. (Ed.). (2004a). *Processing instruction: Theory, research, and commentary*. Mahwah, NJ: Lawrence Erlbaum Associates.

VanPatten, B. (2004b). Input processing in SLA. In B. VanPatten (Ed.), *Processing instruction: Theory, research, and commentary* (pp. 5–31). Mahwah, NJ: Lawrence Erlbaum Associates.

VanPatten, B. (2004c). Input and output in establishing form-meaning connnections. In B. VanPatten, J. Williams, S. Rott, & M. Overstreet (Eds.), *Form-meaning connections in second language acquisition* (pp. 29–47). Mahwah, NJ: Lawrence Erlbaum Associates.

VanPatten, B. (2007). Input processing in adult second language acquisition. In B. VanPatten & J. Williams (Eds.), *Theories in second language acquisition* (pp. 115–135). Mahwah, NJ: Lawrence Erlbaum Associates.

VanPatten, B. (2009). Processing matters in input enhancement. In T. Piske & M. Young-Scholten (Eds.), *Input matters in SLA* (pp. 47–61). Bristol: Multilingual Matters.

VanPatten, B. (2011). Stubborn syntax. In C. Sanz & R. Leow (Eds.), *Implicit and explicit language learning: Conditions, processes, and knowledge in SLA and bilingualism* (pp. 9–21). Washington, DC: Georgetown University Press.

VanPatten, B., & Benati, A. (2010). *Key terms in second language acquisition*. London: Continuum.

VanPatten, B., & Cadierno, T. (1993). Explicit instruction and input processing. *Studies in Second Language Acquisition, 15*(2), 225–244.

VanPatten, B., Keating, G., & Leeser, M. (2012). Missing verbal inflections as a representational problem: Evidence from self-paced reading. *Linguistic Approaches to Bilingualism, 2*(2), 109–140.

VanPatten, B., & Oikkenon, S. (1996). Explanation versus structured input in processing instruction. *Studies in Second Language Acquisition, 18*(4), 495–510.

White, L. (1989). *Universal grammar and L2 acquisition*. Amsterdam: John Benjamins.

White, L. (2003). *Second language acquisition and Universal Grammar*. Cambridge: CUP.

White, L. (2007). Linguistic theory, universal grammar, and second language acquisition. In B. VanPatten & J. Williams (Eds.), *Theories in second language acquisition* (pp. 37–55). Mahwah, NJ: Lawrence Erlbaum Associates.

Williams, J. (2005). *Teaching writing in second and foreign language c lassrooms*. New York, NY: McGraw-Hill.

CHAPTER 2

Input and output in SLA

Applying theories of mental representation and skill

Wynne Wong
Ohio State University

This chapter offers second language (L2) instructors pedagogical perspectives for the position articulated by VanPatten in Chapter 1 of this volume that language consists of two distinct domains: (1) mental representation and (2) the ability to use language (i.e., skill). The author reviews some pedagogical practices that have been influential over the years in light of this perspective and offers L2 instructors ideas for creating classroom activities that help foster the development of these two domains of language. In addition to structured input and structured output activities (which have been well established and researched in SLA circles), the author offers some new ideas to create engaging input and output activities for the L2 classroom. These activities include the use of film as the medium to deliver input as well as to encourage the creation of extended meaningful output.

1. Introduction

In Chapter 1 of this volume, VanPatten argues that before researchers can adequately investigate the impact of instruction on second language acquisition (SLA), researchers and practitioners need to recognize that language development involves (1) the development of a mental representation of the L2 and (2) the ability to use language in real time (i.e., skill). He points out that before researchers can assess the potential effects of instruction, it is first necessary to understand which domain of language they are referring to. Along the same vein, if one accepts the position that language consists of two domains, i.e., mental representation and skill, pedagogical practice must also reflect this distinction in order for it to be effective.

This chapter offers pedagogical perspectives for L2 instructors that reflect the position articulated by VanPatten in chapter one that language consists of two broad domains: (1) mental representation and (2) skill. The author will first briefly review the key points of VanPatten's position as they pertain to L2 instruction. Following this, the author will review some pedagogical practices that have been influential over the years in light of the perspective that language consists of two distinct domains. This chapter concludes by offering some pedagogical activities that use input to help learners develop a mental representation of language as well as activities that are better geared towards developing the ability to use language. In addition to structured input and structured output activities (which have been well established and researched in SLA circles), this chapter offers new ideas for creating engaging input and output activities for the L2 classroom. These activities include the use of film as the medium to deliver input as well as to encourage the creation of extended meaningful output.

2.   Mental representation and skill

The idea that mental representation and skill constitute different components of language acquisition is not a new concept in the field of SLA, but as VanPatten (this volume: 1) argues, this distinction is often overlooked by some SLA scholars and L2 instructors. He proposes that recognizing this distinction may lead to a better understanding of how instruction may impact (or not impact) these different domains and by extension, lead to the development of more effective pedagogical materials.

VanPatten defines mental representation as the abstract, implicit, and underlying linguistic system in a speaker's brain/mind (VanPatten & Benati 2010: 107). These abstract properties of language include the formal domains of language (i.e., syntactic, lexical, phonological, morphological, etc.) as well as certain properties of semantics (VanPatten this volume: 3). This underlying linguistic system exists outside of awareness. By this he means that speakers typically cannot articulate what is in their mental representation. For example, one's mental representation of language allows one to know what is possible in a language as well as what is not possible but a speaker generally (unless they are linguists) cannot explain why (see VanPatten this volume for discussion).

VanPatten argues that mental representation operates on input data and is not amenable to outside influences such as instruction. However, instruction can set up conditions to help it develop, i.e., providing input and the means to process input correctly. VanPatten defines input as samples of language that communicate some kind of message or meaning. It is "not a sample of language to illustrate how language works" (VanPatten this volume: 4).

Skill, in the context of language, refers to "communication in all of its manifestations: interpretation (reading, listening), expression (writing, speaking), and negotiation (conversational interaction, turn taking)" (VanPatten this volume: 8).

Skill develops by engaging in task and context appropriate activities. This means that in order to develop communicative ability in an L2, one must engage in expressing and negotiating meaning. VanPatten postulates that instruction may have an impact on skill development if instruction provides opportunities for learners to engage in task appropriate practices (this volume: 9).

Output is often associated with skill development. No one would argue that in order to speak an L2 fluently and accurately, one needs to practice doing so. However, it is important to point out that output as a form of skill enhancement does not refer to production in which the communication of meaning is absent. Therefore, activities like mechanical drills would not be the kind of "output" that many SLA scholars recognize as being beneficial for fostering accuracy and fluency.

3.   Input, output, and pedagogy

As VanPatten points out, when a distinction between these two domains of language is not made, i.e., mental representation and skill, it is difficult to assess the effectiveness of different instructional practices. In fact, the reason why the roles of input and output have sometimes been misunderstood in some language teaching approaches may in part be due to the failure to understand this distinction. The author reviews some of these pedagogical approaches/methods in regards to the roles of input and output in the next sections.

3.1   Drills

An example of a teaching method that did not make a distinction between mental representation and skill was the Audiolingual Method (ALM), the method that was widely used in the 1960s. Based on structural linguistics and behaviorist psychology, L2 acquisition was viewed as a result of habit formation via repetition and extensive drilling. The role of input was ignored and language production was largely mechanical. As discussed above, this type of production does not qualify as the type of output that is beneficial for SLA, i.e., output tied to the expression and negotiation of meaning. This method was not conducive to building a mental representation of language nor was it effective for developing language skills in the sense of fostering any kind of communicative ability.

In the 1970s, rationalist and mentalist views reconceptualized language as a rule-governed entity. Meaningful practice was advocated over rote learning and many pushed for a more eclectic approach that would combine structural practice with meaningful language use (see the discussion in Wong & VanPattten 2003 and

Wong 2008). A widely used method during this time was a sequence of pedagogical practices articulated by Paulston (1972) which consisted of first giving learners explicit information about a target form followed by a series of production activities. These activities would first begin with mechanical drills, followed by meaningful drills, and finally communicative drills. As with the ALM, this approach also did not make a distinction between mental representation and language use. There was no attention given to input; instruction began with explicit information followed by production. While some attention was given to meaningful output, there was an assumption that learners must first engage in mechanical production before they could be allowed to express meaning in a communicative way. This view is problematic for several reasons. First, before learners can develop communicative ability, they must have some kind of mental representation of the L2 in place. By ignoring input, this method did not help foster the development of a mental representation. In other words, this method required learners to produce or practice what did not yet exist in their mental representation. VanPatten (this volume: 8) points out that in L1 contexts, native speakers normally have a relatively mature mental representation of language before they start working on developing language skills. However, in L2 contexts, there is a tendency to require L2 learners to practice language skills that go beyond what they have in their mental representation. Furthermore, the idea that output must first be mechanical has no empirical support (see Wong & VanPatten 2003 for a discussion). As emphasized here and elsewhere, if communicative ability is the skill that L2 learners are to develop, then they must engage in expressing and negotiating meaning.

3.2   Krashen and input

Krashen (1985) stimulated discussion in the language teaching profession when he put forth his input hypothesis and made the claim that comprehensible input was a necessary and sufficient condition for SLA. Among other things, Krashen's ideas have been criticized for being untestable and unrealistic for many L2 classroom learning contexts, especially in foreign language learning contexts where access to L2 input is much more limited. Citing research from French immersion contexts (e.g., Harley 1993; Harley & Swain 1984; Swain 1985), some scholars pointed out that despite years of receiving comprehensible input, these learners could not obtain certain levels of accuracy for some grammatical features in their production. Therefore, comprehensible input cannot be a sufficient condition.

    If one recasts Krashen's ideas in light of the understanding that language consists of mental representation and skill, his claims appear much more palatable. If acquisition is defined in terms of how accurate L2 learners are in their production of certain grammatical features or how fluent they are, one may argue that input alone is insufficient for some L2 learning contexts and that output may be needed for the development of some of these skills. However, if one takes acquisition to mean the development of a mental representation, then it is much more difficult to criticize Krashen because only processed input is usable for building a mental representation (VanPatten this volume: 6). Therefore, it is important to understand which domain of language one is referring to before one can ascertain whether certain ideas about teaching practices are sound or not.

3.3   Communicative Language Teaching (CLT)

CLT, the mostly widely used approach today in North America and Europe (among other places) made its appearance around the 1980s. CLT is defined as an approach rather than a method because it is based on a philosophy of teaching (rather than a prescribed set of procedures), i.e., that language is tied to the act of communication (Wong 2005: 4). Therefore, while the overarching goal of CLT is the development of communicative competence, CLT may be realized in different ways. Consequently, there exist many types of CLT classrooms. In what has been characterized as the strong form of CLT, there was a tendency to equate CLT with the absence of grammar instruction. Hinkel and Fotos (2002: 4) describe CLT as instruction that does not include "formal grammar instruction" or corrective feedback and associate CLT with giving learners large quantities of "meaning-focused input". At the other extreme, there are some CLT classrooms that remain very form-focused with little attention given to meaning and/or input. In their discussion of CLT, Lee and VanPatten (2003) point out that while students may be given the chance to answer questions that are personalized, many classrooms remain teacher-dominated and accuracy is often emphasized over meaning. Drills remain prevalent in some if not many CLT classrooms. This observation is also documented in Katz and Blythe (2007: 13): "Mechanical exercises, such as drills or fill-in-the-blank activities are not uncommon". Therefore, while the main goal of CLT is to develop communicative competence, one may question whether L2 learners are really being given opportunities to use output to communicate meaning in some CLT classrooms. More importantly, before L2 learners can develop communicative ability in an L2, they must first have some kind of underlying mental representation of the L2. This implies that if instructors want L2 learners to develop communicative ability, instruction must also provide learners with opportunities to help this mental representation develop, i.e., make sure they have access to comprehensible input.

4. Pedagogical implications

If one accepts that L2 development involves both the development of a mental representation and the ability to use language accurately, then L2 instruction should provide opportunities that will help both of these domains develop. This means (1) the availability of input, (2) the means to notice input and to make form-meaning connections, and (3) opportunities to create output that requires the expression and negotiation of meaning. In the next sections, the author explores some pedagogical activities that include these criteria. In addition to structured input activities, readers will find some new ideas for creating engaging input activities for the L2 classroom.

4.1   Activities: Development of mental representation

Because mental representation is dependent on input data, it is critical that learners have access to lots of comprehensible input that encourages them to pay attention to and interpret meaning. If the goal of instruction is to focus on form, this may be best achieved via the use of input-based activities first. Since output has the potential to make L2 learners pay attention to information in input that they may otherwise not notice (e.g., see Swain 1995), output activities may also contribute to developing underlying representation as long as it is sufficiently balanced with adequate input. The following activities are designed to provide learners with input (and in one case also output) and opportunities to process input for meaning.

4.1.1   *Structured input*
Structured input (SI) activities are input activities that are designed to help learners make correct form-meaning connections. These activities are informed by the processing strategies that L2 learners tend to use on their own. These strategies are described in VanPatten's model of input processing (VanPatten 2004). Because learners' own strategies are not always the most efficient, SI activities structure the input in such a way that makes them use better processing strategies to make correct form-meaning connections. Therefore, SI activities help L2 learners derive better intake data for acquisition.

Empirical support for SI activities was first documented in VanPatten and Cadierno (1993). This study showed that SI activities were effective in enabling L2 learners to both interpret and produce target structures (i.e., Spanish object pronouns). The fact that participants were able to produce the target structures even though they never practiced doing so during treatment suggests that these activities were able to affect L2 learners' underlying mental representation. Since this study, a large body of research on SI has surfaced to support the effectiveness of these activities for a variety of languages and grammatical structures (For a recent review, see Benati & Lee 2008). The target structure in the following SI activity is the French subjunctive. The processing problem with the subjunctive is that this form is redundant and therefore not critical for understanding the meaning of a message (See Farley 2001 and Wong 2005 for a discussion). The meaning that the subjunctive form expresses, i.e., doubt, volition, opinion, etc., is already expressed by the main clause as in (1):

(1) *Je doute que Pierre soit riche.*
     I doubt that Pierre *is* (subjunctive) rich.

The form *soit* expresses doubt but this is already expressed by the clause *Je doute que* so the subjunctive form is redundant and has low communicative value (i.e., the form is not important for understanding the meaning of the sentence). Furthermore, because the subjunctive form appears in the middle of a sentence or utterance, this form is not perceptually salient which in turn makes the form more challenging to process (see VanPatten's Sentence Location Principle, 2004: 14).

In the following activity, the input is *structured* in such a way that learners must rely on verb forms in order to determine what meaning is being expressed. What makes this particular SI activity different from some previous SI activities is that it is based on a French language mystery film, *Liaisons* This film was designed to deliver comprehensible input to L2 learners of French.

LES PERSONNAGES DU FILM LIAISONS
Étape 1. Decide if each sentence expresses an opinion, a doubt or certainty based on the characters from the film *Liaisons*.

1. ...*aille* [subjunctive] en France pour l'enterrement de son oncle.
    (...go to France for her uncle's burial.)
    a. Il est évident que Claire (It is evident that Claire)
    b. Il est bon que Claire (It is good that Claire)
2. ...*soit* [subjunctive] une amie de Claire.
    (...be a good friend of Claire's)
    a. Il est merveilleux qu'Abia (It's wonderful that Abia)
    b. On sait qu'Abia (We know that Abia)
3. ...*fait* [indicative] ses devoirs avant de travailler à l'hôtel.
    (...does her homework before working at the hotel.)
    a. Il est évident que Claire (It is evident that Claire)
    b. Il n'est pas certain que Claire (It's not certain that Claire)
4. ...*est* [indicative] français.
    (...is French.)

    a.   Il n'est pas sûr qu'Alexis (It's not sure that Alexis)

    b.   Il est sûr qu'Alexis (It's sure that Alexis)

5. ...*ait* [subjunctive] beaucoup d'amis à Montréal.

    (...has a lot of friends in Montreal.)

    a.   Il est important qu'Abia (It is important that Abia)

    b.   On pense qu'Abia (We think that Abia)

Étape 2. Complete the sentences logically.

1. Je pense que Claire _____. (I think that Claire _____)

2. Il est bizarre qu'Alexis _____. (It is bizarre that Alexis ____)

3. Il est évident qu'Abia _____. (It is evident that Abia ____)

    (Wong, Weber-Fève, Ousselin & VanPatten, 2013: 512)

Étape 1 of the above activity structured the input in such a way that learners must rely on the verb forms in order to determine what meaning is being expressed, i.e., doubt, certainty or opinion. Furthermore, as discussed above, the French subjunctive form is always in the middle of a sentence which makes this form even less salient. By putting the form in initial position, the activity also made the form more perceptually salient. *Étape* 2 is a follow-up step to encourage learners to express meaning with controlled and limited output. What is critical is that activities provide sufficient practice with input before leading learners to output. For more information on how to create SI activities, see Farley (2005) and Wong (2005).

4.1.2 *Discourse scrambling*

Another type of input driven activity is discourse scrambling. Developed by VanPatten and his colleagues at Michigan State University (B. VanPatten, personal communication, January 7, 2012), this activity involves discourse level input that contains sentences that are out of order. The learners' task is to put the sentences in order so that the discourse makes sense. In order to do such a task, learners must pay close attention to meaning. In the following example, film is again used as the medium for the delivery of input. The input comes from a brief scene of the film, *Liaisons* (2012). The protagonist Claire has received a mysterious invitation for a weekend stay at a hotel. She is on the phone with the hotel receptionist to confirm this reservation and to find out who might have made it for her.

UNE RÉSERVATION MYSTERIEUSE

Étape 1. Claire is on the phone with a hotel receptionist concerning the mysterious reservation she received. Put the following in order based on what makes sense. You will verify your responses when watching the scene.

–   Cette fin de semaine...

    (This weekend.)

- Ok. Merci.
  (Ok. Thanks.)
- Vous avez une réservation à mon nom?...
  (Do you have a reservation in my name?)
- Oui, Bonjour.
  (Yes. Hello.)
- Qui a fait la réservation, s'il vous plaît?...
  (Who made the reservation, please?)
- Oui. Samedi et dimanche...
  (Yes. Saturday and Sunday.)
- Je m'appelle Claire Gagner.
  (My name is Claire Gagner.)

Étape 2. Now compare what you wrote with a partner. Did you have the same order? Would you like to modify any of your responses?

Étape 3. Now you will watch this scene. Pay close attention to the scene and check to see if what you wrote is correct.
(adapted from VanPatten, Wong & Weber-Fève, 2011)

In addition to providing opportunities for learners to receive and work with input, this technique also enables instructors to preview language before showing a film to increase comprehension of the language as well as what happens in a movie scene. If the purpose of showing a film segment is to expose learners to specific vocabulary or language forms, this technique will also help make that target vocabulary or grammar more salient when learners later encounter the words or forms in the film. This technique is not limited to film. Instructors can also use short reading passages or dialogs that some language textbooks use to present vocabulary and grammar. Rather than have students take turns reading dialogs in textbooks, instructors can create a discourse scrambling activity from the dialog to help learners process the dialog as input.

4.1.3 *Dictogloss*

Dictoglosses involve cycles of input and output, and require that students work in pairs or in small groups to reconstruct something they hear or read (Wajnryb 1990). If an instructor is using this technique to help learners focus on form, the target structure may be embedded in the text that will be heard or read. A dictogloss (also known as *text reconstruction*) typically involves four stages. In stage one, the instructor introduces the topic of what students will be reconstructing as well as any necessary vocabulary. In stage two, students either hear or see the text they will be reconstructing. If the text is to be read orally, the instructor normally reads the text two times. Some instructors allow students to take notes while they listen to the text. Others may prefer that no notes be taken. If students are allowed to take notes, they should not write complete sentences because this is not a dictation exercise. Their task is to attempt to reconstruct what they heard. If the text is to be displayed (e.g., on a power point slide), it should not be displayed for too long so that students are able to copy or memorize it. In stage three, students attempt to reconstruct what they read or heard the best they can in pairs or in small groups by writing out the text. If they were allowed to take notes, they may make use of their notes. Spelling and grammatical accuracy should be emphasized in their reconstructions. In step four, pairs or groups compare their reconstructed texts with the original version. At the end of the activity, the instructor goes over the text with the class, points out how the target form was used in the text, and addresses any questions. Finally, the instructor asks comprehension or follow-up questions about the text to make sure meaning stays in focus.

Because learners know that they need to reconstruct the text after reading or listening to it, they are required to pay very close attention to this input. Izumi (2002) has postulated that requiring learners to reconstruct texts in addition to receiving input may push learners to process input more deeply than they otherwise might. When learners subsequently compare their reconstructed texts to the original version, they are more likely to notice particular language forms, either because they successfully reproduced them or because certain forms posed challenges for them. Furthermore, because this is a collaborative task and accuracy is a goal, learners are required to negotiate both form and meaning with each other.

The following is an example of a dictogloss task for a low intermediate French class targeting preterit and imperfect verbs:

L'HISTOIRE DE NADIA ET DE FRANÇOIS
Étape 1. You are going to hear a story about how Nadia met her husband. You will hear the story two times. As you listen to the story, take notes about the details of the story but do not write complete sentences. You will compare your notes with your classmates later.

Teacher's Script:
[Quand Nadia, la sœur d'Abia, *avait* 25 ans, elle *habitait* Paris parce qu'elle *étudiait* le journalisme à la Sorbonne. Un jour, Alexandra, une amie dans son cours de communications, lui *a téléphoné*. Alexandra l'*a invitée* à dîner chez elle la veille de Noël. Nadia *a accepté* l'invitation. Chez Alexandra, Nadia *a rencontré* François, le cousin du petit ami d'Alexandra. Nadia *trouvait* François très beau. Trois mois plus tard, François *est devenu* son conjoint.]

Étape 2. Compare your notes with two classmates. Use your notes to reconstruct as accurately as possible the story you just heard.

Étape 3. Your instructor will show you the original story. Compare what your group wrote with the original version. Make any necessary corrections.

Étape 4. Have you or anyone in your family met a soul mate? How did this happen? (Adapted from Wong et al. 2013: 325)

In the next example, the author offers a new twist on dictoglosses by using film as the source of input. As seen earlier, film is an excellent source of authentic L2 input and dictoglosses may be designed around a brief scene of a film for a variation on this type of task (VanPatten et al. 2011). To use film in dictoglosses, the instructor would have students watch a brief scene from a film and then attempt to reconstruct the dialog. After reconstructing the dialog in small groups, students check their answers by watching the scene from the film again.

The following is from the film *Les Invasions barbares* (2003).

[What students see]

In the following scene, Sébastien speaks to a nurse, Suzanne, about the possibility of obtaining a test for his father who has cancer. Watch the scene carefully. You will see it twice. After the second time, you and a partner will reconstruct the part of the scene missing below. After reconstructing your text, you will watch this scene again so you can check your answers.

SUZANNE: Oui, il y en a un à Sherbrooke. Mais il y a des listes d'attente de six, huit mois, des fois un an. Vaut mieux pas y penser. Vous allez à Burlington avec lui aujourd'hui?
SÉBASTIEN:
SUZANNE:
SÉBASTIEN:
SUZANNE:
SÉBASTIEN:
SUZANNE:

[Complete text for students to compare after reconstruction]
SUZANNE: Oui, il y en a un à Sherbrooke. Mais il y a des listes d'attente de six, huit mois, des fois un an. Vaut mieux pas y penser. Vous allez à Burlington avec lui aujourd'hui? (Yes, there is one in Sherbrooke. But there is a waiting list of six, eight months, sometimes a year. Better not think about it. Are you going to Burlington with him today?)
SÉBASTIEN: Oui. (Yes.)
SUZANNE: Là, ils en ont un. (They have one there.)

SÉBASTIEN: Formidable. (Great.)
SUZANNE: Mais c'est très cher. Deux mille dollars US au moins, et il faut payer cash ou avec une carte de credit. (But it's very expensive. Two thousand dollars US at least, and you must pay cash or use a credit card.)
SÉBASTIEN: L'argent, c'est pas un problème. (Money is not a problem.)
SUZANNE: Vous êtes chanceux. (You're lucky.)

An important point to keep in mind when doing dictoglosses is to make sure that the level of the text is appropriate so that learners' processing resources are not overtaxed (VanPatten & Wong 2006). For low beginners, three to four sentences may be sufficient. The above example may be done with first-year French students. Notice sentences are short and vocabulary is relatively basic. Research that support the use of dictoglosses/text reconstructions include Izumi, Bigelow, Fujiwara, Miho, and Fearnow (1999), Izumi and Bigelow (2000), and Izumi (2002).

As discussed previously, while instruction may not directly affect learners' mental representations (VanPatten, this volume), instructors can set up conditions to help its development. Structured input, discourse scrambling, and dictoglosses are some examples (and which are by no means exhaustive) of input activities that provide learners with opportunities to receive and process input to help with this process.

4.2   Activities: Skill development

In addition to developing mental representation, L2 learners also need to develop the ability to use their underlying linguistic system. In order for learners to develop fluency and accuracy in an L2, they need to engage in tasks that require them to create output that is tied to the expression of meaning. The following are a few examples of such tasks.

4.2.1   Structured output tasks

Structured output (SO) tasks are grammar tasks because they require learners to use specific grammatical forms. However, unlike a drill, the expression of meaning is critical. In other words, SO tasks require learners to access a particular language form or structure in order to express meaning (Lee & VanPatten 2003). Additionally, SO tasks require learners to go beyond language practice. SO tasks also require learners to learn new information as a result of engaging in the tasks such as making comparisons or drawing conclusions about various topics.

The following are examples of two SO tasks targeting the French subjunctive.

MES DÉSIRS
Étape 1. What do you desire from the following people? Complete the sentences with the verbs provided.

1. Je veux que mon/ma colocataire (écouter) _____
    (I want that my roommate [to listen] _____)
2. J'aime mieux que mes voisins (s'entendre) _____
    (I want that my neighbors [to get a long] _____)
3. Il vaut mieux que mon ami(e) (sortir) _____
    (It's better that my friend [to go out] _____)
4. Je préfère que mon/ma colocataire (dormir) _____
    (I prefer that my roommate [to sleep]) _____
5. Je veux que ma famille (se sentir) _____
    (I want that my family [to feel] _____)

Étape 2. Compare your answers with a partner. Who is more demanding? You or your partner?)
(Wong et al. 2013: 475)

Note that learners are required to use the subjunctive to express their own meaning as they complete the sentences. In step two, they are asked to compare responses with a partner and to draw a conclusion based on the information exchanged, i.e., Who is more demanding?

The next activity also focuses on the subjunctive but requires freer responses.

LES MEILLEURES SOLUTIONS
Étape 1. Decide if each solution given is a good or bad idea for each problem indicated.

1. les espèces menacées: On interdit aux gens d'aller à la chasse.
    (endangered species: Ban people from hunting.)
2. le réchauffement climatique: On n'a besion de rien faire.
    (global warming: We don't need to do anything.)
3. la faim: Les gens pauvres peuvent manger plus d'aliments OGM.
    (hunger: Poor people can eat more genetically modified foods.)
4. la pollution: On exige que les gens fassent du compost.
    (pollution: Require people to compost.)
5. la pauvrété: On paie plus d'impots.
    (poverty: Pay more taxes)

Étape 2. Show your responses to a partner. Did you have the same responses? For each response where you indicated it was a bad idea, decide what is the best solution to the problem with a partner.
Modèle: la faim (hunger)
    Le gouvernement peut donner aux gens plus d'assistance sociale.
    (Government can give more social aid to people)
(Wong et al. 2013: 509)

This activity gives students the opportunity to use the subjunctive but its goal is not simply to practice the subjunctive. Students' first task is to decide whether each solution is good or bad. Then with a partner, they indicate what they think is the best solution to the bad solutions they identified. Therefore, this task requires students to create output that is tied to expressing meaning and also requires them to negotiate with classmates what they think are the best solutions to certain environmental and social issues.

4.2.2 *Rewrite-a-scene*

Output activities do not need to be tied to grammar goals or target any specific forms. The following example illustrates a creative way to give students an opportunity to engage in more extended writing using film again as the medium. Students first receive input by watching a scene from a film. Following this, in pairs or small groups, they rewrite the scene by altering some of its elements. The following example is taken from a short scene of the film *Paris je t'aime* (2006).

Étape 1. You will watch a scene from the film *Paris je t'aime*. Carol, a middle-aged American woman, visits Paris for the first time. As we see Carol travel through Paris, she shares some of her thoughts and impressions. You will watch this scene twice. The second time you watch it, jot down 5–6 things that Carol shares with viewers.

Étape 2. Share what you wrote with a partner. Did your partner include things you did not?

Étape 3. With your partner, rewrite the scene so that the protagonist is either a male or a female college student rather than a middle-aged woman. What types of thoughts would a college student have visiting Paris for the first time? Would his/her thoughts and impressions be similar or different from Carol's? Would a male student's impressions be different from a female student's impressions?

This activity makes learners pay close attention to the input they get through watching the segment. In order to rewrite the scene so that the protagonist is a male or female student, they need to comprehend the segment well and then reinterpret it through the eyes of a college student. In other words, students are required to process the input well for meaning and then they are pushed to create output by expressing meaning through the perspective of another character.

4.2.3 *Film re-making project*

The scene rewriting activity described above may be taken further by having students not just rewrite a scene but also act in and film their scenes. This type of activity gives students the opportunity to create both extended written and oral output as well as encourage students to use their creativity. The activity in Appendix A is an example of such a task. This project is designed for a second semester French course and is intended to be used as an oral final exam.

The task is for students to remake a 2–3 minute scene from a film that they have been watching in class, *Liaisons* (see Appendix A). Each group selects a scene from the film they want to remake. They may make a faithful adaptation of the scene, alter the genre and/or other elements, or create a new scene. After their scene selection, students work together to write the script in their own words with original language that is appropriate to their level. They receive a group grade on the script and are assessed on creativity and language accuracy among other things (see Appendix B). Because this film portrays cultural and linguistic differences between France and Quebec, they are asked to demonstrate their awareness of these differences in their script writing (see Appendix A point 4). Additionally, students are asked to make sure that each person has relatively the same amount of speaking lines. After writing the script, students film their scene to show in class.

Forty percent of the project grade is an individual grade (Appendix B). Students are assessed individually on their acting (10%) and their language skills: (1) pronunciation/comprehensibility (10%), (2) fluency (10%), and (3) accuracy (10%). This project may also be adapted so that students perform their scenes in class as a play rather than make a film. Regardless of the medium, this type of project gives students the opportunity to engage in extended writing and speaking to help them develop fluency and accuracy in a creative way. Furthermore, instructors may include as part of the assessment other aspects of language learning such as cultural and language awareness.

5.   Conclusion

This chapter offered L2 instructors ideas for creating pedagogical activities that flow from VanPatten's position in chapter one of this volume that language consists of two distinct domains, i.e., the development of a mental representation of language and the ability to use that underlying representation. Some pedagogical practices that have been influential over the years were reviewed in light of this perspective. Because mental representation is dependent on processed input, it was proposed that activities that are best suited for developing underlying representation are activities that provide lots of comprehensible input and those that encourage learners to engage in input processing. Because skill develops by engaging in task and context appropriate activities, communicative ability may be best developed by having learners engage in output activities that require the expression and negotiation of meaning. Well established activities such as structured input and structured output were discussed, and some new ideas (e.g., discourse scrambling, dictoglosses driven by film, scene rewriting, and film re-making) were presented.

To conclude, there are roles for both input and output in the creation of L2 classroom activities. By understanding the nature of these activities and how they work to enhance the development of different language domains (i.e., mental representation or skill), instructors will be better equipped to create opportunities to promote L2 language development in their classrooms.

References

Benati, A. & Lee, J. (Eds). (2008). *Grammar acquisition and processing instruction: Secondary and cumulative effects.* Bristol, UK: Multilingual Matters.

Farley, A. (2001). Authentic processing instruction and the Spanish subjunctive. *Hispania, 84,* 289–299.

Farley, A. (2005). *Structured input: Grammar for the acquisition-oriented classroom.* Boston, MA: McGraw-Hill.

Harley, B. (1993). Instructional strategies and SLA in early French immersion. *Studies in Second Language Acquisition* 15: 245–260.

Harley, B., & Swain, M. (1984). The interlanguage of immersion students and its implication for second language teaching. In A. Davies, C. Criper, & A. Howatt (Eds.), *Interlanguage* (pp. 291–311). Edinburgh: EUP.

Hinkel, E., & Fotos, S. (2002). *New perspectives on grammar teaching in second language classrooms.* Mahwah, NJ: Lawrence Erlbaum Associates.

Izumi, S. (2002). Output, input enhancement, and the noticing hypothesis: An experimental study on ESL Relativization. *Studies in Second Language Acquisition, 24,* 541–577.

Izumi, S., & Bigelow, M. 2000. Does output promote noticing and second language acquisition? *TESOL Quarterly, 34,* 239–278.

Izumi, S., Bigelow, M., Fujiwara, M., & Fearnow, S. (1999). Testing the output hypothesis: Effects of output on noticing and second language acquisition. *Studies in Second Language Acquisition, 21,* 421–452.

Katz, S., & Blyth, C. (2007). *Teaching French grammar in context.* New Haven, CT: Yale University Press.

Krashen, S. (1985). *The input hypothesis: Issues and implications.* London: Longman.

Lee, J. F., & VanPatten, B. (2003). *Making communicative language teaching happen.* New York, NY: McGraw-Hill.

Les invasions barbares. Dir. Denys Arcand. Alliance Atlantis, (2003).

Liaisons. Screenplay by Bill VanPatten & Wynne Wong. Dir. Andrei Campeanu. AT/Media, (2012). Film.

Paulston, C.B. (1972). Structural pattern drills: A classification. In H. Allen & R. Campell (Eds.), *Teaching English as a second language* (pp. 129–138). New York, NY: McGraw Hill.

Paris je t'aime. Prod. Emmanuel Benbihy & Claudie Ossard. La Fabrique de films, (2006).

Swain, M. (1985). Communicative competence: Some roles of comprehensible input and comprehensible output in its development. In S. Gass & C. Madden (Eds.), *Input in second language acquisition* (pp. 235–253). Rowley, MA: Newbury House.

Swain, M. (1995). Three functions of output in second language learning. In G. Cook & B.
Seidlhofer (Eds.), *Principles and practice in applied linguistics: Studies in honor of H. Wid-
dowson,* 125–144. Oxford: OUP.

VanPatten, B. (2004). Input processing in SLA. In B. VanPatten (Ed.), *Processing instruction:
Theory, research, and commentary* (pp. 5–31). Mahwah, NJ: Lawrence Erlbaum Associates.

VanPatten, B., & Benati, A. (2010). *Key terms in second language acquisition.* London: Continuum.

VanPatten, B., & Cadierno, T. (1993). Explicit instruction and input processing. *Studies in Second Language Acquisition, 15*, 225–43.

VanPatten, B., & Wong, W. (2006, April 2). *Grammar without Drills!* Annual Meeting of the
Northeast Conference for the Teaching of Foreign Languages, New York, NY.

VanPatten, B., Wong, W., & Weber-Fève. S. (2011, July 6–9). Beyond soda and popcorn: Using
film to promote language development. Annual Convention of the American Association
of Teachers of French, Montreal, CA.

Wajnryb, R. (1990). *Resource books for teachers: Grammar Dictation.* Oxford: OUP.

Wong, W. (2005). *Input enhancement: From theory and research to the classroom.* New York, NY:
McGraw-Hill.

Wong, W. (2008). Rethinking a focus on grammar – From drills to processing instruction and
meaningful output: Data from the French subjunctive. In J. Watzinger-Tharp & S. Katz
(Eds.), *Conceptions of L2 grammar: Theoretical approaches and their application in the L2
classroom* (pp. 72–92). Boston, MA: Heinle Cengage.

Wong, W., & VanPatten, B. (2003). The Evidence is IN: Drills are OUT. *Foreign Language Annals,
36*, 403–423.

Wong, W., Weber-Fève, S., Ousselin, E., & VanPatten, B. (2013). *Liaisons: An introduction to
French.* Boston, MA: Heinle-Cengage.

Appendix A

In small groups, you will remake a 2–3 minute scene from the film *Liaisons*. Your group is expected to work *together*, and group members are expected to share the work *equally*. You will receive an individual and a group grade for this project. All work is to be completed in FRENCH unless otherwise specified.

Requirements:

1. *Select a scene* to remake. You may also create a completely new scene but the scene must be inspired by the film *Liaisons* and/or have characters from *Liaisons*. You may add additional characters not in the original film such as extras. The finished scene is 2–3 minutes long.
2. *Form your «société de production cinématographique».* By the end of WEEK 7, each group must notify your instructor with: (1) the name of your "société," (2) the names of "les acteurs," and (3) a brief description of the scene.
3. *Elect a "réalisateur/réalisatrice."* This person will be in charge of the filming and/or directing of your scene. Should s/he spend additional "technological" time individually editing the film, s/he will receive extra credit. (See instructor if this applies.)
4. *Write a script.* Everyone is to be involved. Rewrite the dialogue in your own French! Pay attention to cultural authenticity when composing language such as differences between France and Quebec. Make sure each group member has relatively the same amount of speaking lines. Production notes (i.e., stage directions) and the distribution of roles must also be included. The production notes may be in English and should be enclosed in brackets.
5. *Memorize on-screen dialogue.* No scripts (or actors who appear to be extensively reading off of hidden or off-screen cue cards) are allowed!
6. *Use your imagination/creativity.* You may make a faithful adaptation (with level-appropriate dialogue) of your scene, or you may reinvent it by changing its genre, tone, cinematic styling, etc. You may also create a new scene and/or add characters.
7. *Distribution-of-Work Sheet*: Describe the work each member of your group did on this project in English. Make sure each student signs it showing that you are in agreement.
8. *Make a DVD.*

Appendix B

Nom: _____

Société de production: _____

GRADING CRITERIA

	Group Grade	Individual Grade
Script – Distribution of roles listed – Name of *société de production cinématographique* is present – Technical notes – Ideas/content/creativity	/1 /1 /3 /15	X X X X

– Language:
  – original, level appropriate, and accurate
  – evidence of language awareness (e.g., cultural authenticity, culturally appropriate expressions, etc.)
	/12
	/6
		X
		X

Individual contribution to preparation/script	X	/10

Performance
– Costumes/props/sound
– Acting
– Language
  – Pronunciation/comprehensibility
  – Fluency
  – Accuracy
	
	/10
	X
	
	X
	X
	X
		
		X
		/10
		
		/10
		/10
		/10

Time limit respected (2–3 minutes) Distribution-of-Work Sheet included	/1 /1	X X
TOTAL GRADE	/100	

CHAPTER 3

Interaction and the Noun Phrase Accessibility Hierarchy

A study using syntactic priming*

Jennifer Behney and Susan Gass
Youngstown State University and Michigan State University

Following on the extensive findings of the benefits of conversational interaction in second language (L2) learning and the existence of the Accessibility Hierarchy (AH) in L2 learners' acquisition of relative clauses (RCs), this study considers how RC input provided to L2 learners results in greater production of subject (SUBJ) and direct object (DO) RCs in an interactive context. Using a scripted syntactic priming design, 30 learners of Italian engaged in a picture description activity with the researcher. Priming of both SUBJ RCs and DO RCs was found, with a greater number of SUBJ RCs produced throughout the study. Findings are discussed in terms of the AH and RC acquisition.

1. Introduction

Over the past thirty years, much has been written about the interactionist approach (see Gass & Mackey 2006; Gass & Mackey 2007; Mackey & Abbuhl 2006; and Mackey, Abbuhl & Gass, 2012 for recent reviews). Gass and Mackey (2007: 176) point out that, "it is now commonly accepted within the SLA literature that there is a robust connection between interaction and learning". The relationship has been examined with regard to numerous language forms (e.g., Doughty & Varela 1998; Ellis 2007; Ellis, Loewen & Erlam, 2006; Mackey 1999, 2006; Mackey & Philp 1998; McDonough 2007; Muranoi 2000; Philp 2003; Sheen 2007). The results are found for children as well as adults (Mackey & Oliver 2002; Mackey & Silver 2005; Van den Branden 1997); they are valid in classroom as well as laboratory settings

* This is a revised version of a paper presented at the 9th International Congress of the *International Society of Applied Psycholinguistics,* held in June, 2010. We are grateful to Elisa Ghia of the Università degli studi di Pavia, and Matt Scollin, currently at the University of Illinois Urbana-Champaign, for their assistance in collecting data for this study.

(Gass, Mackey & Ross-Feldman 2005, 2011 [see meta-analysis by Mackey & Goo 2007]); and they hold for a range of languages, including French (Ayoun 2001; Swain & Lapkin 1998, 2002), Japanese (Ishida 2004; Iwashita 2003), Korean (Jeon 2007), and Spanish (de la Fuente 2002; Gass & Torres 2005; Leeman 2003). The relationship, however, is not always straightforward and can be mediated by such learner variables as working memory (Mackey, Philp, Egi, Fujii & Tatsumi 2002) and inhibition (Gass, Behney & Uzum 2013). With few exceptions, the literature has not addressed the effect of the input on the selection of linguistic form. This chapter fills that void by considering two forms of relative clauses, one clearly documented to be more basic and more easily learned than the other. The questions are addressed through the of use syntactic priming. In keeping with the goals of the current volume, namely, to focus on innovative research, we consider interaction-based research as our point of departure and use syntactic priming as the methodology to understand how L2 learners make choices about complex and related linguistic forms.

The interactionist approach goes back to the early 1980s with research by Long (1980, 1981), Gass and Varonis (1985, 1994), and Varonis and Gass (1982, 1985). At the core of the interactionist approach is that what happens in conversation impacts learning. In other words, interaction itself facilitates learning by unifying a number of features known to benefit learning, namely, input, feedback, attention, and output. The features are dependent on external factors (e.g., input and feedback) as well as internal factors such as attention. When learners are engaged in a conversation with a native speaker of the target language or a proficient speaker of that language, there are often breakdowns in communication. Such breakdowns are claimed to be beneficial and even part of the process of learning. This is so because the conversation is often put on hold while the participants use a variety of discourse strategies to resolve the problem, for example, clarification requests, recasts, and confirmation requests (see Gass 1997; Gass & Selinker 2008; Gass [with Behney & Plonsky] 2013, and the reviews mentioned above). As a result of negotiation, there is increased input, often clarified through examples or rephrasing, and increased output. Important is the fact that the interaction itself draws learners' attention to parts of the L2 that may be problematic. As Mackey, Abbuhl, and Gass (2012: 10) note, "This constellation of features – interactionally modified input, having the learner's attention drawn to his/her interlanguage and to the formal features of the L2, opportunities to produce output and opportunities to receive feedback – are the core components of the interactional approach...". Gass (1988) also points out that learning is actually a process involving input (as an initial step) and ending with control over linguistic form.

This chapter focuses on input and investigates how the input itself determines the forms a learner selects to produce (output). The significance of output has been dealt with extensively (Swain 1985, 1995, 2005). In particular, there are a number of benefits associated with output among which is the benefit derived from production which "may force the learner to move from semantic processing to syntactic processing" (Swain 1985: 249). In other words, during production, one tests one's knowledge extensively by being forced to put elements in a particular order. Thus, if we know how to elicit output, we know how to increase the potentiality of learning.

In the next two sections we address the structure that we used and the method that we adopted in our investigation of the relationship between input and form selection by L2 learners.

In order to determine whether learners select one linguistic form over another, we selected a syntactic structure with two subparts that are related in both form and meaning. We used hierarchically-related relative clause types, based on the Accessibility Hierarchy (AH), initially proposed by Keenan and Comrie (1977). In its simplest form, the AH, is a typological universal[1] that accounts for differences among languages and that attempts to predict the types of relative clauses that languages can have. The basic principle is that one can predict the types of relative clauses that a given language will have based on this hierarchy which takes as its basic principle the grammatical role of the head noun phrase and its relative clause (RC) modification: subject (SU) > direct object (DO) > indirect object (IO) > oblique (OBL) > genitive (GEN) > object of comparision (OCOMP)[2]. The claim is that predictions can be made such that if a language has a relative clause of type *X*, it will also have any relative clause type higher on the hierarchy, or to the left of type *X*. Thus, if we know that a given language has an OBL (indirect object) RC (e.g., *That's the boy that I gave a book to),* we also know that it has direct object and subject relative clauses, the latter of which are present in most of the world's languages. We cannot predict *a priori* the lowest relative clause type in a given

---

1.   The question of the universality of the NPAH has been brought into question by a series of articles focused on East Asian languages (see SSLA special issue, 2007 [2], in particular, articles by Jeon & Kim, 2007; Ozeki & Shirai, 2007; Yabuki-Soh, 2007; Yip & Matthews, 2007). Because the findings of universality for European languages have been robust and because the subject of investigation of this study involves English learners of Italian, that issue is not addressed in this paper. In broad terms, research on relative clauses suggests that the hierarchy is adhered to, but that such issues as semantics and language specifics play an important role in relative clause acquisition.

2.   Subject relative clause: That's the woman [*who* flew the airplane] (*who* is the subject of the clause). Direct object relative clause: That's the dancer [*whom* I saw in the store] (*whom* is the direct object of its clause). Indirect object relative clause: That's the little boy [to *whom* I gave the stuffed animal] (*whom* is the indirect object of its clause). Object of preposition relative clause: That's my student [*whom* I told you about]. Genitive relative clause: That's my son [*whose child* is two]. Object of comparative: That's the man [*whom* I am taller than].

language; we can only predict RC types on the basis of knowing the presence of a given relative clause type.

The generalizations that stem from the AH have been tested with second language learners in both classroom and lab environments. The findings clearly demonstrate that there is an implication of difficulty (Banfi 2003; Croteau 1995; Doughty 1991; Eckman, Bell & Nelson 1988; Gass 1979, 1982; Keenan & Comrie 1977; Pavesi 1986; Valentini 1992, 1997); learners followed the orderings of the hierarchy with regard to learning and production frequency/order: easiest relative clause types (e.g., subject, direct object) are generally learned earlier than those lower on the hierarchy (e.g., object of comparative). Second, Gass (1980) found that when learners were told to produce RC types lower on the hierarchy, they overwhelmingly produced RC types higher; the reverse was not found. Finally, when instructed on direct objects, but not subject relatives, learners generalize their learning to subject relatives, but not vice versa (e.g., Eckman, Bell & Nelson 1988; Gass 1982). This latter is an important finding in trying to understand the relationship between instruction and typological markedness, as is reflected in the AH.

Because the goal of our study was to examine the selection and production of related structures in conversation and to understand how that production was determined by the input, we adopted syntactic priming as the method for data elicitation. We did this by examining whether direct object relative clauses ("the star that I saw is red"), a relatively difficult structure for L2 learners, can be syntactically primed in L2 learners as opposed to an alternate structure, subject relative clauses ("the star that is red"), which is a less developmentally advanced structure.

Syntactic priming, the tendency to repeat previously uttered or comprehended syntactic structures when an alternate structure is available (Bock 1989), has in recent years become a topic of discussion in the second language (L2) literature (see McDonough & Trofimovich 2009). In general, priming studies have been conducted in laboratory settings without specific regard to ways in which priming occurs in a natural context. With a focus on how learning takes place in interaction, it is appropriate to extend the concept of priming to interactive contexts. There has been a recognition that what happens in natural conversation involving L2 learners can be viewed as a type of priming where learners will produce a form that they hear in previous utterances as opposed to some other alternative utterance. In the past 5–10 years, the phenomenon has also been documented in the SLA literature (see McDonough 2006, who focused on the acquisition of English double-object datives; McDonough & Mackey 2008 where the focus was on English question forms by native speakers of Thai; and Kim & McDonough 2008 who investigated the L2 acquisition of English passive sentences by native speakers of Korean). An example is given in (1) below from McDonough (2006: 182).

(1)   A: The man shows his wife the boot.
      B: A teacher is teaching some kids a game.

To understand this example, learners A and B were involved in a picture description/matching activity. As can be seen, speaker A used a double-object dative to describe a picture. Immediately following this, speaker B used the same construction to describe another picture, even though speaker B could have used a prepositional dative.

The question remains as to which syntactic structures are susceptible to priming and which are less likely to benefit from priming. McDonough (2006) suggested that more complex target structures are susceptible to priming in the L2 and that priming might be partially responsible for the facilitating effect of interaction in L2 acquisition. This is supported by Behney (2008) who found syntactic priming of a more complex target structure of subject relative clauses as opposed to the alternate structure of noun-adjective noun phrases in native English speaking learners of Italian.

In the current study, we focus on language in an interactive context, the locus for much L2 learning, to determine how the input impacts syntactic choice. We use syntactic priming to investigate this issue[3]. The primes were scripted but the context was one that approximated a typical interactive classroom activity.

2.   Research questions

Two research questions guided this study:

1.   Do L2 learners of Italian show evidence of syntactic priming after receiving input containing subject relative clauses and direct object relative clauses?

Given past research on priming, we predict that priming will occur with both subject relative clauses and the more advanced structure of direct object relative clauses among these L2 learners.

2.   In a conversational context (interaction activity), are there more priming effects with subject relative clauses than with direct object relative clauses?

The priming literature states that more difficult or less common structures are more prone to the effects of priming. Hence, the more difficult structure (direct object relatives) is predicted to be more susceptible to priming effects than the easier

---

3.   There is a vast literature on syntactic priming which goes beyond the limits of this study. We refer the reader to a recent book by McDonough and Trofimovich (2009) for a thorough discussion of syntactic priming in the SLA literature.

structure (subject relative clauses). On the other hand, the literature dealing with the AH might predict more priming with subject relative clauses than with direct object relative clauses precisely because it is easier to produce subject relatives.

3.   Method

3.1   Participants

Participants for this study were 32 learners of Italian at two large Midwestern universities. Two participants were removed from the data set because they did not produce any subject or direct object relative clauses. This left us with a total of 30 native English-speaking participants whose data were used for analysis. At the time of data collection, they had completed two years of university-level Italian study. In Table 1 is general information about the 30 participants who remained in the study. There were 19 females and 11 males. The "researcher" consisted of three separate individuals: one native speaker of Italian, one advanced nonnative speaker of Italian, and one nonnative speaker of Italian who had completed three years of Italian study.

3.2   Design

The design of this study was adapted from Cleland and Pickering (2003). It consisted of a picture description task in which the researcher and the participant took turns describing cards with a single colored object (e.g., a blue cloud) to each other and finding the card matching the other's description. The researcher's descriptions were scripted, as in previous studies involving syntactic priming (e.g., Behney 2008; Branigan, Pickering & Cleland 2000; Cleland & Pickering 2003;

Table 1. Participants

N	M age	Gender	Other Ls*	Study Abroad**
30	20.48 (SD = 2.97)	19 females 11 males	Spanish French German Latin Hebrew Japanese	12 participants

*Participants had studied these languages between .5 (in the case of Japanese) and 6 years (in the case of Spanish).

**Two participants had spent two months in Italy; the range for the other 10 was 1 to 4 weeks, with an average of 3.3 weeks.

Hartsuiker, Pickering & Veltkamp 2004; McDonough 2006); that is, the researcher was actually reading the noun phrases with relative clauses (i.e., the *primes*) from the cards in a particular order so that each prime was followed by a card that the participant had to describe (i.e., the *target*). Having the cards ordered in this way also ensured that there were an equal number of subject relative clause (SUBJ RC) primes and direct object relative clause (DO RC) primes, 15 of each. The participant did not know that the researcher was following these scripted cards.

Each card that the participant described contained a prompt that the participant was instructed to use to begin his/her description, so as to ensure that he/she would produce some type of relative clause rather than a simple noun phrase (as in McDonough 2006 and Kim & McDonough 2008 where prompts of the verbs to be used were provided on the participants' cards and in McDonough & Chaikitmongkol 2010 where prompts of question words were provided). As an example, consider the sequence in (2). (The underlined part indicates the prompt written on the participant's card).

(2)   Researcher: *L'albero che è bianco è qui.*
                           The tree that is white is here.
      Participant UM2:   *La nuvola che è azzurro è qui.*
                           The cloud$_{SingFem}$ that is blue$_{SingMasc}$ is here.
      Researcher: *Il triangolo che vedo è azzurro.*
                           The triangle that (I) see is blue.
      Participant UM2:   *Il cerchio che io vedo è rosso.*
                           The circle that I see is red.

3.3   Materials

On each picture card was a single object. In total there were ten objects (squares, triangles, circles, suns, moons, trees, stars, clouds, hearts, and arrows) and each object appeared in 6 colors (red, yellow, blue, gray, white, and black), for a total of 60 cards. In addition, there were 35 filler cards which had pictures of unique objects that could be described without a color adjective, or without any additional description whatsoever (e.g., *Il fiore* "The flower," as there was only one flower in the experiment). Examples of the materials are given in Figure 1.

3.4   Procedure

During the picture description activity, the participants heard 15 SUBJ RC primes and 15 DO RC primes described by the researcher which were followed by 30 target picture cards which the participant had to describe with noun phrase relative

Researcher's card   Participant's card   Filler card
(DO prime)   (target)

| Il triangolo che vedo è azzurro. | La freccia che … | Il fiore |

Figure 1. Picture cards

Table 2. Primes and targets

	Primes (Researcher Cards)	Targets (Participant Cards)
SUBJ RC Primes	15	30 noun phrases
DO RC Primes	15	
Fillers	35	35

clauses. An item in this experiment refers to the researcher's description of a card (the prime) followed by the participant describing a card (the target). We operated with four different item lists which were quasi-randomized by Excel; there were no more than two consecutive items that occurred before one of the 35 fillers. Filler primes were always followed by filler targets. Table 2 below summarizes the primes and targets.

The participant and the researcher sat facing each other at a table with a divider between them, as can be seen in Figure 2.

Each had: (1) a set of matching cards spread out before them and (2) a box of description cards to be described. The researcher took a card from the box of cards and read the prime off the card (e.g., *Il triangolo che è nero è qui.* "The triangle that is black is here."). The participant's task was to find from the cards that were spread out before him/her a card with, in this example, a picture of a black triangle. The participant then put the card in a box that was situated to the side. The participant then took a card from his/her box of cards to be described. On the card was, for example, the prompt *Il cerchio che…* ("The circle that…"). The participant might have said, *Il cerchio che è rosso è qui.* ("The circle that is red is here."). In this case

Figure 2. Experimental set-up (reprinted with permission of Matt Scollin)

the participant used a SUBJ RC in the target as did the researcher in the prime, so syntactic priming has occurred. The researcher then was to find the card with the red circle from the matching set in front of her and put it aside. The researcher then selected the next card from the description set and said, for example, *La stella che vedo è nera.* ("The star that I see is black."). The participant was to find the card with a black star, put it aside, and select the next card from the box of cards to be described. If he/she then said, *Il quadrato che vedo è azzurro.* ("The square that I see is blue."), priming has occurred because it is, like the prime, a DO RC. If, however, the participant described the card with a SUBJ RC (e.g., *Il quadrato che è azzurro è qui.* "The square that is blue is here."), priming has not occurred. This continued until all cards had been described by both researcher and participant. The sessions were recorded and then transcribed.

3.5   Target structure

Relative clause structures in Italian are similar to relative clauses in English, at least with regard to subject and direct object relative clauses. As in English, the relative clause in Italian is introduced by a relative pronoun. In subject relative clauses and direct object relative clauses, the pronoun *che* ("that," "which," "who," "whom") can be used to refer to both human and nonhuman antecedents.

(3) *Lei è la ragazza che lavora con Paolo.*
    She is the girl who works with Paolo.

(4) *Il triangolo che è rosso è qui.*
    The triangle that is red is here.

(5) *L'amico che ho conosciuto alla festa viene da Bergamo.*
    The friend whom I met at the party comes from Bergamo.

(6) *L'albero che vedo è azzurro.*
     The tree that I see is blue.

The relative pronoun *il quale* is also used in subject relative clauses and must be inflected for grammatical gender and number (*il quale, la quale, i quali, le quali*). There were no primes containing *il quale* used in the study, however, and participants did not produce any targets containing *il quale*. Any adjectives inside the relative clause must also be inflected for gender and number (*La stella*$_{\text{SingFem}}$ *che è rossa*$_{\text{SingFem}}$ *è qui. La stella*$_{\text{SingFem}}$ *che vedo è rossa*$_{\text{SingFem}}$.). Errors in gender agreement of the color adjectives were frequent among the participants but were not considered in this study as they were outside of the scope of investigation. This is consistent with other studies conducted within this genre in which unrelated morphological errors were not considered (Kim & McDonough 2008; McDonough 2006; McDonough & Chaikitmongkol 2010).

3.6   Coding

We coded all learner utterances as either SUBJ RC, DO RC, or Other. In coding the targets that the participants produced, we accepted both *La stella che è rossa* ("The star that is red") as well as *La stella che è rossa è qui* ("The star that is red is here") as SUBJ RCs. For DO RC targets, we accepted *La stella che vedo* or *che io vedo è rossa* ("The star that I see is red") as well as *La stella che ho trovato è rossa* ("The star that I found is red"). We coded other structures as *Other*, including simple noun phrases (e.g., *Il triangolo azzurro* "The blue triangle"); noun-verb-adjective clauses (e.g., *Il cuore è nero* "The heart is black"); subject relative clauses lacking a verb (e.g., *La freccia che azzurra* "The arrow that blue"); phrases that did not contain a color adjective (e.g., *Il sole che brucia* "The sun that burns"); and incomprehensible phrases or phrases in languages other than Italian (e.g., *La freccia che alla izquierda bianco* "The arrow that on the [left, Spanish] white" and *La luna che non bianca non it's black sorry* "The moon that no white no [it's black sorry, English]").

3.7   Analysis

Following Cleland and Pickering (2003) and Bernolet, Hartsuiker, and Pickering (2007), we calculated the ratio of the number of DO RC targets produced by participants to the total number of all RCs (SUBJ RCs + DO RCs) produced following DO RC primes and the ratio of the number of DO RC targets produced to the total number of all RCs (SUBJ RCs + DO RCs) produced following SUBJ RC primes for each participant. In order to compare these two DO RC ratios to see what effect the type of prime that the participants received had on their production of DO RC targets, a repeated measures ANOVA was run on the DO RC ratios with the repeated measures variable of Prime Type (either SUBJ RC or DO RC). (The decision to use the DO RC ratios rather than the SUBJ RC ratios was arbitrary since in both cases the difference in Prime Type is the same.)

4. Results

The results are presented in Table 3. The total number of targets produced across participants and items was calculated. As can be seen in the table, more SUBJ RC targets were produced by the participants after SUBJ RC primes (total = 321, M = 10.70 per participant) from the researcher than after DO RC primes (total = 264, M = 8.80 per participant). Similarly, more DO RC targets were produced by participants after DO RC primes (total = 128, M = 4.27 per participant) than after SUBJ RC primes (total = 77, M = 2.57 per participant). The ratio of SUBJ RC targets produced following SUBJ RC primes to the total number of RCs produced was 80.65%, while the ratio of SUBJ RC targets produced following DO RC primes was 67.35%. The ratio of DO RC targets produced following DO RC primes to the total number of RCs produced was 32.65%, while the ratio of DO RC targets produced following SUBJ RC primes was 19.35%. This 13.3% difference of Prime Type was found to be significant in the repeated measures ANOVA; that is, there was a significant main effect of Prime Type, $F(1, 29) = 14.21, p < .001$, $\eta^2 = .33$.

With regard to research question 2 which asked whether the priming effects were greater with subject relative clauses than with direct object relative clauses, the answer appears to be yes. As can be seen from Table 3, when the prime was a SUBJ RC, 80.65% of the responses were SUBJ RCs. On the other hand, when the prime was a DO RC, only 32.65% of the responses followed suit, that is, were DO RCs.

Table 3. Numbers and percentages of targets produced after primes across participants

Prime Type	Target Type				
	SUBJ	DO	Total RCs	Other	Total
SUBJ RC	321 (80.65)	77 (19.35)	398	52	450
DO RC	264 (67.35)	128 (32.65)	392	58	450
Total	585	205	790	110	900

Note. Percentages of types of target produced to total RCs produced appear in parentheses.

5. Discussion

This study questioned the role of input in determining selection of two hierarchically-related forms. The first research question asked whether we would find priming with relative clauses in L2 learners of Italian. In other words, with a relatively complex syntactic structure, can repeated input influence selection/production. Priming did occur with these learners. Specifically, with both SUBJ and DO RCs, there was greater production with priming than without. When the prime was a SUBJ RC, there were 321/398 (80.65%) SUBJ RC responses, but when the prime was a DO RC, there were 264/392 (67.35%) instances of SUBJ RC responses. Similarly, DO RC targets were more common after DO RC primes; when the prime was a DO RC, there were 128/392 (32.65%) DO RC responses, but when the prime was a SUBJ RC, there were 77/398 (19.35%) instances of DO RC responses.

The second research question asked about the interplay between input (priming) and structural difficulty: was there more priming with subject relative clauses than with direct object relative clauses? There were more SUBJ RCs successfully primed (80.65% SUBJ RCs were produced following SUBJ RC primes) than there were DO RCs successfully primed (32.65% of the time DO RC targets were produced following DO RC primes). All things being equal, we would expect SUBJ RC primes to yield a large number of SUBJ RCs (which was the case) and DO RC primes to yield a large number of DO RCs (which was not the case). One can also point to the fact that the SUBJ prime yielded nearly four times as many SUBJ RCs than it did DO RCs, suggesting a strong priming influence. On the other hand, the ratio of DO to SUBJ RCs following a DO RC is approximately 2:1, suggesting a lower priming influence. These results are consistent with past research on the AH which attest to the difficulty of learning structures lower on the hierarchy. In fact, as noted earlier, Gass (1979, 1980) found that even when participants were given explicit instructions to produce DO RCs, there was a strong tendency to produce SUBJ RCs. Yet, this was not the case when given instructions to produce SUBJ RCS; changes to RC types other than subject rarely occurred.

Conversation provides a forum for frequent use of a structure, giving learners the opportunity to adopt that form in subsequent speech. This phenomenon provides the underpinnings of previous investigations of priming as relevant to the context of learning. Priming has been shown to have an effect in the L2 in a wide range of syntactic structures, some simple and some more complex (Behney 2008; Kim & McDonough 2008; McDonough 2006; McDonough & Mackey 2008; McDonough & Chaikitmongkol 2010). As was the case with studies by McDonough and Mackey, McDonough and Chaikitmongkol, and Behney, we have used structural difficulty as a variable, reflected through the AH. We found that the extent of the effect of priming interacts with the complexity of the structure such that priming of a simpler structure has a greater effect than priming with a more complex structure. An additional point to note is that there is an interesting effect of priming in the predicted direction, outlined by the Accessibility Hierarchy with the occurrence of more priming of SUBJ RCs than of DO RCs. Priming does have an effect on production, however, just not as great an effect as the hierarchy itself. SUBJ RC primes promote both SUBJ RC and DO RC targets. However, the influence in the other direction is not as strong. DO RC primes do produce DO RC targets, but they also produce a large number of SUBJ RC targets.

There are a number of issues that would benefit from further investigation. One limitation in the current study is that for practical purposes the "researcher" consisted of three different individuals. One of the researchers was a native speaker of Italian who carried out the study with 9 of the participants; another researcher was an advanced nonnative speaker of Italian who carried out the study with 18 of the participants; and the third researcher was an undergraduate student who had completed three years of Italian study and who carried out the study with only 3 of the participants. As suggested by Behney (2008), the level of L2 proficiency of the researcher may have affected how likely the participants were to show priming. Although there were too few participants with two of the researchers to run a statistical comparison of the amount of priming that occurred with each researcher, it is interesting to note the differences in the ratios of primed targets to relative clauses produced. As described in the Results there was an overall 13.3% difference of prime type. When that difference is broken down by researcher, we see that there was a 28.82% difference of prime type with the native speaking Italian researcher, a 5.64% difference with the advanced nonnative speaking researcher, and a 3.79% difference with the student researcher. Clearly, the researcher may play a role in the amount of priming that can occur in L2 interaction; whether the research involves a true confederate scripting design or the use of a scripted interlocutor who is clearly more proficient than the participants should be investigated in future studies.

Second is the question of the naturally-occurring context of priming. Our data came from scripts and, therefore, we do not know what happens in other environments, although we did use an activity that is not uncommon in second and foreign language classrooms. What we do know, however, is that learners typically "take from" utterances of teachers and utterances of other learners, often through a process of negotiation as is illustrated in example (7) (taken from Gass & Varonis 1989: 81).

(7) Hiroko: A man is uh drinking c-coffee or tea uh with the saucer of the uh uh coffee set is uh in his uh knee

     Izumi: in *him* knee

Hiroko:	uh on *his* knee
Izumi:	yeah
Hiroko:	on *his* knee.
Izumi:	so sorry. On *his* knee

In this example, Hiroko says *in his knee* with Izumi responding with an incorrect form, *in him knee*. Hiroko maintains the original form in terms of the pronominal case. Presumably, as a result of the negotiation, and multiple exemplars of the correct modifier *his*, Izumi drops her alternative choice of *him* and adopts *his* as the preferred choice. Whether this prompts further appropriate use of case is an open question. The issue of lab versus natural/classroom contexts was investigated by Gass, Mackey, and Ross-Feldman (2005, 2011). Their study looked at negotiation in lab versus classroom contexts finding that the differences are not great. Rather, negotiation is dependent on task type and not context.

A third issue relates to proficiency. We did not have an independent measure of proficiency, primarily because proficiency was not a variable. Rather, we used seat time as a way of describing the approximate and relative level of the learners, which we feel is "low-level." This, of course, is subjective; one person's low-level can be another's intermediate. What would be useful in future studies is to determine if the same pattern found in the current study holds for learners who have greater control over both of the alternative structures.

Finally, we did not have baseline data of RC production of this group of learners. We opted not to test our learners on the structure in question due to the fact that the testing itself might have served as a forum for learning. Relative clauses had been introduced during their two years of Italian university study so the structure itself was not new to them at the time of data collection. We further relied on the extensive literature of L2 RC acquisition which shows a clear preference in production and learning order that reflects the AH. Further exploration of the knowledge-base background would clearly be useful.

6.   What about pedagogy?

This chapter explores the use of syntactic priming in an interaction-based activity. Despite the fact that for practical reasons, data were not collected in a classroom environment, the activity used is one that is typical of second/foreign language classrooms. The research conducted in this study provides a unique and innovative perspective on the learning of complex structures combining priming and interaction. It is clear that syntactic priming as a pedagogical intervention has its benefits, although, for reasons detailed above and below, we feel that because of the novelty of this research program, specific recommendations are premature.

7. Conclusion

At early stages of learning (as was the case in the current study), priming, or extensive input, possibly through a conversational context, can aid when learning a complex structure, although clearly, we do not have specific data of what these particular learners would have done without priming. Past research suggests that there is very little ability to use DO relative clauses at this level, so we do have reason to believe that the 32.65% level of DO relative clauses is, in part, due to the priming received.

We investigated the extent to which priming or extensive input can be an aid in learning complex structures. This research needs to be furthered with other relative clause types (e.g., indirect objects). A question that awaits further investigation has to do with the directionality of priming. In previous instructional studies (e.g., Eckman, Bell & Nelson 1988; Gass 1982) instruction on DO RCs resulted in learning DO and SUBJ relative clauses, but learning in the opposite direction did not occur. The results from the current study suggest that the same phenomenon occurs with priming: When learners were supplied with SUBJ RC primes, a small number of DO RC targets were produced, but when they were supplied with DO RC primes, a large number of SUBJ RCs were produced. A more systematic study with only primes of one type (SUBJ RCs or DO RCs) being supplied to the learners (as McDonough 2006 did in Experiment 2 with only double object datives) would more fully answer the question of the direction of generalizability.

In sum, we have shown that natural learning paths and structural difficulty can be at odds with the effects of priming and extensive use of structures.

References

Ayoun, D. (2001). The role of negative and positive feedback in the second language acquisition of the passé composé and imparfait. *The Modern Language Journal, 85*, 226–243.

Banfi, E. (2003). Alcune caratteristiche della frase relativa cinese e frasi relative nell'italiano di cinesi. In E. Banfi (Ed.), *L'italiano L2 di cinesi. Percorsi acquisitionali,* 92–119. Milan: Franco Angeli.

Behney, J. (2008, October). L2 syntactic priming of Italian relative clauses. Poster session presented at the Second Language Research Forum (SLRF) Conference, University of Hawai'i Manoa, Honolulu, HI.

Bernolet, S., Hartsuiker, R.J., & Pickering, M.J. (2007). Shared syntactic representations in bilinguals: Evidence for the role of word-order repetition. *Journal of Experimental Psychology-Learning Memory and Cognition, 33*, 931–949.

Bock, K. (1989). Closed-class immanence in sentence production. *Cognition, 31,* 163–186.

Branigan, H., Pickering, M., & Cleland, A. (2000). Syntactic co-ordination in dialogue. *Cognition, 75*, B13–B25.

Cleland, A., & Pickering, M. (2003). The use of lexical and syntactic information in language production: Evidence from the priming of noun-phrase structure. *Journal of Memory and Language, 49*, 214–230.

Croteau, K. (1995). Second language acquisition of relative clause structures by learners of Italian. In F. Eckman, D. Highland, P.W. Lee, J. Mileham, & R. R. Weber (Eds.), *Second language acquisition theory and pedagogy* (pp. 115–128). Mahwah, NJ: Lawrence Erlbaum Associates.

de la Fuente, M. (2002). Negotiation and oral acquisition of L2 vocabulary: The roles of input and output in the receptive and productive acquisition of words. *Studies in Second Language Acquisition, 24*, 81–112.

Doughty, C. (1991). Second language instruction does make a difference: Evidence from an empirical study of SL relativization. *Studies in Second Language Acquisition, 13*(4), 431–469.

Doughty, C., & Varela, E. (1998). Communicative focus on form. In C.J. Doughty & J. Williams (Eds), *Focus on form in classroom second language acquisition*, 114–138. Cambridge: CUP.

Eckman, F., Bell, L., & Nelson, D. (1988). On the generalization of relative clause instruction in the acquisition of English as a second language. *Applied Linguistics, 9*(1), 1–20.

Ellis, R. (2007). The differential effects of corrective feedback on two grammatical structures. In A. Mackey (Ed.), *Conversational interaction in second language acquisition: A collection of empirical studies* (pp. 339–360). Oxford: OUP.

Ellis, R., Loewen, S., & Erlam, R. (2006). Implicit and explicit corrective feedback and the acquisition of L2 grammar. *Studies in Second Language Acquisition, 28*, 339–368.

Gass, S. (1979). Language transfer and universal grammatical relations. *Language Learning, 29*(2), 327–345.

Gass, S. (1980). An investigaton of syntactic transfer in adult L2 learners. In R. Scarcella & S. Krashen (Eds.), *Research in second language acquisition* (pp. 143–141). Rowley, MA: Newbury House.

Gass, S. (1982). From theory to practice. In M. Hines & W.E. Rutherford (eds),*On TESOL '81. Selected papers from the Fifteenth Annual Conference of Teachers of English to Speakers of Other Languages, Detroit, Michigan, March 3–8, 1981* (pp. 120–139). Washington, DC: TESOL.

Gass, S. (1988). Integrating research areas: A framework for second language studies. *Applied Linguistics, 9*(2), 198–217.

Gass, S. (1997). *Input, interaction and the development of second languages.* Mahwah, NJ: Lawrence Erlbaum Associates.

Gass, S., Behney, J., & Uzum, B. (2013). Inhibitory control, working memory, and L2 interaction gains. In K. Droździał-Szelest & M. Pawlak (Eds.), *Psycholinguistic and sociolinguistic perspectives on second language learning and teaching.* Berlin: Springer.

Gass, S., & Mackey, A. (2006). *Input, Interaction and Output: An Overview.* In K. Bardovi-Harlig & Z. Dörnyei (Eds.). *AILA Review, 19,* 3–17.

Gass, S., & Mackey, A. (2007). Input, interaction, and output in second language acquisition. In B. VanPatten, & J. Williams (Eds.),*Theories in second language acquisition: An introduction,* 175–200. Mahwah, NJ: Lawrence Erlbaum Associates.

Gass, S., Mackey, A., & Ross-Feldman, L. (2005). Task-based interactions in classroom and laboratory settings. *Language Learning, 55,* 575–611.

Gass, S., Mackey, A., & Ross-Feldman, L. (2011). Task-based interactions in classroom and laboratory settings. *Language Learning, 61*(Supplement 1), 189–200. [Reprint of 2005]

Gass, S., & Selinker, L. (2008). *Second language acquisition: An introductory course* [3rd Edition]. New York, NY: Routledge.

Gass, S., & Torres, M. (2005). Attention when? An investigation of the ordering effect of input and interaction. *Studies in Second Language Acquisition, 27,* 1–31.

Gass, S., Behney, J., & Plonsky, L. (2013). *Second language acquisition: An introductory course.* New York, NY: Routledge.

Gass, S., & Varonis, E. (1985). Variation in native speaker speech modification to non-native speakers. *Studies in Second Language Acquisition, 7,* 37–57.

Gass, S., & Varonis, E. (1989). Incorporated repairs in NNS discourse. In M. Eisenstein (Ed.), *Variation and second language acquisition* (pp. 71–86). New York, NY: Plenum.

Gass, S., & Varonis, E. (1994). Input, interaction, and second language production. *Studies in Second Language Acquisition, 16,* 283–302.

Hartsuiker, R., Pickering, M.J., & Veltkamp, E. (2004). Is syntax separate or shared between languages? Cross-linguistic syntactic priming in Spanish-English bilinguals. *Psychological Science, 15*(6), 409–414.

Ishida, M. (2004). Effects of recasts on the acquisition of the aspectual form of -te i (ru) by learners of Japanese as a foreign language. *Language Learning, 54,* 311–394.

Iwashita, N. (2003). Negative feedback and positive feedback in task-based interaction: Differential effects of L2 development. *Studies in Second Language Acquisition, 25,* 1–36.

Jeon, K. (2007). Interaction-driven L2 learning: Characterizing linguistic development. In A. Mackey (Ed.), *Conversation interaction in second language acquisition: A collection of empirical studies* (pp. 379–403). Oxford: OUP.

Jeon, K.S., & Kim, H.-Y. (2007). Noun Phrase Accessibility Hierarchy in head-internal and head-external relativization in L2 Korean. *Studies in Second Language Acquisition, 29*(2), 253–276.

Keenan, E., & Comrie, B. (1977). Noun phrase accessibility and Universal Grammar. *Linguistic Inquiry, 8*(1), 63–99.

Kim, Y., & McDonough, K. (2008). Learners' production of passives during syntactic priming activities. *Applied Linguistics, 29,* 149–154.

Leeman, J. (2003). Recasts and L2 development: Beyond negative evidence. *Studies in Second Language Acquisition, 25,* 37–63.

Long, M. (1980). *Input, interaction and second language acquisition.* Unpublished PhD dissertation, University of California.

Long, M. (1981). Input, interaction, and second language acquisition. In H. Winitz (Ed.), *Native language and foreign language acquisition. Annals of the New York Academy of Science, 379,* 259–278.

Mackey, A. (1999). Input, interaction, and second language development: An empirical study of question formation in ESL. *Studies in Second Language Acquisition, 21,* 557–587.

Mackey, A. (2006). Feedback, noticing and instructed second language learning. *Applied Linguistics, 27,* 405–430.

Mackey, A., & Abbuhl, R. (2006). Input and interaction. In C. Sanz (Ed.), *Mind and context in adult second language acquisition: Methods, theory, and practice* (pp. 207–233). Washington, DC: Georgetown University Press.

Mackey, A., Abbuhl, R., & Gass, S. (2012). Interactionist approach. In S. Gass & A. Mackey (Eds), *Handbook of second language acquisition,* 7–23. New York, NY: Routledge.

Mackey, A., & Goo, J. (2007). Interaction research in SLA: A meta-analysis and research synthesis. In A. Mackey (Ed.), *Conversational interaction in second language acquisition: A collection of empirical studies* (pp. 407–452). Oxford: OUP.

Mackey, A., & Oliver, R. (2002). Interactional feedback and children's L2 development. *System, 30,* 459–477.

Mackey, A., & Philp, J. (1998). Conversational interaction and second language development: Recasts, responses, and red herrings? *Modern Language Journal, 82,* 338–356.

Mackey, A., Philp, J., Egi, T., Fujii, A., & Tatsumi, T. (2002). Individual differences in working memory, noticing of interactional feedback, and L2 development. In P. Robinson (Ed.), *Individual differences and instructed language learning* (pp. 181–210). Amsterdam: John Benjamins.

Mackey, A., & Silver, R. (2005). Interactional tasks and English L2 learning by immigrant children in Singapore. *System, 33,* 239–260.

McDonough, K. (2006). Interaction and syntactic priming. *Studies in Second Language Acquisition, 28,* 179–207.

McDonough, K. (2007). Interactional feedback and the emergence of simple past activity verbs in L2 English. In A. Mackey (Ed.),*Conversational interaction in second language acquisition: A collection of empirical studies* (pp. 323–338). Oxford: OUP.

McDonough, K., & Chaikitmongkol, W. (2010). Collaborative syntactic priming activities and EFL learners' production of *wh*-questions. *The Canadian Modern Language Review/La revue canadienne des langues vivantes, 66,* 817–841.

McDonough, K., & Mackey, A. (2008). Syntactic priming and ESL question development. *Studies in Second Language Acquisition, 30,* 31–47.

McDonough, K., & Trofimovich, P. (2009). *Using priming methods in second language research.* New York, NY: Routledge.

Muranoi, H. (2000). Focus on form through interaction enhancement: Integrating formal instruction into a communicative task in EFL classrooms. *Language Learning, 50,* 617–673.

Ozeki, H., & Shirai, Y. (2007). Does the noun phrase accessibility hierarchy predict the difficulty order in the acquisition of Japanese relative clauses? *Studies in Second Language Acquisition, 29*(2), 169–196.

Pavesi, M. (1986). Markedness, discoursal modes, and relative clause formation in a formal and an informal context. *Studies in Second Language Acquisition, 81*(1), 38–55.

Philp, J. (2003). Constraints on "noticing the gap": Non-native speakers' noticing of recasts in NS-NNS interaction. *Studies in Second Language Acquisition, 25,* 99–126.

Sheen, Y. (2007). The effects of corrective feedback, language aptitude and learner attitudes on the acquisition of English articles. In A. Mackey (Ed.), *Conversational interaction in second language acquisition: A series of empirical studies* (pp. 301–322). Oxford: OUP.

Swain, M. (1985). Communicative competence: Some roles of comprehensible input and comprehensible output in its development. In S. Gass & C. Madden (Eds.), *Input in second language acquisition* (pp. 235–253). Rowley, MA: Newbury House.

Swain, M. (1995). Three functions of output in second language learning. In G. Cook & B. Seidlhofer (Eds.), *Principle and practice in applied linguistics* (pp. 125–144). Oxford: OUP.

Swain, M. (2005). The output hypothesis: Theory and research. In E. Hinkel (Ed.), *Handbook of research in second language teaching and learning* (pp. 471–483). Mahwah, NJ: Lawrence Erlbaum Associates.

Swain, M., & Lapkin, S. (1998). Interaction and second language learning: Two adolescent French immersion students working together. *The Modern Language Journal, 82*, 320–337.

Swain, M., & Lapkin, S. (2002). Talking it through: Two French immersion learners' response to reformulation. *International Journal of Education Research, 37*, 285–304.

Valentini, A. (1992). *L'italiano dei Cinesi. Questioni di Sintassi.* Milan: Guerini Studio.

Valentini, A. (1997). Frasi relative in italiano L2. *Linguistica e Filologia, 5*, 195–221.

Van den Branden, K. (1997). Effects of negotiation of language learners' output. *Language Learning, 47*, 589–636.

Varonis, E., & Gass, S. (1982). The comprehensibility of non-native speech. *Studies in Second Language Acquisition, 4*, 114–136.

Varonis, E., & Gass, S. (1985). Non–native/non–native conversations: A model for negotiation of meaning. *Applied Linguistics, 6*, 71–90.

Yabuki-Soh, N. (2007). Teaching relative clauses in Japanese: Exploring alternative types of instruction and the projection effect. *Studies in Second Language Acquisition, 29*(2), 219–252.

Yip, V., & Matthews, S. (2007). Relative clauses in Cantonese-English bilingual children: Typological challenges and processing motivations. *Studies in Second Language Acquisition, 29*(2), 277–300.

CHAPTER 4

Generative approaches and the competing systems hypothesis

Formal acquisition to pedagogical application

Drew Long and Jason Rothman
University of Florida and University of Reading

In this chapter, we ponder why highly advanced tutored learners perform differently than their naturalistic L2 counterparts at the same level of proficiency in certain, predictable contexts. The Competing Systems Hypothesis (CSH) (Rothman 2008) attempts to explain some of these differences, appealing to the deterministic role played by pedagogically-designed metalinguistic knowledge that only tutored learners have. We will review one study done to test the CSH, Rothman (2008), which compares and contrasts near-native tutored and naturalistic L2 learners of Spanish in the domains of grammatical (viewpoint) aspect. Using Rothman's (2008) findings as an example, we will outline how one can reduce the gap between linguistic descriptive grammars and pedagogical grammars in an accessible and usable way for language teaching.

1. Introduction

Despite many compelling reasons to expect the contrary, there is a substantial disconnect between linguistic theory and generative empirical acquisition research on the one hand, and pedagogical research and practice on the other. It would be wrong to assume, however, that this disconnect is unknown to generative linguists and/or language education professionals or that this divide exists by mere happenstance. It is not always clear how empirical psycholinguistic research can be applied directly to the reality of the dynamic L2 classroom setting[1]. Psycholinguistic

---

1. There is a substantial literature about the divide between theory, research and practice within applied linguistics/SLA, which we acknowledge and do not intend to ignore by not incorporating it more fully in the text (e.g. Ellis, R. (2010); Pica, T. (1997); Lightbown, P.M. (2000); Spada (2005). While such work shares in many ways the essence of the spirit of what we attempt to bring to light herein, there are important differences that render the cases covered not fully

research, the fundamental motivation of which is to understand how the mind/ brain represents and processes language, is not necessarily associated by many from outside the discipline or even within with providing the kinds of answers that are useful in the classroom. To be sure, uncovering how second languages are represented in the mind and how second languages are processed does nothing to change the practical variables that language teachers have to confront on a daily basis. However, this does not mean that such findings are not relevant for the classroom. From the point of view of the generative acquisitionist, there are at least two reasons for the disconnect between language acquisition/processing research and language teaching (see also Rothman 2008, 2010; VanPatten 2010; Whong 2011; Gil, Marsden & Whong to appear). First, the underlying cognitive processes involved in second language acquisition are far from well understood. Psycholinguists are therefore well occupied with the prevailing questions presented in their own paradigms and do not commonly consider the practical implications of their claims. Furthermore, psycholinguists who do not normally engage in applied linguistics proper are often uninformed as to the contemporary questions of language education research, a case of academic isolation which makes the task of contributing to an inherently related field less than straightforward. Moreover, in

---

commensurable, ranging from paradigmatic assumptions regarding the nature of language and its representation itself, the role that explicit knowledge and teaching might have for acquisition proper and the type of research done and/or reviewed to elucidate the larger points. For example, Lightbown (2000) attempts to demonstrate how the large amount of SLA research conducted on pedagogical questions has contributed to a greater understanding of historic generalizations on classroom language learning, but also to encourage caution in applying SLA research to pedagogy. Lightbown's main purpose, however, is to point out that much SLA research has been conducted in the classroom to identify and understand the roles of the different participants in classroom interaction, the impact of certain types of instruction, and factors which promote or inhibit learning. Spada (2005), as another example, explores issues and challenges inherent to research programs in instructed SLA settings (focus on classroom research and its application). She explores what she considers an 'ethical challenge' – the relevance of research for pedagogical practice – and she offers suggestions on how to support researchers and teachers in making links between research and practice more meaningful. Like Lightbown, she cautions against the overeager application of this research, with all its complicating variables, to making generalizations about pedagogy. What we all share in common is the recognition for the need to highlight the role that SLA research could play in establishing realistic expectations for classroom learners and language teachers. However, our goal is to attempt to do this from a generative linguistic perspective, which inevitably departs from coverage of research attempting to make a similar argument via meta-analyses of SLA research on processes in the classroom per se ("the linguistic, cognitive, pedagogical and social influences fostering or hindering classroom SLA"). Rather, like Bruhn de Garavito's chapter in this volume, our focus is to test generative theoretical generalizations (that hold in specific linguistic contexts) experimentally and ponder how such can be incorporated to tangible classroom impacts.

an effort to remain as unbiased as possible, generative language acquisition experts often ignore pedagogical implications that their research might reveal. Rightly or wrongly, this practice stems from the mindset that pedagogical implications of formal linguistic research can only be an artifact of first revealing the cognitive underpinnings of the cognitive and linguistic processes themselves.

Under the above scenario, generative language acquisition research and language pedagogy overlap in areas of seeming mutual exclusivity. The generative linguist cannot be concerned with facilitating acquisition like the pedagogue, but rather seeks to understand its mental constitution and the role that neurological maturation might play on the limits of adult language acquisition and processing potentials. Formal acquisition research is thus primarily concerned with determining what is cognitively possible for adult minds in ideal situations of access to high quality input. Alternatively, the pedagogue is obliged to deal with the realities of the most common locus of adult language acquisition, that is, language learning in the confines of a classroom setting. In such loci, quality and quantity issues related to input abound in a less than ideal sense (see e.g., Rothman & Guijarro-Fuentes 2010), among many other deterministic linguistic, cognitive and affective factors. As a result, it is not as crucial to the pedagogue to know what the brain is able to do or to understand precisely to what extent and why child and adult language acquisition and processing seem to differ, but rather to know how to maximize the effectiveness of the classroom learning experience given what classroom learners are likely to have available to them. Maintaining the essence of Krashen's (1982) learning vs. acquisition distinction from the 1970s (see Krashen 1982 for a summary), which has spawned significant changes to language classrooms (cf. Lightbown 2000 *inter alia*), many formal acquisitionists believe that explicit metalinguistic knowledge cannot alter the acquisition process – that is, the metalinguistic knowledge itself cannot become part of the underlying grammatical competence (see e.g. Schwartz & Gubala-Ryzak 1992, but see Slabakova 2008). This does not mean that pedagogical rules are not helpful at some level, learned in the truest sense of the word or stored in the mind/brain of individuals. Rather, it is maintained that such knowledge embodies a system of metalinguistic norms which are learned, stored and applied at a more conscious level than the underlying procedural knowledge associated with true competence, which is an unconscious system of linguistic mental representation/computation.

A final reason for the disconnect has to do with the inevitable difficulty in explaining the jargon, abstraction, working assumptions and the like of one discipline to people who work in a complementary field yet view the same object of inquiry in very different ways. Of course, this is true in both directions implicated here. In principle, any teacher could be trained in generative grammar and any generative linguist could be trained in language education research. The point to be made is that for one to really understand the impact of the current literature in either field and then attempt a meaningful integration, one must be trained with the background in both fields to do so. For both the formal linguist and language teacher, language itself is a tool of the trade; however, how they view this tool is often different in signifact ways. For some language teachers, any given language is often viewed as a static entity to which the labels *correct* and *incorrect* can be applied somewhat straightforwardly. To this end, any given language has a set grammar that can be described in mostly binary terms that are readily amenable to the teaching of so-called rules. For formal linguists, language is simply not that straightforward and need not be since it is viewed as a cognitively based system of mental computation that brings together form to meaning in ways that are universally delimited by internal factors (either domain-specific, domain-general or a combination of both).

Regardless of the underlying reasons for the lack of communication between linguistics and language teaching, few would deny that a language teacher who is more aware of the subtleties of linguistic structures of the language she is teaching and of key issues in the general understanding of adult language acquisition would make a more effective teacher. Most language teachers are not trained in formal linguistics despite compelling reasons to expect they could benefit from such training. Understanding language acquisition in terms of how the brain/ mind processes and represents language can unlock latent facilitative skills of the language teacher in ways that cannot be appreciated until one is trained in the linguistic and cognitive sciences. It is equally true that most generative acquisitionists and language processing experts are not trained in classroom education sciences. If making connections between the two fields is to become meaningful then training in both directions is necessary. With all of this in mind, we endeavor herein to make connections between generative linguistic studies of adult second language (L2) acquisition and language teaching, by showing how the former can inform the latter in tangible ways. Our goal is to highlight the role that generative SLA research could play in establishing realistic expectations for classroom learners and language teachers, paralling similar attempts made in, for example, instructed SLA and other areas of applied SLA (see e.g. Lightbown 2000, Spada 2005; Ellis 2010).

While many generative studies have highlighted persistent differences in production that set apart even highly advanced L2 speakers from native speakers – putting aside the inherent comparative fallacy of comparing L2 learners against a benchmark of monolinguals, e.g., Bley-Vroman 1983 – relatively little research has addressed the equally persistent if less obvious distinctions that differentiate two kinds of L2 learners: highly advanced tutored (classroom) learners and highly advanced naturalistic learners. Though highly advanced L2 learners in general have been shown capable of attaining a native or near-native morphosyntactic competence (see White 2003 inter alia), the question that arises is why tutored learners perform differently than naturalistic L2 learners in specific, perhaps highly predictable contexts (see Rothman 2008 inter alia). Moreover, we endeavor to hypothesize how addressing this query from a generative perspective can and should be used in the domain of language teaching. One hypothesis that purports to explain some of these differences is the Competing Systems Hypothesis (CSH) (Rothman 2008), which contends that the very presence in the tutored L2 learner's mind of two co-existing grammars for the L2, one based on learned explicit pedagogical (metalinguistic) knowledge and the other the naturalistically acquired one, leads to residual performance differences (see Section 2.0 for details). It is claimed that oversimplification in classroom instruction can lead to the formation of a static system of learned rules that are imprecise in their description of how the actual target grammar operates[2].

This separate metalinguistic system is hypothesized to compete for primacy with the naturally acquired generative L2 grammar, especially in contexts that favor a reliance on metalinguistic knowledge (e.g. when being tested). Thus, the CSH predicts differences in production unique to tutored L2 learners in instances when these two grammars are in conflict, and that such differences will relate to pedagogical overgeneralizations. An even stronger case for the CSH is made if poverty-of-the-stimulus (POS) effects can be shown in both learner groups; such evidence would remove the confound of a difference between the two groups in underlying competence and reinforce the plausibility of a competing pedagogical system which deviates production in the case of the tutored learners. This is so since POS knowledge is argued to only be obtained as a byproduct of true acquisition, i.e. not stochastic learning, and thus is indicative of target underlying representation at the level of actual competence (cf. e.g. Schwartz & Sprouse 2000; Rothman & Iverson 2008). Consequently, if tutored learners can show appropriate POS knowledge, like naturalistic learners, despite making production errors, unlike naturalistic learners, that can be likened to metalinguistic knowledge then this would be consistent with the proposal that there are two systems at play in the tutored L2 learners.

---

2.   We concur with Diane Larsen Freeman who stated in a published interview that: "*Rules can be useful, but rules are form-based and are usually stated in inflexible ways. However, that is not how language works. Language exists for the expression and interpretation of meaning, and that includes grammatical meaning*". Although our understanding of language acquisition and its representation differ significantly from Larsen-Freeman, we join her in advocating that one needs to "*teach reasons so that students understand that language is the way it is*" (Pérez-Llantada & Larsen-Freeman 2007).

In the following sections, we start by detailing more concretely the CSH and review one study done to test the CSH, Rothman (2008), which compares and contrasts near-native tutored and naturalistic L2 learners of Spanish in the domain of grammatical aspect. In this case, it is shown how pedagogical rules oversimplify actual grammatical competence for this domain and how such oversimplifications can lead to performance differences on subtle semantic nuances in a predictable way for the classroom L2 learners only. The remainder of the chapter, then, takes this study as the point of departure to discuss how a pedagogy informed by theoretical linguistics can be designed. Further to this epistemological discussion, referring back to the grammatical domain examined in Rothman (2008) as a mere example, we will outline how one can reduce the gap between linguistic descriptive grammars and pedagogical grammars in an accessible and usable way for language teachers. In other words, we endeavor to show how informing language teachers of the overgeneralizations that they are likely unaware they are providing can reduce the incongruity that is passed along to learners between actual grammatical competence and an imprecise system of metalinguistic knowledge.

2. The Competing Systems Hypothesis

Building on Felix's Competition Model of the early 1980s (e.g. Felix 1985), Rothman (2008) proposed and tested the Competing Systems Hypothesis (CSH)[3]. As the name suggests, the CSH proposes that some (divergent) L2 performance behavior, even at the highest levels of L2 proficiency, can be explained by a competition of separate L2 mental linguistic systems. What does the CSH intend by a competition of two grammars?

Much SLA research over the past decades has highlighted the role that grammatical competition plays in L2 acquisition. In most cases, however, when SLA researchers refer to such competition they are referring to the interaction between the first grammar (L1) and the emerging interlanguage grammar for the L2. Although different paradigmatic approaches use various labels, e.g. transfer, influence, inhibition or L1 entrenchment, most SLA theories propose a deterministic role for the L1 in the L2 learning task at the level of grammatical representation and/or processing. Given the foci of the CSH, it is technically agnostic with respect

---

3. We wish to point out that the larger claims we make towards fomenting increased integration and dialogue between formal linguistics and language teaching are not contingent upon the CSH itself, but rather can and do exist independently of it.

to the role L1 influence/transfer has on the process of interlanguage development.[4] The CSH's predictions focus on pedagogically-based residual optionality in ultimate attainment that cannot be linked back to L1 influence. As a result, the role that the L1 has played in the initial stages and L2 developmental sequencing is simply not in the scope of its discussion. The two grammars to which the CSH refers are definitively both grammars for the L2, albeit of a different nature.

The proposed two grammars at stake are the system of underlying grammatical competence for the L2 and a separate system of learned metalinguistic knowledge, learned explicitly via classroom teaching. Because the CSH is a theory that assumes a Universal Grammar (UG) approach to understanding linguistic representation and its acquisition (see Chomsky 2007 for review), the first system is assumed to obtain on the basis of available target input and its interaction with UG[5]. The second system is the byproduct of explicit training in the L2, given specifically designed pedagogical explanations.

We assume *a priori* that there is a difference between *acquisition* and *learning* and we share in the UG contention that what is learned, in the truest sense of that word, does not come to affect or alter the underlying acquired system. In our view, however, it is fair to use the term grammar to refer to both systems even if this departs from the traditional notion of what a grammar is in linguistic terms. Reasonably, one might take exception to the label "grammar" in reference to the second system. After all, the term "grammar" in formal linguistics traditionally applies uniquely to the unconscious system of competence. It would be reasonable, then, to reject the second system as a grammar per se since the learned system is outside the underlying L2 competence. We do not deny this position, but wish to point out that at the level of highly advanced L2 proficiency addressed by the CSH,

---

4.   The CSH is agnostic in the sense that it does not address L1 influence at all, not because its author believes L1 transfer does not obtain as suggested by Flynn 1987 and Epstein et al. 1996. The CSH does not comment on L1 influence in interlanguage development because it is not a hypothesis about the process of development, but rather a hypothesis that seeks to explain some L2 behavior at the level of L2 ultimate attainment.

5.   We acknowledge that many details are put aside here, for ease of exposition and space limitations, related to learning constraints on L2 competence potentials, even when assuming, as we do, full access to UG in adulthood. For example, as Full Transfer/Full Access (Schwartz & Sprouse 1996) contends, L1 transfer can block some parsing failures, the process through which the transition from an L1 representation to the target L2 via access to UG accessibility occurs. See White (2003) for a discussion of this and similar issues related to L2 convergence from the UG perspective. Furthermore, we also wish to point out that the CSH can be compatible with other theories of L2 grammatical representation, such as emergentism (e.g. O'Grady 2006), if one assumes that underlying grammar representation obtains in a similar way as it does in L1 acquisition and is thus distinct from the conscious learning of explicit rules to which L2 learners in a classroom setting are clearly exposed and do learn.

this system of learned metalinguistic knowledge, like underlying grammatical competence, is likely to be quite comprehensive and have a true mental status. Crucially and more importantly, this system is likely to no longer be (completely) conscious to the learner, but would have passed from declarative memory to a system that is more proceduralized within the mind. If this is on the right track, then like actual competence, this second system is/can be an unconscious system (or unconsciously applied in real time) that serves as a secondary filter, at least for performance[6]. A second reason to call it a grammar derives from the spirit of what we are attempting to do herein, this being the building of bridges between linguistic researchers and language teachers. Since language teachers usually consider metalinguistic knowledge to be a faithful representation of what grammar is, using this label also facilitates the discussion at the heart of this endeavor.

To the extent that what is acquired at the level of linguistic representation is faithfully represented by descriptive pedagogical rules, it is difficult to tease these two systems apart. To be sure, an inability to tease apart the two systems because the explicit rules result in the same surface (output) performance as the actual competence of course does not mean that there are not separate systems at play. To test the CSH, then, one needs to identify where explicit rules fail to reflect the actual target grammar. Pedagogical rules often under or even overestimate the actual mental representation of a given property, a fact that underscores the need for linguistics to inform language pedagogy more directly, as we will see described for one specific domain of grammar in Section 2.1. In such cases, testable predictions according to the CSH can be made, summarized in this quote:

> In addition to other interceding factors, the present hypothesis [CSH] claims that pedagogical simplifications form a separate system of learned knowledge and that this system can override linguistic competence (the generative system) of the L2 learner at the level of performance. These separate systems remain intact through advanced stages and essentially provide two filters for linguistic performance. This means that even when interlanguage reaches a steady-state in advanced learners that is representationally native-like in particular domains, the learned knowledge system can intercede, especially in highly monitored output, resulting in systematic errors. The prediction, therefore, is that once grammatical properties have been acquired at the mental representation level this system can interfere with production, but not comprehension. This explains how learners can have knowledge of semantic entailments of particular morphosyntactic properties at proficiency levels where they do not use the corollary overt forms entirely like natives. I call this hypothesis the Competing Systems Hypothesis (Rothman 2008: 85–6).

---

6.   How this happens, to the extent it does, is not important. For example, does it become a habit from repetition? Does it become a part of long term memory? What is crucial here is that proceduralization of metalinguistic knowledge does not enter or alter the language modules and thus the underlying linguistic representation.

Insofar as the CSH claims that specific L2 asymmetries can be predicted to stem from explicit pedagogical rules that imprecisely over- or underestimate the actual target L2 grammar, the same patterns should *not* be observed in naturalistic L2 learners of the same high proficiency levels, as naturalistic L2 learners should not have had access to the hypothesized source of asymmetrical behavior. In other words, naturalistic learners do not get the explicit rules that tutored L2 learners do[7]. As a result, "this hypothesis is falsifiable if the errors observed are not isolated to tutored learners, since naturalistic learners would not have such a separate system (Rothman 2008: 85–86)." We will see how these assertions translate into the methodologies used to test the usefulness of the CSH.

To be clear, the CSH is not a hypothesis intended to explain all L2 differences in ultimate attainment; rather, it joins several other hypotheses offered to explain specific divergent behaviors in learners who otherwise show very high levels of L2 attainment. One welcome contribution of the CSH is that it endeavors to bridge the gap between formal acquisition theory and language teaching. In the remaining sections, we will present one study that shows support for the CSH, after which we will explore how to apply what the CSH suggests towards building a more informed pedagogy for language teaching in adulthood.

2.1 Rothman (2008)

Rothman (2008) chose to examine grammatical aspect in this study, due to its salience in L2 Spanish as a common point of pedagogical oversimplification. Grammatical aspect, otherwise known as viewpoint aspect, refers to the speaker's perspective on the boundedness in time of an event: bounded [+perfective] (i.e., 'closed', 'completed') or unbounded: [−perfective] (i.e., 'not completed') (see e.g., Depraetere 1995; Giorgi & Pianesi 1997; Smith 1991). In Spanish, this distinction is encoded morphologically in two distinct paradigms: preterit [+perfective] and imperfect [−perfective].

(1) PRETERIT
     Roberto dijo la verdad.
     Roberto told the truth.

(2) IMPERFECT
     Roberto decía la verdad.
     Roberto was telling/used to tell the truth.

---

7.   We do not intend to suggest that naturalistic learners are never offered "rules" by native speakers with whom they interact or do not attempt to form their own version of descriptive rules. However, whatever "rules" naturalistic learners receive are, in the majority of cases, sure to be qualitatively and quantitatively different from tutored learners whose entire process of learning is formulated around rules of this type.

By contrast in English, the [+-perfective] aspect distinction is not realized morphologically. In English, there is one morphological simple past which can be used in bounded and unbounded contexts, as seen in (3) and (4).

(3)   John called his mother yesterday. [+perfective]
(4)   John called his mother every day as a young adult. [–perfective]

Past characterizations of progressive or habitual actions [–perfective] are instead conveyed a number of different ways in English: using modal verbs, such as 'used to' and 'would', the copula ('be') + gerund constructions or by attaching an adverbial modifier, such as 'always' or 'every day', to an action described using simple past morphology. In other words, the simple past in English can convey two possible interpretations, as either an episodic (3) or an iterative reading (4).

Conversely, in Spanish, only the imperfect can convey two types of readings – still different from the two readings of the simple past in English – as either a progressive (5) or iterative (6) action.

(5)   *Jorge caminaba a la escuela cuando vio el accidente.*
       Jorge was walking to school when he saw the accident.

(6)   *Jorge siempre caminaba al parque antes de tomar su café.*
       Jorge always walked to the park before drinking his coffee.

Summarizing these crucial distinctions, the Spanish form closest in function to the simple past in English, the preterit, can only support an episodic reading, as opposed to the dual interpretations in English, while the Spanish imperfect, a synthetic morphological paradigm which doesn't exist in English, can support multiple interpretations of a different nature. These form-to-meaning differences are summarized in Figure 1 below from Slabakova and Montrul (2003: 172).

Pedagogical descriptions of the preterit and imperfect for English learners generally depict these as discrete semantic entities to be defined lexically via English translation equivalencies rather than linguistic tools to distinguish distinctions along a common scale of aspectual perspective. Consequently, in some cases subtle semantic distinctions may be lost for the tutored learner. For example, the verb *haber* is commonly taught to default to the imperfect. Although it might not

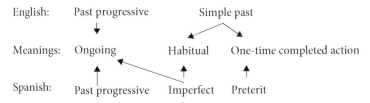

Figure 1. Form-to-meaning mappings

be clear to a linguistically untrained person why this is so, it likely has to do with the fact that haber is lexically a stative predicate and as such maps mostly naturally to [–perfective] aspect. This overgeneralization, however, is unable to account for the production and interpretation of example (7), in which the preterit is used to anchor the boundedness of the temporal reference.

(7) *Hubo varias manifestaciones en aquella época.*
     There were various demonstrations during that time period.

While native-like use of preterit and imperfect morphology in all contexts by English learners of L2 Spanish is the exception rather than the rule, even for advanced learners, contexts such as those exemplified in (7) provide an appropriate stage to test the predictions of the CSH by comparing tutored L2 learners to naturalistic learners of equal proficiency. The CSH predicts that only the tutored learners, who have access to oversimplified pedagogical rules, will deviate from the native speakers.

Rothman tested three participant groups: (i) a Spanish native control group, (ii) a group of highly advanced tutored English learners of L2 Spanish and (iii) a group of highly advanced naturalistic learners of L2 Spanish. All of the participants in groups (i) and (ii) were sampled from university-level instructors of Spanish from two U.S. universities. As university instructors, the tutored learners were very familiar with pedagogical Spanish grammars. Conversely, all of the naturalistic learners in group (iii) learned Spanish in a naturalistic environment as adults without ever receiving formal instruction.

The study employed two types of tests: a cloze paragraph multiple-choice test and a fill-in-the-blank production task. The multiple-choice task consisted of a fairy tale written in Spanish from a pedagogical website. The test provided binary choices, either the preterit or the imperfect, for verbs in the story. The test was designed such that the appropriate responses coincided with canonical pedagogical explanations of the preterit and imperfect. The aspect production task consisted of a series of sentences in which the subjects were required to fill in blank spaces with either the preterit or the imperfect. The task was designed to include cases in which the appropriate responses were those which contradicted traditional pedagogical explanations.

On the multiple-choice task, both the naturalistic and tutored learners performed well, performing with no statistical difference as compared to the native controls. However, those few tokens in which tutored learners' selection of the preterit and imperfect varied from the native speaker group and the naturalistic L2 group involved copula verbs or common English translation equivalencies, both of which coincided with pedagogical oversimplification.

On the production task, the tutored learners showed significant deviation from the native speaker group, producing the preterit and imperfect differently than the natives 25% of the time on average. As a single figure, however, this average does not depict the actual range of deviation demonstrated by individual tutored learners, from 0% to 58.3%. In fact, 25% of the tutored learner group performed within the range of the native speakers, suggesting that a low probability of convergence on native-like competency does not preclude successful convergence in some tutored learners. On the other hand, the naturalistic learners demonstrated only a 2.27% divergence from the native speaker consensuses and coincided with a far greater intra-group consistency, a range of only 0% to 8.3%.

In conclusion, a pattern to tutored L2 learner target-deviancy was revealed. In line with the predictions of the CSH, tutored L2 learners demonstrated deviation from native speakers (NSs) and highly advanced non-native speakers (NNSs) in selecting between the preterit and imperfect in specific, predictable contexts. Summarizing, the tutored L2 learners deviated from the NSs – and the naturalistic learners – in selecting between the preterit and imperfect in accordance with the predictions of the CSH. This deviation manifested in three specific contexts: (a) with commonly used stative verbs (e.g., *ser, haber*), (b) verbs whose preterit and imperfect contrast is taught lexically by means of English translation equivalents (e.g., *sabia* = "I knew" vs. *supe* = "I found out"; *quería* = "I wanted" vs. *quise* = "I tried") and (c) after adverbials that are taught as default triggers to either the preterit or the imperfect form (e.g., *siempre* – "always", *cuando* – "when"). By contrast, the naturalistic learners performed like the NSs on both tasks. Since tutored learners only deviated in the three contexts that can be attributed to imprecise pedagogical rules, Rothman cited formal instruction as the variable that accounted for the difference between the naturalistic and tutored learners.

3.   Reducing the gap: Towards a theoretical linguistically informed pedagogy

Now that we have seen supporting evidence for the CSH in the study presented above, the question becomes one of how we can use this knowledge in a practical sense to improve second language teaching. Rothman (2008) made no attempt to build such bridges, concerned primarily with uncovering one (of many) predictable source(s) of L2 performance divergence even and especially in L2ers with high overall proficiency. Simply put, the idea was to test a hypothesis about why some L2 behavior obtains the way it does. In this regard, the endeavor set out in Rothman (2008) was seemingly successful. Showing that a likely source of some specific L2 difference is concomitant to the way in which language is explicitly taught is, however, much more useful than merely for the sake of understanding performance variables more deeply. If the CSH is on the right track, there is value in what it reveals. That some performance issues obtain as a byproduct of the inflexible nature of rules imparted in the way language is taught is a welcome finding, precisely because it highlights something tangible that can be done to ameliorate some performance issues.

The solution to the problem appears to be relatively unproblematic: do away with the imprecision of explicit grammatical rules in the sense that Larsen-Freeman advocates (see footnote 2 above). In principle, this should be an easy task; however, in reality it is not. One easy solution would be to simply remove all teaching of explicit grammatical rules from the foreign language classroom. Indeed, some methodologies over the past decades have essentially eradicated the teaching of explicit grammar in the classroom, such as those that apply the tenets of the communicative teaching approach in the most extreme sense. However, expecting that this can be done on a large-scale basis is impractical. Explicit teaching of grammar, in our view, is fine and even helpful in many ways that are not readily appreciated. However, the act of teaching grammar is itself representative of the unnatural nature of the classroom learning situation since children are obviously not taught language in such a manner. To be sure, teaching second languages in the classroom setting is a necessary endeavor given real world realities. Ideally all L2ers would in a situation where they could absorb a second language in the ways children do; however, most adult language learners obviously cannot abandon their lives to become immersed naturalistic learners. As a result, the vast majority of L2 learning must happen (or at least take place at some point) in a classroom setting. That this is necessary, however, does not make it natural. Secondly, given the limitations that the classroom situation brings to quantity of input and the meaningful contextualization of input to which L2ers are exposed, teaching of grammatical rules might help L2ers notice things in the limited input they receive that would otherwise go unnoticed. Following from the theory we work in as generative linguists, we should clarify that by 'noticing' we mean an unconscious process by which input that would not otherwise cause a parsing failure achieves the status of doing so (see Slabakova's 2008 Bottleneck Hypothesis for tangible suggestions along these lines). Thirdly, although not necessary, metalinguistic knowledge allows adults to make use of the L2 more quickly and seemingly satiates the typical adult's need to understand, if not have some control over, the process of learning. And so, we do not take the position that grammar rules should not be taught explicitly; we simply propose that they be taught less inflexibly and more reflective of the linguistic reasons for which a property obtains the way it does. Of course this is everyone's goal and, we ponder, the extent to which most language teachers are aware that they might in fact not be doing this already.

In passing along inflexible rules one believes to be correct, one inevitably passes along the impression they reflect. And so, the simple abstract solution we proposed is not so simple after all. What needs to be done, then, is to provide training to teachers in the linguistic sciences on at least two fronts: (a) explain to them what we know about language as a cognitive system and second language acquisition and (b) provide them with linguistically precise rules of the target grammar, as well as tangible proof that they are not presently armed with such precise tools without some training in linguistics. We should add that in order for (a) and (b) to happen meaningfully, formal linguists must also be trained in education science to understand the real needs of language teachers and students and how to best incorporate cognitive research into practical pedagogical forms. Given space limitations, we will focus on (b) in the remainder of the chapter. *3.1 Why are the rules we teach not precise?*

Discussing the grammar of language X should be relatively uncomplicated. However, there are at least three types of grammars one could use to describe language X: descriptive, prescriptive and pedagogical grammars. At times, these grammar types result in very conflicting claims when talking about the same property, a confusing and illogical ambiguity for language teachers, language learners and linguists alike. For reasons articulated below, linguistics only validates the first type of grammar. Being aware of the differences in these types of grammars and understanding their goals is an important first step towards understanding the limitations of each and determining how a relationship between linguistics and language teaching can be beneficial.

3.1.1   *Prescriptive grammars*

Prescriptive grammars foment so-called "grammatical" rules that are created on the basis of some venerated (and subjective) norm, usually the "standard" or "educated version" of the language. Who decides that one cannot end a "proper" sentence with a preposition in English when it is clear that all native speakers do so in everyday speech? In fact native speakers of English from all dialects typically end the vast majority of relevant sentences with the preposition at the end. This contrasts sharply with a language like Italian where preposition stranding is truly ungrammatical to the extent that native speakers simply cannot produce them and/or have difficulty in parsing such sentences. Rules belonging to prescriptive grammar are violated ubiquitously, especially in everyday speech. Interestingly, prescriptivism is rejected by all formal linguists. The pedagogue's prescriptive grammar is a byproduct of most educators' inculcation in the idea that language standards, however arbitrary and far from actual day-to-day language use, define the most correct, and therefore most prestigious, form of a language.

3.1.2   *Pedagogical grammars*

Pedagogical grammars are grammars of the type offered in any foreign language textbook for non-native speakers and the ones that are advanced by L2 teachers. These are the types of rules that the CSH warns can be clandestinely imprecise. Pedagogical grammar rules are not natural rules, but rather are compiled on the basis of two things: (a) non-linguistic, surface-level descriptions of the target L2 grammar and (b) purposeful design grounded in direct and indirect comparisons between the target L2 language and the native language of the audience. With especially (b) in mind, it is easy to appreciate how pedagogical grammars cannot be completely accurate. Such would be to assume that Hebrew, for example, is based on English or vice versa depending on the consumer audience. This immediately explains why specific pedagogical grammars have limited audiences. For example, the leading Italian textbooks sold in the US, even if written entirely in Italian, would not find a good market in Spain, France or Portugal since what is explained in these books is based on a comparison to English, which in the context of these countries is rendered invalid. Referring back to the property studied in Rothman (2008), grammatical aspect in the past tense, learners of Italian in Spain, France and Portugal would not need the same types of explanations nor could they be the same as the ones given in the US since the L1 comparison is quite different: Spanish, French and Portuguese encode perfectivity in the past in much the same way. In addition to highlighting similarities and differences between the first language and the target second language, pedagogical grammars offer rules of general design usually based on frequency that attempt to approximate usage trends but which are often inaccurate overall. As we have noted, Rothman (2008) showed that the teaching of imprecise defaults such as the imperfect should go after adverbs denoting repetition or long periods of duration such as *siempre* 'always' and *a menudo* 'often,' creates performance problems.

3.1.3   *Descriptive grammars*

Descriptive grammars seek to describe what can be observed in the speech of native speakers and what native speakers may intuit as possible and impossible sentences of their native language through judgments. This is the grammar to which linguists subscribe; that is, formal linguists are charged with describing what native speakers know about their grammar and language in general and functional linguists concern themselves with what speakers do with the grammar they have. Descriptive grammars do not tell people what is acceptable; they merely describe how people actually speak and use their internal grammar. Moreover, if a descriptive grammar makes reference to the unconscious rules of native speakers, then it is at the same time proposing an explanatory model to describe the internal grammar of an individual speaker. In this sense, then, the formal linguist tries to uncover the internal regularities of the language and explain what every native speaker knows implicitly in an explicit way. Let us consider the following example sentences with this question in mind: can the bold words be co-referential?

(1)   a.   **Cindy** knows that **she** is going to win the prize.
       b.   **She** knows that **Cindy** is going to win the prize.

How do native speakers of English know that in (a) *Cindy* and *she* can be the same person (co-referential), but not in (b) where they must be different people (disjoint reference). Furthermore, why should this be? From the point of view of a pedagogical grammar, such information only enters conscious thought when it is relevant for the L1–L2 pairing – for example, when English and Korean are combined, since these words operate differently in those languages. From a prescriptive grammar view, facts like this are simply ignored, but a descriptive grammar confronts these facts and explains them straightforwardly. A descriptive analysis observes that *Cindy* and *she* are types of nouns, both are subjects, and these subjects can apparently be in either matrix (main clausal) or embedded clause positions, though their interpretations for co-reference are dependent on an interplay of the order in which they appear relative to one another and their word type. Many details aside (see Chomsky 1981 for details), pronouns (*she*) have a different status than proper names (*Cindy*), and their binding abilities for co-reference are affected as such.

The point we wish to underscore is that knowledge of this last type of grammar might prove quite useful to language instructors as it goes beyond typological comparisons of one language to the other and offers an understanding as to why the target language works as it does. An additional benefit of understanding the target grammar past the limitations of prescriptive and pedagogical analyses is that it approximates more closely the type of unconscious knowledge that native speakers have for the target language, thus avoiding overgeneralizations that happen as a result of pedagogical description. In the next section, we will demonstrate how explanations of grammatical properties based on descriptive grammars can be made available in usable terms to teachers.

4.   **Towards an empirically informed pedagogy: Grammatical aspect explanations from a descriptive grammar**

As reviewed in Section 2 above, the research done in Rothman (2008) studied the domain of grammatical aspect in L2 Spanish, noting that several related pedagogical rules that are inflexibly presented give rise to target-deviant behavior in L2 performance. What this study did not do, however, is attempt to demonstrate how this could be ameliorated, if not avoided altogether, by modifying the information imparted to teachers about grammatical aspect in such a manner that they can incorporate the linguistic nature of grammatical aspect more accurately into how this contrast is taught. It should be uncontroversial to state that the linguistic concept of aspect is not introduced in SLA instruction to learners. However, such concepts are seldom brought to the attention of language teachers unless they are students of linguistics themselves as many are. As a result, the Preterit/Imperfect contrast is most often taught in absolute terms and in line with English/Spanish contrast equivalencies as discussed in Section 2 above. In general, such explanations hold true, but they are hardly absolute. The idea we wish to put forth is that L2 explanations that appeal too heavily to comparisons with the L1 are destined to fall short, especially when the L1 is very different from the L2 for the property of focus. Related to grammatical aspect in the scenario presented in Rothman (2008) as a mere example (see chapters in Gil, Marsden and Whong's (to appear) book for other properties and other language combinations), we are essentially concerned with how English and Spanish map three semantic meanings to past morphology, as schematized in Figure 1 in Section 2 below. Although perfectivity in English, unlike Spanish, is not encoded in uniquely dedicated morphemes, the related semantics itself is of course available.

Since, in English, past habitual and one time completed actions employ the same morphology, generalizations are taught to learners to compensate for this difference. English learners of L2 Spanish are told that repetitions, habitual events and events with long duration take imperfective morphology, and past events that happen once take perfective morphology. To bolster such explanations, learners are often provided with lists of trigger words that denote the aforementioned categorizations such as *siempre* -"always" (requires the imperfect) and *una vez* – "one time" (requires the preterit). Such explanations and the associated trigger words work most of the time, though certainly not always as it is perfectly grammatical and felicitous to use the preterit with the word 'always'. Furthermore, the preterit/ imperfect distinction of particular verbs is more difficult to explain. Often, the preterit/imperfect distinction for these verbs is taught lexically in line with their translatability to English equivalents. Needless to say, Spanish is not a translation of English. As a result, explanations dependent on translation equivalency will, in due course, meet with the inevitability of failing to account for what they seek to explain with 100% accuracy. For example, the verb *saber,* see example (2) below, is commonly taught as meaning *to know* in the imperfect and *to find out* in the preterit (similar examples abound). Accordingly, this translation-based explanation is unable to account for the interpretation of example (2), in which the Preterit is not only used meaning *to know* but also follows *siempre*.

(2) *Siempre supiste que yo te lo pediría.*
     You always knew that I would ask you for it.

Although the Preterit and Imperfect forms of certain verbs are, by far, more likely to be translated differently into English, it is inaccurate to claim that in every possible context, the preterit of these verbs will be equivalent to English translation value *X*, whereas the imperfect of the same verbs is equivalent to value *Y*. In other words, it is not that the meaning of the verb itself changes, but that the aspect may be more accurately conveyed through a different English translation. Thus, instead of saying that *supe* must mean *I found out* and *sabía* must mean *I knew*, students could be taught in an accessible way that what is really happening is that the verb *saber*, which is stative in the imperfect (and thus atelic), becomes an achievement (and thus is telic) in the preterit. And so, in both forms the verb still means "to know" it is just that the preterit is inchoative in nature and marks the beginning point of knowing (i.e. from that point on), which often happens to nicely correlate to the English phrasal verb "to find out". However, the meaning of the verb itself does not actually change, as the translation technique of teaching the difference would suggest.

What teachers of Spanish need to understand related to this property is that the difference between the preterit and imperfect past tenses is a surface (morphological) reflex of formal linguistic (syntactic and semantic) notions related to how the viewpoint of the speaker is represented with respect to the boundedness of the event's completion. In simpler terms, the speaker's use of the preterit indicates her point of view that the event represented by the verb is bounded in a specific, fixed instance of time. On the other hand, her use of the imperfect would indicate her perspective that the time-frame of the event represented by the verb is unbounded in the past. This covers *all* uses of the preterit and imperfect without further stipulation. If this distinction were explained in such a way that teachers and students of Spanish find it functionally useful, then it is conceivably that the predominant overgeneralizations in the form of imprecise pedagogical rules would no longer be necessary. Linguistic descriptive analyses are necessary to form the basis of accurate explanations of the type we just offered. To create them and/or understand them, knowledge of the basic tenets of the linguistic sciences is necessary. To this aim, future teachers of foreign languages should be encouraged to engage in formal linguistic training as part of their education. Furthermore, we are in need of textbook authors who are themselves better trained in linguistics and language acquisition – or, in the case that they are, they should be encouraged to incorporate more directly such training into pedagogical formulation and textbook design. Of course, this can only be done if there is a market for such materials. It is our hope that discussions such as the one offered herein help to create such a market.

5.   Conclusion

In this chapter, we attempted to make connections between generative linguistic approaches to second language acquisition and the practical side of second language learning in a classroom setting. To build such bridges, we presented evidence supporting the Competing Systems Hypothesis (CSH) and went beyond the intent of the original study. That is, Rothman (2008) proposed the CSH to test whether or not imprecise pedagogical rules can have an effect on L2 performance at high levels of L2 proficiency. Rothman was uniquely interested in understanding L2 performance; consequently, an answer to the narrow question he proposed via the CSH was sufficient. However, our goal in this chapter has been to take the answer to this query and bring it to practice for second language learning. If indeed we have positive evidence that linguistic imprecision in pedagogical explanation can lead to the formation of a separate filtering system in classroom learners which promotes indefinite target-deviant L2 performance, then it seems reasonable to endeavor to dispose of the imprecision, especially when together linguists and teachers are armed with the complimentary expertise to do so. In essence, to reduce the consequences for tutored learners under traditional pedagogy as noted by the CSH, we must reduce the space between descriptive linguistic grammars and pedagogical grammars. Since teachers are generally not exposed to such grammars, a first step towards reducing this space would be twofold: (a) to encourage, if not require, teachers of foreign languages to be trained in linguistic descriptive grammars and to be shown why and for what contexts the other types of grammars exist (pedagogical and prescriptive grammars) and (b) for linguists to create accessible descriptive grammars that are usable for teachers and L2 learners alike who are not necessarily trained in formal linguistics. To be clear, the main problem, as we see it, lies only in the lack of earnest attempts at present to do what we suggest. Teachers and linguistic researchers are of course equally capable of understanding what the others do and uncovering, together and separately, the latent connections we have discussed as well as the benefits of opening a dialogue. The issue is this one of access, in both directions, to the others' resources and agendas. Once these connections are established, the next logical step would be to make practical pedagogies inclusive of textbooks and other supportive material that is accurate to descriptive grammars and functional for its audience.

It is important to state that what is proposed herein is not limited to the direct benefit formal linguistic description could have for the teaching of aspect in L2 Spanish, but should equally apply to all properties of any target language taught as an L2 to adult learners. We believe that thedisconnect between formal acquisition studies and language teaching has gone on for far too long and we are inspired by the connections that have begun to be made in this area in the past few years. To be fair, not all that is studied in formal acquisition is pertinent to language teaching and vice versa; however, where obvious overlap exists, communication between these two interrelated fields should be strengthened.

References

Bley-Vroman, R. (1983). The Comparative fallacy in interlanguage studies: The case of systematicity. *Language Learning, 33,* 1–17.

Chomsky, N. (1981). *Lectures on government and binding: The Pisa lectures.* The Hague: Mouton.

Chomsky, N. (2007). Of mind and language. *Biolinguistics, 1,* 9–27.

Depraetere, I. (1995). On the necessity of distinguishing between (un)boundedness and (a)telicity. *Linguistics and Philosophy, 18,* 1–19.

Ellis, R. (2010). Second language acquisition, teacher education and language pedagogy. *Language Teaching, 43*(02), 182–201.

Epstein S.D., Flynn, S., & Martohardjono, G. (1996). Second language acquisition: Theoretical and experimental issues in contemporary research. *Behavioral and Brain Sciences, 1,* 677–758.

Felix, S. (1985). More evidence on competing cognitive systems. *Second Language Research, 1,* 147–172.

Flynn, S. (1987). *Parameter-setting model of L2 acquisition.* Dordrecht: Kluwer.

Gil, K.-H, Marsden, H., & Whong, M. (To appear). *Universal Grammar and the language classroom.* Dordrecht: Springer.

Giorgi, A., & Pianesi F. (1997). *Tense and aspect: From semantics to morphosyntax.* Oxford: OUP.

Krashen, S. (1982). *Principles and practice in second language acquisition.* Oxford: Pergamon.

Lightbown, P.M. (2000). Anniversary article. Classroom SLA research and second language teaching. *Applied Linguistics, 21*(4), 431–462.

O'Grady, W. (2006). The syntax of quantification in SLA: An emergentist approach. In M. Grantham O'Brien, C. Shea, & J. Archibald (Eds.),*Proceedings of the 8th Generative Approaches to Second Language Acquisition Conference (GASLA 2006)* (pp. 98–113). Somerville, MA: Cascadilla Press.

Pérez-Llantada, M.C., & Larsen-Freeman, D. (2007). New trends in grammar teaching: Issues and applications: An interview with Prof. Diane Larsen-Freeman. *Atlantis, 29*(1), 157–163.

Pica, T. (1997). Second language acquisition research methods. *Encyclopedia of Language and Education, 8,* 89–99.

Rothman, J. (2008). Aspectual selection in adult L2 Spanish and the competing systems hypothesis: When pedagogical and linguistic rules conflict. *Languages in Contrast, 8*(1), 74–106.

Rothman, J. (2010). Theoretical linguistics meets pedagogical practice: Pronominal subject use in Spanish as a second language (L2) as an example. *Hispania, 93*(1), 52–65.

Rothman, J., & Guijarro-Fuentes, P. (2010). Input quality matters: Some comments on input type and age-effects in adult SLA. *Applied Linguistics, 31*(2), 301–306.

Rothman, J., & Iverson, M. (2008). Poverty-of-the-stimulus and L2 epistemology: Considering L2 knowledge of aspectual phrasal semantics. *Language Acquisition: A Journal of Developmental Linguistics, 15*(4), 270–314.

Schwartz, B.D., & Gubala-Ryzak, M. (1992). Learnability and grammar re-organization in L2A: Against negative evidence causing the unlearning of verb movement. *Second Language Research, 8,* 1–38.

Schwartz, B.D., & Sprouse, R. (1996). L2 cognitive states and the full transfer/full access model. *Second Language Research, 12,* 40–72.

Schwartz, B.D., & Sprouse, R. (2000). When syntactic theories evolve: Consequences for L2 acquisition research. In J. Archibald (Ed.), *Second language acquisition and linguistic theory,* 156–186. Oxford: Blackwell.

Slabakova, R. (2008). *Meaning in the second language.* Berlin: De Gruyter.

Slabakova, R., & Montrul, S. (2003). Genericity and aspect in L2 acquisition. *Language Acquisition, 11,* 165–196.

Smith, C.S. (1991). *The parameter of aspect* [2nd edition 1997]. Dordrecht: Kluwer.

Spada, N. (2005). Conditions and challenges in developing school based SLA research programs. *The Modern Language Journal, 89*(3), 328–338.

VanPatten, B. (2010). Some verbs are more perfect than others: Why learners have difficulty with ser and estar and what it means for instruction. *Hispania, 93,* 29–38.

White, L. (2003). *Second language acquisition and Universal Grammar.* Cambridge: CUP.

Whong, M. (2011). *Language teaching: Linguistic theory in practice.* Edinburgh: EUP.

CHAPTER 5

Why theory and research are important for the practice of teaching

The case of mood choice in Spanish relative clauses

Joyce Bruhn de Garavito
Western University

Theoretical approaches to second language research suggest that the interaction between different linguistic modules may be at the root of many difficulties faced by learners. The choice of mood in relative clauses in Spanish illustrates the problem given that, in order to be proficient in this area, speakers must know what the two moods, indicative and subjunctive, bring to the meaning of the sentences (semantics) and what the contribution of the context is (pragmatics). Based on results of research carried out by generative linguists on the acquisition of mood selection in relative clauses, this paper argues that the results of theoretically based research that looks at questions such as these has an important contribution to make to language teaching, bridging the gap between generative linguistic approaches to SLA and pedagogy.

1. Introduction

Generative approaches to second language acquisition often address the issue of how the human mind/brain comes to know what it does know. For this reason many of the questions researchers are focused on relate to what the learner of a second language brings to the task, whether it be a set of universal principles (UG) in conjunction with knowledge of the first language or something altogether different. The answer to this question will in turn inform us as to whether knowledge of the target language by a second language learner is similar (Schwartz & Sprouse 1996, among others), or fundamentally different from the knowledge of a native speaker (Bley-Vroman 1989). If differences are found we aim at finding out what they are and what causes them.

The questions addressed by those interested in language pedagogy, on the other hand, are more pragmatic in nature: how best to use the resources available to the teacher to guide the learner to be able to communicate as easily as possible in the target language. It is generally accepted that some sort of knowledge is necessary for communication to be possible, but the exact nature of this knowledge is less important than the end result: speaking, understanding, reading and writing the target language at a certain level of proficiency. So, for example, in their seminal article, Canale & Swain (1980) speak about four types of competences that together constitute communicative competence, one of which is linguistic competence. These authors then insist that the difference between competence and performance is irrelevant to the main problem, the attaining of a certain level of communicative abilities. In contrast, generativists only focus on linguistic competence and, although much of their evidence comes from performance, attempt to answer only questions about knowledge.

The idea that several competencies are involved under the umbrella of communicative competence has been fruitful for language pedagogy and second language research. For generative linguists the language faculty is made up of several modules that may correspond up to a certain point to the competencies referred to by Canale and Swain. Lexical items, which carry their own meaning, are combined into phrases and sentences in the syntactic module, and features such as tense and number are added as part of the morphology. These phrases or sentences are then interpreted or assigned a meaning in the semantic module, a meaning that cannot be reduced to the sum of the meanings of the individual words (Slabakova 2010). At the same time, the phrase or sentence must be pronounced, that is, a phonological form must be assigned to it. It is customary for generative linguistics to think of these domains or modules as constituting the grammar of a language. Pragmatics is the module which contributes additional meaning leading to a more precise interpretation depending on context or knowledge of the world. For example, suppose I say 'The teachers kept the children in because they were very rowdy'. How do I assign an interpretation to 'they'? Among other things, I need lexical and syntactic knowledge to help me identify 'they' as a pronoun and the subject of the sentence. Semantics will tell me that pronouns such as these generally refer back to an antecedent in a previous clause. However, how do I decide between 'the teachers' and 'the children' as the phrase the pronoun is referring back to? From the point of view of the syntax, both are possible. I therefore use context and my knowledge of the world to resolve the ambiguity: children are generally rowdy, teachers are not. If the context changes, so does my interpretation. Think of 'The striking teachers were arrested by the police because they were very rowdy'.

The question of how the different modules interact with each other and how these interactions may make the learning task easier or more difficult is not obvious. Clearly, for example, a certain degree of control over the pragmatics of a language is important for communication, but how does the pragmatics interact with the syntax, the morphology, and the semantics of a language? In recent years research conducted within the generative approach has led to the suggestion that interfaces between different domains, that is, areas in which different linguistic modules interact with each other, may be particularly vulnerable in different ways and under different learning conditions, including early bilingualism (Hulk & Müller 2000; Müller & Hulk 2001), language attrition due to contact (Montrul 2002), and second language acquisition (Sorace 1993). For some researchers, the interface is precisely the place where fossilization occurs and the source of non-convergence in L2 speakers. This is the view elaborated primarily in Sorace's work (Sorace 2011), who claims that learners can acquire the morphosyntax but sometimes face great obstacles with regards to interpretation. This often results in so-called residual optionality, that is, the fact that even very advanced learners sometimes use non-target forms at the same time as target forms, at least some of the time.

2. Interfaces

We have defined interfaces as the space in which different linguistic modules interact with each other. This is illustrated in Figure 1, adapted from White (2009).

As Figure 1 shows, not all interfaces are equal. If we consider the middle box the grammar proper, then relations between the phonology and the syntax on the one hand and between the syntax and the semantics on the other, or between the lexicon and any of the other modules, are all internal to the grammar, they are internal interfaces. Not so the pragmatics, whose interface with the other components is external.

Many researchers working within generative-based theoretical approaches to second language acquisition have recently focused on the possibility that interfaces between different modules of the grammar may be particularly vulnerable in the sense that they lead to residual optionality even at near-native stages (Interface Hypothesis, Sorace 2011), that is, even very advanced speakers of a second language may occasionally use forms that are not appropriate in the second language. White (2011) suggests interfaces may be problematic at earlier stages as well.

	Lexicon	
Articulatory-Perceptual System	Phonology Semantics	Conceptual-Intentional System (including pragmatics)
	Syntax	

Figure 1. Articulatory/perceptual – Conceptual/intentional Interface

One of the first suggestions that interfaces might be problematic in several types of acquisition comes from studies on simultaneous bilingualism. Although we now know that early bilinguals are very good at keeping their languages apart (Genesee 1988; Paradis & Genesee 1997), it is also well known that transfer is possible, indeed probable. Hulk and Müller (2000) and Müller and Hulk (2001) argued that crosslinguistic influence between the languages of a bilingual depended on three main factors: whether the two languages seemed to overlap in a particular area, whether there was apparent structural ambiguity in one of the languages, and whether the grammar interfaced with a module such as pragmatics. Interfaces have since been extensively examined in attrition (Belletti & Leonini 2004; Montrul 2004; Tsimpli, Sorace, Heycock, & Filiaci 2004), second language acquisition (Borgonovo, Bruhn de Garavito, Guijarro-Fuentes, Prévost & Valenzuela 2006; Bruhn de Garavito & Valenzuela 2008; Lozano 2006); and bilingualism (Serratrice 2007; Serratrice, Sorace & Paoli 2004) with many reporting non-convergence or residual optionality at advanced and near native levels. One of the questions that has arisen is whether all types of interfaces cause problems or whether only external interfaces are at the root of the difficulties learners face. In fact, it is possible that multiple interfaces are even more problematic (Hopp 2009).

Why should interfaces be more vulnerable? Sorace (2011: 12) argues that the problem is better understood "if one considers that speakers need to acquire the following:

1. knowledge of the structure and of the mapping conditions that operate within interface conditions, and
2. the processing principles that apply in the real-time integration of information from different domains."

In other words, we need to know whether there is a problem with how knowledge is represented in the mind, in particular how particular forms map onto or relate in the different modules, or whether we are dealing with greater difficulty due to processing exigencies, or maybe both. The answer to this question is still a matter of debate well beyond the scope of this chapter.

One of the areas that has been studied most in regards to gaining an understanding of how mapping, i.e. production or interpretation, of a structure may be subject to interface conditions, is the use of overt and null pronouns in Romance languages such as Italian and Spanish (see work by Sorace and colleagues in particular). As is well known, in these languages it is not obligatory to express the subject overtly, as shown in (2a). In English, however, an explicit subject is obligatory, as the contrast between the translation of the Spanish sentence in (2a) and the ungrammaticality of (2b) shows.

(2) a. Llegué   tarde.
         arrived-I late
         'I arrived late.'

     b. *Arrived late.

The interpretation and production of null subjects constitutes a prime example of an interface condition. On the one hand, we have the syntactic phenomenon, the omission of subject pronouns. On the other, there are pragmatic conditions that constrain the use of explicit and null subjects. In general, overt subject pronouns are used to express focus on the subject or for disambiguating a referent in the discourse, as the examples in (3) show. In (3a), the use of an overt pronoun is infelicitous (marked with #) because the two people referred to have just been mentioned and there is no contrast implied. Most monolingual native speakers would omit the subject pronoun here. In (3b) there is contrast, two people are sick but only one of them came in to work, and therefore the pronoun is necessary.

(3) a. María y Julia no vinieron hoy. #Ellas/Ø estarán enfermas.
         'María and Julia did not come today. They must be sick.'

     b. Marta y yo estamos enfermas, pero yo/#Ø sí vine a la oficina.
         Marta and I are sick, but I did come to the office.

It is generally agreed that the syntax of null pronouns is acquirable without much difficulty; in fact learners drop subjects quite early on. However, the pragmatic constraints are far more problematic, as has been shown for many types of acquisition, including early bilingualism (Paradis & Navarro 2003; Serratrice 2007; Sorace, Serratrice, Filiaci & Baldo 2009), L1 attrition (Montrul 2004; Tsimpli, Sorace, Heycock & Filiaci 2004), and second language acquisition (Belletti, Bennati, & Sorace 2007; Montrul & Rodríguez Louro 2006; Sorace & Filiaci 2006). Focusing on the second language acquisition of null and overt subjects Rothman (2009) conducted an experiment in which he first ascertained whether participants had acquired the syntax of null subjects by testing their interpretation of the subject of embedded clauses under certain conditions. Null subject languages have the interesting property, first noticed by Montalbetti (1984), that both the null subject and an explicit pronoun in an embedded clause can be interpreted ambiguously, referring either back to the subject of the main clause or to a third party. However, this ambiguity disappears if the subject of the main clause is a quantifier such as *every* or an interrogative such as *who*. In these cases the only interpretation possible for a third person pronoun is to refer to a third party, although the null subject will still be ambiguous. This phenomenon has been found valid for many types of languages including Japanese (Kanno 1997). Rothman (2009) argued that the acquisition of this contrast between null and overt subjects by second language learners can be taken as evidence that they know the syntax. For the second part of his experiment he only looked at those individuals that had passed the syntax test. For the main task, learners were asked to choose between a null or an overt subject, a choice that relied solely on pragmatics. Although participants were able to pass the syntactic test, they had great difficulty on the pragmatic test. This again shows that interface conditions may be particularly difficult for second language learners (see also Rothman 2010). Although I am not focusing on subject pronouns here, it is interesting to note that, in general, Spanish textbooks barely mention the fact that Spanish allows null subjects. More problematic, however, is that the pragmatic conditions are never practiced in any way whatsoever, giving learners the impression that use of overt/null subjects is arbitrary.

Similar studies have been carried out on the interpretation and use of articles in both Spanish and English (Ionin, Montrul, & Crivos, forthcoming). The syntax of English distinguishes between subjects interpreted as generic, which may be realized without an article ('Lions are fierce'), and specific reference subjects that take an article ('The lions are fierce'). Spanish, on the other hand, does not generally allow subjects without an article (*Leones son feroces), so a sentence in which the noun phrase includes an article can be interpreted as either generic or specific (Los leones son feroces 'Ø The lions are fierce'). Again, participants in Ionin et al.'s study have some trouble with the interpretation.

This chapter focuses on a third example of an interface, the choice of the subjunctive or the indicative in relative clauses. The next section describes what the choice implies, that is – what the learners' task is – before moving on to results of previous research on the subject.

3.   The use of mood in relative clauses

One of the main difficulties learners face when taking Spanish courses is the choice of mood, whether the subjunctive or the indicative, in embedded clauses. This is understandable given that there are a number of factors involved, some of which are quite subtle depending as they do on semantic and pragmatic distinctions that even linguists have trouble defining exhaustively. Furthermore, the determining factors are generally not found in the embedded clause but rather in the main clause, thus leading to a long distance dependency.

From a theoretical point of view, mood distinctions have been studied mostly in the verbal complement domain (Kempchinsky 1986; Picallo 1985; Progovac 1993; Rochette 1988). In sentential arguments of predicates, the presence of subjunctive mood can be linked to two different mechanisms. In the first, mood is the result of lexical selection; in these cases there are no mood alternations, in other words, choice of the incorrect mood leads to ungrammaticality. For example, volitional predicates such as *to want* select the subjunctive in their complements and, as a result, indicative is ungrammatical in this context:

(4) a. Quiero que vengas.
         want-I that come-you-subj.
         'I want you to come.'

     b. *Quiero que vienes.
         want-I that come-you-ind.
         'I want you to come.'

The second mechanism is often referred to as polarity subjunctive. In these cases the subjunctive is possible due to the presence of negation or interrogation in a sentence with a verb that normally selects indicative (5). In most of these cases both moods can alternate without ungrammaticality. The difference between the two moods is interpretational, in other words, the speaker is trying to convey a semantic distinction that is signalled by the difference in mood. With indicative, the speaker signals that the embedded proposition is presupposed and with subjunctive there is lack of presupposition (Borgonovo 2003; Giorgi & Pianesi 1997; Quer 2002, among others).

(5) a. No dijo que habías llegado/hubieras llegado.
         (s/he) not said that (you) had-ind. arrived/ had-subj arrived.
         'S/he didn't say you'd arrived.'

     b. No cree que Patricia es/sea simpática.
         (s/he) not believe that Patricia is-ind/is-subj nice
         'S/he doesn't believe Patricia is nice.'

Modal distinctions are also found in adverbial and relative clauses (Pérez Saldanya 1999). In relative clauses, the focus of this chapter, the phenomenon patterns with polarity subjunctive in that grammaticality is not at stake; rather, interpretation is, as shown in (6).

(6) El estudiante que ha/   haya   terminado puede irse.
     the student   who has-ind /has-subj finished   may   leave
     'The student who has finished may leave.'

The use of the indicative in (6) indicates that there is a particular student that has finished, while the use of the subjunctive refers to any student who has met the condition of having finished. The two interpretations signalled by mood depend on the referential properties of the noun phrase (NP) modified by the relative:

indicative correlates with specificity of the NP and subjunctive, with non-specificity (Farkas 1985; Kampers-Manhe 1991; Pérez Saldanya 1999; Quer 2001).

What is crucial for the specific or non-specific interpretation of a noun phrase is context. Intensional contexts, those that convey a difference in the degree of certainty, allow a non-specific interpretation of noun phrases universally. Such contexts include future, negation, interrogatives, imperatives, and use of intensional (e.g. *necesitar* 'need') and modal (*querer*) verbs. The non-specific interpretation is ruled out in other environments, typically those that relate something that has taken place, as seen by the impossibility of having a subjunctive relative inside the NP in (7).

(7)   Salió un estudiante que *haya/había terminado el examen.
       left a student that had-subj/had-ind finished the exam
       'A student that had finished the exam left'

Besides mood, (non) specificity can be marked in other ways including the type of determiner, with indefinite determiners being more easily interpreted as non-specific than definite ones; the presence or absence of a determiner (bare nouns tend to be interpreted as non-specific in Spanish); and the presence or absence of the preposition *a* which is used in Spanish to mark direct objects which are animate, generally [+human], and [+specific] (Torrego 1998). The problem is that these additional ways of marking specificity do not correlate exactly with the use of the subjunctive, which can appear in relative clauses with a definite antecedent or one that does not refer to a [+human] entity.

The brief description of the subjunctive in relative clauses is useful because it allows us to see what the learner's task will be to successfully acquire the ability to control the semantic distinctions allowed by mood alternations, thus increasing communicative competence. Learners have to extract from the input (or from instruction) knowledge of the difference in form between the subjunctive and the indicative (morphology); the presence of this distinction mainly in embedded clauses and the fact that the choice depends on factors present in the main clause (syntax); the fact that the choice of the subjunctive or the indicative in relative clauses depends on the specific/non specific interpretation of the antecedent (semantics); and the importance of the context (pragmatics). Unlike the use of mood in most complement clauses, the choice of subjunctive or indicative in relative clauses will never lead to ungrammaticality. Crucially, the input will include both subjunctive and indicative in embedded clauses that modify a noun phrase, so frequency cannot be a good indicator. In the classroom the input may include explicit explanation and perhaps correction. However, given the semantic and pragmatic factors involved, focus on form in the traditional sense will not be sufficient given that 'form' generally refers to lexical, morphological or syntactic components of the grammar. The learner must be exposed to situations where the choice has clear semantic and pragmatic impact. It has to matter, for example, whether I am looking for a particular book or any book that meets a particular condition. The question is whether this actually happens, and in fact whether it is possible at all. In the next section we will examine what research can tell us about the learnability of the choice of mood in relative clauses.

4.   Specific vs. non-specific: Is interpretation learnable?

Collentine (1995; 2003; 2010) has conducted research on the acquisition of the subjunctive although not necessarily focusing on relative clauses. Collentine (1995: 122) asks whether, given the amount of time we spend teaching this mood, it is "reasonable to anticipate that, by the end of the intermediate level, our learners will reach a developmental stage at which mood-selection instruction can be effective?". He continues stating that the results of his empirical study show that 'intermediate level learners do not reach a point in their development at which they would have the appropriate *linguistic foundation* with which to fully benefit from mood-selection instruction.' He argues convincingly that learners have trouble with complex syntactic structures, including embedded clauses. As we shall see below, this claim has fallen on deaf ears at least when it comes to textbook writers.

The acquisition of the subjunctive in complement clauses is somewhat easier than relative clauses for two reasons: the input is relatively straightforward, with only some sociolinguistic variation, and the rules are also relatively clear cut, use of the incorrect mood leads to ungrammaticality. As we saw, relative clauses are far more complex. Learners have to be able to control the morphology associated with the indicative and the subjunctive, and map the use of the one or other mood onto the correct interpretation of the specificity of the head of the relative clause, which actually lies outside the embedded clause. In other words, the learners have to deal with morphology, syntax, semantics and pragmatics. Is this an impossible task? Should we simply stop trying to help students produce and interpret relative clauses?

Borgonovo, Bruhn de Garavito and Prévost (2007, submitted) examined knowledge of the conditions that rule mood choice in relative clauses with three groups, a Spanish native speaker control group and two groups of English speaking learners of Spanish who had all begun to learn their second language after the age of puberty. Following a placement test participants were assigned to an intermediate group (n = 14) and an advanced group (n = 13). The advanced group consisted of second language speakers that had used the language for communication for an average of 10 years, while the intermediate group, who were studying in Mexico, had only used it on average for two years. The authors argued that interface conditions are acquirable, following work by Dekydtspotter, Sprouse, & Thyre (2000), Borgonovo and Prévost (2003) and others. As we shall see, the results partially supported this claim.

The full set of tasks included a grammaticality judgement task that tested knowledge of the use of the subjunctive in complement clauses with volitional verbs (subjunctive) and relative clauses in which only the indicative was possible because the context referred to an event that had taken place. This test served to disqualify any learners who were not able to distinguish between the two moods.

The main test was a truth value judgement task in which speakers were given a short scenario in English that served to establish the specificity of the head noun phrase. This was followed by two minimal pair sentences that differed as to the presence of the subjunctive or the indicative in the relative clause. Learners were asked to judge on a scale from +2 to –2 whether these sentences were appropriate or not. The Truth Value Judgement Task is illustrated in (8) and (9). Note that all DP heads were introduced with an indefinite article to force the speaker to focus on the context.

(8) It is Marisol's birthday. Her friends don't know what to get her, so they ask her boyfriend. He says:
   a. Marisol quiere un perfume que anuncien en la televisión.
       Marisol wants a perfume that they announce-subj on television
   b. √Marisol quiere un perfume que anuncian en la televisión.
       Marisol wants a perfume that they announce-ind on television

(9) I must spend a week in a hotel, but I cannot leave my dog alone at home. The problem is that most hotels don't allow pets in the rooms. I ask a friend of mine:
   a. √¿Conoces un hotel que acepte perros?
       know-you a hotel that accept-subj dogs
   b. ¿Conoces un hotel que acepta perros?
       know-you a hotel that accept-Ind dogs

The task examined contexts that, as we mentioned above, allow non-specific interpretations across languages. These are illustrated in the following examples.

   a. Environments created by strong intensional predicates, e.g. *want* and *need*:

(10) Queremos una casa   que tenga   vista al   mar.
      want.1P   a   house that has.Subj view over sea
      'We want a house that has an ocean view'

b. Negation:

(11) No conozco a nadie   que entienda   esta derivación.
      neg know   *a* nobody that understands this derivation
      'I don't know anybody who understands this derivation.'

c. Imperatives:

(12) Lee un libro que te   haga   pensar alguna vez!
      read a   book that you make.Subj think   some   time
      'Read a book that makes you think, once in a while'

d. Future:

(13) Escribiré   un libro que denuncie   este escándalo.
      write.FUT.1s a   book that expose.Subj this scandal
      'I'll write a book that exposes this scandal'

e. Modal verbs:

(14) Pueden enviar unos agentes que no   estén   de uniforme.
      can.3s send   some agents that neg be.Subj of uniform
      'They can send agents that are not in uniform'

f. Interrogatives

(15) ¿Sabes de algún estudiante que   hable catalán?
      know. 2s of   some   student that   speak.Subj Catalan
      'Do you know any student that speaks Catalan?

The summary of the results is illustrated in Figure 2.

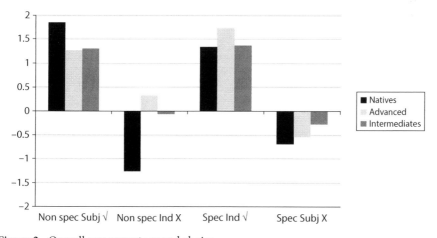

Figure 2. Overall responses to mood choice

Recall that judgements on this task were between a maximum acceptance of +2 and total rejection of –2. Overall, both the intermediate and the advanced learners made the correct distinctions in both the specific and non specific contexts and the difference between their responses to the different contexts was significant. However, as Figure 2 shows, although both learner groups clearly prefer the subjunctive in non-specific contexts, their acceptance of the indicative was significantly different from the native speakers' clear rejection of this mood.

Figure 3 shows the mean responses to non-specific contexts broken down for each of the categories.

Examining the responses for the individual categories confirms the overall impression given in Figure 2. The native speakers strongly accept the subjunctive in non-specific contexts and strongly reject the indicative. The two non-native groups clearly treat the inappropriate use of the indicative in these contexts in a different way than the native speakers, they exhibit a tendency to accept the indicative more frequently. In fact, the advanced speakers make a significant distinction between the two moods only in the case of strong intensional predicates, the future and interrogatives. The intermediates actually make a significant difference in more cases, with strong intensional predicates, future, interrogative, imperative and modal contexts. There does not appear to be progress as proficiency increases, and we find a great deal of variability.

Figure 4 shows the responses for specific contexts.

The first thing to notice in Figure 4 is that the native speakers show some variability, particularly in the interrogative and modal contexts. In the case of the interrogative there is no significant difference between their responses with indicative and subjunctive.

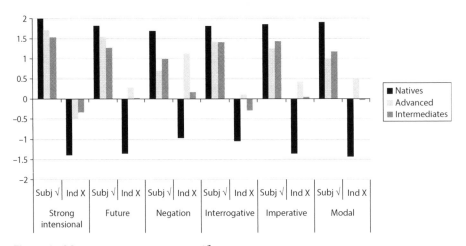

Figure 3. Mean responses to non-specific contexts

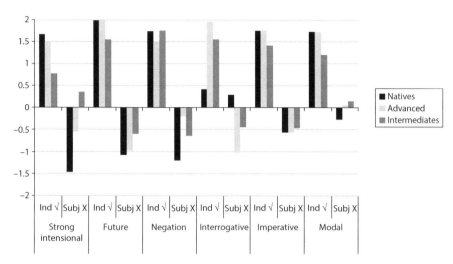

Figure 4. Mean responses to specific contexts

Turning now to the second language groups, we find significant differences between the responses to indicative and subjunctive in all cases, in fact their responses to interrogative sentences are closer to what is expected than for the native speakers. The intermediate learners also produce significant differences in all types except strong intensionals. Like the other two groups, their rejection of the subjunctive in the case of modals is low. We seem to find progression based on proficiency.

To summarize this study, we find that learners seem to deal more easily with specific contexts in which their appropriate choice of the indicative is strong and their rejection of the subjunctive seems on a par with the native speaker responses. Non-specific contexts are more problematic, with the subjunctive generally preferred but the indicative rejected less frequently. We could say there is a tendency among the second language learners to choose the indicative. However, learning has clearly taken place, the responses are far from random. It is interesting to note that similar results were found by Iverson, Kempchinsky, and Rothman (2008) in their study on the acquisition of negative polarity subjunctives.

As we shall see below, mood choice in relative clauses is taught in most courses, including at the beginning level. However, the different types of contexts are not, so it is particularly interesting to note that these learners seem on their way to acquiring the distinctions. On the one hand they are not learning exactly what is taught, but they are acquiring knowledge that is not taught (see Bruhn de Garavito 1997 for a similar conclusion).

5.   Approach to relative clauses in textbooks

In this section we will examine two introductory and one advanced textbook. We have chosen these not because we wish to criticize them in particular or because they are particularly bad. In fact, they have many interesting qualities, they are very recent and they are used across North America. However, they follow a very traditional methodology, and, as we shall see, their approach is very similar. In this respect they do not differ from at least 15 other textbooks that we have examined. The two beginning texts are *¡Hola Amigos!* (Jarvis, Lebredo, Mena-Ayllón, Rowinsky-Geurts & Steward 2012) and *Vistas* (Blanco & Donley 2005). The intermediate level Spanish textbook is *Imagina. Español sin barreras* (Blanco & Tocaimaza-Hatch 2011).

Both in the beginning and in the intermediate level textbooks it is customary to present the subjunctive in complement clauses first, followed by relative clauses and or adverbial adjuncts. For example, *Vistas* includes 18 lessons that go from greetings all the way to hypothetical *if* clauses. The morphology related to the subjunctive is first presented with formal commands in Chapter 12, and in the same chapter the use of the subjunctive 'with verbs of will and influence'. Chapter 13 goes on to verbs of emotion and doubt or disbelief, and end with the subjunctive with conjunctions (adjuncts). Relative clauses, referred to as adjective clauses, are presented in Chapter 14. *¡Hola amigos!* contains 12 lessons with an optional final chapter. The subjunctive mood is introduced in Lesson 11 in complement clauses, and in lesson 12 we find 'Subjunctive to express indefiniteness and nonexistence' (286). As for the intermediate textbook, *Imagina* includes 10 chapters, the subjunctive in complement clauses is found in lesson 3 and in relative clauses in lesson 4. It is important to note that focus on embedded clauses, whether indicative or subjunctive, only begins with the introduction of the subjunctive.

Turning now to how these representative textbooks go about teaching mood choice in relative clauses *¡Hola Amigos!* provides the greatest amount of context because the chapter is introduced by a dialogue about two friends that are searching for a hotel. This gives the learner the opportunity to contrast sentences such as *We have to find a hotel that* +subjunctive; *There is no hotel that* + subjunctive; *There are many hotels that* + indicative. The explanation regarding the use of mood says 'The subjunctive is always used in the subordinate clause when the main clause refers to something or someone that is indefinite, unspecified, hypothetical, or nonexistent.' (286). There is a small attention grabber box on the side that explains the indicative is used for existent, definite or specified persons or things. The explanations are followed by several examples that are not contextualized. Finally, there is a page of exercises.

Vistas is quite similar although there is less context provided. Like *¡Hola Amigos!* there is an introduction that states 'You will now learn how the subjunctive can be used in adjective clauses to express that the existence of someone or something is uncertain or indefinite' (434). This is followed by more detailed explanations with examples that contrast use of the subjunctive and the indicative. Finally we find exercises that include filling the blanks with the correct form in sentences without context, sentence forming from a list of words, and classified ads that do provide a context.

The more advanced course book does almost exactly the same as the introductory texts. The introduction states that "When an adjective clause describes an antecedent that is known to exist, use the indicative. When the antecedent is unknown or uncertain, use the subjunctive." (134) This is followed by examples of the contrasting use of the moods presented in sentences devoid of context, and further explanations regarding negative and indefinite words as antecedents, the use of the differential object marking in relation to "hypothetical persons" (135), and the use of the two moods in questions. The explanations are followed by exercises including fill-in-the-blanks and sentence completion tasks. Finally, there is a section titled *Comunicación* that permits the production of semi-controlled use of the two moods. In all three textbooks, upon finishing the exercises, we move onto a different grammar point altogether.

It is important to note that there is a long tradition of teaching Spanish in this way. But we must ask ourselves what students understand of these explanations. As a student I am told I should use the subjunctive to refer to someone or something that is nonexistent, do I use it to speak about unicorns and fairies? What is an adjective clause? What does it mean to say that someone or something's existence is indefinite? And what is an antecedent? This is not a critique of traditional teaching: it is quite possible that adult students feel the need to understand consciously the rules of the language. It is also probable that many instructors feel more comfortable explaining rules because it is less risky. But I think we should at least try to meet the students at their level, and not speak in terms that should be reserved for specialists. As we saw above, the choice of mood cannot be boiled down to a grammar point that is placed, like a brick on a wall that is under construction, in the mind of the learner, to then move on to some other brick to place. We have known for years, maybe centuries, that language is a system that needs to evolve in the mind of the learner. You do not first install the present tense, then move on to the past tense and install it, and so on, because when we learn the past tense our use of the present tense must change.

When teaching mood distinctions in Spanish relative clauses it is essential to understand the complexity of the problem for the learner (see VanPatten 2010 for a similar argument). The learner has to acquire the morphology of the subjunctive and the indicative, the syntax that permits the formation of relative clauses, the semantics associated with the subjunctive in contrast to the indicative, and finally, the learner has to infer the pragmatics, to put herself/himself in the mind of the person they are speaking to in order to understand the very subtle differences being conveyed, differences that are probably expressed in their first language in a different way.

6. Discussion and conclusions

In this paper we have begun by examining the complexity associated with the choice of subjunctive or indicative in Spanish relative clauses. A learner has to make the connection between the mood used in the embedded clause and the interpretation of the head noun phrase in the main clause. In order to make this connection the learner has to be aware of the morphology, the ending on the verb that distinguishes the different moods; s/he has to be aware of possible clues to the interpretation, such as the presence/absence of differential object marking and the form of the determiner; crucially, however, the learner has to extract the interpretation as either specific or non-specific from the context. Thus acquisition of the subjunctive lies at the interface of several modules, including internal modules such as morphology, syntax and semantics, and external modules such as pragmatics. Although communicative approaches have emphasized the importance of different types of competences or abilities that a learner may aspire to acquire, the fact is that these abilities are often, as in the present case, tied to one another. Also, as in many cases, linguistic competence, in terms of Canale and Swain (1980), is somehow central to acquiring the other abilities. This is not to say that this paper is defending the position that we must overtly teach grammar, rather we are stating that the lexicon and the grammar, including the morphology, the syntax and the semantics, have to be somehow acquired, and that the process can be very complex, whether we practice naturalistic approaches or not.

Assuming the complexity of the task in hand, we have asked whether it is possible to accomplish it: in other words, we must consider the question of learnability. Researchers into second language acquisition can provide us with results that may be important in the decision making process of language professionals. Collentine (1995; 2003) has suggested that learners should have reached a level in which they can process embedded clauses before they are introduced to distinctions such as the subjunctive. It is notable that no Spanish textbook ever offers the students the opportunity to practice embedded clauses using the tenses they already know before introducing them to the subjunctive. Collentine's suggestion is not only based on empirical data but is also eminently reasonable. After all, embedded clauses involve at a minimum a great deal more structure to process than simple clauses. This would be relatively easy to incorporate into a course. Instead of introducing the subjunctive in an introductory level we could include contextualized practice on all types of embedded clauses. Once the learner is comfortable understanding and producing subordinate and relative clauses they may be ready to acquire mood choice.

Work by Borgonovo, Bruhn de Garavito and Prévost (2007; submitted; see also 2005) suggests that mood choice in relative clauses is learnable at higher levels, but not all contexts are learned at the same time: rather the results suggest that it spreads through the grammar of the individual so that certain contexts may have almost reached native-like intuitions while the distinction is not at all clear in others. What is absolutely certain is that there is a disconnect between the approach taken by most textbooks and what needs to be accomplished by the learners. Completing two or three pages of exercises will not lead to acquisition and therefore the type of introduction found in most Spanish textbooks does not constitute the best use of valuable class time. Again, all indications are that the choice of mood in relative clauses should not be taught in an introductory course. At the intermediate stage some contrasts may be presented, but perhaps not all possible contexts.

An understanding of the problems involved in the acquisition of mood choice in relative clauses also leads to the conclusion that it should always be taught within a context. It is almost impossible to clearly explain the difference between a specific interpretation of a noun phrase and a non-specific interpretation, and even if we manage to do this it is not at all certain the learner will be able to apply what has been understood consciously to processing complex clauses. Whether it is through visual aids, dialogues, short stories, or other activities, the learner has to be given the opportunity of receiving a great deal of contextualized input, and perhaps producing contextualized output. Manipulating a list of sentences that have no connection one to the other, as is done in many textbooks, is not an effective way of guiding the learner towards mastery of a distinction of such complexity. This is not a particularly new idea, as most applied linguists will point out, but it bears repeating.

To summarize, research that has been mainly carried out with theoretical questions in mind has been shown to be applicable to practical problems such as language teaching. An examination of this type of questioning may inform us as to the nature of what is being acquired which leads to an understanding of when it is possible to acquire it and some suggestions on how it should be presented. Of course this will always be only part of the picture, we have to take into consideration many other factors such as individual variation between learners, their goals and motivation in learning the language, the uses to which they put the language, the society in which the language is taught, etc. Language teaching has to feed off of many different methodologies and disciplines. However, there is no reason to reject a particular approach because we decide a priori that it has nothing to tell us. It is important to establish a dialogue between language teaching professionals and generative linguistics. As argued by Gil, Marsden, and Whong (to appear), the more classroom instruction is underpinned by an understanding of theoretical principles, the more effective it will be.

Reference

Belletti, A., Bennati, E., & Sorace, A. (2007). Theoretical and developmental issues in the syntax of subjects: Evidence from near-native Italian. *Natural Language and Linguistic Theory, 25*, 657–689.

Belletti, A., & Leonini, C. (2004). Subject inversion in L2 Italian. *Eurosla Yearbook 4*, 95–118.

Blanco, J.A., & Redwine Donley, P. (2005). *Vistas. Introducción a la lengua española*. Boston, MA: Vista Higher Learning.

Blanco, J.A., & Tocaimaza-Hatch, C.C. (with García, P.N.) (2011). *Imagina. Español sin barreras*. Boston, MA: Vista Higher Learning.

Bley-Vroman, R. (1989). What is the logical problem of foreign language learning? In S. Gass & J. Schachter (Eds.), *Linguistic perspectives on second language acquisition* (pp. 41–68). Cambridge: CUP.

Borgonovo, C. (2003). Mood and focus. In J. Quer, J. Schroten, M. Scorretti, P. Sleeman, & E. Verheugd (Eds.), *Romance languages and linguistic theory 2001: Selected papers from 'Going Romance', Amsterdam, 6–8 December 2001* (pp. 17–30). Amsterdam: John Benjamins.

Borgonovo, C., Bruhn de Garavito, J., Guijarro-Fuentes, P., Prévost, P. & Valenzuela, E. (2006). Specificity in Spanish: The syntax/semantics interface in SLA. *Eurosla Yearbook, 6*, 57–78.

Borgonovo, C., Bruhn de Garavito, J., & Prévost, P. (2005). Acquisition of mood distinctions in L2 Spanish. In A. Burgos, M.R. Clark-Cotton, & H.S. (Eds.), *Proceedings of the 29th Boston University Conference on Language Development (BUCLD)* (pp. 97–108). Somerville, MA: Cascadilla Press.

Borgonovo, C., Bruhn de Garavito, J., & Prévost, P. (2007). The acquisition of mood distinctions in L2 Spanish relative clauses. Paper presented at the Hispanic Linguistics Symposium, San Antonio, TX.

Borgonovo, C., Bruhn de Garavito, J., & Prévost, P. (Submitted). Mood selection in relative clauses: Interfaces and variability. *Studies in Second Language Acquisition*.

Borgonovo, C., & Prévost, P. (2003). Knowledge of polarity subjunctive in L2 Spanish. In B. Beachley, A. Brown, & F. Conlin (Eds.), *Proceedings of the 27th Boston University Conference on Language Development*, Vol. 1 (pp. 150–161). Somerville, MA: Cascadila Press.

Bruhn de Garavito, J.L.S. (1997). Verb complementation, coreference and tense in the acquisition of Spanish as a second language. In W.R. Glass & A.T. Pérez-Leroux (Eds.),*Contemporary perspectives on the acquisition of Spanish*, Vol. 1 (pp. 167–188). Somerville, MA: Cascadilla Press.

Bruhn de Garavito, J., & Valenzuela, E. (2008). Eventive and stative passives in Spanish L2 acquisition: A matter of aspect. *Bilingualism: Language and Cognition, 11*(3), 323–336.

Canale, M., & Swain, M. (1980). Theoretical bases of communicative approaches to second language teaching and testing. *Applied Linguistics, 1*, 1–47.

Collentine, J. (1995). The development of complex syntax and mood selection abilities by intermediate-level learners of Spanish. *Hispania, 78*, 122–135.

Collentine, J. (2003). The development of subjunctive and complex-syntactic abilities among foreign language learners of Spanish. In B.A. Lafford & R. Salaberry (Eds.), *Spanish second language acquisition. State of the science* (pp. 74–97). Washington DC: Georgetown University Press.

Collentine, J. (2010). The acquisition and teaching of the Spanish subjunctive: An update on current findings. *Hispania, 93*, 39–51.

Dekydtspotter, L., Sprouse, R.A., & Thyre, R. (2000). The interpretation of quantification at a distance in English-French interlanguage: Domain specificity and second language acquisition. *Language Acquisition, 8*, 265–320.

Farkas, D. (1985). *Intensional descriptions and the Romance subjunctive mood*. New York, NY: Garland.

Genesee, F. (1988). Early bilingual development: one language or two? *Journal of Child Language, 16*, 161–179.

Gil, K.-h., Marsden, H., & Whong, M. (To appear). Generative second language acquisition and language pedagogy. In K.-H. Gil, H. Marsden, & M. Whong (Eds.), *Universal Grammar and the second language classroom*. Dordrecht: Springer.

Giorgi, A., & Pianesi, F. (1997). *Tense and aspect: From semantics to morphosyntax*. Oxford: OUP.

Hopp, H. (2009). Ultimate attainment at the interfaces in second language acquisition: Off-line and on-line performance. *Bilingualism: Language and Cognition, 12*, 463–483.

Hulk, A., & Müller, N. (2000). Bilingual first langauge acquisition at the interface between syntax and pragmatics. *Bilingualism: Language and Cognition, 3*(3), 227–244.

Ionin, T., Montrul, S., & Crivos, M. (Forthcoming). A bidirectional study on the acquisition of plural NP interpretation in English and Spanish. *Applied Psycholinguistics*.

Iverson, M., Kempchinsky, P., & Rothman, J. (2008). Interface vulnerability and knowledge of the subjunctive/indicative distinction with negated epistemic predicates in L2 Spanish. *EUROSLA Yearbook, 8*, 135–163.

Jarvis, A.C., Lebredo, R., Mena-Ayllón, F., Rowinsky-Geurts, M., & Stewart, R.L. (2012). *¡Hola amigos!* [2nd Canadian edition]. Scarborough, ON: Nelson Education.

Kampers-Manhe, B. (1991). *L'opposition subjonctif-indicatif dans les relatives*. Unpublished PhD dissertation, University of Groningen.

Kanno, K. (1997). The acquisition of null and overt pronominals in Japanese by English speakers. *Second Language Research, 13*(3), 265–287.

Kempchinsky, P.M. (1986). *Romance subjunctive clauses and logical form*. Unpublished PhD dissertation, UCLA.

Lozano, C. (2006). Focus and split-intransitivity: the acquisition of word order alternations in non-native Spanish. *Second Language Research, 22*(2), 145–187.

Montalbetti, M. (1984). *After binding: On the interpretation of pronouns*. Unpublished PhD dissertation, MIT.

Montrul, S. (2002). Incomplete acquisition and attrition of Spanish tense/aspect distinctions in adult bilinguals. *Bilingualism: Language and Cognition, 5*(1), 39–68.

Montrul, S. (2004). Subject and object expression in Spanish heritage speakers: A case of morpho-syntactic convergence. *Bilingualism: Language and Cognition, 7*(2), 125–142.

Montrul, S., & Rodríguez Louro, C. (2006). Beyond the syntax of the Null Subject Parameter: A look at the discourse-pragmatic distribution of null and overt subjects by L2 learners of Spanish. In V. Torrens & L. Escobar (Eds.),*The acquisition of syntax in Romance languages* (pp. 401–418). Amsterdam: John Benjamins.

Müller, N., & Hulk, A. (2001). Crosslinguistic influence in bilingual language acquisition: Italian and French as recipient languages. *Bilingualism: Language and Cognition, 4*, 1–21.

Paradis, J., & Genesee, F. (1997). On continuity and the emergence of functional categories in bilingual first-language acquisition. *Language Acquisition, 18*, 91–124.

Paradis, J., & Navarro, S. (2003). Subject realization and crosslinguistic interference in the bilingual acquisition of Spanish and English: What is the role of input? *Journal of Child Language, 30*, 1–23.

Pérez Saldanya, M. (1999). El modo en las subordinadas relativas y adverbiales. In I. Bosque & V. Demonte (Eds.), *Gramática descriptiva de la lengua* española (pp. 3253–3323). Madrid: Espasa Calpe.

Picallo, C. (1985). *Opaque domains*. Unpublished PhD dissertation, The City University of New York.

Progovac, L. (1993). Subjunctive: The (mis)behavior of anaphora and negative polarity. *The Linguistic Review, 10*, 37–59.

Quer, J. (2001). Interpreting mood. *Probus, 13*, 81–111.

Quer, J. (2002). Spanish L2 grammars of mood: On interfaces and learnability. In J. Costa & M.J. Freitas (Eds.), *Proceedings of GALA 2001* (pp. 189–195). Lisbon: Associacao Portuguesa de Linguistics.

Rochette, A. (1988). *Semantic and Syntactic Aspects of Romance Sentential Complementation.* Unpublished PhD dissertation, MIT.

Rothman, J. (2009). Pragmatic deficits with syntactic consequences?: L2 pronominal subjects and the syntax-pragmatics interface. *Journal of Pragmatics, 41*, 951–973.

Rothman, J. (2010). Theoretical linguistics meets pedagogical practice: Pronominal subject use in Spanish as a second language (L2) as an example. *Hispania*, 93, 52–65.

Schwartz, B.D. & Sprouse, R. (1996). L2 cognitive states and the Full Transfer/Full Access model. *Second Language Research,* 12(1), 40–72.

Serratrice, L. (2007). Cross-linguistic influence in the interpretation of anaphoric and cataphoric pronouns in English–Italian bilingual children. *Bilingualism: Language and Cognition, 10*, 225–238.

Serratrice, L., Sorace, A., & Paoli, S. (2004). Transfer at the syntax-pragmatics interface: Subjects and objects in Italian-English bilingual and monolingual acquisition. *Bilingualism: Language and Cognition, 7*(3), 183–205.

Slabakova, R. (2010). Semantic theory and second language acquisition. *Annual Review of Applied Linguistics, 30*, 231–247.

Sorace, A. (1993). Incomplete and divergent representations of unaccusativity in non-native grammars of Italian. *Second Language Research, 9*, 22–48.

Sorace, A. (2011). Pinning down the concept of "interface" in bilingualism. *Linguistic Approaches to Bilingualism, 1*(1), 1–33.

Sorace, A., & Filiaci, F. (2006). Anaphora resolution in near-native speakers of Italian. *Second Language Research, 22*, 339–368.

Sorace, A. Serratrice, L. Filiaci, F., & Baldo, M. (2009). Discourse conditions on subject pronoun realization: Testing the linguistic intuitions of older bilingual children. *Lingua, 119*(3), 460–477.

Torrego, E. (1998). *The dependencies of objects*. Cambridge, MA: the MIT Press.

Tsimpli, I.-M., Sorace, A., Heycock, C., & Filiaci, F. (2004). First language attrition and syntactic subjects: A study of Greek and Italian near-native speakers of English. *International Journal of Bilingualism, 8*(3), 257–277.

VanPatten, B. (2010). Some verbs are more perfect tha others: Why learners have difficulty with *ser* and *estar* and what it means for instruction. *Hispania, 93*, 29–38.

White, L. (2009). Grammatical theory: Interfaces and L2 knowledge. In W.C. Ritchie & T.K. Bhatia (Eds.), *The new handbook of second language acquisition* (pp. 49–65). Bingley: Emerald.

White, L. (2011). The interface hypothesis. How far does it extend? *Linguistic Approaches to Bilingualism, 1*(1), 108–110.

CHAPTER 6

Input-based incremental vocabulary instruction for the L2 classroom

Joe Barcroft
Washington University in St. Louis

This chapter reviews theoretical and research foundations of input-based incremental (IBI) vocabulary instruction (Barcroft 2004a, 2005, 2012) and exhibits how the IBI approach can be used to promote effective second language (L2) vocabulary instruction. It first considers key concepts (such as processing resource allocation) and pivotal research findings (such as the effects of sentence writing [Barcroft 2004a; Wong & Pyun 2012] and copying target words [Barcroft 2006] on L2 word learning), that underlie the approach. It then discusses ten principles of IBI vocabulary instruction (e.g., *Use meaning-bearing comprehensible input when presenting new words*) and provides a checklist for designing IBI vocabulary lessons. Finally, a sample IBI vocabulary lesson is presented along with an explanation of how the lesson incorporates various IBI principles.

1. Introduction

What is the most effective way to teach vocabulary in a second language (L2)? When addressing this question, it is important to consider how different options for providing *input* (samples of the target language) and assigning different types of tasks (e.g., writing a target word in an original sentence) affect learning different aspects of word knowledge, including word form, word meaning (e.g., L2-specific meanings), form-meaning mapping, and other types of knowledge, such as *collocation* (how words tend to co-appear with other words at rates that are greater than chance), over time. Fortunately, there is a growing body of research on *lexical input processing* (how learners process words and lexical phrases as input) demonstrating how L2 vocabulary learning is affected when target words are presented in the input in different ways and when learners are required to perform different types of tasks as they are exposed to target words in the input.

Overall, research on lexical input processing has drawn attention to the importance of allowing learners to process L2 words presented using the most well suited type of input possible without requiring them to perform tasks that detract from their ability to process the target words as input. For example, Barcroft and Sommers (2005) found that presenting target L2 words in acoustically varied formats led to substantial gains in L2 word form learning: increases from 38 to 64% using multiple talkers instead of a single talker and from 45 to 61% using multiple speaking styles produced by a single talker. Barcroft (2004a), on the other hand, found that requiring learners to write target words in original sentences yielded approximately *half* as much productive L2 word learning as compared to when target words were presented as input without assigning any additional task. The implications of these two sets of findings for instruction are clear: increase talker and speaking-style variability when presenting new L2 words but do not require learners to write the new words in sentences, at least with regard to learning novel form during the initial stages of learning a new word.

This chapter focuses on *input-based incremental (IBI) vocabulary instruction*, an approach to L2 vocabulary instruction that is grounded in theory and research on lexical input processing and that incorporates concrete research findings related to L2 vocabulary learning across the board. As such, it is an approach that is consistent with research findings such those mentioned above – the effectiveness of including talker and speaking-style variability when presenting target words as input and the ineffectiveness of writing target words in sentences during the initial stages of L2 word form learning – while avoiding relying on "intuition" or "hunches" when it comes to L2 vocabulary instruction. A number of the research findings that underlie the IBI approach may seem "counterintuitive" by traditional standards, such as with regard to the effects of sentence writing mentioned above or the negative effects of copying target words when they are presented as input during the initial stages of learning new words (Barcroft 2006), but findings such as these provide us with important opportunities to rethink our "world view" as it relates to L2 vocabulary instruction and to make the adjustments needed to provide learners with improved learning conditions and better opportunities to acquire L2 vocabulary over time.

There are a variety of approaches to instructed vocabulary acquisition. For example, Terrell's (1986) Binding/Access framework emphasizes activities that promote mental processes involved in linking form and meaning without translation. As another example, Nation (2001) has advocated the inclusion of four strands – meaning-focused input, language-focused learning, meaning-focused output, and fluency development – within a program that involves both intentional and incidental vocabulary learning. Approaches such as these have provided language instructors with specific types of activities and components of curricular design that can promote vocabulary learning in an effective manner. IBI vocabulary instruction is unique, however, in that it provides a comprehensive approach that emphasizes incremental but thorough attention to different aspects of word knowledge over time while being consistent with a variety of research findings related to lexical input processing, such as those discussed in this chapter. These findings concern the effects of specific tasks, such as semantically and structurally oriented tasks and opportunities for target word retrieval, as well as the effects of specific learning conditions, particularly with regard to how target vocabulary is presented as input.

The IBI approach is also grounded theoretically on multiple fronts. For example, IBI provisions for presenting target words frequently in the input and for using meaning-bearing input are consistent with the emergentist perspective on how learners build up knowledge not only of individual word forms but also of formulaic sequences and the collocational properties of words over time (see, e.g., Ellis 2006). As a second example, many task-related research findings that underlie the IBI approach speak to, from a theoretical perspective, the importance of *specificity* (or being specific) with regard to processing type when predicting learning outcomes. Tasks that invoke semantically oriented processing can be expected to facilitate semantically oriented learning (when the semantically oriented learning is not overly redundant with previously known semantic information), but these tasks (and the semantically oriented processing they invoke) should not be expected to be effective at promoting form-oriented learning. The idea that semantically or meaning-oriented "deeper" processing should lead to improved word form learning is inconsistent with this theoretical position and the research findings that support it. As a third example, input-related research findings related to the positive effects of acoustically varied input on word form learning suggest that non-linguistic indexical properties of speech promote the development of more distributed and robust mental representation of word forms (see Barcroft & Sommers, 2005; Sommers & Barcroft, 2007). As a final example, the IBI approach takes into account the important distinction between output *with* versus *without* access to meaning (see Lee & VanPatten, 2003; VanPatten 2003). The effects of these two types of output have been found to be quite different when it comes to language acquisition, including language acquisition at the word level, as research reviewed in this chapter demonstrates. Whereas output without access to meaning can impede learners' abilities to process target words as input, output with access to meaning facilitates their ability to encode and retain target words because opportunities for word retrieval strengthen mental connections for the target words in question. Theoretical foundations such as these underlie the IBI approach and constitute important reasons for adopting it.

The rest of the chapter is divided into four sections. Section 1 explains the research and theory that led to the development of IBI instruction. Section 2 presents and discusses ten principles of IBI vocabulary instruction. Section 3 introduces and explains a seven-item checklist for developing IBI vocabulary lessons. Section 4 presents a sample IBI vocabulary lesson along with commentary on how the IBI principles are incorporated in the lesson.

2.   Lexical input processing: Theory, research, and instruction

In the study of language acquisition, *input* refers to samples of a target language to which a language learner is exposed. Examples of input range from spoken and written stories, a series of individual sentences, or even individual words. Krashen (1985) proposed that input with structures slightly beyond one's current level of competence ($i + 1$) promotes L2 development. Other researchers have focused more on input processing (IP), conversion of input to intake, integration, and system change in their work (Gass 1997; VanPatten 1996).

Input and IP can be analyzed at multiple levels with regard to the acquisition of different types of linguistic structures. Suppose that an L2 learner of Spanish hears the following: *Quiero que vengas conmigo a una fiesta el sábado después de la ponencia* 'I want you to come to a party with me Saturday after the lecture.' This example of sentence-level input provides a great deal of information about Spanish as a linguistic system, such as how *-o* marks first-person singular and *-as* second-person singular and how *vengas* is the subjunctive form of the verb *venir* 'to come.' At the lexical level, there are word forms and a context from which their meanings might be inferred. The meaning of *ponencia* 'lecture' might be inferred, for example, if the learner already knows that there will be a lecture on Saturday. Oftentimes we are exposed to isolated lexical items as input as well: *La ventana... La puerta no... Sí, la ventana. La ventana... Así es. Ábrela. La ventana.* 'The window... Yes, the window... The window. Not the door. That's it. Open it. The window.' Interestingly, Brent and Siskind (2001) found that up to 9% of child-directed speech (input) consisted of individual lexical items, indicating that the quantity of this type of input is not trivial. What is critical, however, is that whether new words appear in sentences or as isolated items, they must be processed as input or they cannot be learned.

To date, research on IP and L2 acquisition has focused more on sentence-level IP and grammar acquisition more than other levels of IP and other aspects of acquisition. In recent years, however, researchers have become increasingly interested in *lexical IP*, or how learners process words (*word-level IP*) and lexical phrases (including idiomatic expressions) as input. In order to learn a new

L2 word, a learner must (1) encode and retain the form of the new word; (2) activate an appropriate semantic representation for the word, including L2-specific meanings and usage patterns (collocations, connotative meanings, etc.) and the word's syntactic functions; and (3) map the form of the word onto the appropriate semantic representation of the word. Research on lexical IP has identified how a number of different types of tasks and different types of input affect how learners allocate their limited (cognitive) processing resources toward one or more of these three components of word learning.

In the study of L2 lexical IP, the term *processing resource allocation* refers to how learners distribute their limited cognitive processing capacities toward different aspects of learning new words, such as word form, word meaning, and form-meaning mapping. Research on lexical IP has demonstrated that different types of tasks and methods of presenting target words as input can cause learners to allocate processing resources differentially toward one or more of these three key components of word learning, such as with regard to the relationship between form-oriented and semantically oriented types of processing and learning.

This theoretical perspective regarding the importance of distinguishing between different types of processing and learning is at odds with another line of thinking that maintains that focusing extensively on the semantic or meaning-related properties of a target word should be an effective method of L2 vocabulary learning. The origin of this line of thinking is connected to a particular application of ideas about the levels of processing (LOP) and human memory (Craik & Lockhart 1972). According to the LOP framework, activities that involve semantically oriented "deeper" processing lead to better memory than activities that involve structurally oriented "shallower" processing. Following an unqualified extension of LOP to the realm of L2 vocabulary learning, one might argue that semantically oriented tasks such as sentence writing, assessing one's feelings about the meaning of words, and addressing questions about word meanings should facilitate L2 word form learning. However, studies have demonstrated that requiring any one of these three tasks leads to *decreased* intentional L2 word form learning when compared to presenting new L2 words as input alone without requiring learners to perform any additional task (Barcroft 2004a, 2002, 2003 respectively).

In light of such findings, it is appropriate to consider alternative theoretical perspectives on human memory, such as *transfer appropriate processing* (TAP) (Morris, Bransford & Franks 1977), for their potential applicability to L2 vocabulary learning. According to TAP, the effect of a variable on memory depends on the nature of the task performed at study and at test such that semantic orientation should facilitate performance on subsequent semantically oriented tasks and structural orientation should facilitate performance on subsequent structurally oriented tasks. Barcroft (2002) proposed the *type of processing – resource allocation*

(*TOPRA*) model, which is consistent with the TAP approach, to depict how different types of processing produce different types of learning outcomes. Three versions of the model appear in Figure 1. In each version, the thicker outer lines remain stable because they represent the restricted amount of processing resources available to a learner. The inside lines can move, however, as different types of processing and corresponding types of learning increase or decrease, the basic idea being that each type of processing exhausts processing resources. As one type of processing increases due to a specific type of task demand, others must decrease in order to accommodate. The amount and type of learning that ultimately takes place will reflect this kind of trade-off.

The TOPRA model can be used to predict how different types of processing should affect learning for distinct components of word knowledge, such as word form, word meaning, and form-meaning mapping. Whereas Version A (in Figure 1) is the general version of the model, Version B focuses on processing for word meaning, word form, and form-meaning mapping, and Version C focuses on the semantic and formal components of word learning. Version C demonstrates most clearly the prediction that (when processing demands are sufficiently high) increased semantic processing can increase learning for the semantic (including conceptual) properties of words while decreasing learning for their formal properties. Word form learning decreases under these conditions because fewer processing resources remain available to process word form. Therefore, the *decreased* intentional L2 word form learning associated with semantically oriented tasks like sentence writing, assessing one's feelings about the meaning of words, and addressing questions (respectively, Barcroft 2004a, 2002, 2003), as discussed above, are consistent with the predictions of the TOPRA model. Interestingly, in a partial replication of Barcroft's (2004a) study, Wong and Pyun (2012) found that decreases in L2 vocabulary learning associated with sentence writing were more pronounced among English-speaking L2 learners when the L2 in question was Korean as compared to when it was French, potentially due to the increased distance (and increased novelty when it comes to word form, particularly written word forms) between English and Korean. This finding makes sense from the TOPRA perspective given that sentence writing as a semantically oriented task is expected to detract from form-oriented processing and learning.

Barcroft (2002) reported one particularly telling demonstration of why it is critical to specify type of processing when predicting learning outcomes regarding the effects of semantically oriented versus structurally oriented tasks on intentional L2 vocabulary learning. The study compared the effects of making pleasantness ratings about the meanings of target words (a semantically oriented task that required indicating on a rating scale how pleasant the referent of each target word made each participant feel) versus counting the number of letters in target words

A. General version: Types of processing and learning

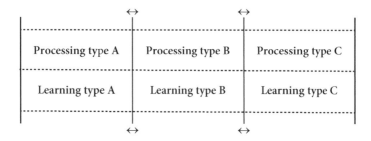

B. Components of vocabulary learning: Semantic, formal, and mapping

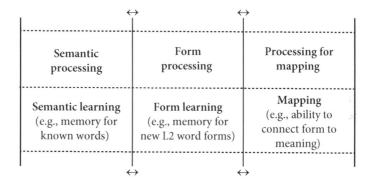

C. Semantic and formal components of vocabulary learning

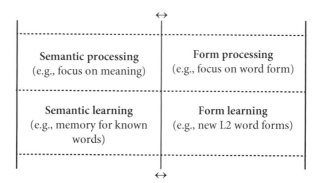

Figure 1. Type of Processing – Resource Allocation (TOPRA) Model

(a structurally oriented task) on intentional L2 vocabulary learning among English-speaking learners of L2 Spanish. All of the participants were asked to do their best to learn 24 new Spanish words while viewing word-picture pairs on a screen. For 8 words, they performed the semantic task; for another 8 words, they performed the structural task; and for another 8 words they performed no task (word groups and learning conditions were counterbalanced). Among the posttests they completed after the learning phase were two *free recall tasks* for which the participants simply attempted to recall words that they could remember, first in Spanish, the L2 they were learning, and then in English, a language they had already acquired.

As depicted in Figure 2, the free recall results were wholly consistent with the predictions of the TOPRA model. Spanish free recall scores were higher for the letter-counting (+structural) task than for the pleasantness-ratings (+semantic) task, but English free recall was higher for the pleasantness-ratings (+semantic) task than for the letter-counting (+structural) task. As predicted by the TOPRA model, the increased semantic processing invoked by the semantic task decreased processing resources that otherwise could have been allocated toward encoding the new L2 word forms. The effect on the left side of Figure 2 for English free recall depicts a *standard LOP effect*, whereas the effect on the right side for Spanish (L2) free recall is an *inverse LOP effect*. In other words, semantically oriented "deeper" processing can function like a double-edged sword when compared to form-oriented "shallower" processing; the former leads to better memory for previously acquired ("known") words but worse memory for novel L2 word forms.

Interestingly, the importance of specifying *type* of processing when predicting learning outcomes also goes beyond intentional L2 vocabulary learning. In a study on L2 vocabulary during reading, Barcroft (2009) found that requiring learners to generate L1 synonyms (a semantically oriented task) during vocabulary learning reduced L2 word learning in both intentional and incidentally oriented contexts as compared to no-semantic-task conditions. In the study, Spanish-speaking learners of English ($N = 114$) at low-intermediate ($n = 59$) and high-intermediate ($n = 55$) levels read an English passage containing ten new English words translated in the text. Four conditions were examined: I. "Read for meaning." II. "Read for meaning

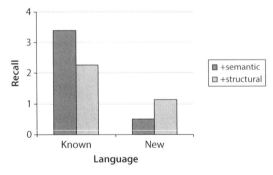

Figure 2. Effects of making pleasantness ratings (+semantic) versus letter counting (+structural) on free recall in a known language (English) and a new language (L2 Spanish)

and generate Spanish synonyms for the translated words." III. "Read for meaning and attempt to learn the translated words." IV. "Read for meaning, attempt to learn the translated words, and generate Spanish synonyms for these words."

The results of the study indicated significantly higher scores for the intentional over incidentally oriented condition and significantly lower scores when participants were required to generate synonyms. The negative effects of synonym generation appeared in both the intentional and incidental conditions with no significant interaction between condition and task. These findings, which are depicted in Figure 3, provide additional support for the TOPRA model and suggest that its predictions about the potential negative effects of semantically oriented tasks can extend beyond intentional into incidentally oriented contexts of vocabulary learning. They also favor asking students to instruct learners to make specific efforts to learn new words in a reading from a pedagogical perspective.

In another study on incidentally oriented vocabulary learning among Japanese speakers learning L2 English, Kida (2010) included a semantically oriented condition in which participants made pleasantness ratings. This semantically oriented task yielded significantly lower vocabulary learning scores when compared to a structurally oriented (phonological) task, and there was no statistically significant difference in performance of the group that performed the semantically oriented task and the performance of a no-task control group. Actual means were lower for the semantically oriented task as compared to the no-task control, but the difference did not reach statistical significance. Clearly, the semantically oriented pleasantness-ratings task was not effective at promoting learning of the novel word forms whereas the form-oriented structural task was more effective at doing so.

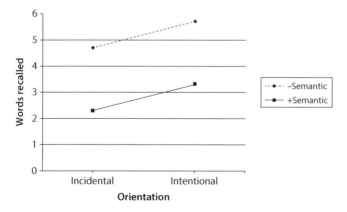

Figure 3. Negative effects of L1 synonym generation (+semantic) on incidental and intentional L2 vocabulary learning during reading

In addition to research on the effects of semantic versus structurally oriented tasks and their processing and learning counterparts, lexical IP research also has examined the effects of having learners perform other types of tasks during intentional L2 vocabulary learning. For example, Barcroft (2006) demonstrated that requiring learners to copy L2 words (when they appeared with pictures of their referents) decreased word learning as compared to when they were not asked to copy the words. Other studies, however, have demonstrated that allowing learners to attempt to retrieve target words on their own after they have been exposed to the words as input positively affects L2 word learning (Barcroft 2007; McNamara & Healy 1995; Royer 1973). These combined findings exhibit how two tasks that may appear somewhat "similar" on the surface can be very different in their true nature and therefore yield very different effects on L2 vocabulary learning. The copying task constituted a type of output *without* access to meaning that can detract from learners' ability to process target words as input whereas the retrieval task was a type of access *with* access to meaning (see Lee & VanPatten 2003, VanPatten 2003) that positively affects consolidation of target word forms in memory (see Barcroft 2007 for further discussion 2007).

In addition to the various tasks discussed thus far, research on lexical IP is also interested in the relationship between the type of input to which learners are exposed and how well they learn L2 vocabulary. Two types of input that have been found to affect L2 vocabulary learning positively are (a) input that includes increased numbers of exposures to target words and (b) input with increased talker, speaking-style, and speaking-rate variability (and increased fundamental-frequency variability for speakers of a tonal language). The rest of this section discusses research on these two types of input.

To begin, consider the role of number of exposures to target words in the input. One of the most basic findings in memory research is the positive effect of increasing number of repetitions. As Greene (1992: 132) has pointed out: "All other things being equal, our memory for information will depend on the number of times that we have encountered or studied it." When other internal variables such as working memory span and other external variables such as stimulus (input) quality are held constant, increasing the number of times that an individual is exposed to a stimulus increases our memory for the stimulus in question. Over a century ago, Ebbinghaus (1885) provided evidence of how memory for stimuli improves according to the number of times one is exposed to the stimuli. Since that time, memory researchers have investigated how the effect of repetition tends to function as a *learning curve*, a graph that depicts the gradually increasing positive effect of repetition (on an X axis) on amount of learning (on a Y axis). As Greene (1992: 132–133) explains, the prototypical learning curve is *monotonic* (the curve goes in one direction, upward, only) and *negatively accelerated* ("the rate of the upward movement is always slowing down"). The positive effects of increased exposure to target words can be readily observed both in the L2 classroom and in research on L2 vocabulary learning. To provide just one example, Hulstijn, Hollander, and Greidanus (1996) found that increased exposures to target words improved L2 vocabulary learning during reading.

In addition to increasing exposure frequency, another adjustment that can be made when presenting target words as input is to increase the number of talkers, speaking styles, or speaking rates used when presenting target words as input. Barcroft and Sommers (2005) and Sommers and Barcroft (2007) asked English speakers to attempt to learn 24 new words in Spanish in a series of experiments. All of the participants were presented with each target word 6 times for the same amount of time. During the learning phase, the participants were exposed to 8 of the words in each of three different learning conditions: no variability, moderate variability, and high variability. In the no-variability conditions, all 6 repetitions of each word were spoken by the same talker (or in the same speaking style or at the same rate). In the moderate-variability conditions, 2 repetitions of each word were spoken by 3 different talkers (or in 3 different speaking styles or at 3 different rates). In the high-variability conditions, 1 repetition of each word was spoken by 6 different talkers (or in 6 different speaking styles or at 6 different speaking rates). After the learning phase in each experiment, the participants were tested on picture-to-Spanish cued recall and Spanish-to-English cued as measures of vocabulary learning. Both their accuracy and latency, or reaction time (in milliseconds), were measured.

In all three experiments, positive additive effects were observed such that vocabulary learning was higher in the moderate-variability condition as compared to the no-variability condition and higher in the high-variability condition as compared to both the moderate- and low-variability conditions. Figure 4 depicts the accuracy results for talker variability. The results for speaking-style and speaking-rate variability followed a similar pattern of positive additive effects. From a theoretical perspective, the researchers noted that these findings were consistent with the proposal that the non-linguistic *indexical* properties of speech (such as information about talker, the style of speech of the speaker, and the speaking rate) are encoded during word learning and lead to more distributed representations of lexical form when these indexical properties are varied during the presentation of target vocabulary as input.

However, the results also indicated that amplitude and fundamental-frequency (F0) variability produced null effects, at least for native speakers of English. From a theoretical perspective, the researchers interpreted these findings by proposing the *extended phonetic relevance hypothesis* (see also Sommers, Nygaard & Pisoni 1994 on the phonetic relevance hypothesis with regard to speech perception), which posits that only sources of variability that are phonetically relevant will have a positive effect on word form learning. Interestingly, in a study designed

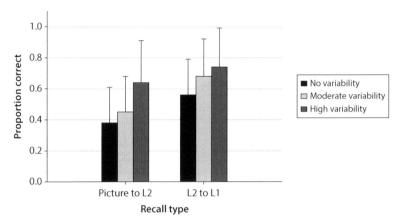

Figure 4. Effects of talker variability on L2 vocabulary learning based on picture-to-L2 and L2-to-L1 recall combined (error bars = standard deviations of the mean)

specifically to test the extended phonetic relevance hypothesis, Barcroft and Sommers (2012) found positive additive effects of F0 variability on L2 vocabulary learning among bilingual speakers of Zapotec (a tonal language) and Spanish but null effects of F0 variability on L2 vocabulary learning among speakers of Spanish (not a tonal language) who did not speak any tonal language. These findings suggest that because F0 was phonetically relevant only to the Zapotec speakers in the study, only the Zapotec speakers benefited from F0 variability, as is consistent with the extended phonetic relevance hypothesis.

3.   Summary of key implications of research

The research findings on lexical IP reviewed in this section clarify a number of points about L2 vocabulary learning:

1. Repeated exposure to target words in the input is beneficial to learning new words successfully.
2. Target words can be presented in a manner that enhances their learnability, such as by using multiple talkers, speaking styles, or speaking rates (and multiple F0s for speakers of a tonal language) when presenting them.
3. Semantically elaborative tasks can detract from L2 word learning (when compared to presenting target words as input without requiring any additional task) during the initial stages of word learning because they exhaust processing resources that otherwise could be directed toward encoding new word forms and making appropriate form-meaning mappings. This implication is

consistent with predictions of the TOPRA model regarding the relationship between different types of processing and expected learning outcomes.

4. A tasks that require producing output without access to meaning, such as copying words while attempting to learn them, can decrease word learning effectiveness.

5. Although forced output without access to meaning can impact L2 vocabulary learning negatively, opportunities to retrieve target words after some initial word-level IP has taken place can impact positively on our ability to learn L2 words.

Each of these points was taken into consideration in the development of the IBI approach.

4. Ten principles of IBI vocabulary instruction

The ten principles of input-based incremental (IBI) vocabulary instruction appear in Table 1. Barcroft (2004b) discussed some of these principles of a previous version of the IBI approach. Barcroft (2005) discussed nine of these principles while focusing on vocabulary instruction for L2 Spanish. The previous version of Principle 8 (from Barcroft 2005) was *Respect different stages of the development of vocabulary knowledge*, which has been changed to *Promote learning L2-specific word meanings and usage over time* in order to focus more proactively on helping learners to move through different stages of development with regard to L2-specific aspects of knowledge and usage. Because the approach was designed to be comprehensive, some of the principles may seem more "self-evident" (e.g., Principles 1 and 10) than others. The ties of other principles to the critical role of input in language learning and to specific theories and research findings (e.g., Principles 2, 5, 6, and 7) should also be apparent. Each principle is discussed in order in the rest of this section.

Table 1. Ten Principles of IBI Vocabulary Instruction

1. Develop and implement a vocabulary acquisition plan.
2. Present new words frequently and repeatedly in the input.
3. Promote both intentional and incidental vocabulary learning.
4. Use meaning-bearing comprehensible input when presenting new words.
5. Present new words in an enhanced manner.
6. Limit forced output without access to meaning during the initial stages.
7. Limit forced semantic elaboration during the initial stages.
8. Promote learning L2-specific word meanings and usage over time.
9. Progress from less demanding to more demanding activities over time.
10. Apply research findings with direct implications for vocabulary instruction.

Principle 1 affirms the importance of having a plan for L2 vocabulary learning, which includes selecting target words. While this principle may be one of the more self-evident ones, it is important to include because planning is critical and, unfortunately, oftentimes not put into practice when it comes to curricular design and classroom instruction. One option to consider in planning is to make use of word frequency in the target language (see, e.g., Nation 2001, for discussion of research in this area), such as when one focuses on the 2000 or 3000 or 5000 most frequently used words. Schmitt (2010) provides a useful summary of key issues related to measuring vocabulary and vocabulary size, including references for a number of readily available vocabulary size assessment instruments. Another issue related to Principle 1 is the extent to which a course syllabus is going to be lexically oriented. Grammar has been emphasized more than vocabulary in L2 instruction from a historical perspective (Zimmerman 1997), but many researchers, such as Willis (1990; cf. Sinclair & Renouf 1988) and Lewis (1993, 1997), have called for developing much more lexically oriented syllabi. Finally, on a larger scale, conducting an L2 needs analysis (see, e.g., Long, 2005) can be useful when determining target vocabulary within any program of language instruction.

Principle 2 advocates taking advantage of the benefits of increased exposure (Key Implication 1 from the previous section). The benefit of increased exposure is one of the most ubiquitous findings in research on memory and other areas of inquiry related to learning, including L2 vocabulary learning. For example, as mentioned previously, Hulstijn, Hollander, and Greidanus (1996) reported that Dutch-speaking learners of French learned more L2 vocabulary during reading when they were exposed to target words 3 times instead of only once. Kida (2010) also found a positive effect for 3 exposures over 1 exposure in a study on incidental L2 vocabulary learning during reading among Japanese-speaking learners of L2 English. It is not always the case that instructors attend carefully to the number of times target words are presented in written texts or spoken input, but findings such as these clearly indicate the value of doing so and making efforts to increase frequency of exposure to target words.

Principle 3 calls for promoting both intentional and incidental vocabulary learning. Relying on incidental vocabulary learning (and "indirect instruction") alone can lead to fewer gains in vocabulary learning as compared to when intentional vocabulary learning activities (and "direct instruction") are included. For example, Paribakht and Wesche (1997) demonstrated that combining direct instruction with incidentally oriented instruction can be more effective than relying on incidental learning alone. Intentional orientation alone can also have a positive effect on L2 vocabulary learning during reading. Hulstijn (1992, Experiment V) found that L2 learners who had been informed that they would be tested on target word meanings after a reading picked up more word meanings than learners who were not instructed to do so. Positive effects of this nature were also observed in Barcroft's (2009) study: learners in intentional-orientation conditions learned more words than learners in the incidentally oriented conditions. In other words, if instructors ask their students to attempt to learn new words that they encounter in a reading and let them know that they will be tested on them, the students are likely to learn more new words from the reading in question.

Principle 4 argues for using meaning-bearing comprehensible input when presenting new words. At a very basic level, this principle makes sense because if the meanings of target words are not activated, how can learners map novel forms to their meanings? They would not be able to do so. This principle follows Krashen (1985) by affirming that meaning-bearing comprehensible input is a necessary ingredient for successful SLA. Krashen's position that input at the level of $i + 1$ (slightly above one's current level of competence) is what is needed for L2 acquisition is also pertinent here. The more *in*comprehensible input is, the less likely a learner can infer the meaning of a new word. IBI vocabulary lessons should be consistently meaning-oriented and engaging. They also should regularly provide learners with opportunities to learn new information; in other words, they can be substantially content-based.

From an emergentist theoretical perspective, the use of sentence- and discourse-level meaning-bearing and comprehensible input when presenting target words allows learners to engage in the critical process of *chunking*, which refers to how we mentally group items (such as words) that co-occur in a language. Learners need to be exposed to sentence- and discourse-level input for this to occur because single-word input (although in no way trivial in and of itself) does not provide sufficient evidence to learners regarding how words tend to co-occur. Consider, for example, the following input segment that includes the possible target words *mug* and *scalding*: *This is a coffee mug. It looks like the coffee in the mug is really hot. When coffee is really hot, what is it called? Scalding. Scalding hot coffee. What else can be scalding? ... Right, water. Scalding water or scalding hot water. If you touch scalding hot water, you definitely can get burned.* This example demonstrates not only how a target word can be presented frequently in the input while still having the input be meaning-oriented but also how meaning-bearing input allows learners to associate words that tend to co-occur in a language, such as *scalding, hot*, and *coffee* and *scalding, hot,* and *water* in English. Evidence of co-occurrence of this nature comes from the input. Without sufficiently meaning-bearing and comprehensible input, learners would be left to their own devices to guess which words in a language tend to co-occur or not.

Principle 5 calls for enhancement of target vocabulary when it appears in the input. Enhancement can take on a number of forms. These include textual enhancement techniques such as increasing the font size of target words or bolding or underlining them. Other techniques may go beyond simple enhancement and be more related to altering a text and providing the meaning of target words. Hulstijn, Hollander, and Greidanus (1996), for example, found that including definitions of words in marginal glosses positively affected L2 vocabulary learning during reading. In the spoken mode, target vocabulary can be spoken in a particularly clear voice or in a slower voice so that learners have better opportunities to perceive the word forms in question. Additionally, as explained previously, the use of increased talker, speaking-style, and speaking-rate variability (and F0 variability for speakers of tonal languages) has been found to substantially positive (and additive) effects on L2 vocabulary learning in the spoken mode (Barcroft & Sommers 2005; Sommers & Barcroft 2007; Barcroft & Sommers 2012). Utilizing techniques such as these when presenting target vocabulary in the input should pay off when it comes to amount of vocabulary learned within a given period of time (as is consistent with Key Implication 2 from the previous section).

Principles 6 and 7 are tied to decreases in vocabulary learning observed when learners are required to engage in excessive semantic processing of a redundant nature or to produce output without access to meaning during the initial stages of learning L2 words (Key Implications 3 and 4 from the previous section). These two principles are supported by research reviewed in the previous section demonstrating the negative effects of semantically elaborative tasks such as sentence writing, attending to questions about the meaning of target words, making pleasantness ratings, synonym generation, the output-oriented task of word copying (a form of output without access to meaning). The IBI approach advocates restricting the extent to which these types of activities are used during the initial stages of learning new words. However, with regard to semantically oriented tasks in particular, if the task in question focuses on L2-specific meanings or usage of a target word or expression that are distinct from L1 meanings and usage, this task should be more beneficial than a semantically oriented task that focuses on areas where there is overlap in meaning and usage because the former will allow learners to focus on *new* as opposed to redundant information on the semantic front.

Principles 8 and 9 are central to the IBI approach given their particular emphasis on the *incremental* nature of vocabulary learning. Principle 8 calls for activities that promote learning L2-specific word meanings and usage at the appropriate time. Typically, activities of this nature will come after a learner has had an opportunity to process a target word form as input and has learned more general meanings and usage of the word that are not specific to the L2, but one also may focus on meanings and usage of this nature at the early stages instead of focusing on redundant meanings (based on L1 knowledge). For example, an English-speaking learner of L2 Spanish may learn that *cambiar* means 'to change' but then also needs to learn that the same verb can be used to mean 'to cash,' as in *cambiar un cheque* 'to cash a check' (the Spanish-speaking learner of English needs to learn the opposite, that is, to learn the distinction between "to change" and "to cash"). The same L2 learner of Spanish also may come to realize that the Spanish word *burro* 'donkey' can be used in an expression such as *el burro hablando (al conejo) de orejas* 'the donkey talking (to the rabbit) about ears' to express the idea of 'the pot calling the kettle black' and in so doing continue to expand her or his knowledge of L2-specific meanings (connotative or otherwise) and usage. IBI lessons incorporate activities that help to promote this type of expanded knowledge of L2-specific meanings and usage over time.

Principle 9 points out that what may not be effective in Step 1 of a vocabulary lesson may be much more effective at a later point in time. Words need to be used in a fluent manner and in a variety of meaning-oriented contexts. Therefore, different types of semantically elaborative and output-oriented activities may be appropriate once a learner has had sufficient opportunities to process new words as input. In other words, the question is not *whether* to include semantically elaborative and output-oriented activities but *when* to include them, in consideration of learners' developmental stages with regard to different aspects of word knowledge. Additionally, in designing one or more series of tasks for an IBI lesson, it may be beneficial to consider theoretical proposals and research related to task complexity and task difficulty, such as those of Robinson (e.g., 2001, 2003), noting also that one can include the principles and general approach of IBI vocabulary instruction seamlessly within task-based instruction and communicative language teaching.

Finally, Principle 10 proposes that L2 instructors (and program directors, course coordinators, and developers of L2 instructional materials) should stay abreast of any research findings that have direct implications for L2 vocabulary instruction. Whereas the other nine principles of the IBI approach are proposed to be basic and foundational when it comes to effective L2 vocabulary instruction, Principle 10 suggests continuing to inform oneself about new research findings that have immediate implications for improving L2 vocabulary instruction within the larger approach described here. Table 2 presents a series of research findings that can be viewed as falling into this category, including the positive effects of opportunities for target word retrieval (Key Implication 5 from the previous section), the positive effects of using nonvocal, classical background music when presenting target words, and the negative effects of presenting words in semantically based sets (likely due to the effects of interference), among others.

Table 2. Other Research Findings with Direct Implications for Vocabulary Instruction

Study	Finding
Barcroft, 2007a; McNamara & Healy, 1995; Royer, 1973	Positive effects of allowing learners opportunities to attempt to generate target words on their own
De Groot (2006)	Positive effects of nonvocal, classical background music (Bach's fourth Brandenburg concerto with flutes, a violin, and string instruments in the study)
Finkbeiner & Nicol (2003); Tinkham (1997)	Negative effects of presenting words in semantically based sets
Luppescu & Day (1995)	Positive effects of bilingual dictionary use (as compared no dictionary use) on vocabulary learning during reading
Pulido (2009)	Reading abilities and background knowledge on a topic are an indicator of ability to infer new word meanings during reading.
Other studies ...	*Add many applicable research findings to this list and incorporate them as appropriate when designing IBI vocabulary lessons...*

5.   A checklist for designing IBI lessons

Figure 5 presents a checklist for designing effective vocabulary instruction lessons. The checklist draws attention to key tenets of the IBI approach, in particular, presenting target vocabulary repeatedly in the input during the initial stages and a gradually increasing the difficulty of tasks over time. Numbers 2 and 3 on the checklist also serve as reminders to make the lessons meaningful, interactive, and informative. Anyone designing an IBI lesson can make use of this checklist. When completing the checklist, if you find that you cannot check a particular item, it should not be difficult to go back and make adjustments to the lesson so as to be able to check the item in question.

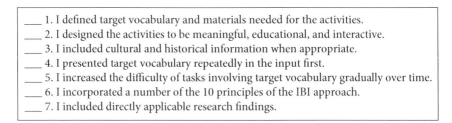

Figure 5. Checklist for Designing IBI Lessons

6.   A sample IBI lesson

This section presents a modified version of a sample IBI vocabulary lesson designed by Barcroft and McBride (2011) and presented at the 2011 MIDTESOL Conference in St. Louis, Missouri. IBI lessons involve multiple activities that are connected to a main topic. The lesson presented here is also followed by explanation and analysis regarding how specific IBI principles are incorporated. The topic of this sample lesson is the current political landscape in the USA.

The lesson would be appropriate for L2 English learners at an advanced level provided that they do not already know the target words in question. The learners could be in one of a variety of different types of classes, such as a conversation class or a class that focuses on English for special purposes. The original list of target words was selected by asking an L2 English instructor to provide a vocabulary list from a recent reading in a course on advanced-level intensive English. The theme we selected to teach these words was the current political situation in the United States. Other themes would be appropriate as well, such as a theme related to economics, but a theme related to politics was clearly one viable option. In light of findings about the potentially negative effects of presenting words in semantically oriented sets (Finkbeiner & Nicol 2003; Tinkham 1997), even though the original set of words do not form as tight of a semantic set as those tested in studies in this area, we replaced four of the original target words with four other words from completely different semantic areas. Replacement of this sort need not always be as extreme as in the case here, but the example shows how target words from completely different semantic areas can be incorporated within one coherent theme-oriented lesson. Finally, this sample lesson includes 12 target words, but this number certainly could be increased. Barcroft (2012), for example, presents (in book format) fourteen sample IBI lessons, each of which has 20 target words or more. Ultimately, decisions about how many target words to select and how much time to dedicate to each step in the lesson (e.g., how slow to proceed when presenting target words in the input and how many times to repeat the target words) should be made by instructors (and course coordinators, etc.) in consideration of the students with whom they are working and the goals they have for vocabulary learning for the particular language course in question.

6.1   Sample lesson

The Current Political Landscape in the USA

Selection of Target Words. Underlined words were removed from original list in order to expand the semantic range; bolded words were added to replace them:

ramification, reputation, proactive, <u>ethics</u>, conscience, covert, inadvertently, <u>investi-</u>
<u>gation</u>, <u>consumer</u>, legitimate, verify, <u>campaign</u>, **cranberry, to punt, plateau, wheel-**
barrow

Target Words. *ramification, reputation, proactive, conscience, covert, inadver-*
tently, legitimate, verify, cranberry, to punt, plateau, wheelbarrow

Step 1. Prepare a computer-based presentation with 12 pictures (in slides) that
depict or are related to each of the 12 target words. (Even though it may be more
difficult to find pictures for some of the words, such as *covert* and *legitimate*, the
input provided by the instructor can help to fill in gaps. In our lesson, for example,
the slide for *covert* included a clip-art drawing of a man that looks like a spy [wear-
ing spy glasses and so forth]; the slide for *legitimate* included a picture of a box for
a "legitimate" version of a software program.) Present all of the target words as
input while showing the picture file at the front of the class. Go through the slides
several times so that the students have opportunities to hear each target word
while viewing its corresponding picture several times. Vary the rate at which you
pronounce the target words on different repetitions.

For example: *This is a CRANBERRY. A cranberry is a small, red fruit that grows*
on bushes like this. Cranberries have a sharp taste, so usually people don't eat them
by themselves. One of the most common things with cranberries is cranberry juice.
Have any of you ever had cranberry juice? .... [next picture] This picture is associated
with the word RAMIFICATION. A ramification is the result of something, oftentimes
the result of something negative. Ramifications are the other negative consequences of
an action. In the comic strip here, you can see that the little boy has to deal with the
ramifications of not listening to his coach. The crowd is a bit "judgmental" about his
performance. Do you understand the meaning of ramification? [next picture] The
word PROACTIVE is an adjective. To be proactive means to anticipate a future event
and take action to avoid negative consequences. A proactive person gets things done
ahead of time and doesn't wait until something bad happens and there is an emer-
gency. You can be proactive with your health, or with your work. [next picture]. Your
CONSCIENCE is that part of you that tries to be a good person. People who have a
"clean conscience" are people who know they have done the right thing. Someone who
has a "heavy conscience" feels bad because he or she has done something wrong and
knows it. [next picture] The next picture is making reference to another adjective: the
word COVERT. Covert means shhhh, something to do with a secret. Usually we talk
of covert operations, like when spies participate in a covert operation. If something is
covert, you don't tell other people about it. Do you understand? [next picture]
INADVERTENTLY describes actions that you didn't mean to do. Another way to say
this might be to say "not on purpose" or "unintentionally" or "by accident." If you
inadvertently delete a file from a computer, oops, it is not what you meant to do, so
you did it inadvertently. [next picture] LEGITIMATE means "real" or "genuine." It is

the opposite of "false." Sometimes my students don't come to class and do not have a legitimate excuse. Other times my students have legitimate excuses. A legitimate excuse would be if you had to go to the doctor on emergency. That would be a legitimate reason for not coming to class...

Step 2. Complete an activity in which students match the written forms of the 12 target words to their corresponding pictures using the same picture file from Step 1. Provide each student with a list of the 12 target words (in random order) with blank spaces to the right of each word. Have each picture (the same pictures used in Step 1) appear (in some random order) with a letter below each picture or say each letter as the picture appears. Students should write the letter of each picture next to the word it to which it refers.

Step 3. Provide definitions of each target word to the entire class and ask them to try to recall each target word. Before beginning this activity, tell the students to wait until you ask for the one before they say anything. Wait about 3 seconds after each definition before asking for the word so that all students have an opportunity to try to recall each word.

For example: *This adverb is used to describe when someone does something without intending to do so. [Wait 3 seconds]. What is it?* [Wait for answers]. *Good... Inadvertently. Right. OK, next word. A vehicle that has only one wheel; it is commonly used to move items from one place to another during gardening.* [Wait 3 seconds] *What is it? Good... Wheelbarrow. That's right. OK, next word...*

Step 4. Provide students with a sheet that contains written definitions of all 12 target words and ask them to do their best to write all of them next to their corresponding definitions.

Step 5. Complete a "Charade" activity in which students act out one target word each while others try to guess what the word is. Even though the list includes vocabulary that is abstract (with only three concrete nouns), there is always a way to attempt to depict the words. The challenge in depicting the more abstract terms can be part of the fun of the activity.

Step 6. Have students work in pairs and attempt to create (and write) original sentences related to the topic of the current political situation in the United States. Each sentence should contain at least 3 of the 12 target words in the list. Have the words appear on a screen at the front of the class without their definitions so that the students can work from this list.

Step 7. Have a discussion about the students' views on current national political situation in the US. As appropriate, involve some of the 12 target words. After the discussion, mention that there will be a brief vocabulary quiz on the 12 words at the beginning of the next class.

Step 8. At the beginning of the next class, give the students a practice quiz on the 12 target words. The quiz should provide definitions for each of the 12 words and ask that the students produce each target word form. Go over all of the answers after students have finished. Below is an example of the quiz:

1. Conforming to the law or to rules; authentic, genuine.

   _____

2. A consequence of an action or event, especially when complex or unwelcome.

   _____

3. The beliefs or opinions that are generally held about someone or something.

   _____

4. Reach a state of little or no change after a time of activity or progress; to cause to remain at a stable level, especially to prevent from rising or progressing.

   _____

5. A small cart with a single wheel at the front and two supporting legs and two handles at the rear, used typically for carrying loads in building work or gardening.

   _____

6. A small, red, acid berry used in cooking; the red, acid fruit or berry used in making sauce, relish, jelly, or juice.

   _____

7. Creating or controlling a situation by causing something to happen rather than responding to it after it has happened; tending to initiate change rather than reacting to events.

   _____

8. An inner feeling or voice viewed as acting as a guide to the rightness or wrongness of one's behavior; the awareness of a moral or ethical aspect to one's conduct together with the urge to prefer right over wrong.

   _____

9. Without knowledge or intention; marked by unintentional lack of care.

   _____

10. Make sure or demonstrate that something is true or justified; swear to, support a statement by affidavit.

    _____

11. A kick in which the ball is dropped from the hands and kicked before it touches the ground; to propel (a ball).

    _____

12. Not openly acknowledged or displayed.

    _____

Step 9. After going over the answers to the quiz from Step 7, have students look at their answers and think of whether they have heard any alternative definitions or uses of the target words and alternate forms (different word classes, etc.) not covered so far. Working with the students, discuss and clarify appropriate alternative uses and meanings and commonly used alternate word classes.

For example: *So far we have talked about the word "legitimate" as an adjective, but it can also be used as a verb. "To legitimate" means to make something become justified or lawful. Can you think of any examples of how it can be used as a verb?.... So far we have focused primarily on the word "reputation" as a noun, but its adjective form "reputable" is also fairly commonly used. A business can be reputable, for example, if it has a good reputation....*

Step 10. Ask students if they think that they could create a story in which all of the target words could be used. Ask them what the theme of the story might be and which words might be difficult to incorporate in the story. Then tell students that you have prepared a story in which all of the words could be used. Provide them with the story with blank spaces where each target word should appear and ask them to try to fill in the blanks in order to complete the story. The story could be presented on paper to each student or at a screen at the front of the class with numbered blanks. Below is an example of a story with blanks for target words:

WORD LIST: cranberry/ramification/reputation/proactive/conscience/inadvertently/legitimate /to verify/to punt/plateau/wheelbarrow/covert

An Afternoon of Diversions from Work

I try to be _____ about my health. Instead of waiting to get sick, I try to eat healthy and exercise. I've been told that _____ juice is very healthy, so the other day, while I was reading the newspaper online, I was drinking some. Unfortunately, while doing that, I _____ knocked my glass of juice over. It spilled all over my laptop computer and damaged the computer. I couldn't believe it! I had a lot of work I had to do that afternoon. I decided that I could just use my roommate's computer. In general, I try not to use my roommate's things, but this time I had a _____ reason for making an exception. I felt that I could use his computer while still keeping a clean _____. I turned on his computer, and it asked for me to choose an account. I chose Bob's, but then it asked me to _____ my identity by providing the password. Since I didn't know what that was, I decided to use instead the "guest account." It opened up. On the desktop was that stock photo of a countryside scene with a _____ full of flowers parked in front of a simple, wooden house, a vision that made me realize that I had succeeded in my somewhat "_____" operation to obtain access to my roommate's computer.

So then I was finally able to access my email, where I discovered a message sent two days ago from a friend. I have a _____ for not responding to emails on time. I opened the email and saw my friend's travel photos, including beautiful shots of _____ *and other features of New Mexico's rocky landscape.*

Right then, I was startled by the sound of something hitting the window. I jumped out of my seat and went to see the source of the interruption. Apparently, someone had tried _____*a football and had aimed poorly. That distracted me for a while, and when I returned to the computer, I realized that it was already after 3 pm! I know that putting off important work can have serious* _____*, so I closed my email and got to work.*

6.2   Explanation and analysis of sample lesson

The following explanation and analysis addresses how each of the ten IBI principles are related to the sample lesson.

Principle 1. A lesson such as this one fits within a language program that has includes a carefully developed plan for vocabulary acquisition. This plan should include a series of lessons designed to promote the acquisition of specific sets of target words over time. The plan may involve considering word frequency and different thresholds for coverage in texts and spoken discourse, and the target words included in this sample lesson should be a subset of the larger list of target vocabulary included in the plan.

Principle 2. Steps 1, 3, 5, 7, and 9 clearly demonstrate Principle 2 as they ensure that the target words will be presented frequently and repeatedly in the input in the lesson. In Step 1, the instructor produces the target words *frequently* while talking about a computer-based picture file in a presentation program. The consistent repetition of the target words in the input may seem exaggerated, but to the extent that the forms of these words are novel to the learners, and this may be the case to a large degree, the repetition should be beneficial. The fact that target words appear in the input again in Steps 3, 5, 7, and 9 demonstrate how the target words appear *repeatedly* over time. The target words appear in the input when they are spoken by students in Steps 3 and 5 and when they are spoken by both the instructor and the students in Steps 7 and 9. This variety of target-word-focused input flood provides learners with numerous opportunities to process the target words as input and to retain them.

Principle 3. While this particular lesson focuses largely on intentional vocabulary learning when it comes to the target words, it also provides learners with a number of opportunities to pick up other vocabulary incidentally. During the steps in which the instructor is presenting input and other steps in which the class is discussing the theme at hand (e.g., Step 7), other vocabulary that is new to the learners may appear, providing opportunities for learners to pick up this vocabulary as well. Activities can be designed to promote learning target vocabulary incidentally as well, such as when key terms appear in a novel or other type of reading that has been assigned, but in the present sample lesson, learners are encouraged and directed to learn the target vocabulary intentionally to a large extent.

Principle 4. Steps 1, 3, 5, 7, and 9 not only ensure that target vocabulary is presented frequently and repeatedly in the input, they also provide input that it is consistently meaning-bearing. It is meaning-bearing because the meaning of the words is focused on, as is the larger theme in question. The instructor also should work to make the input as comprehensible as possible. Repetition of the target words in and of itself should help to achieve this goal because repetition is one of the many features that help to make input more comprehensible, but other features, such as including visuals, comprehension checks, and rephrasing should help to make the input more comprehensible as well. Note in particular how these features are included in the sample input provided for Step 1, such as the following comprehension checks *Have any of you ever had CRANBERRY juice?* and *Do you understand the meaning of RAMIFICATION?* An instructor can make adjustments in the input being provided based on student responses to questions such as these.

Principle 5. To the extent that the instructor enhances the presentation of target words by stressing them, pronouncing them very clearly, or both in Steps 1 and 3, Principle 5 is being incorporated. The indication in Step 1 to pronounce the target words at varying rates also can be considered a form of input enhancement. Varying the rate or the speaking style used when presenting the words as input can have positive effects on retention, as research on acoustic variability and L2 vocabulary learning indicates.

Principle 6. The heavy emphasis in Step 1's presenting the target words in the input without requiring learners to produce output without access to meaning follows Principle 6. The target words are presented to the learners in the input, but the learners are not asked to copy them. In this way, learners can focus on processing the target words as input without being required to exhaust limited processing resources for a parroting type of output. This provision is different from when they are asked to attempt to retrieve the target words on their own in Steps 3, 4, 5, and 8. Retrieving target words on one's own is a form of output *with* access to meaning; it presupposes that a learner has had opportunities to process the target words as input previously (because a learner cannot retrieve a target word if it has never been presented in the input previously).

Principle 7. The avoidance of forced semantic elaboration in the first five steps of the lesson is consistent with Principle 7. It is not until Step 6 that students are asked to utilize the target words in a sentence-writing activity related to the theme of the lesson. It is not that semantic elaboration is always a "bad idea." Instead, what matters is that one should not involve learners in semantically elaborative tasks and expect those tasks to be effective for learning novel word forms. The TOPRA model depicts why such an expectation would be erroneous.

Principle 8. Step 9 is consistent with Principle 8 in that it promotes learning L2-appropriate meanings and usage. The extent to which those exemplified here are L2-specific depends on the L1s of the learners. If the instructor knows the L1s in question, she or he can target meanings and usage that are novel.. Secondary meanings and alternative forms of target words (including other word classes, such as *reputation* and *reputable*) are considered after learners have had opportunities to process the novel words as input and to work with a limited set of meanings and uses.

Principle 9. The gradual progression of the steps from less to more demanding tasks over time is consistent with Principle 9. In Step 1, learners are processing input, which itself is demanding, but learners are asked *only* to listen and process the input (and respond to brief comprehension checks). In Step 2, they are asked to do a matching task with the target words, but this task is less demanding than when they are asked to produce the target words on their own in Step 4. Steps 6 and 7 are more demanding in that they go beyond focus on the target words themselves and require learners to make use of the target words to write sentences (Step 6) and have a discussion (Step 7) related to the larger theme of the lesson. Fortunately, these more demanding tasks come after the learners have had numerous opportunities to process the target words as input and to focus on the target words without being asked to make use of them while performing other tasks. Additional steps also could be added to the lesson. These steps could focus on theme-related expansion activities, for example, while still being consistent with Principle 9 given their placement within the overall order of the steps.

Principle 10. The word selection process and Steps 3, 4, 8, and 10 demonstrate Principle 10 by incorporating two research findings that are directly applicable to vocabulary instruction. Studies by Tinkham (1997) and Finkbeiner and Nicol (2003) have demonstrated that learning words in thematic sets is more effective than learning words in semantic sets. Therefore, even though the original set of words do not form as tight of a semantic set as those tested in these studies, the word-selection process involved replacing four of the target words with other words in order to expand the semantic range of the target vocabulary. Other studies by Royer (1973), McNamara and Healy (1995), and Barcroft (2007a) have demonstrated the positive effects of providing opportunities to retrieve target words (after they have been presented in the input), and Steps 3, 4, 8, and 10 all provide learners with these types of opportunities. Steps 4, 8, and 10 do so by asking learners to work individually to attempt to retrieve the target words whereas Step 3 does so by asking the class to work together to try to retrieve target words. Incorporating readily applicable research findings such as these in lessons should help to promote vocabulary learning effectively.

From a larger perspective, note three key points about this sample lesson. First, consider the thoroughness of this lesson when it comes to providing learners with opportunities to process target words as input and to learn L2-specific and meanings and usage of target words. The opportunities provided for learners to retrieve target words on their own – a readily applicable research finding as per Principle 10 – are also extensive. Even if the exposures to the target words as input and retrieval opportunities were reduced, they may still be sufficient to allow many learners to learn and retain the target words in question. Second, the overall sequencing of the activities provides learners with opportunities to learn the target words before they are asked to use them in discussion related to the larger theme of the lesson. This provision should allow learners to discuss the theme more effectively and make it more enjoyable (and less frustrating due to having insufficient vocabulary knowledge pertinent to the topic) to discuss the theme.

Third, the lesson is consistent with the seven items in the checklist for designing IBI vocabulary lessons. (1) The target vocabulary and materials needed for the activities are defined. (2) The activities are designed the activities to be meaningful, educational (albeit based on information generated largely from other students about the current political situation in the USA in this case; additional teacher-generated information certainly could be added), and interactive. (3) The activities included cultural and historical information when appropriate, in this case with regard to the political system and current political situation in the USA. (4) Target vocabulary appeared repeatedly in the input first *before* learners were asked to use the target vocabulary on their own. (5) The difficulty of tasks involving target vocabulary gradually increased over time. (6) The lesson incorporated a number of the 10 principles of the IBI approach, as explained above in the explanation and analysis of the principles. Finally, (7) the lesson included additional directly applicable research findings, as suggested by Principle 10. In this case, the two research findings concerned the benefits of (a) using more thematically as opposed to semantically oriented sets of target words and (b) providing opportunities for target word retrieval.

7.   Summary and conclusion

In summary, the approach to L2 vocabulary instruction described in this chapter is supported by a substantially large body of research, in particular, research on lexical input processing. Concrete research findings on the lack of effectiveness of tasks such as sentence writing, word copying, and addressing questions related to the meaning of target words during the early stages of learning words underlie key principles of the IBI approach (Principles 6 and 7 in these cases). The approach is also theoretically grounded in several key areas, such as with regard to (a) the emergentist perspective on frequency effects in language learning and learning formulaic properties of words; (b) transfer appropriate processing and the importance of *specificity* in processing type when predicting learning outcomes, as visually depicted by the TOPRA model; (c) the proposal that acoustically varied input can promote more distributed mental representations of developing lexical representations; and (d) the differential impact of output *with* versus *without* access to meaning in language learning.

Supported by research and theory in this manner, the ten principles of IBI vocabulary instruction advocate frequent exposure to target vocabulary in meaning-bearing and (largely) comprehensible input and avoidance of semantic elaboration and output without access to meaning during the early stages of learning new words. The approach also advocates a gradual build-up in the extent to which learners are asked to make use of target words in different types of tasks, which themselves should increase gradually in difficulty over time so that learners have sufficient opportunities to process target words as input before they are asked to make use of the target words. Other principles, such as Principle 1 regarding having a vocabulary acquisition plan, help to make the IBI approach more comprehensive as opposed to being a series of isolated suggestions only.

The checklist provided in this chapter was designed to provide instructors with a useful tool when creating IBI lessons on their own. The sample lesson was included to provide a clearer idea of what IBI vocabulary lessons look like. For readers interested in viewing more sample lessons, Barcroft (2012) provides fourteen IBI lessons, some of which use multiple sources of input and some of which use reading as a primary source of input.

It is hoped that the present chapter and other available IBI-related resources are useful to instructors, language program directors, developers of instructional materials, and others interested in the IBI approach. As new research findings on L2 vocabulary learning continue to accrue, the list of readily applicable research findings available for the application of Principle 10 should continue to grow as well. Undoubtedly, new technologies also will provide new means for presenting input and implementing different aspects of the IBI approach. However, as Barcroft (2012) has pointed out, there are at least five tenets of IBI vocabulary instruction that are foundational and are unlikely to change. These concern the critical roles of (1) planning for vocabulary instruction and learning; (2) provision of target vocabulary as input and consideration of issues in lexical input processing; (3) specificity when predicting the relationship between task type, processing type, and expected learning outcomes; (4) the incremental nature of vocabulary learning; and (5) the importance of teaching all aspects of L2 word knowledge, including L2-specific meanings and usage, over time. The principles related to these tenets, in combination with the openness of Principle 10, are designed to provide the approach with both a rudder and a sail as research in this area continues to expand.

References

Barcroft, J. (2002). Semantic and structural elaboration in L2 lexical acquisition. *Language Learning, 52*, 323–363 DOI: 10.1111/0023-8333.00186.

Barcroft, J. (2003). Effects of questions about word meaning during L2 lexical learning. *The Modern Language Journal, 87*, 546–561.

Barcroft, J. (2004a). Effects of sentence writing in L2 lexical acquisition. *Second Language Research, 20*, 303–334.

Barcroft, J. (2004b). Second language vocabulary learning: A lexical input processing approach. *Foreign Language Annals, 37*, 200–208.

Barcroft, J. (2005). La enseñanza del vocabulario en español como segunda lengua [Vocabulary instruction in Spanish as a second language]. *Hispania, 88*, 568–583.

Barcroft, J. (2006). Can writing a new word detract from learning it? More negative effects of forced output during vocabulary learning. *Second Language Research, 22*, 487–497.

Barcroft, J. (2007). Effects of opportunities for word retrieval during second language vocabulary learning. *Language Learning, 57*, 35–56.

Barcroft, J. (2009). Effects of synonym generation on incidental and intentional vocabulary learning during second language reading. *TESOL Quarterly, 43*, 79–103.

Barcroft, J. (2012). *Input-based Incremental Vocabulary Instruction.* Alexandria, VA: TESOL Publications.

Barcroft, J., & McBride, K. (2011, October). Teaching and Learning Vocabulary: What Recent Research Tells Us. Paper presented at the MIDTESOL Conference, St. Louis, MO on October 14, 2011.

Barcroft, J., & Sommers, M.S. (2005). Effects of acoustic variability on second language vocabulary learning. *Studies in Second Language Acquisition, 27*, 387–414.

Barcroft, J., & Sommers, M.S. (2012, March). New evidence in support of the extended phonetic relevance hypothesis: FO variability improves L2 (Russian) vocabulary learning for speakers of a tonal language (Zapotec). Paper presented at the Georgetown University Roundtable on Languages and Linguistics on March 9, 2012.

Brent, M.R., & Siskind, J.M. (2001). The role of exposure to isolated words in early vocabulary development. *Cognition, 81*, B33–B-44.

Craik, F.I.M., & Lockhart, R.S. (1972). Levels of processing: A framework for memory research. *Journal of Verbal Learning and Verbal Behavior, 11*, 671–684.

de Groot, A.M.B. (2006). Effects of stimulus characteristics and background music on foreign language vocabulary learning and forgetting. *Language Learning, 56*, 463–506.

Ebbinghaus, H. (1885). Memory: A contribution to experimental psychology. Available online at <http://psychclassics.yorku.ca/Ebbinghaus/index.htm>.

Ellis, N. (2006). Cognitive perspectives on SLA. The Associative-Cognitive CREED. *AILA Review, 19*, 100–121.

Finkbeiner, M., & Nicol, J. 2003. Semantic category effects in second language word learning. *Applied Psycholinguistics, 24*, 369–383.

Gass, S. (1997). *Input, interaction, and the second language learner.* Mahwah, NJ: Lawrence Erlbaum Associates.

Greene, R.L. (1992). *Human memory. Paradigms and paradoxes.* Hillsdale, NJ: Lawrence Erlbaum Associates.

Hulstijn, J.H. (1992). Retention of inferred and given word meanings: Experiments in incidental learning. In P.J.L. Arnaud & H. Béjoint (Eds.), *Vocabulary and applied linguistics* (pp. 113–125). London: Macmillan.

Hulstijn, J.H., Hollander, M. & Greidanus, T. 1996. Incidental vocabulary learning by advanced foreign language students: The influence of marginal glosses, dictionary use, and recurrence of unknown words. *Modern Language Journal, 80*, 327–339.

Kida, S. (2010). The role of quality and quantity of vocabulary processing in incidental L2 vocabulary acquisition through reading. Paper presented on March 7, 2010 at the Annual Conference of the American Association of Applied Linguistics in Atlanta GA.

Krashen, S. (1985). *The input hypothesis: Issues and implications.* New York, NY: Longman.

Lee, J.F., & VanPatten, B. (2003). *Making communicative language teaching happen* [2nd edition]. New York, NY: McGraw-Hill.

Lewis, M. (1993). *The lexical approach: The state of ELT and the way forward.* Hove, UK: Language Teaching Publications.

Lewis, M. (1997). Pedagogical implications of the lexical approach. In J. Coady & T. Huckin (Eds.), *Second language vocabulary acquisition* (pp. 255–270). Cambridge: CUP.

Long, M. (Ed.). (2005). *Second language needs analysis.* Cambridge: CUP.

Luppescu, S., & Day, R.R. 1995. Reading dictionaries, and vocabulary learning. In B. Harley (Ed.), *Lexical issues in language learning* (pp. 229–251). Amsterdam: John Benjamins.

McNamara, D.S., & Healy, A.F. (1995). A generation advantage for multiplication skill training and nonword vocabulary acquisition. In A.F. Healy & L.E. Bourne, Jr. (Eds.), *Learning and memory of knowledge and skills: Durability and specificity* (pp. 132–169). Sage, CA: Thousand Oaks.

Morris, C.D., Bransford, J.D., & Franks, J.J. (1977). Levels of processing versus transfer appropriate processing. *Journal of Verbal Learning and Verbal Behavior, 16*, 519–533.

Nation, I.S.P.(2001). *Learning Vocabulary in Another Language.* Cambridge: CUP.

Paribakht, T.S., & Wesche, M. (1997). Vocabulary enhancement activities and reading for meaning in second language vocabulary acquisition. In J. Coady & T. Huckin (Eds.), *Second language vocabulary a*cquisition (pp. 174–200). Amsterdam: John Benjamins.

Pulido, D. (2009). How involved are American L2 learners of Spanish in lexical input processing tasks during reading? *Studies in Second Language Acquisition, 31*, 31–58.

Robinson, P. (2001). Task complexity, task difficulty, and task production: Exploring interactions in a componential framework. *Applied Linguistics, 22*, 27–57.

Robinson, P. (2003). The Cognition Hypothesis, task design and adult task-based language learning. *Second Language Studies, 21*, 45–107.

Royer, J.M. (1973). Memory effects for test-like events during acquisition of foreign language vocabulary. *Psychological Reports, 32*, 195–198.

Schmitt, N. (2010). *Researching vocabulary: A vocabulary research manual.* Basingstoke: Palgrave Macmillan.

Sinclair, J.M., & Renouf, A. (1988). A lexical syllabus for language learning. In R. Carter & M. McCarthy (Eds), *Vocabulary and language teaching* (pp. 140–158). Harlow: Longman.

Sommers, M., & Barcroft, J. (2007). An integrated account of the effects of acoustic variability in L1 and L2: Evidence from amplitude, fundamental frequency, and speaking rate variability. *Applied Psycholinguistics, 28*, 231–249.

Sommers, M.S., Nygaard, L.C, & Pisoni, D.B. (1994). Stimulus variability and spoken word recognition. I. Effects of variability in speaking rate and overall amplitude. *Journal of the Acoustical Society of America, 96*, 1314–1324.

Terrell, T. (1986). Acquisition in the natural approach: The binding/access framework. *Modern Language Journal*, 70, 213–27.

Tinkham, T. (1997). The effects of semantic and thematic clustering on the learning of second language vocabulary learning. *Second Language Research, 13*, 138–163.

VanPatten, B. (1996). *Input processing and grammar instruction: Theory and research.* Norwood, NJ: Ablex.

VanPatten, B. (2003). *From input to output: An instructor's guide to second language acquisition.* New York, NY: McGraw-Hill.

Willis, D. (1990). *The lexical syllabus: A new approach to language teaching.* London: Collins ELT.

Wong, W., & Pyun, D.O. (2012). The effects of sentence writing on L2 French and Korean lexical retention. *The Canadian Modern Language Review, 68*, 164–189.

Zimmerman, C. (1997). Historical trends in second language vocabulary instruction. In J. Coady & T. Huckin (Eds.), *Second language vocabulary acquisition* (pp. 5–19). Cambridge: CUP.

CHAPTER 7

Experimentalized CALL for adult second language learners

Nora Presson, Colleen Davy and Brian MacWhinney
Carnegie Mellon University

Improvements in computer technology have opened up new possibilities for integrating web-based language learning with classroom practice. In particular, experimental computer-assisted language learning (eCALL) methods can make student learning more efficient, while also providing detailed data for second language acquisition theories and models. Studies show that eCALL systems that target basic language skills can lead to significant learning gains after only two or three hours of practice, with gains retained months later. Training in basic skills can be supplemented by online methods for using Internet media, map tours, subtitled video, chat rooms, and learning games. All these systems can be linked to classroom teaching to provide deeper support for second language learning.[1]

1. Introduction

Rapid advances in computer technology have stimulated a wide array of new approaches to computer-assisted language learning (CALL). There have been underlying improvements in bandwidth, connectivity, operating systems, processors, programming languages, and high-resolution touch screens. These improvements have been accompanied by the growth of online resources such as games, dictionaries, grammars, translators, multilingual media, and Wiki pages. Based on these developments and the advent of ubiquitous computing, software for second language learning is now moving away from the desktop to mobile devices such as iOS and Android. Integrating these new capabilities with traditional classroom language teaching poses major new challenges and opens up fascinating possibilities for researchers, as well as for teachers, developers, and learners. Using these new methods, researchers can gather data in the laboratory and over the web that will help us understand the actual process of second language learning, as it occurs

1. This work was supported by NSF grant SBE-0836012 to the Pittsburgh Science of Learning Center.

in both instructed and naturalistic situations. However, to realize these new potentials, researchers, learners, and instructors must reconfigure their relations and roles in order to work in a new, more collaborative manner.

This chapter examines the ways in which computerized second language (L2) instruction can incorporate established experimental methodology as well as newer methods in dynamic assessment (Cen, Koedinger et al. 2006) to produce demonstrable improvements in learning. This work is important for two reasons. First, it can provide concrete, fully implemented methods for improving instruction. Second, it can provide detailed data, collected systematically over the web, that permit the formulation of more precise accounts of the language learning process. We will refer to this method as eCALL (experimentalized computer-assisted language learning). We begin by explaining the logic of eCALL system development. Next, we show how eCALL systems can address issues in SLA regarding stages of development, patterns of error and correct usage, the role of explicit corrective feedback, practice effects, training based on student modelling, and the provision of explicit rule instruction. After that, we examine methods for automating lesson creation and data collection in eCALL. Then, we examine current limitations of eCALL, ways of addressing these limitations, and future possibilities for research and pedagogy in computerized contexts. Our analysis will examine how these interventions can be used to improve student learning, and how these interventions can allow second language acquisition (SLA) researchers to develop more accurate models of second language learning and processing informed by these new types of data.

Work in the CALL tradition has explored ways in which computers can be used to provide language instruction. Comparative studies (Chenoweth, Ushida et al. 2006) have shown that full computer-based courses (see examples at learner. org or oli.cmu.edu) can produce learning outcomes comparable to those obtained from classroom teaching. However, full course systems tend to integrate a wide variety of activities in ways that make it difficult to track details of the learning of particular skills, such as vocabulary, grammar, dictation, and pronunciation. In contrast, eCALL is designed to configure separate modules for training in these basic skills. For these basic skill activities, computers excel in their ability to provide carefully selected learning targets and to score, tabulate, and analyze student responses. In many cases, computers can make accurate diagnoses of student errors and provide proper diagnostic feedback. Computers can store a virtually unlimited trial history from which they can construct full profiles, learning curves, and error analyses. As we will see in Section 4, students can also rely on computers to locate written materials in the second language, listen to L2 radio broadcasts, watch video in L2, correspond in L2 chat rooms, and explore the L2 physical and cultural environment.

However, there are limits to what computers can do. Computer speech recognition is still too imprecise to permit good recognition of learners' oral productions, and this limits the ways in which computers can deliver articulatory training or engage in conversation. Fortunately, instructors excel exactly in those areas where computers are the weakest. Ideally, learners could use computers for what they do best and could interact with instructors for what they do best. However, for this division of labor to operate properly, instructors must interact with the researchers developing online materials to ensure that they interleave correctly with classroom materials and textbooks. The eCALL materials we discuss here are configured to link to the specific vocabulary, grammatical forms, or pronunciation skills targeted by the textbook selected by each individual instructor. These methods that place the instructor in control of the coordination of eCALL with other materials to produce an integrated treatment of all linguistic subsystems and areas of content both inside and outside the classroom.

To test the efficacy of educational interventions, one must collect controlled experimental data. However, not all CALL methods generate such data. Often CALL programs fail to achieve random assignment or involve other violations of internal validity, making it difficult to draw reliable conclusions about the efficacy of specific interventions and their implications for L2 processing and learning. Fortunately, experimental evaluation of training interventions is becoming increasingly frequent (Felix 2005), as researchers come to realize that eCALL evaluation serves not only to validate interventions but also to improve future implementations.

In addition to showing the effectiveness of a particular training activity, experimental evaluation can test specific predictions of particular language learning models. MacWhinney (1995) noted that it is possible to configure computerized training in basic skills so that learners are assigned randomly to treatment conditions. However, extracting valid experimental data from online learning systems also requires that students engage fully with the tasks. This engagement can only happen if teachers, students, and researchers have a shared vision of the importance of such an intervention providing computerized training in basic skills. Once this consensus has been achieved, eCALL research and instruction can progress on a solid footing. However, achieving this consensus requires experimenters to consider carefully how eCALL instruction can mesh with the pedagogical goals of classroom practice.

Training through eCALL offers the promise of providing a continually improving baseline of instructional quality. By refining and improving existing models on the basis of ongoing experimentation, we can ratchet up the quality of instruction, even as we continue to collect data that will improve our understanding of the basic cognitive mechanisms underlying second language learning. The iterative process in which theory informs intervention and interventions inform theory can provide a solid basis for improving the science of second language acquisition.

Training with eCALL can be applied in either online instruction or laboratory "pull-out" experiments in which classroom learners visit the controlled laboratory setting for data collection. Examples of the latter include studies of phonological contrasts (Edwards and Zampini 2008), the use of context to interpret prosodic cues (Hardison 2005), or studies with naïve beginners of the type we will discuss later in this paper. The advantage of laboratory eCALL is that there is less need to fit in closely with the classroom syllabus and it is easier to guarantee that subjects are focused clearly on the task at hand. However, integrated or "in vivo" eCALL (Koedinger 2011) has greater relevance to the actual process of instruction, particularly if the eCALL lessons are closely linked to the materials covered in the classroom. Moreover, it is often easier to recruit large numbers of participants for online eCALL training, facilitating the design of more sophisticated comparisons within an experiment.

Current eCALL systems maintain many features of earlier CALL systems, of which they are a natural outgrowth. In the past, "the majority of CALL uses were limited, in form, to drill and practice exercises" (Liu, Moore et al. 2002). Although current eCALL applications continue to emphasize the role of practice and repetition, there have been important additions in terms of improved multimedia support, ubiquitous Internet connectivity, individualized student tracking, logging of responses for instructor tracking, and creation of uniform data sets for analysis by researchers. At the same time, there has also been an upsurge in open-ended computerized methods such as games, subtitled video, and real-world activities provide computerized support systems that go far beyond the CALL systems of the past. It is important to realize that what is novel about eCALL is not the specific methods used in particular tutors or modules, but the ability to extract experimentally valid data that can inform the construction of a system that integrates learning resources, the classroom, and the community through the web. We are clearly not yet there and the studies we will examine here are just first steps in the direction of this very ambitious research program.

2.   eCALL examination of SLA principles

From the viewpoint of SLA research, eCALL can be regarded as a method for examining pedagogical principles that can accelerate second language learning. The effect is cyclical: the pedagogical principles used in the field of SLA can be applied to eCALL training programs, which can then in turn refine and test those principles, thus adding to our knowledge base, which can be used to improve eCALL methods. In this section, we consider work that explores the role of four important instructional factors: the provision of immediate explicit corrective feedback, modeling of student knowledge, repeated practice, and explicit instruction. In Section 4, we discuss ways of studying more interactive feedback types, such as negotiation of meaning in chat rooms, usage patterns in mobile computing, or the computerized analysis of conversations recorded in naturalistic settings.

2.1   Corrective feedback in the classroom

Corrective feedback (CF) can be a key engine for learning in the classroom (Bangert-Drowns, Kulik et al. 1991; Ellis 2009). Classroom CF can come in many forms, and recent experiments and meta-analyses (Lyster 2004; Sato and Lyster 2012; Lyster, Saito et al. 2013) have demonstrated the complexity of the effects of these forms of CF. These analyses have distinguished (1) written vs. oral feedback, (2) implicit vs. explicit correction (prompts and recasts vs. metalinguistic correction), (3) instructor feedback vs. peer feedback, (4) high vs low working memory learners, and (5) younger vs. older learners. Analyses of classroom interactions have shown that, within the larger categories of prompts, recasts, and explicit correction, there are further variations in terms of conversational structure and instructional impact. These analyses have been informed by the theories of noticing (Schmidt 1993), focus on form (Long 2000), input processing (Robinson 1995), the output hypothesis (Swain 2005), skill theory (DeKeyser 2007), the procedural/declarative distinction (Morgan-Short and Ullman 2011), monitoring theory (Levelt 1989), and retrieval theory (de Bot 1996; Karpicke and Roediger 2006).

2.2   Corrective feedback in eCALL

Given the interactive complexity of these forces, successful delivery of optimal levels of CF in the classroom may require a high level of instructor skill and engagement. Instructors must quickly diagnose the nature of the learner error, choose a feedback method, and then possibly interrupt the flow of classroom interaction, leading to violations of normal conversational practice (Gardner and Wagner 2005). Providing CF through the computer can address some of these problems. When the computer provides CF, learners may be frustrated, but they will not suffer any embarrassment. More importantly, the speed of computer processing makes it possible to quickly compose feedback contingent on the nature of the learner's response, personal learner characteristics, instructional theory, and instructional goals. Moreover, during interactions in a classroom, learners are being constantly exposed to errors that they themselves may never make, whereas the errors being corrected by the computer are ones that are specifically a problem for the individual learner interacting with the program.

Recent literature on cognitive tutors in math and science domains demonstrates the added power of immediate corrective feedback that is targeted at specific student performance errors (Koedinger, Anderson et al. 1997). By integrating a practice interface with an underlying cognitive model of correct and incorrect ("buggy") student knowledge, alternative feedback messages can be constructed to match the type of misconception a student is likely to have given his or her behavioral performance. For example, a student answering the question "2 – 4 =?" with "6" probably does not understand the symbol for subtraction, whereas one answering "2" may not understand that order matters in subtraction.

It is important to consider how the use of CF in eCALL can be informed by the rich literature on classroom feedback methods reviewed briefly in the last section. There are some findings from that literature that cannot apply directly. For example, the contrast between spoken and written feedback in eCALL is different from that in the classroom, because written feedback can be provided immediately by the computer with great diagnostic accuracy. Also, the comparison between instructor feedback and peer feedback would only be relevant in the eCALL context if lessons were configured within a social space. This is an interesting possibility, but not one which has yet been explored. However, there are three findings from classroom CF literature that may well apply to the eCALL context. First, the evidence for better uptake of CF in the form of prompts by younger learners (Lyster and Saito 2010) could suggest that eCALL instruction that targets younger learners should emphasize this form of CF. Second, the relation between high working memory capacity (WMC) and the ability to benefit from recasts (Sagarra 2007; Goo 2012) may also operate in the eCALL context. Third, the potential advantage of prompts over explicit correction in the classroom might possibly extend to eCALL instruction (Sanz and Morgan-Short 2004).

In the eCALL context, the difference between explicit corrective feedback and recasts is not as sharp as in the classroom context. This is because recasting only really makes sense as a conversational move. For example, if the learner translates *you went to the store* into Spanish as *tú fui al mercado*, the computer's response would be *tú fuiste al mercado* in which the first person verb *fui* is restated or recast as *fuiste*. The computer's response could be characterized as a recast, but it could equally well be viewed as explicit corrective feedback, particularly if the word *fuiste* is highlighted. Thus, the contrast between recasts and explicit correction may not be as sharp or interesting in eCALL as in classroom-based research.

On the other hand, the implementation of feedback through prompts in an eCALL program could be more interesting. First, recent classroom research has suggested that prompts may be more effective than recasts in promoting learning

(Ammar and Spada 2006; Ellis, Loewen et al. 2006; Ellis 2007; Sheen 2007; Yang and Lyster 2010). Second, implementing prompts through the computer is relatively easy. The standard method here is just to say *please try again*, but the computer can also deliver a simple repetition with a question mark at the end, clarification requests such as *pardon* or partial feedback that repeats the correct segment and asks the student to revise the incorrect segment. Third, there are good theoretical reasons to explore the role of prompts in eCALL. Tutorial design theory (Koedinger, Pavlik et al. 2008) has characterized this issue as "the assistance dilemma". The dilemma here is how to decide when instruction should provide information and assistance to students and when it should request students to generate this information. On the one hand, assistance can function as scaffolding, but on the other hand it can serve as a crutch. Similarly, asking students to generate their own correct forms can function as effective teaching or it can lead to confusion and imposition of an unnecessary cognitive load. Both Koedinger et al. and Long (1997) conclude, reasonably enough, that the answer to this dilemma depends largely on details of the material to be learned, as well as characteristics of the learner.

In practice, the study of contrasting effects of CF in eCALL is still in its infancy. The work we will consider here has only been able to examine a few segments of this general problem space. One area of emphasis has been on the effects of diagnostic CF, as opposed to simple correctness feedback. Zhang examined this contrast in the context of a system called the PinyinTutor (http://talkbank.org/pinyin) that helps learners of Chinese practice the dictation into Pinyin of Chinese words and phrases. Analyses of the effectiveness of this system showed that the experimental group that received diagnostic CF attained an 18% improvement in accuracy, as opposed to the control group subjects who received simple correctness feedback and who attained a 10% improvement across the duration of the study. This advantage for the training group was highly significant. In this task, there are many possible errors: the letters typed could be an illegal sequence in the Pinyin system, the initial or final sound of either syllable could be incorrect, there could be an incorrect number of syllables in the student response, and the tone of one or both syllables could be incorrect. In the diagnostic version of the program, students are given feedback regarding the exact nature of each error type. Moreover, each of these errors leads to different predictions about what the student needs to know, as well as different estimates of his or her current knowledge state (Gordon & Kowalski in press). In this system, response and latency data collected by the Flash program are transferred to servers at Carnegie Mellon University (CMU) for ongoing computation of adaptive feedback. The PinyinTutor data are also sent to the CMU DataShop repository (http://pslcdatashop.web.cmu.edu) for further offline analysis and possible future reanalysis. Providing correctness feedback immediately after the student types an answer makes correcting mistakes easier, and is important for student uptake (Ellis 2009), but this basic feedback can be supplemented by diagnostic CF targeted at the specific component of Pinyin typing that led to the error.

Speech recognition technology also has the potential to provide immediate feedback on pronunciation, a feature that requires a particular type of feedback "that does not rely on the student's own perception" (Ehsani and Knodt 1998). Refinement of pronunciation requires an outside observer to monitor and provide corrective feedback, as speakers are often unable to compare their pronunciation to a model. Cucchiarini, Neri and Strik (2009) further suggest that feedback on pronunciation should be (a) in a stress-free environment, (b) in real-time, and (c) individualized for each speaker. Computer software kits like EduSpeak® (Franco, Bratt et al. 2010) use phone-level mispronunciation detectors that, when they are able to produce reliable transcriptions, are comparable to human raters, and can provide feedback in real time and based on individual performance. These kits can be used to replace native speaker human listeners, which are often in short supply for second language learners. Speech recognition can also be used for the automatic scoring of oral fluency by focusing on temporal dynamics of speech, such as word count, length and rate of speech, and so on. The SpeechRaterTM system uses this information, as well as rough estimates of number of repetitions and corrections, to provide real-time feedback to speakers on their oral performance (Zechner, Higgins et al. 2009). Speech recognition systems can provide feedback on both segmental (phonemes or syllables) and suprasegmental (prosody and intonation) features of the language (see Ehsani & Knodt 1998 for an overview).

2.3   Explicit rule instruction

In addition to varying the content of feedback, computers can implement different levels of explicitness in the presentation of linguistic patterns and rules. The value of explicit metalinguistic information for adult learners is a central and ongoing question in SLA theory. Meta-analyses (Norris and Ortega 2000; Spada and Tomita 2010) have indicated a general positive effect for explicit rule presentation. In an earlier review of this issue, MacWhinney (1997) concluded that explicit rule instruction was most useful when the rule to be learned was quite simple. In such cases, the rule can be kept active in working memory and used to match to incoming positive exemplars, thereby consolidating learning on both the explicit and implicit levels (MacWhinney 2012). For example, in a computerized study of the learning of the Spanish counterfactual conditional, Rosa and Leow (2004) found that the most effective instruction involved explicit corrective rule feedback concurrent with each test trial. The rule governing this construction in Spanish is fairly complex, but Rosa and Leow were able to formulate it on computer screens in a way that was concrete and memorable (p. 196).

A major problem with the conclusions reached in these meta-analyses is that the studies involved have typically involved untimed measures that may not assess the proceduralization of the relevant skills. When evaluated in this way, explicit instruction could be viewed as "teaching to the test." It is clear that research needs to disentangle the effects of explicit rule instruction from the testing of these effects. There are at least three ways in which this can be done. One is to administer posttests that require generalization of the newly acquired knowledge to constructions not involved in the training. For example, training of French gender marking on the article should be able to support improvement in gender marking on the adjective. Generalization tests of this type are rare, but they can prove quite useful in assessing this issue. A second way of testing generalization is to examine changes in speed of processing. We report some initial attempts in this direction below. A third way is to examine retention. Many of the studies discussed here have administered repeated posttests across intervals of weeks and months to assess long-term retention. The assumption here is that explicit rule formulations should be more prone to loss than implicit or proceduralized learning.

To illustrate how we can approach this issue, consider two multi-session eCALL training experiments for novice learners of French learning to categorize nouns by grammatical gender (Presson and MacWhinney 2012). In these experiments, the rules for the orthographic cues to gender (e.g., words ending in -age are almost always masculine) were presented in an eCALL tutorial. Learners selected the gender and received correctness feedback with either no additional information, explicit orthographic cue statements (e.g., -age -> le), or highlighting of the relevant ending. The computerized training interface allowed for immediate feedback, randomization to feedback conditions, automatic data logging, and monitoring of participant progress. By computerizing the task, we were also able to test the prediction that, although explicit feedback might lead to better performance and greater retention after delay, this advantage could come at the cost of less rapid performance under time pressure, due to the additional time required to process explicit information. To that end, the program presented post-tests both with and without a time pressure constraint (a response deadline of 1400ms). This additional testing condition clearly showed that explicit cue feedback not only led to better learning and retention with no time pressure, but that explicit cue feedback led to greater accuracy even with a time pressure constraint, and that the addition of time pressure during training did not make a difference in the amount of improvement, suggesting there may be less of a trade-off between learning explicit cues or rules and rapid online behavioral performance than often assumed. This study also showed that, with only 90 minutes of practice, learners' ability to judge the gender of French words rose from 62% accuracy to 78% accuracy. Moreover, this ability was retained two months later, even though these novice learners were receiving no further exposure to French in the interval. The validity of the cues involved in this training was between 90% and 97%. However, this means that there are still some exceptions, and the training did not include the exception words. Thus, a fuller study of learning of French gender in future experiments will need to include both training on the valid cue patterns and additional training on exception words to see how well the two types of training can be integrated.

2.4   Repeated practice and student modeling

CALL programs are well adapted to the task of providing practice in component language skills. At the very beginning of experimental psychology, Ebbinghaus learned about the ways in which memory for new items and associations could be promoted by distributed practice that focused on the generation of remembered items. The role for such graduated interval recall and generation in vocabulary learning has been studied frequently since then (Pimsleur 1967; Royce 1973; McNamara and Healy 1995; Barcroft 2007). A particular variant form of eCALL focuses specifically on the optimization of practice scheduling, using graduated interval recall. An example of this is Pavlik and Anderson's (2008) English-Japanese vocabulary program that demonstrated that practice is most efficient when the interval between practice trials starts small and gradually increases. Their program models ongoing advances in student knowledge to optimize the practice schedule and select practice trials accordingly. In this approach, a general group-based model of learning efficiency over spacing intervals is combined with past student data to estimate the current strength of student knowledge. Modelling these processes can determine when to present practice trials in order to lead to the greatest learning gains. The organization of vocabulary learning through graduated interval recall is only one of many features of eCALL design that can potentially lead to faster and better word learning. Barcroft (this volume) provides a thorough analysis of the many other factors that can support this process in terms of his input-based incremental (IBI) approach. These factors can be realized through eCALL systems that emphasize meaningfully resonant (MacWhinney, 2012) links between words in terms of paradigmatic associations, sensory associations, derivation, synonyms, and sentential context.

In addition to diagnosing the learner's knowledge state from behavioral responses, eCALL programs can allow for the integration of data from previous student behavior to improve feedback and trial selection. Zhao (2012) created an eCALL tutor to provide instruction on correct use of the English article system. She first created a list of cues for selecting which article (*a, an, the,* or no article) to use in various contexts. In particular, she differentiated between cues that are rule-based (e.g., when introducing new information into the conversation, use the indefinite article "*a*", as in "I just bought a new car.") and those that are feature-based (e.g., when giving a street name, do not use an article, as in "turn onto Fifth Avenue" instead of "turn onto the Fifth Avenue"). By tracing student performance on practice trials with each type of cue, she found that students could acquire proper use of rule-based cues easily without explicit instruction, but explicit instruction was needed for learning of feature-based cues. After only three hours of using the English Article Tutor, students showed a 23% improvement in accuracy of article selection, moving from 53% accuracy to 76% accuracy (where chance accuracy is 33%).

In addition to feedback based on simple trial-by-trial error diagnosis, recent interventions outside the language domain (most notably Cognitive Tutor Algebra; Koedinger, Anderson, Hadley, & Mark 1997) diagnose student misconceptions with a quantitative model of student knowledge based on past performance. In this approach, immediate feedback can be responsive to specific estimates of a student's knowledge state. It can also take into account prior errors and help-seeking behavior in estimating the probability that a student has a specific wrong idea, thereby making remediation easier and more targeted to the individual student. Of course, the strategy of targeting feedback to specific learner errors and characteristics is not novel in eCALL – rather, it is a foundation of teacher expertise, as instructors track student performance and give appropriate feedback, as they deem necessary. It remains to be seen, however, to what degree adding specifically quantitative model-based individualized feedback can increase the amount of learning in a language task, especially because the quality of any targeted feedback is dependent on the quality of the underlying model. As theoretical descriptions of learner behavior and common errors continue to improve, so too can the effect of implementing individualized feedback in a computer training context.

In addition to training on grammar and vocabulary, computers can also be used to practice speaking. As described above, advances in speech recognition technology have allowed language learners to practice their pronunciation even without a teacher (for an overview of the use of speech recognition in language learning, see Eskenazi 2009). However, even without the use of speech recognition, speaking practice with a computer has shown to lead to improvements in both fluency and accuracy of speech. Yoshimura and MacWhinney (2007) had English learners of Japanese repeatedly read Japanese sentences and recite them from memory. They heard a sentence spoken by a native Japanese speaker, then read the sentence aloud six times, then repeated it from memory three times. Through these repetitions, they not only began to repeat the sentences with greater fluency but showed improvements in phonological accuracy of their repetitions as well.

Davy and MacWhinney (in preparation) used a task in which adult English learners of Spanish listened to a native Spanish speaker and repeat what they hear multiple times. They found that this procedure leads to greater accuracy and fluency on later sentence production tasks compared to untrained sentences. Learners benefitted more from training that allowed them to practice complex sentences in separate phrasal groups than through complete sentence repetition. The study also showed how fluency training can be controlled through picture stimuli, thereby eliminating any reliance on pure echoic production of sentences (Erlam 2006).

Computerized practice is also useful in longer speaking tasks. De Jong and Perfetti (2011) created a computerized program to guide adult ESL students through the 4/3/2 task, an activity in which students are given a topic to talk about for four minutes, then three minutes, and finally two minutes. Traditionally this task is done with a partner, with the speaker giving the speech to three different people. However, de Jong and Perfetti found that students not only showed increased accuracy and fluency with each practice during the training period, but increased in fluency from pre-test and post-test, where the tests were completely unrelated speaking activities on untrained topics.

3. Automating trial generation and data collection

In addition to their aid in the rigorous control of pedagogically relevant variables, computers can also ease the arduous processes of material creation and data collection and analysis. In this next section we consider the use of computers in automatizing tasks that, when done by hand, can be prohibitively time-consuming: the generation of practice and testing materials, and data logging.

3.1 Automatic generation of materials

Technology can also aid in the generation of eCALL materials, either for practice (Brown and Eskenazi 2004; Heilman, Zhao et al. 2008) or testing (Feeney and Heilman 2008; Pino and Eskenazi 2009). This generation can be a difficult and time-consuming task for teachers and researchers, who must consider elements such as student level, relevant interests, subject matter, and representation of certain target vocabulary items or grammatical elements. Any degree of computerized automation of this task would be a great help to educators as they could then devote the time spent creating tests and training materials to other instructional activities.

For example, the REAP Project (or REAder's Practice) is designed to provide extensive reading practice for ESL learners, with the goal of increasing vocabulary.

This project scrapes the Internet for reading passages containing vocabulary from the Academic Word List (Coxhead 2000). The passages are then analyzed for content information and reading level so that students can read on topics that are both interesting for them and at a level appropriate for them. Whereas some of the passages are screened, either by researchers or by the students, many are simply mined and presented directly to students. The REAP Project also works to semi-automate the process of creating assessments to check whether students were reading the text, and measure vocabulary knowledge. For example, Feeney and Heilman (2008) discovered that simply by generating a list of unique words that appeared in the text and asking students to choose between that list and a similar list that also contains random words, they can see whether the students are actually reading. Student performance on this task correlated significantly with post-reading vocabulary assessments, suggesting that reading the passages leads to vocabulary growth.

Another example of semi-automated generation of practice trials comes from an L2 preposition tutor asking learners to move objects around a virtual room by following instructions presented in the L2 using spatial prepositions (Presson, MacWhinney et al. 2010) – available at http://talkbank.org/SLA/prepositions). For example, a learner can see (in Spanish) "Pick up the ball to the left of the plant and put it on the sink" and would click the object (ball) to move it to the target location (on the sink). The goal of this training intervention was to use spatial and enactment cues to strengthen the gains from practice comprehending preposition words. The tutor itself was created by manually segmenting target areas around each object (e.g., "above" and "under") such that many objects could be arranged into multiple configurations. For example, a fixed object such as a chair, or a movable object such as a ball, could have another object to its left or right, above or below it, or more generally near it. Therefore, using those manual specifications, the program was able to automatically generate a much larger number of room scenes, each containing several fixed and movable objects that could be manipulated when following L2 instructions. This trial generation would have been extremely difficult if each individual trial had to be created separately and by hand, and the degree of automation results in a practically unlimited number of trials from a relatively limited practice set (although a greater variety of objects and locations could be highly beneficial to motivation and generalization).

In addition to generating natural language stimuli for real learners, computerization also aids in the generation of artificial and miniature languages that can be used to conduct tightly controlled laboratory studies of language learning processes (Opitz and Friederici 2007; Morgan-Short, Sanz et al. 2010). These statistically reliable but sometimes complex stimuli can allow for systematic manipulation of language frequency and structure, as well as the processing difficulty for naive

learners. For example, de Graaff (1997) used an artificial language in a computerized training paradigm to show that explicit instruction improved L2 grammar
learning relative to no explicit instruction, and that this advantage was present for
both simple and complex grammatical structures, and for both morphology and
syntax. In this case, computerization was used to "optimally control the input and
exposure" (p. 253), reflecting the advantage of both artificial grammar and computerized training.

3.2   Data logging

A core feature of eCALL is the capacity to log learner performance, instantaneously and automatically. With Internet connectivity, data from remote access to training materials can be logged to a central repository, and can be easily exported,
manipulated, and analyzed. Without automatic logging, an experimenter often
must code and log all responses manually, and sometimes must use coarse aggre-
gate data (e.g., time to finish taking a test) instead of fine-grained trial- or student
action-level data (e.g., time to finish each problem independently), which provide
more detailed information about student behavior. Earlier, we noted how data
from the PinyinTutor system (Zhang 2009) is transmitted continually to servers at
CMU. This system is now in use at 40 locations internationally, yielding semester-
long learning records from 3844 students. As these data come in, they are collected
into web pages that allow each instructor to monitor the usage and progress of
each of their students. These scores can be used as a component of the class grade,
thereby freeing the instructor from the task of grading pinyin dictation assign-
ments. At the same time, the computer provides students with summary scores
that allow them to track their own progress.

The benefit of automatic logging is especially clear in the emerging field of the
neuroscience of second language learning. In running a neuroimaging experiment, brain data must be matched to the behavioral events that trigger or reflect
the activation being recorded. This correspondence allows researchers to analyze
the brain correlates of behavioral and perceptual events, which can provide key
evidence into the mechanisms of second language learning (Hernandez, Hofmann
et al. 2007; Abutalebi 2008; Osterhout, Poliakov et al. 2008; van Hell and Tokowicz
2010). Without a fine-grained temporal log of behavioral events and stimulus presentation, used to tag events on the resulting brain data, it would be difficult or
impossible to associate changes in brain activity to events in the world. For
example, Morgan-Short and colleagues (2010) showed different event-related potential (ERP) responses in high and low proficiency L2 learners for noun-article
and noun-adjective agreement errors in a computer-generated artificial grammar,
which was possible because of the ability to match automatically generated

time-stamped stimulus presentation logs (thereby differentiating signals from article and adjective trials) to corresponding ERP data.

3.3   Limitations to computerization

Although eCALL expands the scope of interventions and data collection beyond what is possible with non-computerized training, there are important limitations in current technology that make it difficult or impossible to shift all language training to the computer.

First, although speech recognition technology continues to advance, it is not yet reliable enough to be used alone as an automated feedback mechanism for second language learners. Systems that use speech recognition must anticipate a certain rate of failure, either in terms of *misses* (saying the speech is correct when it's not) or *false alarms* (saying the speech is incorrect when it's not). To minimize frustration on the part of the user, programmers typically will err on the side of maximizing misses. Even given this bias, there will still be some frustrating false alarms to sounds that are acceptable, but which are judged as unacceptable. As a result, speech recognition cannot always be a reliable source for pronunciation training. In addition, speech recognition cannot yet support the interpretation of full sentence input. There have been a few programs that have attempted to create immersion-like speaking environments, but in order to make speech recognition possible, they must use highly constrained tasks, such as providing a question for the student to answer and a list of different possible answers to choose from. The speech detection mechanism can then choose which possible answer was uttered and give feedback. However, the answers must be different enough that the speech detection can choose between them, limiting the usefulness of this program (for an overview of spoken dialogue systems, see Eskenazi 2009). These limitations in speech recognition technology mean that training activities that improve comprehension (which does not require but can include speech output) are easier to computerize with automatic feedback than interventions targeted at oral production (which is necessarily dependent on speech output).

Second, the interactional aspects of language acquisition are difficult to replicate on the computer. It is generally accepted (Long 1983; Long 1996; Gass, Mackey et al. 1998) that there are clear benefits of conversational interaction with native speakers. In the Unified Competition Model, MacWhinney (2012) argues that, in order to maximize second language learning progress, we want to couple the benefits of eCALL with the benefits of conversational interaction. There are many benefits from conversational interaction for both comprehension (VanPatten 2011) and production . Moreover, social participation can support acculturation (Pavlenko and Lantolf 2000; Firth and Wagner 2007), the growth of the use of L2 for inner speech or "thinking in the second language", and improved motivation for learning (Dörnyei 2009). However, providing socially supportive contexts for learners can be a challenge. Chat sites like LiveMocha (http://www.livemocha.com) or systems such as Second Life (http://secondlife.com/destination/chinese-island) provide one solution to this problem, using computer access as a way to facilitate learner connection to human interlocutors rather than attempting to automatize or simulate naturalistic conversation. There is evidence that realtime computer-mediated communication (CMC) in chat rooms leads to higher levels of learner output. It has also been suggested that CMC may provide opportunities for negotiation of meaning of the type observed in face-to-face interactions (Varonis and Gass 1985). However, Peterson (2006) found that these systems produce only low levels of meaning negotiation. In terms of the overall effects of chat rooms, there have been no controlled studies, and student reactions to these systems are often mixed (Yao 2009; Peterson 2010).

Finally, the cost of setup and implementation of computerized training serve as limitations to the rapid spread of this technology. During the early stages of development, programming and equipment costs are a central obstacle to constructing eCALL exercises. The REAP Project (Heilman, Juffs et al. 2007), for example, requires the scanning of potential reading activities for appropriateness and student interest. Although the program can scrape the Internet for content, at this stage in its development the intervention is dependent on human readers to screen that content to ensure its appropriateness for the study. Creating models of student knowledge, such as the ones used in Cognitive Tutor Algebra (Koedinger, Anderson, Hadley & Mark 1997) requires a relatively large up-front investment to develop, test, and refine a usable model to track student learning. These models are domain-specific, meaning that each skill requires its own model, which must be developed from basic principles. In the language domain, this means that each language requires its own model and that transfer between language models may be limited. In addition, speech recognition programs also often require the initial loading in of expected speech to use for comparison to the inputs (Eskenazi 2009). However, there are also costs to traditional classroom or interactive activities, namely the human capital required to create interactive contexts or administer those activities. In the long run, computerized training may save time and human capital, but the up-front investment continues to be a consideration for educators and researchers alike.

4.   Future directions in eCALL

As we learn how to take advantage of these ongoing technological advances, we can begin to see how to configure eCALL in interestingly novel ways. In particular, we can develop eCALL methods for (1) studying large data sets, (2) tracking usage patterns in non-experimental settings with mobile devices, and (3) recording data from naturalistic interactions.

4.1   Experiments with large data sets

One key opportunity provided by eCALL exercises is the ability to collect massive amounts of data from a broad learner population. Advances in data mining and model discovery algorithms can improve the scope of analysis possible with existing data. In addition, the possibility of collecting data from a large number of learners (e.g., releasing publicly usable mobile training activities) gives leverage to test not only the main effects of instructional variables on learning effectiveness, but also the interactions, both simple and higher order, that require substantially more statistical power to effectively test than is often available in traditional lab or classroom experiments. This can allow researchers to expand language models beyond the positive effect of, for example, explicit instruction, to include the interaction of those effects with other instructional properties and individual differences.

For example, in two experiments using a training intervention for typing conjugated Spanish verbs at the very early stages (first and third semester) of undergraduate classroom instruction, data were collected from over 1000 learners across multiple training and testing sessions, resulting in a massive database of written production accuracy data (Presson et al. 2013). Learners completed 90 minutes of training (three 30-minute sessions over one month) typing conjugated verbs. Learners in first semester Spanish benefitted the most from this training, improving their accuracy rate by about 28%. Learners were provided with correctness feedback and the correct target response. The training task included several different verb contrasts, designed to test the prediction that accuracy in conjugation was predictable from properties of the verb (e.g., type frequency) and instruction (e.g., instructional sequence): present compared to past (preterite) tense, fully regular compared to subregular (stem and spelling change) verbs, and default -ar compared to non-default -er and -ir verbs in a fully crossed design. The large dataset showed higher-order interactions reflecting the fact that difficulty factors (e.g., preterite tense is harder than present tense) were sometimes additive (e.g., preterite tense non-ar verbs were harder than preterite tense -ar verbs, which in turn were harder than present tense non-ar verbs), and revealed that both baseline accuracy and the amount of improvement after training can be predicted by a combination of these verb properties.

By collecting trial-level data, and by automatically logging student performance, the marginal cost of collecting data from additional learners is greatly reduced, and collecting larger and systematically sampled datasets becomes easier. By collecting over 75,000 observations of student production of conjugated Spanish verbs, this computerized training intervention provided data painting a detailed picture of the interaction of verb properties in increasing not only the baseline difficulty of conjugation, but also the size of gains after training. The large sample size meant that such a dataset was possible using a test that took only 5–10 minutes per student. The pattern of data in this case both emphasizes the need for an explicitly developmental model of production of verb morphology and makes future predictions about which verbs should be most targeted in production training.

In addition, large datasets have the statistical power to begin to make more productive inferences from null effects than is typically possible. In a comparison of explicit feedback and analogy to a familiar example, three separate experiments with varying sample size showed a null difference in amount of improvement for all verb types (Presson et al. 2013). In a typical classroom or laboratory sample, it would be difficult to make inferences from this null effect; however, given both the large sample sizes and replication across samples in the computerized, large-scale training context, these effects can be taken as suggestive evidence that the two interventions were equally effective (i.e., the true effect size of the difference is negligible). This result suggests that the mechanism of improvement after training is the provision of correctness feedback itself, and that the additional information of an example or rule statement was either not useful or equally useful across these samples, and this suggestion is only meaningful in the context of large samples and multiple replications.

4.2   Mobile computing and usage patterns

Increasingly, the future of CALL and eCALL will be linked to the use of mobile devices. With the introduction of devices such as the iPhone, the iPad, and the Android tablets, the very meaning of "computer" has begun to shift. As computing devices become smaller, more mobile, and more ubiquitous, there will be more and more ways to use these technologies in socially flexible contexts. One of the largest disadvantages faced by adult second language learners is the greatly reduced time on task for a classroom learner compared to a child first language learner. This difference in time on task may be a major force producing positive outcomes for study abroad programs (DeKeyser 2007). By providing more such opportunities to practice L2 skills, ubiquitous computing can also improve learning outcomes. Currently, learners can use the iPad to access gamelike applications for vocabulary training such as uTalk or MindSnacks. Links to many of these applications can be found at (http://talkbank.org/SLA/ipad.html). If the tablet is linked to the Internet through either wireless or a cellular network, it can be used to listen to audio or watch television on L2 websites. Beyond that, teachers can configure contextualized lessons using systems such as Google Earth tours or map-based games systems (Hoshino, Saito et al. 2009) that direct the learner through specific interactions in the community. At this point, the focus of eCALL program development and research will shift to careful coordination of basic skills training with support of mobile computing by the classroom instructor. This coordination will require an increasingly close collaboration between researchers, programmers, and instructors.

There are many strategies that commercial training programs use to increase motivation: game-like features such as scoring mechanisms and social collaboration, prioritizing graphic design, adaptive difficulty, and de-emphasis of explicit grammar instruction, to name a few. However, we must be cautious in applying all of these features indiscriminately, as it remains to be seen whether such manipulations of the training environment can improve learner compliance to a training regimen, and whether they improve or harm learner outcomes in various language skills.

In addition to locally stored computer software, the Internet also allows for the creation of websites (therefore accessible on multiple hardware systems) that can provide instruction or practice. Websites like Memrise (http://www.memrise.com) or Anki (http://ankisrs.net) are centered around vocabulary drills, allowing users to review vocabulary at any time on their computers or mobile devices, either by using provided "decks" of words or by creating their own custom lists. Memrise in particular leverages research on gaming features (Aleven, Myers et al. 2008), practice scheduling (Pavlik and Anderson 2008), and encoding elaboration (Craik and Lockhart 1972; Ellis 1995; Barcroft 2002; Barcroft and Sommers 2005) to teach and practice vocabulary in a number of languages. The social collaborative nature of the program also allows any user to create a vocabulary list, allowing learners of any language to use the site. Websites that are free to use and readily available provide ample opportunities for language learners to receive instruction and practice their target language at any time and place, and have the potential to become a huge source of data for further research on computer-supported language learning.

Given these new technological possibilities, we can begin to think in terms of an extended eCALL system that incorporates all of these learning methods within a single platform. Let us refer to this integrated platform as the Language Partner. This system can be programmed using HTML5 and the Google Web Toolkit (GWT) so that it can run equally well on mobile devices or desktop computers, both relying on information transmitted over WiFi connections to the Internet. This system will include many of the components described earlier: basic skills and vocabulary tutors, games, interactive media access, and situated learning activities. The various facilities will continually record student usage patterns and responses that will be logged into DataShop files for subsequent student modelling and linkage to classroom activities. Figure 1 illustrates the general shape of a Language Partner system.

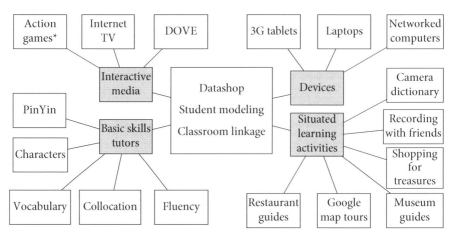

Figure 1. The Language Partner System

4.3   Computerized studies of naturalistic interactions

An important component of the Language Partner is the use of mobile devices to obtain photos, videos, and recordings of interactions in the community. The goal here is for the student to record real-life interactions of the type promoted in the Språkskap Project (Clark, Wagner et al. 2011) for later analysis in the classroom. For example, a learner of Icelandic recorded her interactions in a bakery in Rejkjavik. These data were transcribed and the transcripts were linked to audio records. The resulting corpus, called IceBase, was used by Guðrún Theodórsdóttir as the basis for her dissertation in the Conversation Analysis framework. These data are available to researchers from http://talkbank.org. By using applications such as *Recorder* in the iPad, or recording H.264 movies, learners can record interactions with native speakers in sites such as restaurants, museum tours, excursions, or homes. Like the Icelandic corpus, these records can then be analyzed either for pedagogical or research purposes. In the classroom, these materials could help students understand conversational practices, pragmatic norms, linguistic forms, and methods for negotiating meaning. For researchers, the corpora can be analyzed by programs such as CLAN (MacWhinney, Fromm et al. in press) for automatic lexical and morphosyntactic analysis or Praat (Boersma and Weenink 1996) and Phon for phonological analysis (Rose and MacWhinney in press). Within Praat, researchers (de Jong and Wempe 2009) are developing methods for linking transcripts to audio at the word level. Once these methods are available, we will be able to conduct increasingly powerful analyses for fluency and phonological accuracy.

5. Conclusion

Technology has always expanded the realm of the possible in human learning and education. Advances such as the printing press, the telephone, the motion picture, and the television have all had their impact on second language learning. The desktop computer, the Internet, and tablet computing are now further transforming how we can learn second languages. Constant access to mobile training exercises, complex algorithmic modelling of student behavior, immediate feedback, subtitled video, and automated trial selection and randomization, among other advances, can help adult learners compensate for the often challenging and difficult circumstances that confront them when beginning to learn a second language. Here, we have presented the results from studies examining the use of computer tutors for both novice learners and in real course contexts. We have shown that these methods can lead to rapid increases in competence for features such as French gender assignment, English article usage, Spanish fluency, Spanish verb conjugation, and Pinyin dictation. However, the full power of this approach will not be realized until a much fuller set of resources is created for each relevant language. Once these resources become available, they can lead to a revolution in SLA research and theory, as we automatically log data, adapt student feedback, and conduct large-scale experiments with relatively low cost. Ideally these advances in theory, experimentation, and training can be coordinated with best practices from classroom pedagogy to lead to breakthroughs in the learning of second languages.

References

Abutalebi, J. (2008). Neural aspects of second language representation and language control. Acta Psychologica, 128, 466–478.

Aleven, V., Eben Myers, E., Easterday, M., & Ogan, A. (2008). Toward a framework for the analysis and design of educational games. In G. Biswas, D. Carr, Y.S. Chee, & W.Y. Hwang (Eds.), Proceedings of the 3rd IEEE Conference on Digital Game and Intelligent Toy-Enhanced Learning (pp. 69–76). Los Alamitos, IEEE Computer Society.

Ammar, A., & Spada, N. (2006). One size fits all? Recasts, prompts, and L2 learning. Studies in Second Language Acquisition, 28, 543–574.

Bangert-Drowns, R., Kulik, C.-L., Kulik, J.A., & Morgan, M.T. (1991). The instructional effects of feedback in test-like events. Review of Educational Research, 61: 213–238.

Barcroft, J. (2002). Semantic and structural elaboration in L2 lexical acquisition. Language Learning, 52, 323–363.

Barcroft, J. (2007). Effects of opportunities for word retrieval during second language vocabulary learning. Language Learning, 57, 35–56.

Barcroft, J., & Sommers, M. (2005). Effects of acoustic variability on second language vocabulary learning. Studies in Second Language Acquisition, 27, 387–414.

Boersma, P., & Weenink, D. (1996). Praat, A system for doing phonetics by computer. Tech. Rep. 132. Amsterdam: Institute of Phonetic Sciences of the University of Amsterdam.

Brown, J., & Eskenazi, M. (2004). Retrieval of authentic documents for reader-specific lexical practice. InSTIL/IOCALL Symposium, Venice.

Cen, H., Koedinger, K., & Junker B. (2006). A general method for cognitive model evaluation and improvement. Intelligent Tutoring Systems, 164–175.

Chenoweth, A., Ushida, E., & Murday, K. (2006). Student learning in hybrid French and Spanish courses: An overview of language online. CALICO Journal, 24, 115–145.

Clark, B., Wagner, J., Lindemalm, K., & Bendt, O. (2011). Språkskap: Supporting second language learning in the wild. INCLUDE 11. Available on: <http://soda.swedish-ict.se/5446/1/F514_1578.PDF>

Coxhead, A. (2000). A new academic word list. TESOL Quarterly, 34, 213–238.

Craik, F.I.M., & Lockhart, R.S. (1972). Levels of processing: A framework for memory research. Journal of Verbal Learning and Verbal Behavior, 11, 671–684.

Cucchiarini, C., Neri, A., & Strik, H. (2009). Oralprodiciency training in Dutch L2: The contribution of ASR-based corrective feedback. Speech Communication, 51, 853–863.

Davy, C., & MacWhinney, B. (In preparation). Fluency training through picture description.

de Bot, K. (1996). The psycholinguistics of the output hypothesis. Language Learning, 46, 529–555.

de Graaff, R. (1997). The eXperanto experiment: Effects of explicit instruction on second language acquisition. Studies in Second Language Acquisition, 19, 249–275.

de Jong, N., & Perfetti, C. (2011). Fluency training in the ESL classroom: An experimental study of fluency development and proceduralization. Language Learning, 61, 533–568.

de Jong, N., & Wempe, T.O.N. (2009). Praat script to detect syllable nuclei and measure speech rate automatically. Behavior Research Methods, 41, 385–390.

DeKeyser, R. (Ed.). (2007). Practice in a second language: Perspectives from applied linguistics and cognitive psychology. Cambridge: CUP.

DeKeyser, R. (2007). Study abroad as foreign language practice. In R. DeKeyser, Practice in a second language: Perspectives from applied linguistics and cognitive psychology (pp. 208–226). Cambridge: CUP.

Dörnyei, Z. (2009). The psychology of second language acquisition. Oxford: OUP.

Edwards, J., & Zampini, M. (Eds.). (2008). Phonology and second language acquisition. Amsterdam: John Benjamins.

Ehsani, F., & Knodt, E. (1998). Speech technology in computer-aided learning: Strengths and limitations of a new CALL paradigm. Language Learning and Technology, 2, 45–60.

Ellis, N.C. (1995). The psychology of foreign language vocabulary acquisition and its implications for CALL. International Journal of Computer Assisted Language Learning, 8, 103–128.

Ellis, R. (2007). The differential effects of corrective feedback on two grammatical structures. In A. Mackey (Ed.), Conversational interaction in second language acquisition: A collection of empirical studies (pp. 339–360). Oxford: OUP.

Ellis, R. (2009). Corrective feedback and teacher development. L2 Journal, 1, 3–18.

Ellis, R., Loewen, S., & Erlam, R. (2006). Implicit and explicit corrective feedback and the acquisition of L2 grammar. Studies in Second Language Acquisition, 28, 339–368.

Erlam, R. (2006). Elicited imitation as a measure of L2 implicit knowledge: An empirical validation study. Applied Linguistics, 27, 464–491.

Eskenazi, M. (2009). An overview of spoken language technology for education. Speech Communication, 51, 832–844.

Feeney, C., & Heilman, M. (2008). Automatically generating and validating reading-check questions. Ninth International Conference on Intelligent Tutoring Systems.

Felix, U. (2005). Analyzing recent CALL effectiveness research: Towards a common agenda. Computer Assisted Language Learning, 18, 1–32.

Firth, A., & Wagner, J. (2007). Second/foreign language learning as a social accomplishment: Elaborations on a reconceptualized SLA. Modern Language Journal, 91, 800–819.

Franco, H., Bratt, H., Rossier, R., Venkata Rao, G., Shriberg, E., Abrash, E. & Precoda, K. (2010). EduSpeak®: A speech recognition and pronunciation scoring toolkit for computer-aided language learning applications. Language Testing, 27, 401–418.

Gardner, R., & Wagner, J. (2005). Second language conversations. London: Continuum.

Gass, S., A. Mackey, & Pica, T. (1998). The role of input and interaction in second language acquisition: An introduction. Modern Language Journal, 82, 299–307.

Goo, J. (2012). Corrective feedback and working memory capacity in interaction-driven L2 learning. Studies in Second Language Acquisition, 34, 445–474.

Hardison, D. (2005). Contexutualized computer-based L2 prosody training: Evaluating the effects of discourse context and video input. CALICO Journal, 22, 175–190.

Heilman, M., Juffs, A., & Eskenazi, M. (2007). Choosing reading passages for vocabulary learning by topic to increase intrinsic motivation. 13th International Conference on Artificial Intelligence in Education. Marina del Rey, CA.

Heilman, M., Zhao, L., Pino, J. & Eskenazi, M. (2008). Retrieval of Reading Materials for Vocabulary and Reading Practice. The 3rd Workshop on Innovative Use of NLP for Building Educational Applications, Association for Computational Linguistics.

Hernandez, A.E., Hofmann, & J., Kotz, S. (2007). Age of acquisition modulates neural activity for both regular and irregular syntactic functions. NeuroImage, 36, 912–923.

Hoshino, J., Saito, T., & Kazuto, S. (2009). Task-based second language learning game system. In Proceedings of the 8th International Conference on Entertainment Computing (pp. 323–324). Paris: Springer.

Karpicke, J., & Roediger, H. (2006). Repeated retrieval during learning is the key to long-term retention. Journal of Memory and Language, 57, 151–162.

Koedinger, K.R. (2011). Bridging the lab and the field with /in vivo/ experimentation. Society for Research on Educational Effectiveness (SREE).

Koedinger, K.R., Anderson, J., Hadley, W., & Mark, M. (1997). Intelligent tutoring goes to school in the big city. International Journal of Artificial Intelligence in Education, 8, 30–43.

Koedinger, K.R., Pavlik, P., Mclaren, B., & Aleven, V. (2008). Is it better to give than to receive? The assistance dilemma as a fundamental unsolved problem in the cognitive science of learning and instruction. In B.C. Love, K. McRae & V.M. Sloutsky (Eds.), Proceedings of the 30th Annual Conference of the Cognitive Science Society, Austin, TX, Cognitive Science Society (pp. 2155–2160).

Kowalski, J., Gordon, G., & MacWhinney, B. (in press). Refining an assessment for improving dictation skills of Chinese syllables. Journal of Educational Data Mining.

Levelt, W.J.M. (1989). Speaking: From intention to articulation. Cambridge, MA: The MIT Press.

Liu, M., Z. Moore, Graham, L., & Lee, S. (2002). A look at the research on computer-based technology use in second language learning: A review of the literature from 1990–2000. Journal of Research on Technology in Education, 34, 250–273.

Long, M. (1983). Native speaker/non-native speaker conversation and the negotiation of comprehensible input. Applied Linguistics, 4, 126–141.

Long, M. (1996). The role of the linguistic environment in second language acquisition. In W.C. Ritchie & T.K. Bhatia (Eds.), Handbook of second language acquisition (pp. 413–468). New York, NY: Academic Press.

Long, M. (1997). Problems in SLA. Mahwah, NJ: Lawrence Erlbaum Associates.

Long, M. (2000). Focus on form in task-based language teaching. In R. Lambert & E. Shohamy (Eds.), Language policy and pedagogy: Essays in honor of A. Ronald Walton (pp. 179–192). Amsterdam: John Benjamins.

Lyster, R. (2004). Differential effects of prompts and recasts in form-focused instruction. Studies in Second Language Acquisition, 26, 399–432.

Lyster, R., Saito, K., & Sato, M. (2013). Oral corrective feedback in second language classrooms. Language Teaching, 46, 1–40.

Lyster, R. & Saito, T. (2010). Oral feedback in classroom SLA. Studies in Second Language Acquisition, 32, 265–302.

MacWhinney, B. (1995). Evaluating foreign language tutoring systems. In V.M. Holland, J.D. Kaplan & M.R. Sams (Eds.), Intelligent language tutors: Theory shaping technology (pp. 317–326). Mahwah, NJ: Lawrence Erlbaum Associates.

MacWhinney, B. (1997). Implicit and explicit processes. Studies in Second Language Acquisition, 19, 277–281.

MacWhinney, B. (2012). The logic of the Unified Model. In S. Gass & A. Mackey (Eds.), The Routledge handbook of second language acquisition (pp. 211–227). New York, NY: Routledge.

MacWhinney, B., Fromm, D., Forbes, & Holland, A. (In press). AphasiaBank: Data and Methods. In N. Mueller & M. Ball (Eds.), Research methods in clinical linguistics and phonetics (pp. 268–287). New York, NY: Wiley.

McNamara, D.S., & Healy, A.F. (1995). A generation advantage for multiplication skill training and nonword vocabulary acquisition. In A.F. Healy & L.E. Bourne (Eds.), Learning and memory of knowledge and skills: Durability and specificity (pp. 132–169). Thousand Oaks, CA: Sage.

Morgan-Short, K., Sanz, C., Steinhauer, K., & Ullmann, M.T. (2010). Second language acquisition of gender agreement in explicit and implicit training conditions: An event-related potential study. Language Learning, 60, 154–193.

Morgan-Short, K., & Ullman, M.T. (2011). The neurocognition of second language. In S. Gass & A. Mackey (Eds.), The Routledge handbook of second language acquisition (pp. 282–300). New York, NY: Routledge.

Norris, J.M., & Ortega, L (2000). Effectiveness of L2 instruction: A research synthesis and quantitative meta-analysis. Language Learning, 50, 417–528.

Opitz, B., & Friederici, A. (2007). Neural basis of processing sequential and hierarchical syntactic structures. Human Brain Mapping, 28, 585–592.

Osterhout, L., Poliakov, A., Inoue, K, McLauglin, J., Valentine, G., Pitkanen, I., Frenck-Mestre, C., & Hirshensohn, J. (2008). Second-language learning and changes in the brain. Journal of Neurolinguistics, 21, 509–521.

Pavlenko, A., & Lantolf, J. (2000). Second language learning as participation and the (re)construction of selves. In A. Pavlenko & J. Lantolf, Sociocultural theory and second language learning (pp. 155–178). Oxford: OUP.

Pavlik, P.I. & Anderson, J. (2008). Using a model to compute the optimal schedule of practice. Journal of Experimental Psychology: Applied, 14, 101–117.

Peterson, M. (2006). Learner interaction management in an avatar and chat-based virtual world. Computer Assisted Language Learning, 19, 79–103.

Peterson, M. (2010). Computerized games and simulations in computer-assisted language learning: A meta-analysis of research. Simulation and Gaming: An Interdisciplinary Journal, 41(1): 72–93.

Pimsleur, P. (1967). A memory schedule. Modern Language Journal, 51, 73–75.

Pino, J., & Eskenazi, M. (2009). Semi-automatic generation of cloze question distractors' effect of students' L1. SLaTE Workshop on Speech and Language Technology in Education. Pittsburgh, PA.

Presson, N., Sagarra, N., MacWhinney, B., & Kowalski, J. (2013). Compositional production in Spanish second language conjugation. Bilingualism: Language and Cognition.

Presson, N., & MacWhinney, B. (2012). Learning grammatical gender: The use of rules by novice learners. Applied Psycholinguistics.

Presson, N., MacWhinney, B., & Heilman, M. (2010). A simulated environment for the embodied learning of Spanish prepositions. Second Language Research Forum, University of Maryland.

Robinson, P. (1995). Attention, memory, and the noticing hypothesis. Language Learning, 45, 285–331.

Rosa, E.M., & R. P. Leow (2004). Computerized task-based exposure, explicitness, type of feedback, and Spanish L2 development. Modern Language Journal, 88, 192–216.

Rose, Y., & MacWhinney, B. (In press). The Phon and PhonBank initiatives.

Royce, J.M. (1973). Memory effects for test-like events during acquisition of foreign language vocabulary. Psychological Reports, 32, 195–198.

Sagarra, N. (2007). From CALL to face-to-face interaction: The effect of computer-delivered recasts and working memory on L2 development. In A. Mackey (Ed.), Conversational interaction in second language acquisition: A collection of empirical studies (pp. 229–248). Oxford: OUP.

Sanz, C., & Morgan-Short, K. (2004). Positive evidence versus explicit rule presentation and explicit negative feedback: A computer-assisted study. Language Learning, 54, 35–78.

Sato, M., & Lyster, R. (2012). Peer interaction and corrective fedback for accuracy and fluency development. Studies in Second Language Acquisition, 34, 591–626.

Schmidt, R. (1993). Awareness and second language acquisition. Annual Review of Applied Linguistics, 13, 206–226.

Sheen, Y. (2007). The effects of corrective feedback, language aptitude, and learner attitudes on the acquisition of English articles. In A. Mackey (Ed.), Conversational interaction in second language acquisition: A collection of empirical studies (pp. 301–322). Oxford: OUP.

Spada, N. & Tomita, Y. (2010). Interactions between type of instruction and type of language features: A meta-analysis. Language Learning, 60, 263–308.

Swain, M. (2005). The output hypothesis: Theory and research. In E. Hinkel (Ed.), Handbook of research in second language teaching and learning (pp. 471–484). Mahwah, NJ: Lawrence Erlbaum Associates.

van Hell, J., & Tokowicz, N. (2010). Event-related brain potentials and second language learning: Syntactic processing in late L2 learners at different L2 proficiency levels. Second Language Research, 26, 43–74.

VanPatten, B. (2011). Input processing. In S. Gass & A. Mackey (Eds.), The Routledge handbook of second language acquisition. New York, NY: Routledge.

Varonis, E., & Gass, S. (1985). Non-native/Non-native conversations: A model for negotiating meaning. Applied Linguistics, 6, 71–91.

Yang, Y., & Lyster, R. (2010). Effects of form-focused practice and feedback on Chinese EFL learners' acquisition of regular and irregular past tense forms. Studies in Second Language Acquisition, 32, 235–263.

Yao, T.-c. (2009). The current status of Chinese CALL in the United States. Journal of Chinese Language Teachers Association, 44, 1–23.

Yoshimura, Y., & MacWhinney, B. (2007). The effect of oral repetition in L2 speech fluency: System for an experimental tool and a language tutor. SLATE Conference (pp. 25–28).

Zechner, K., Higgins, D., Xi, X. & Williamson, D.M. (2009). Automatic scoring of nonnative spontaneous speech in tests of spoken English. Speech Communication, 51, 883–895.

Zhang, Y. (2009). A tutor for learning Chinese sounds through pinyin. Modern Languages. Pittsburgh, Carnegie Mellon University.

Zhao, Y. (2012). Explicitness, cue competition, and knowledge tracing: A tutorial system for second language learning of English article usage. Modern Languages. Pittsburgh, Carnegie Mellon University.

CHAPTER 8

Accounting for variability in L2 data

Type of knowledge, task effects, and linguistic structure*

Silvia Perpiñán
Western University

This chapter examines variability in L2 data and isolates two factors that have a significant impact on L2 performance: task modality and linguistic structure. A group of native speakers of Spanish and two groups of intermediate L2 Spanish learners (L1 English and L1 Arabic) completed an oral and a written production task which elicited direct object and oblique Spanish relative clauses. Results indicated that not only did modality have a significant effect on the results, as previously stated (Bialystok 1982; Tarone 1983), arguably because oral and written tasks tap into different types of knowledge (Ellis 2005); but also that linguistic structure was a robust determinant in the speakers' results, showing that linguistic and cognitive approaches can inform each other.

1. Introduction

Independently from the theoretical framework, the ultimate purpose of second language acquisition (SLA) research is to describe the nature of second language linguistic knowledge. Generally speaking, we aim to illustrate how this knowledge develops and how this second language may become an automatic, efficient system. According to Van Patten (2002), the acquisition of a second language implies the creation of an *implicit linguistic system*, which usually entails a long and complex process. This implicit linguistic system, be it of a first or a second language, is commonly defined in the generative tradition as linguistic *competence* (Chomsky

* I would like to thank the participants that completed this study as well as the institutions where they were tested for their help, especially Dar Loughat and the Instituto Cervantes in Tetouan, Morocco. Also, I would like to thank Ileana Paul for reading previous versions of the manuscript, four anonymous reviewers for their helpful comments and suggestions, as well as John W. Schwieter for his great job as editor of this volume. All remaining errors and misconceptions are of course mine.

1965) or *mental representation of grammar* (White 2003). It basically refers to an idealized, abstract linguistic capacity. From a cognitive approach to second language acquisition, the abstract, unconscious knowledge is generally termed *implicit knowledge*. However, implicit knowledge and competence are not equivalent concepts because competence refers to a somehow ideal representation of language (as opposed to *performance*, which is the actual use of the language), whereas for cognitive psychologists there is not such a thing as "ideal" knowledge versus "actual" knowledge. Instead, linguistic knowledge is defined in terms of the processes or characteristics involved, mostly whether it occurs at the level of consciousness (*explicit knowledge)* or below the level consciousness (*implicit knowledge).* Given the common purpose of generative and cognitive research in SLA, to describe the nature of L2 linguistic knowledge, but considering the differences in the fields, this study aims to investigate whether cognitive approaches to SLA can inform linguistic studies and vice versa. The present study is exploratory in nature and it attempts to discover what type of knowledge is measured in each experimental task and how task design, type of knowledge, and linguistic structure interact. Ultimately, it aims to give an explanation of variability in native and second language knowledge and use.

2.   Background and motivation

Linguistic competence, by definition, cannot be observed. As a result, we have to take measurements of performance as indicators of competence. This is one of the great paradoxes in the field of experimental second language research from a generative perspective: aiming to describe linguistic competence, a highly abstract entity, through performance, "the actual use of language in concrete situations" (Chomsky 1965: 4). Positions such as the Missing Surface Inflection Hypothesis (Prévost & White 2000), although not explicitly stated that way, can be interpreted as an explanation for the apparent mismatches between competence and performance. The Missing Surface Inflection Hypothesis, specifically proposed to account for variability in L2 inflectional morphology (Haznedar & Schwartz 1997; Lardiere 1998a, b) argues that correspondence among certain grammatical modules might not be totally flawless. In particular, it proposes that "morphological variability may be attributable to ongoing problems with language use, rather than to a failure to acquire abstract morphosyntax or to an impairment in grammatical representation" (White 2003: 179). Under this view, different tasks may generate different results since they tap into different modules or different uses of the language. Therefore, it is conceivable and in fact common to find divergent results among tasks. For example, White (2002), in her case study of a Turkish L2 learner of English, found that while the speaker's oral production of determiners was inconsistent, her use of determiners in other tasks was more accurate.

Given these difficulties when testing linguistic competence, and on the basis of its exceptionally abstract nature, authors such as DeKeyser (2009) conclude that the traditional competence/performance distinction is neither informative nor useful for the study of second language knowledge. Instead, he considers that for assessing L2 knowledge in a given point in time and exploring how L2 learners acquire and use this knowledge, the explicit/implicit distinction is the most functional one. Therefore, from the cognitive perspective, divergent outcomes could be derived from the type of knowledge involved in each task.

In order to assess the type of knowledge that each task taps into, linguistic knowledge needs to be describable. With this purpose in mind, Ellis (2004) identified seven characteristics that illustrate each type of knowledge. Implicit knowledge is intuitive, procedural, systematic, automatic, accessed when the learner is performing fluently, not verbalizable, and potentially only learnable within the critical period; explicit knowledge, on the other hand, is conscious, declarative, inconsistent, accessible through controlled processing, accessed when the learner experiences certain difficulty, verbalizable, and learnable at any age. Later, Ellis (2005) tried to operationalize these constructs of L2 implicit and explicit knowledge and also a series of characteristics that later could be correlated to the tests designed to measure L2 knowledge. The specific features of linguistic knowledge related to the way L2 learners perform in experimental tasks are summarized in Table 1. Essentially, implicit knowledge is engaged in tasks in which there is not much time available to reflect consciously on the answer, and when the focus of the task is kept primarily on the meaning. Conversely, explicit knowledge is engaged when a task allows for time to reflect and apply grammatical rules and when

Table 1. Operationalizing the constructs of L2 implicit and explicit knowledge (from Ellis 2005)

Criterion	Implicit Knowledge	Explicit Knowledge
Degree of awareness	Response according to feel	Response using rules
Time available	Time pressure	No time pressure
Focus of attention	Primary focus on meaning	Primary focus on form
Systematicity	Consistent responses	Variable responses
Certainty	High degree of certainty in responses	Low degree of certainty in responses
Metalinguistic knowledge	Metalinguistic knowledge not required	Metalinguistic knowledge encouraged
Learnability	Early learning favored	Late, form-focused instruction favored

the task is focused on form more than on meaning. We will later use these criteria to isolate the type of knowledge that is involved in the tasks analyzed in this study.

Whether explicit knowledge interacts with, becomes, or converts into implicit knowledge has been a long discussed topic. We can summarize the interface debate into three main theoretical positions: the noninterface position (Hulstijn 2002; Paradis 2009), which proposes that implicit/explicit knowledge are located in different areas of the brain and one can never become the other; the strong interface position (Sharwood Smith 1981, DeKeyser 1998), which assumes that with practice, explicit knowledge can become implicit knowledge; and the weak interface position (Ellis 1993), which proposes that under certain circumstances, the two types of knowledge can interact. Since the purpose of this paper is to account for variability in L2 knowledge, we will not go into further detail regarding the conversion of one type of knowledge into the other.

3. Accounting for variability

The previous section has shown that depending on the theoretical tenets assumed, differences in results can be accounted for by different constructs: for instance, variability in experimental results, from a generative perspective, can reflect mismatches between grammatical modules or between competence and performance; from a cognitive perspective, it can be the result of using different types of knowledge in each task.

Variability has long been described as one of the defining properties and hard-to-explain phenomenoa of second language grammars going back to the early stages of the field (Bialystok 1982; Sorace 1984; Tarone 1983, 1985). Different approaches and explanations have been put forward in order to understand both the nature of this variability as well as the factors and contexts that promote it. For instance, Tarone (1983) found that L2 learners' production of syntactic and phonological structures systematically varied according to the task used for elicitation. This variation can be problematic when describing the properties of interlanguage grammars since conclusions may be contingent on the experimental methodology.

Similarly, Bialystok (1982) considered variability when measuring second language proficiency in a variety of tasks, in oral and written modality (structural exercises, a discourse completion task, an interview role play, and a debate) and structures (modal verbs and different types of interrogatives). She reported different results depending on the task situations and the demands each task required. Furthermore, she concluded that differences among L2 groups were not only the manifestation of quantitative differences, but also an indication of qualitative differences, namely whether the linguistic knowledge required for completing the task was "analysed" or "unanalysed", associating type of knowledge with the specific demands of each task. As we have seen, this observation would be refined some years later by Ellis (2005).

Further research on the effect of modality in L2 learners' performance (Johnson 1992; Murphy 1997; Wong 2001) and more generally Penney (1989), emphasized the asymmetries between visual or written modality versus aural modality in language performance. In particular, Penney (1989) and Murphy (1997) explained the general difficulties in the aural condition assuming two separate processing systems in the cognitive skills of the speakers, one for auditory material and another one for visual material. Nonetheless, none of these studies except for Murphy (1987), took into account together with the modality effect, the linguistic structure investigated. Murphy (1987) showed that it is in the ungrammatical sentences, in her study subjancency violations, where the modality effects are most pronounced. The present study builds into this line of research providing new data on the interaction between modality and linguistic structure in the L2 learners' performance.

We need to take into consideration that in the literature about L2 pedagogy and classroom second language research, the term *task* is usually employed with a related yet, slightly different denotation. In those cases, it usually refers to task-based instruction in which learners actually *do* something with the target language. That type of 'task' connotation is the one mostly employed in the studies about complexity, accuracy and fluency (CAF) in second language research (Ellis 2003; Housen & Kuiken 2009; Robinson 2011; Skehan 1998). For instance, with this sense of 'task', Kuiken and Vedder (2008) investigated whether cognitive task complexity was associated to linguistic performance in L2 learners. They examined two written tasks with different levels of complexity in 91 Dutch learners of Italian and 76 Dutch learners of French and found there was an effect of task complexity on accuracy. In particular, their results indicated that the more complex the task was, the lesser the number of errors were found. However, no significant relationship was found between task complexity and syntactic or lexical performance. These data partially support the Cognition Hypothesis (Robinson 2005), which proposes that increasing task complexity promotes awareness and attention in the learners resulting in greater linguistic complexity and higher accuracy.

Regarding Spanish as a second language, the language under investigation in this study, Sanz (1997) isolated several factors that could affect language performance. In particular, she investigated production of clitic pronouns and found significant differences according to modality and amount of production required. Results indicated that the more context the L2 learner had and longer sentences they had to write (amount), the less accurate the production was. She also found significantly better results in written than in oral production (modality). Within a processing framework, she interpreted these results in terms of demands in the capacity system: the more material the learner needed to process, the less accurate the production was; also, the less amount of time available, the more problematic the processing. Consequently, she concluded that the oral mode makes more demands on the production system than the written mode.

More recently, task effects have also been reported in processing tests, in which on-line data (reaction times, eye movement measurements, ERPs) varied according to the specific demands of the tasks. For instance, Leeser, Brandl and Weissglass (2011) investigated gender agreement and subject-verb inversion in L2 Spanish through self-paced reading tasks and found different results depending on the secondary task included. In particular, the intermediate L2 learners showed on-line sensitivity to gender agreement violations when reading the target sentences if the secondary task required making a grammaticality judgment, but no sensitivity was found if the secondary task was a comprehension question. No significant results were found for subject-verb inversion in wh-questions. Therefore, if the secondary task was a more metalinguistic task, the L2 learner seemed to be more likely to look for ungrammaticalities. Moreover, this sensitivity not only depended on the task but also on the linguistic structure investigated.

In short, it is apparent that there are several factors that generate variability in a second language, among them methodology. Therefore, it is important to evaluate the way abstract concepts such as the implicit/explicit knowledge or the competence/performance distinctions are measured. This is not a trivial question in experimental second language research since in numerous occasions quantitative data determine the description of the L2 linguistic system. Little work has been done in this respect, with the exception of Ellis (2004, 2005), Ellis & Loewen (2007), Isemonger (2007), and more recently Bowles (2011) for heritage speakers. The purpose of these studies was to legitimate the tasks researchers employ to measure abstract concepts as well as to assess the type of knowledge each task elicits.

Ellis (2005) conducted a psychometric study in which he attempted to establish operational definitions of implicit and explicit knowledge and associate them with independent measurements. In particular, he tested 91 learners of L2 English and 20 native speakers in 17 grammatical structures with 5 different tests. These tests were an oral imitation test with grammatical and ungrammatical structures, an oral retelling narrative test, a timed and an untimed grammaticality judgment test with grammatical and ungrammatical sentences, and a metalinguistic test. In the metalinguistic test, participants had to select the rule that would account for the errors they were presented with, and later produce examples of certain grammatical structures and identify grammatical parts in sentences. Taking into account the criteria discussed earlier that distinguish implicit and explicit knowledge

Table 2. Psychometric study relating implicit/explicit knowledge with tasks (adapted from Ellis 2005)

Results Ellis (2005) Bowles (2011)	Factor A (≈ implicit knowledge)			Factor B (≈ explicit knowledge)	
Criterion	Imitation	Oral Narrative	Timed GJT	Untimed GJT	Metalanguage
Degree of awareness	Feel	Feel	Feel	Rule	Rule
Time available	Pressured	Pressured	Pressured	Unpressured	Unpressured
Focus of attention	Meaning	Meaning	Form	Form	Form
Metalinguistic knowledge	No	No	No	Yes	Yes

(Table 1), Ellis correlated these characteristics with the tasks and determined that the scores from the oral imitation task, the oral narrative and the timed grammaticality judgment task loaded on one factor, whereas the metalinguistic task and the ungrammatical sentences from the untimed GJT loaded on a different factor. Ellis understood these factors as representing implicit and explicit knowledge, respectively. Bowles (2011) corroborated these findings for Spanish not only in L2 learners but also in heritage speakers. Table 2 summarizes the different criteria used to describe implicit/explicit knowledge correlated with the tasks.

In sum, the oral tasks (the oral imitation and the narrative task), and the tasks that have time restrictions to be completed (the imitation task, narration, and the timed GJT) seem to tap more into the implicit knowledge of the L2 learners. On the other hand, the tasks that have an indefinite amount of time to be completed and require more reflection about the form and the language employed tap more into explicit knowledge. Given these findings, the motivation for this study is to combine these results with the effect of the linguistic structure under investigation: direct object and oblique relative clauses.

4. The current study

Inasmuch as methodology seems to be a significant factor in the variability found in L2 learners' results, the general research question for this study is: Can we isolate other variables that may also affect L2 learners' results? In particular, this study examines the effect of two factors in L2 learners' variability: task modality and linguistic structure. Notice that the purpose of this study is not to replicate or validate Ellis's results, or previous research that showed how modality affected the L2 learners' performance. Rather, taking them as a very valid explanation for variability in L2 knowledge, the aim of this study is to add another factor into the equation: the linguistic structure under investigation. It is in this sense that a more formal approach to the study of second language acquisition, that is, a linguistic approach to SLA, can inform cognitive approaches to SLA and vice versa.

In particular, this study investigates knowledge of L2 Spanish relative clauses and its variability regarding production modality and syntactic function. Relative clauses are a linguistic structure extensively investigated in SLA research, in L2 English (Gass 1979, 1984; Hamilton 1994; Hawkins 1989; Hyltenstam 1984, among others; see R. Ellis 2008: 563–575 for a comprehensive review), and more recently in Asian Languages (see special issue in *Studies in Second Language Acquisition* 29, 2007), but not so much in L2 Spanish with the exception of Liceras (1981, 1986).

4.1   The linguistic phenomenon

A relative clause (RC) is an embedded clause that modifies a noun. In this study, only restrictive RCs will be investigated, which are the ones that delimit the meaning of the noun. Relative clauses are usually classified by the syntactic function of the relative pronoun (or gap or operator, depending on the linguistic analysis[1]), and in this study we are concerned with direct object (1) and oblique (2) relative clauses.

(1)   La canción que cantó Juan es mi preferida.
       The song REL sang Juan is my favorite
       'The song that John sang is my favorite.'

(2)   La chica de la que dependía María es muy guapa
       The girl of the REL depended María is very pretty
       'The girl on whom María depended is very pretty.'

Direct Object (DO) relative clauses in Spanish are formed by displacing the constituent that is the direct object of the embedded verb outside its original clause. In order to link the displaced element with the embedded clause, a complementizer (or a relative pronoun, depending on the analysis) is inserted. For Spanish relative clauses, the most common complementizer is *que* 'that'. In English and Arabic, direct object RCs can be constructed in a very similar way, through *wh*-movement and a relative pronoun or complementizer. However, Arabic also accepts a

---

1.   Despite the fact that this study incorporates the linguistic factor into the equation, we believe that technical details regarding the linguistic analysis of the *wh*-movement involved in relative clauses are not necessary for the ultimate purpose of this investigation. For a more detailed analysis of Spanish relative clauses, see Brucart (1992, 1999); Gallego (2006); Rivero (1980, 1982); Suñer (1998, 2000).

non-movement version, which is in fact the most common strategy, in which the head of the relative clause is not moved but base-generated and linked with the embedded clause through a resumptive pronoun, as in *The song that John sang it is my favorite*. As for oblique relative clauses, in standard Spanish the obligatory preposition must move along with the relative pronoun, as in (2). This syntactic phenomenon is called Pied-Piping and unlike in Moroccan Arabic or English, where it also exists, it is the only option for forming oblique RCs in standard Spanish. In English, on the other hand, one can also leave the preposition behind in its original position, a phenomenon called Preposition Stranding, as in *The girl that Mary depended **on** is very pretty*. In Arabic, there is also a form in which there is no movement and a resumptive pronoun is inserted after the preposition in the embedded clause: *The girl that Mary depended **on her** is very pretty*.

The acquisition of relative clauses has been widely studied after the famous Noun Phrase Accessibility Hierarchy (NPAH) proposed by Keenan and Comrie (1977). This hierarchy ranks relative clauses according to two main considerations: crosslinguistic or typological evidence and frequency of the relative pronoun (or gap) function. Drawing on a crosslinguistic survey, the NPAH predicts that subject relative clauses (relative clauses where the gap is in the subject position) are the least difficult and most frequent, followed by the direct object relative clauses, the dative relative clauses and so on. The proposed order of accessibility is represented in (3).

(3)   Noun Phrase Accessibility Hierarchy (NPAH)
      Subject > Direct Object > Dative > Oblique > Genitive > Object of
      Comparison

Furthermore, Keenan & Comrie suggested that this hierarchy reflects the psychological ease of relative clause comprehension, and as such it is logical to think that it can also have implications for order of acquisition. In fact, several L2 studies have corroborated this hypothesis (e.g. Gass 1979, 1984; Hawkins 1989; Tarallo and Myhill, 1983).

Gass (1979) studied a total of 188 students learning English as a second language. Their linguistic backgrounds were quite diverse; their native languages were Italian, Arabic, Portuguese, Farsi, French, Thai, Chinese, Korean, and Japanese. Nonetheless, no results are reported according to the native languages of the students. All subjects completed three tasks: a free composition, a sentence combining task and a grammaticality judgment task. The overall results showed that the L2 production of relative clauses, except for the case of genitive, can be correctly predicted by the NPAH. Gass claimed that the genitive did not conform to the hierarchy proposal possibly because of the salience of the relative pronoun *whose*. Similar results were found in an instructional intervention study (Gass 1984), which corroborated the psychological and implicational validity of the NPAH for L2 learnability. Then, the prediction was that if knowledge of a difficult structure (lower in the hierarchy) is acquired, it automatically generalizes to a related easier structure (higher in the hierarchy).

In Spanish, Liceras (1981, 1986, 1988) conducted a series of studies testing the markedness theory for SLA and found that regardless of the assumed marked character of preposition stranding, 43% of beginner learners accepted the construction. Nonetheless, L2 learners easily recovered from it and rates of acceptance of preposition stranding dramatically dropped in intermediate and advanced learners. This fact made Liceras (1986) conclude that nonnative learners do not include marked structures in their grammars.

Another study that compared the acquisition of relative clauses in different syntactic positions is that of Guasti and Cardinaletti (2003). These authors explored the acquisition of relative clauses by French and Italian children, ages 4;5 to 10;00 with two oral production tasks. Their results found that subject relative clauses were produced not only when targeted, but also instead of other types of RCs; resumptive pronouns were quite frequent; and relatives that needed a preposition and a relative pronoun (Pied-Piping) such as Indirect Object, genitive or locative relative clauses were generally introduced only by the complementizer *che/que* and recurrently followed by a resumptive pronoun, instead of being introduced by Pied-Piping as in standard Italian and French. These results led Guasti and Cardinaletti to conclude that oblique relatives with Pied-Piping are learnt later in life, during schooling, through explicit teaching. They further proposed that in Romance languages there are two types of relative clauses: the conventional ones, with Pied-Piping and relative pronouns, and the non-standard relatives that mostly employ the complementizer.

To my knowledge, there is not a comparable study on the acquisition of Spanish relative clauses in L1, but nothing indicates that the results would be very different from those from Guasti and Cardinaletti (2003), since the three Romance languages share the main common linguistic properties in this respect. However, one observation is in place regarding standard and non-standard RCs in Spanish. Unlike French or Italian, Spanish oblique RCs with Pied-Piping can be formed with two types of connectors: the unstressed *que*[2] ('that'), and the stressed relative pronouns *cual/ quien* ('which/who(m)'), the latter being the only equivalent option in the other Romance languages. In that sense, Spanish clearly shows how oblique RCs formed with

---

2.   There is a debate in the Spanish linguistics literature regarding the status of this *que* in oblique relative clauses. Brucart (1992) proposes a unified analysis considering this *que* always a complementizer, whereas Suñer (2000) believes that in this context it is a real relative pronoun. However, this issue goes beyond the scope of this paper and will not be discussed any further.

stressed relative pronouns (*cual/quien*) belong to the formal register and as such, probably in the realm of pure explicit knowledge. On the other hand, it is harder to conclude that all forms of Spanish Pied-Piping draw exclusively on explicit knowledge, since it is the only 'grammatical' form, at least according to prescriptive grammars. Although there is certain tendency in Spanish to avoid Pied-Piping RCs in oral speech, using resumptive relatives instead (Lope Blanch 1984; Suñer 1998)[3] or subject RCs, it is hard to assert that Pied-Piping relatives are never produced by less educated native speakers. Therefore, it is logic to assume that, acknowledging that these structures are learned later in life, probably helped by explicit instruction; at least more frequent Spanish Pied-Piping -the one formed with *que-*, at some point needs to become part of the implicit knowledge of native speakers.

Following these facts, we could predict for this study that direct object relative clauses, since they are more common and easier to process (Keenan & Comrie 1977), will also be easier to acquire than oblique relative clauses. In addition, if some relative clauses formed through Pied-Piping are part of our explicit knowledge, developed later in life, as proposed by Guasti & Cardinaletti (2003), then we could expect better results on this structure in the written task compared to the oral task.

4.2   Participants

A group of native speakers of Spanish (*n* = 20) acting as a control group and one group of intermediate learners of L2 Spanish completed the study (*n* = 42). The L2 learners came from two different linguistic backgrounds, half of them (*n* = 21) had Moroccan Arabic as their native language and the other half (*n*= 21) had English as their native language. The L2 learners as well as 8 of the native speakers were tested in their country of origin, either the US, Morocco, or Spain; the remaining native speakers were tested in the US. All L2 learners were enrolled in low-to upper intermediate Spanish courses at the time of testing (mean age = 23.8 years old), and they were college students, except for two participants who worked as civil servants in Morocco. The control group consisted of native speakers of Spanish (*n* = 20), from different dialectal varieties: one Argentinean, one Colombian, one Costa Rican, one Mexican, one Venezuelan, and fifteen speakers of Castillian Spanish. The structures under consideration do not exhibit dialectal variation in Spanish, so having native speakers from different Spanish-speaking varieties

---

3.   The *Nueva Gramática de la Lengua Española* (2010) explicitly recommends avoiding them: "aparecen en la lengua oral de muchos países hispanohablantes, pero no son propias de los registros formales ni, en general, de la expresión cuidada, por lo que se recomienda evitarlas." (RAE 2010: 839). My translation: '[the resumptive relatives] appear in the oral language of many Spanish-speaking countries but they do not belong to formal registers or, generally speaking, to a careful expression. Therefore, it is recommended to avoid them.'

should not be an issue. The native speakers' mean age at the time of testing was 32.25. They were all college graduates, except for two of them. Most participants received monetary compensation for participating in the study.

4.3   Materials

The first test administered was a proficiency test, which also served as a screening tool. This test was completed one or two weeks before the experimental tasks. The experimental tasks relevant to this study are an oral and a written production task, administered in this order. These were preceded by other tasks including an oral picture description task and two on-line self-paced reading tasks, not reported here. All tasks were conducted individually with the researcher in a quiet room. The following sections explain in more detail the characteristics of the proficiency test and the two experimental tasks of this study.

4.3.1   *Proficiency task*

The proficiency test consisted of a slightly modified version of the standardized grammar section of the superior level of the Diploma de Español como Lengua Extranjera (DELE) created by the Instituto Cervantes (21 points), and part of the vocabulary test (19 points). The maximum score for these two sections combined was 40 points. The grammar section was slightly modified so it included some questions to check that participants knew the argument structure of the verbs used in the experimental tasks, in particular, whether the verb required a preposition. If participants did not know the correct subcategorization frame of the prepositional verb, then they were not included in the study. This screening measure affected 64% of the initial L2 learners' pool, and only 42 out of 116 were selected to complete the experimental tasks.

4.3.2   *Oral production task*

Participants were presented with a scenario (two pairs of pictures) on a computer screen along with some information describing each image. The information was written on the screen and read out loud by the researcher. After that, the next slide consisted of a selection of the previous image with a question they needed to answer. The beginning of each response sentence was provided to make sure that the extracted constituent for each sentence was the expected one. In order to tap a more implicit response, the participants were instructed to complete the sentence orally as fast as possible with the information they were given. All responses were recorded with a digital recorder through a headphone microphone set that participants wore during the entirety of the oral experiment. Later, the recordings were transcribed and coded according to the structure produced.

There were a total of 12 experimental situations and each situation consisted of two slides. There were 6 scenarios eliciting oblique relative clauses, and 6 eliciting direct object relative clauses. One model scenario of each syntactic structure and a practice situation were provided before the experiment started. Example (4) targeted an oblique relative clause, and the situation in (5) aimed to elicit a direct object relative clause. The fragment of the sentence in italics in (4b, 5b), only provided in the sample scenario, is the expected response. As stated before, all the information was presented in oral and in written format so we could ensure that non-native speakers would not have problems recalling the information they needed to construct the relative clauses.

(4)   Situation exemplifying an oblique relative clause context.

    a.   Slide 1 introducing the situation

Ejemplo

Los compañeros se ríen del chico.
'The classmates REFL laugh at-the boy.'

    b.   Slide 2 eliciting a prepositional Relative Clause

Ejemplo

Los compañeros se ríen del chico
'The classmates REFL laugh at-the boy.'

¿Quién es este chico?
'Who is this boy?

Este   es el chico.... *del   que se   ríen los compañeros.*
This   is   the boy...   at-the that REFL laugh the classmates.
'This is the boy at whom the classmates laugh.'

(5) Situation exemplifying a direct object relative clause context.

    a. Slide 1 introducing the situation

La chica está cortando verduras.
'The girl is cutting vegetables.'

    b. Slide 2 eliciting a Direct Object Relative Clause

   **Ejemplo**

La chica está cortando verduras.
'The girl is cutting vegetables.'

¿Qué es esto?
'What is this?

Estas son las verduras.... *que está cortando la chica.*
These are the vegetables... that is cutting the girl
'These are the vegetables that the girl is cutting.'

4.3.3 *Written production task*

In this paper and pencil task, participants were presented with two independent sentences and these two sentences shared one constituent. Participants were instructed to combine the two sentences keeping the same meaning but not saying again the repeated constituent. The beginning of the target new sentence was indicated to ensure that the participants used the intended constituent as the head of the complex sentence. There was no limit of time to complete the task and one example of each type of structure was provided. The first example demonstrated a prepositional construction and thus, a Pied-Piped relative clause; the second exemplified a transitive construction. The experiment included 6 items that elicited oblique RCs and 5 items targeting direct object RCs. Examples are shown in (6) below.

(6) Examples provided in written sentence-combining task:

    a. El parque es muy bonito. Cada tarde iba a ese parque.
       El parque <u>al que iba cada tarde</u> es muy bonito.
       'The park is very nice. Each afternoon (I) went to that park.
       The park <u>to which (I) went each afternoon</u> is very nice.'

    b. Esa canción es mi preferida. Juan cantó esa canción.
       La canción <u>que cantó Juan</u> es mi preferida.
       'This song is my favorite. Juan sang that song.
       The song <u>that Juan sang</u> is my favorite.'

It must be clarified that in the case of direct object RCs, in both tasks, oral and written, the intended extracted element was always a [−human] constituent. The reasoning for this is to avoid the use of the personal 'a', an obligatory preposition (or case marker) that introduces [+human] direct objects in Spanish. This procedure controlled for the target appearance of Pied-Piping RCs only in the oblique contexts.

5. Results

5.1   Results proficiency task

All participants completed the same proficiency test, which consisted of a superior grammar section and a vocabulary section from the official exam of the Instituto Cervantes (DELE). The maximum score for the two sections is 40, and native speakers, as expected, scored very highly ($M = 39.60$; $SD = .68$). The L2 learners had an average equivalent to an intermediate/upper-intermediate level proficiency ($M = 25.86$; $SD = 7.99$), with a relatively wide distribution, which will allow us to correlate the results according to their proficiency level if needed. As for linguistic background, the English group$_1$ had a slightly higher score than the Arabic group$_2$ ($M_1 = 26.05$ vs. $M_2 = 25.67$), and the Arabic group had a wider distribution ($SD_1 = 7.32$ vs. $SD_2 = 8.79$). A one-way ANOVA indicated a significant effect by group $F(2,59) = 28.74$, $p < .001$, and a post-hoc Tukey HSD test revealed that the only different group was the control group ($p < .001$). The two L2 learner groups did not differ significantly ($p = .98$).

5.2   Results production tasks

In order for the data to be compared, results from the two tasks will be presented together. Also, despite the fact that the proficiency test failed to find any difference between the two types of L2 learners, the statistical analysis per group revealed significant differences between the two groups in some respects. For this reason, and in an attempt to isolate the possible effects of different variables, the analyses and the descriptive statistics have been carried out by group.

A total of 1426 sentences were produced, the oral production task generated 744 sentences and the written task produced 682 sentences. These were coded according to the structure produced and the type of connector used (stressed or unstressed). In the context of oblique RCs, the participants mostly produced Pied-Piping RCs, Null Preposition RCs, and subject RCs. For instance, native # 61 dropped the obligatory preposition producing the ungrammatical "*Esta es la cuidadora que la niña cuenta para hacer la tarta*" ('This is the caregiver that the girl counts to make the cake'). In addition, as a result of L1 transfer, English speakers also produced some ungrammatical RCs with preposition stranding (13% of the time), and the Arabic speakers produced resumptive relatives (17% of the time). In the context of Direct Object RCs there was less variation and more accurate responses, with some resumptive relatives in the case of Arabic speakers (around 10% of the time), such as in "*Esta la caja que el chico la carga*" (Subject # 44, 'This the box that the boy loads it'), and some overextension of Pied-Piping by the English group[4]. Also, some natives and Arabic speakers produced subject RCs in the form of passive sentences in this context, as native #71 who produced "*Los libros que son ordenados por la bibliotecaria*" ('The books that are organized by the librarian') instead of producing a Direct Object RC.

For the purpose of this study, and to make it more comparable with the studies from the cognitive approach, only target (or 'correct') responses will be considered. That means that only direct object RCs in transitive contexts and Pied-Piped relatives in oblique contexts were included in the statistical analysis. Therefore, accuracy of target responses reported in percentages will be the dependent variable. The coding of oral data presented several challenges because oral speech is characterized by hesitations, pauses, corrections, etc. Since the objective of the oral task was to create a more spontaneous context to generate relative clauses, in the event of a correction, the criterion followed was that only the first structure produced by the participant was considered. It must be said, though, that corrections of a full sentence were quite scarce and affected less than 5% of the production;

---

4.   This overextension could be interpreted as a hypercorrection effect. Participants were aware of the difficulty of Pied-Piping and as a result, they overproduced it in inappropriate contexts.

most corrections were in the selection of the relative pronoun. For example, Arabic Subject # 41 produced: "Esta es la entrenadora quien confía ... en quien confían los niños" (*'This is the coach who trusts... on whom the children trust'*); this sentence was coded as a subject RC and not as an oblique RC; then, this sentence was a non-target response. On the other hand, if a sentence presented Pied-Piping but with an incorrect preposition (*en* instead of *de* or *con*, mostly because of L1 transfer), that sentence was coded as 'correct' because the participant still produced a Pied-Piped relative clause structure. For example, English speaker #21 produced: 'La enfermera en que la chica depende" (*'The nurse on whom the girl depends'*), but the correct preposition in Spanish is *'de'* and not *'en'*.

Mean percentages of target responses as well as their standard deviations are displayed in Table 3.

Results showed a strong effect of modality: oral production consistently presented fewer target-like structures than written modality across participants. For instance, in the control group, 98% of written responses were correct versus 92% in the oral task. The difference is still more acute in the Arabic group, with 51% of correct responses in the oral task whereas the target responses in the written task are over 65%. This observation is corroborated by the results of a repeated measures ANOVA with modality (oral vs. written), syntactic structure (direct object vs. oblique) as within-subjects independent variables, and group (control vs. English vs. Arabic) as between-subjects factor. Results indicated a main effect for modality $F(1, 59) = 13.37, p < .001, \eta^2 = .185$; and this main effect did not interact with group (modality $*$ group $= F(2, 59) = 1.36, p > .1, \eta^2 = .044$) because modality equally affected all groups. However, a more detailed within-subjects analysis by group indicated that modality was a significant factor in the native speakers $F(1, 19) = 7.97$, $p = .011, \eta^2 = .296$ and in the Arabic group $F(1, 20) = 5.5, p = .029, \eta^2 = .216$ but not in the English group in which it is only marginally significant $F(1, 20) = 3.626$, $p = .071, \eta^2 = .153$. Nonetheless, despite the fact that Arabic speakers follow the trend of the native speakers, having a strong effect of modality, the English speakers are consistently more accurate than the Arabic speakers, regardless of their comparable proficiency as measured by the standardized proficiency test.

Table 3. Frequency of target responses per group and modality

Group	Modality	
	Oral	Written
Native (*n* = 20)	91.67 (10.12)	98.08 (4.93)
English Speakers (*n* = 21)	69.05 (23.59)	74.21 (28.11)
Arabic Speakers (*n* = 21)	51.59 (35.32)	65.32 (32.03)
Total L2 learners (*n* = 42)	60.32 (30.95)	69.76 (30.10)

Table 4. Frequency of target responses per modality, syntactic structure and group

Group	Oral Task		Written Task	
	Direct Object	Oblique	Direct Object	Oblique
Native (n = 20)	94.17 (13.55)	89.17 (17.33)	97.00 (7.33)	99.17 (3.73)
English Speakers (n = 21)	81.75 (27.34)	56.35 (43.61)	85.71 (24.61)	62.70 (47.70)
Arabic Speakers (n = 21)	68.25 (38.69)	34.92 (41.47)	83.81 (33.83)	46.83 (43.98)
Total L2 learners (n = 42)	75 (33.79)	45.64 (43.41)	84.76 (29.24)	54.76 (46.02)

If we factor in the linguistic structure, the effect on the data is even stronger, and variability gets more prevalent in the results. The frequencies per modality and syntactic structures are shown on Table 4.

The repeated measures ANOVA showed a robust main effect for syntactic structure $F(1, 59) = 18.67$, $p < .0001$, $\eta^2 = .240$, and a significant interaction of structure and group $F(2, 59) = 4.435$, $p = .016$, $\eta^2 = .131$, but structure did not interact with modality ($p > .5$), showing that they are independent factors and that both significantly affected the performance of the L2 learners. There was no three-way interaction. Similarly to the effect we observed regarding modality, that is, the oral task consistently getting worse results than the written counterpart, now we can also observe that oblique relativization is consistently more difficult to produce than direct object relativization. For instance, English speakers got accuracy scores 20% lower in the oblique position than in the DO function; this difference increases to more than 30% in the case of Arabic speakers. The within-subjects analysis per group showed that while syntactic structure is not a significant effect in the control group $F(1, 19) = .283$, $p > .5$, $\eta^2 = .015$, it is significant in both experimental groups, in the English group $F(1, 20) = 4.857$, $p = .039$, $\eta^2 = .195$ and remarkably in the Arabic group $F(1, 20) = 19.217$, $p < .0001$, $\eta^2 = .490$.

As for proficiency, Pearson correlations between proficiency and correct responses by modality showed that while performance in the L1 English group is highly associated with proficiency in both oral and written tasks, oral: $r = .781$, p (one-tailed) $< .001$; written: $r = .755$, p (one-tailed) $< .001$; proficiency of the L1 Arabic group is weakly correlated with their performance, oral task: $r = .381$, p (one-tailed) $= .044$; written task: $r = .348$, p (one-tailed) $= .061$. However, when we factor in the linguistic structure, the results seem to point towards somehow different conclusions: correct responses in the Direct Object RC context in the oral task are not associated with the proficiency of either of the experimental groups

($p > .05$), but they moderately correlated in the written task in the case of the L1 English speakers, $r = .470$, p (one-tailed) $= .016$, but not in the case of L1 Arabic speakers ($p > .05$). On the other hand, Oblique RCs are moderately correlated in all tasks and across participants (correlations range from $r = .450$ to $r = .659$), all of them were significant at the .05 alpha level.

Finally, if we take into consideration the type of relative pronoun produced, we can observe that there is not much difference in the use of stressed or un-stressed relative pronouns between the oral and written in the case of the native speakers (22% use of stressed relative pronouns in the written task vs. 23.5% in the oral task). However, the differences are considerable in the L2 learners' groups, with significantly higher rates of usage of formal stressed pronouns *quien/cual* in the written task than in the oral task. The English speakers produced 26% of for-mal relative pronouns in the oral task vs. 47% in the written task; similarly, the Arabic speakers produced 34% of formal relative pronouns in the oral task vs. 51% in the written task.

6.   Discussion

Overall, results have indicated a strong effect of modality, with more accurate re-sults in the written task than in the oral task. Moreover, we have found a robust effect of linguistic structure in the L2 learners, with more target responses in the direct object context than in the oblique one. These two results were not unex-pected. We have seen that oral tasks usually obtain fewer correct responses than similar tasks in the written modality (Murphy 1997; Sanz 1997; Wong 2001). As Sanz proposed, this effect is probably because the oral mode puts more pressure and more demands on the production system than the written modality does, and for this reason, oral data are more costly. Our results showed that this cost effect is not exclusive to L2 learners since the native speakers also dispayed a modality ef-fect in their results, with significantly better results in the written task compared to the oral one. The fact that modality was also significant in the native group is somehow unexpected and seems to indicate that the modality effect is not related to a lack of competence or a mismatch between performance and grammatical knowledge, since we cannot assume an impaired grammatical representation in the case of the native speakers. This result seems to corroborate Penney's (1989) proposal regarding the independence of the two systems when processing audi-tory and visual stimuli. Another way to interpret this result is by arguing that Pied-Piping in oblique RCs is a costly operation, and then, in a more spontaneous and demanding context such as the oral task, other non-standard forms of oblique relatives may rise. This reasoning would go in line with the rationale behind

Keenan & Comrie's Accessibility Hierarchy in which they propose that resumptive RCs (outside the hierarchy) are overall easier to process than gap relatives; and that oblique RCs are one of hardest positions to operationalize within the hierarchy. This would also explain the tendency of avoiding Pied-Piping in native oral speech, as the *Nueva Gramática de la Lengua Española* admits but disapproves of. Besides, it is interesting to note that the oral modality is more costly not only to L2 learners but also to native speakers, who are not using a developing L2 grammar and, in fact, half of whom are monolinguals. This seems to suggest that the task modality effect is not the product of dealing with two languages. There is a well-established trend of thinking which proposes that bilingualism, despite the fact of its proven benefits on general cognition (Bialystok 2009), can result in an extra cognitive cost that may produce certain (temporal) inefficiency, particularly in bilingual processing (Clahsen & Felser 2006; Sorace 2011). This is not the case here since native speakers, even the monolingual ones, demostrate this task effect. Notice that the purpose of this study is not to explain why L2 learners are not 100% accurate, but to account for systematic variability within the data. As a consequence, if the task effect cannot be explained because of the disparities between competence and performance, or because of the extra processing load of handling two languages, we could ask whether that effect is the result of using different types of knowledge in each task, as proposed by Ellis (2005).

Oral tasks, which usually do not allow for unlimited time, do not require a large amount of metalinguistic knowledge, and are focused mostly on meaning, tap into implicit knowledge. However, the oral task employed here was quite form-oriented since it targeted a particular structure. Nevertheless, we assume that an oral task always involves more implicit knowledge than a written one. Implicit knowledge, which is intuitive, unconscious, systematic, and procedural, is the typical native linguistic knowledge. It is the one naturally available to everybody who acquires a language by the age of 5 (Paradis 2009). After that period, more declarative, explicit knowledge is used in acquiring a language. Therefore, the fact that the native speakers behaved more poorly in a task that required them to use more implicit knowledge, their natural type of linguistic knowledge, needs further explanation. Explicit knowledge, on the other hand, is declarative, inconsistent, controlled, verbalizable, and learnable at any age. Following Ellis (2005), we assume that this is the type of knowledge primarily engaged in the written task. Some of these characteristics may help us understand why the written task obtained better results than the oral task. For instance, the fact that explicit knowledge is more controlled can explain a more accurate and conscious performance. However, explicit knowledge is also assumed to be more inconsistent and less systematic than implicit knowledge, but our results do not show larger standard deviations in the written task compared to the oral, as would be expected (Zobl

1995). On the contrary, the oral task presented more variability than the written task, especially in the case of the native speakers. It is generally assumed that explicit knowledge is more variable than implicit knowledge because it is less reliable, more based on grammatical rules and less automatized than implicit knowledge. Since we do not suppose an impaired grammatical competence in native speakers, the fact that native speakers are presenting variability in their results makes us wonder whether that variability is truly displaying performance errors, or whether the production of relative clauses, particularly oblique RCs, requires the use of an explicit rule even in adults speakers, as Guasti & Cardinaletti (2003) proposed for children, and hence the better results in the written task. If the rule was completely internalized, then it would be used systematically and be part of the implicit knowledge. This does not seem to be completely the case.

We can provide a broader explanation for these results by taking into account the linguistic structure under investigation. The first relevant piece of information about relative clauses is that they are structures learned late in life. Children start producing them around 3 years of age, but do not master them until several years later (Guasti 2002). If relative clauses are learned late in life in the L1, they may as well be learned late in the L2. And as indicated in Table 1, late-learned, form-focused structures belong more to the explicit knowledge of the speakers. This piece of information, together with the extra processing cost that oral tasks seem to impose on the system, can explain why production of relative clauses is overall more accurate in the written task, particularly in the case of oblique RCs. Therefore, it is only through the combination of different yet complementary approaches to the study of SLA, in the case at hand, the cognitive perspective and the linguistics knowledge, that we can understand better these data.

Furthermore, not all syntactic positions are acquired at the same pace, and parallel to the Noun Phrase Accessibility Hierarchy (Keenan & Comrie 1977), some syntactic positions are easier to acquire than others. For instance, relative clauses that require Pied-Piping are usually avoided in L1 production between the ages 3–6 (Labelle 1990), and not accepted in comprehension during those ages, at least in English (McDaniel, McKee & Bersntein 1998). Actually, the native speakers also avoided Pied Piping in some cases and produced non-target subject RCs instead. The results of this study clearly showed a main effect for syntactic structure, with oblique RCs being harder to produce than direct object RCs, as predicted by the Accessibility Hierarchy. Given that DO relative clauses are acquired earlier than oblique relative clauses, and that according to the results, proficiency only correlates with accuracy in the oblique RCs; we could reach the conclusion that the L2 learners have already gained mastery in Direct Object RCs, but not quite yet in oblique RCs. For this reason, we can observe a significant correlation between the overall L2 language proficiency and their development (measured in accuracy rates) in oblique RCs, This means that as their language proficiency improves, they also improve their skills in oblique RC formation. And since we do not observe this progression in the DO relative clauses results, we could conclude that the L2 learners have already reached a relatively stable level of DO relative clauses competence.

In order to understand the overall low percentages of correct responses in the production of relative clauses, we need to have a look at the participants' responses, especially at the replacements of target prepositional relative clauses. For instance, L2 learners as well as native speakers formed oblique relative clauses without the obligatory preposition, a phenomenon called Null-Prep (Klein 1993), as in *This is the man that John depends. This phenomenon was found in approximately 20% of the L2 responses. Also, English speakers transferred Preposition Stranding (ca. 15%), and Arabic speakers transferred strong resumptive pronouns from their L1 (ca. 15–20%). These results have at least two interpretations, not mutually exclusive. The first one is that the L2 learners do not have sufficient knowledge to produce oblique relative clauses; that is, they have a syntactic deficit in their L2 grammars, as proposed by Klein (2004). On the other hand, if we were to adopt Guasti & Cardinaletti's (2003) 'strong' position on the L1 acquisition of relative clauses in Romance languages, we could conclude that Pied-Piping oblique relative clauses are in some way artificial and belong to a formal variety of the language. If this were also the case in Spanish, we could easily explain why native speakers behaved in a more target-like manner in the written (explicit) than in the oral task (implicit). If relative clauses, especially the oblique relative clauses, need to be learned in school, probably by a semi-formal rule, it is understandable that their use is more consistent in a written task rather than in an oral task, since it is allegedly linguistic knowledge belonging to the declarative memory. It is an empirical question whether that explicit, metalinguistic knowledge, through use and practice becomes implicit linguistic competence. If, on the other hand, we adopt a weaker position on the acquisition of Spanish relative clauses, assuming that only Pied-Piping with stressed relative pronouns belongs to explicit knowledge and considering Pied-Piping with *que* part of the implicit knowledge of the speakers, then we need to resort to the typological linguistic information (Keenan & Comrie 1977) to understand why oblique relative clauses are overall more difficult to process and produce than direct object relative clauses. In fact, one could hypothesize that, given the type of linguistic structure and its two proposed versions for Romance languages (the standard one with strong relative pronouns and pied-piping, more appropriate for written and formal discourses; and the colloquial version with complementizers and resumptive pronouns), these structures may permanently belong to different types of knowledge. In particular, the formal, standard version would be allocated to explicit knowledge, or in neurolinguistics terms, to declarative memory; whereas the colloquial version of the RCs would be part of the implicit knowledge or procedural memory. In any case, whether we accept the strong or the weak version of the 'explicitness' of oblique relative clauses in Spanish, it is undeniable, at least in this case, the need to take the linguistic variables into account when providing a cognitive explanation for the data. Only when considering both theoretical approaches, we can better account for the complexity, variation and interaction in the data and reflect on how modality and the type of knowledge involved impact on the linguistic structure and vice versa.

7.   Conclusions and pedagogical implications

This study has isolated two variables that can account for variability in L2 learners' results, and also, to a certain degree, in native data. It has proved that task modality, that is, whether the task is completed orally or in a written format, had a significant effect on the results. In particular, it showed that L2 learners and native speakers alike behaved in a more target-like way in the written modality and systematically had fewer correct responses in the oral task. This finding has been explained as the result of using different types of knowledge in each task. Crucially, the type of knowledge employed is contingent on the type of linguistic structure under investigation; hence the importance of considering both, cognitive and linguistic approaches when exploring developing L2 grammars. We assumed that relative clauses, especially oblique relative clauses, have two versions, a colloquial, informal one on the one hand; and a standard, formal one, on the other hand. The standard, formal version, which involves stressed relative pronouns and Pied-Piping is learned late in life through an explicit rule (Guasti & Cardinaletti 2003), and as such, it is argued to belong to the speakers' explicit knowledge or their declarative memory. The informal version, which involves the complementizer *que* would belong to the implicit, procedural memory. Consequently, we found more standard results in written modality than in oral modality, because explicit knowledge is mainly engaged in written tasks. On the other hand, fewer target responses were found in the oral task because in this modality the speakers tend to employ more implicit knowledge. This is particularly true in the case of L2 learners, who not only had significantly better results in the written modality, but also used twice as much stressed relative pronouns (the formal version, also in their L1s) in the written task compared to the oral task. These findings indicate that they are somehow aware of the standard version of forming RCs, and that they seem to be more accurate when they use this version. Moreover, these findings have pedagogical implications for L2 language teaching and learning and require a reflection on the type of input and instruction these L2 learners are receiving. Observing the differences between the use of stressed relative pronouns in the L2 learners (around 50% of the time when Pied-Piping occurred in the written task) and the use native speakers do of them (around 22% of the time with Pied-Piping in the written task), it is evident that these formal stressed relative pronouns are explicitly taught in class. However, these are still difficult to use in spontaneous speech; therefore, their use diminishes in the oral task and so does the overall accuracy. Given these facts, my advice would be to teach all types of relative clauses only with *que,* the most natural and simplest way, and introduce the stressed relative pronouns only when the L2 learners fully understand all types of relativization structures. This way, with a unifying approach to all relative clauses, we can simplify the already difficult task of mastering relative clauses. Moreover, and since relative clauses are complex, late-learned linguistic structures, which require explicit formal rules to be fully mastered even in first language acquisition, it is advisable to teach them with a focus on form approach. Also, and following the Noun Phrase Accessibility Hierarchy (Keenan & Comrie 1977), direct object relative clauses need to be presented before prepositional relative clauses.

Finally, this study has also attested the complexity of acquiring prepositions. It not only was difficult to find for this experiment L2 learners that knew the correct subcategorization frame for the target prepositional verbs; but also, testing only the learners that already demonstrated knowledge of the preposition did not guarantee correct oblique relativization. This result clearly shows the difficulty of gaining mastery in functional categories, particularly if these categories do not significantly contribute to the overall meaning of the sentence, as it is most of the cases with prepositions. For this reason, it is advisable to teach prepositional verbs always together with their subcategorization frame, so the L2 learner can memorize the verb with its corresponding preposition as an atomic lexical item. Furthermore, this result regarding prepositions indicates that the difficulty in acquiring functional categories is not an exclusive characteristic of L2 learners whose native language does not present that particular functional category, as previously proposed (Hawkins & Chan 1997). Instead, these data suggest that acquiring functional categories is an inherent challenge in L2 grammars, independently from the L1 properties. Therefore, special emphasis should be laid on the explicit teaching of prepositions, and immediate positive transfer of their knowledge should not be anticipated.

References

Bialystok, E. (1982). On the relationship between knowing and using linguistic forms. *Applied Linguistics, 3*(3), 181–206.

Bialystok, E. (2009). Bilingualism: The good, the bad, and the indifferent. *Bilingualism: Language and Cognition, 12*(1): 3–11.

Bowles, M.A. (2011). Measuring implicit and explicit linguistic knowledge: What can heritage language learners contribute? *Studies in Second Language Acquisition 33*(2): 247–271.

Brucart, J.M. (1992). Some asymmetries in the functioning of relative pronouns in Spanish. *Catalan Working Papers in Linguistics,* 113–143.

Brucart, J.M. (1999). La estructura del sintagma nominal: Las oraciones de relativo. In I. Bosque & V. Demonte (Eds.),*Gramática descriptiva de la lengua española, Colección Nebrija y Bello,* 395–522. Madrid: Espasa.

Clahsen, H., & Felser, C. (2006). Grammatical processing in language learners. *Applied Psycholinguistics, 27*(1), 3–42.

DeKeyser, R. (1998). Beyond focus on form: Cognitive perspectives on learning and practicing second language grammar. In C. Doughty & J. Williams (Eds.), *Focus on form in classroom second language acquisition* (pp. 42–63). Cambridge: CUP.

DeKeyser, R. (2009). Cognitive-psychological processes in second language learning. In C. Doughty & M.H. Long (Eds.),*The handbook of language teaching* (pp. 119–138). Hoboken, NJ: Wiley-Blackwell.

Ellis, R. (1993). The structural syllabus and second language acquisition. *TESOL Quarterly, 27*(1), 91–113.

Ellis, R. (2003). *Task-based language learning and teaching.* Oxford: OUP.

Ellis, R. (2004). The definition and measurement of L2 explicit knowledge. *Language Learning, 54*(2), 227–275.

Ellis, R. (2005). Measuring implicit and explicit knowledge of a second language: A psychometric study. *Studies in Second Language Acquisition 27*(2): 141–172.

Ellis, R. (2008). *The Study of second language acquisition* [2nd edition]. Oxford: OUP.

Ellis, R., & Loewen, S. (2007). Confirming the operational definitions of explicit and implicit knowledge in Ellis (2005): Responding to Isemonger. *Studies in Second Language Acquisition, 29*(1), 119–126.

Gallego, J. A. (2006). T-to-C movement in relative clauses. In J. Doetjes & P. González (Eds.), *Romance languages and linguistic theory. Selected papers from "Going Romance" 2004* (pp. 143–170). Amsterdam: John Benjamins.

Gass, S. (1979). Language transfer and universal grammatical relations. *Language Learning, 29*(2), 327–344.

Gass, S. (1984). A review of Interlanguage Syntax: Language Transfer and Language Universals. *Language Learning, 34*(2), 115–131.

Guasti, M.T. (2002). *Language acquisition: The growth of grammar.* Cambridge, MA: The MIT Press.

Guasti, M.T., & Cardinaletti, A. (2003). Relative clause formation in Romance child's production. *Probus, 15*(1): 47–89.

Hamilton, R.L. (1994). Is implicational generalization unidirectional and maximal? Evidence from relativization instruction in a second language. *Language Learning, 44*(1), 123–157.

Hawkins, R. (1989). Do second language learners acquire restrictive relative clauses on the basis of relational or configurational information? The acquisition of French subject, direct object and genitive restrictive relative clauses by second language learners. *Second Language Research, 5*(2), 156–188.

Hawkins, R., & Chan, C.Y. (1997). The partial availability of Universal Grammar in second language acquisition: The "Failed Functional Features Hypothesis". *Second Language Research, 13*(3), 187–226.

Haznedar, B., & Schwartz, B.D. (1997). Are there optional infinitives in child L2 acquisition? *Proceedings of the Annual Boston University Conference on Language Development, 21*(1), 257–268.

Housen, A. & Kuiken, F. (2009). Complexity, accuracy, and fluency in second language acquisition. *Applied Linguistics, 30*(4), 461–473. doi:10.1093/applin/amp048

Hulstijn, J. (2002). Towards a unified account of the representation, processing and acquisition of second language knowledge. *Second Language Research, 18*(3), 193–223.

Hyltenstam, K. (1984). The use of typological markedness conditions as predictors in second language acquisition: The case of pronominal copies in relative clauses. In R.W. Andersen (Ed.), *Second languages: A cross-linguistic perspective.* Rowley, MA: Newbury House.

Keenan, E.L., & Comrie, B. (1977). Noun phrase accessibility and Universal Grammar. *Linguistic Inquiry, 8*(1), 63–99.

Klein, E.C. (1993). *Toward second language acquisition: A study of null-prep.* Studies in Theoretical Psycholinguistics. Dordrecht: Kluwer.

Klein, E.C. (2004). Beyond syntax: Performance factors in L2 behavior. In B. VanPatten, J. Williams, S. Rott, & M. Overstreet (Eds.), *Form-meaning connections in second language acquisition* (pp. 155–177). Mahwah, NJ: Lawrence Erlbaum Associates.

Kuiken, F., & Vedder, I. (2008). Cognitive task complexity and written output in Italian and French as a foreign language. *Journal of Second Language Writing, 17*(1), 48–60.

Isemonger, I.M. (2007). Operational definitions of explicit and implicit knowledge: Response to R. Ellis (2005) and Some Recommendations for Future Research in This Area. *Studies in Second Language Acquisition, 29*(1), 101–118.

Johnson, J.S. (1992). Critical period effects in second language acquisition: The effect of written versus auditory materials on the assessment of grammatical competence. *Language Learning, 42*(2), 217–248.

Labelle, M. (1990). Predication, WH-movement, and the development of relative clauses. *Language Acquisition, 1*(1), 95–119.

Lardiere, D. (1998a). Case and tense in the "fossilized" steady state. *Second Language Research, 14*(1), 1–26.

Lardiere, D. (1998b). Dissociating syntax from morphology in a divergent L2 end-state grammar. *Second Language Research, 14*(4), 359–375.

Leeser, M.J., Brandl, A., & Weissglass, C. (2011). Task effects in second language sentence processing research. In P. Trofimovich & K. McDonough (Eds.), *Applying priming methods to L2 learning, teaching and research: Insights from psycholinguistics,*179–198. Amsterdam: John Benjamins.

Liceras, J. (1981). Markedness and permeability in interlanguage systems. *Working Papers in Linguistics, 2,* 123–150. Toronto, ON: University of Toronto.

Liceras, J. (1986). *Linguistic theory and second language acquisition: The Spanish nonnative grammar of English speakers.* Tübingen: Narr.

Liceras, J. (1988). Learnability: Delimiting the domain of core grammar as distinct from the marked periphery. In S. Flynn & W.A. O'Neil (Eds.), *Linguistic theory in second language acquisition* (pp. 199–224). Berlin: Springer.

Lope Blanch, J.M. (1984). Depronominalization of the relatives. *Hispanic Linguistics, 1*(2), 257–272.

McDaniel, D., McKee, C., & Bernstein, J.B. (1998). How children's relatives solve a problem for minimalism. *Language, 74*(2), 308–334.

Murphy, V. (1997). The effect of modality on a grammaticality judgement task. *Second Language Research, 13*(1), 34–65.

Paradis, M. (2009). *Declarative and procedural determinants of second languages.* Amsterdam: John Benjamins.

Penney, C.G. (1989). Modality effects and the structure of short-term verbal memory. *Memory & Cognition, 17*(4), 398–422.

Prévost, P., & White, L. (2000). Missing surface inflection or impairment in second language acquisition? Evidence from tense and agreement. *Second Language Research, 16*(2), 103–133.

Real Academia Española, & Asociación de Academias de la Lengua Española. (2010). *Nueva gramática de la Lengua Española.* Real Academia de la Lengua Espanola.

Rivero, M.L. (1980). That-relatives and deletion in COMP in Spanish. *Cahiers linguistiques d'Ottawa 9,* 383–399.

Rivero, M.L. (1982). Restrictive relatives with que. *Nueva Revista de Filología Hispánica, 31*(2), 195–234.

Robinson, P. (2005). Cognitive complexity and task sequencing: Studies in a componential framework for second language task design. *IRAL, 43*(1), 1–32.

Robinson, P. (Ed.). (2011). *Task-based language learning.* Hoboken, NJ: John Wiley and Sons.

Sanz, C. (1997). Experimental tasks in SLA research: Amount of production, modality, memory, and production processes. In W.R. Glass & A.T. Perez-Leroux (Eds.), *Contemporary perspectives on the acquisition of Spanish: Production, processing and comprehesion,* Vol. 2 (pp. 41–56). Somerville, MA: Cascadilla.

Sharwood Smith, M. (1981). Consciousness-raising and the second language learner. *Applied Linguistics, 2*(2), 159–168.

Skehan, P. (19980. Task-based instruction. *Annual Review of Applied Linguistics, 18,* 268–286.

Sorace, A. (1984). Knowledge and usage in learning a second language: An interpretation of variability. *Travaux neuchatelois de linguistique (TRANEL) 7*(Oct), 43–92.

Sorace, A. (2011). Pinning down the concept of interface in bilingualism. *Linguistic Approaches to Bilingualism, 1*(1), 1–33. doi:10.1075/lab.1.1.01sor

Suñer, M. (1998). Resumptive restrictive relatives: A crosslinguistic perspective. *Language, 74*(2), 335–364.

Suñer, M. (2000). Some thoughts on Que: Description, theory, and L2. *Hispania, 83*(4), 867–876.

Tarallo, F., & Myhill, J. (1983). Interference and natural language processing in second language acquisition. *Language Learning, 33*(1), 55–76.

Tarone, E.E. (1983). On the variability of interlanguage systems. *Applied Linguistics, 4*(2), 142–164.

Tarone, E.E. (1985). Variability in interlanguage use: A study of style-shifting in morphology and syntax. *Language Learning, 35*(3), 373–403.

VanPatten, B. (2002). *From input to output: A teacher's guide to second language acquisition.* New York, NY: McGraw-Hill.

White, L. (2002). Morphological variability in endstate L2 grammars: The question of L1 influence. *Proceedings of the Annual Boston University Conference on Language Development, 26*(2), 758–768.

White, L. (2003). *Second language acquisition and Universal Grammar.* Cambridge: CUP.

Wong, W. (2001). Modality and attention to meaning and form in the input. *Studies in Second Language Acquisition, 23*(3), 345–368.

Zobl, H. (1995). Converging evidence for the "Acquisition-Learning" distinction. *Applied Linguistics, 16*(1), 35–56.

CHAPTER 9

The development of tense and aspect morphology in child and adult heritage speakers*

Alejandro Cuza*, Rocío Pérez-Tattam**, Elizabeth Barajas*, Lauren Miller* and Claudia Sadowski*
Purdue University* and Swansea University**

This cross-sectional study examines the production of tense and aspect morphology in child and adult heritage Spanish, with the view of informing the development of pedagogical interventions in Spanish language for child and adult heritage Spanish speakers. We compare natural production data from Spanish/English bilingual speakers with monolingual children and adults matched by age. Results show a preference for the production of the preterite as opposed to the imperfect among the older bilingual children, compared to younger children and adults, suggesting L1 attrition in the life span. We argue that the overproduction of preterite tense might be due to semantic transfer from English and morphosemantic restructuring of the aspectual system. The imperfect tense remains underdeveloped across all age groups in the bilingual population, and competes with present tense in adulthood, suggesting incomplete development. Based on these results, we discuss important pedagogical implications for the teaching of aspectual distinctions in heritage Spanish. Finally, we conclude that both L1 attrition and incomplete acquisition play a fundamental role in heritage language development, depending on the type of linguistic knowledge, which has an impact on the Spanish language teaching practices to be adopted for child and adult heritage speakers.

* We would like to thank Esmeralda Cruz, Marilu Castillo, Fernando Llanos, and Joshua Frank for their assistance with different aspects of this project. We are also extremely grateful to the two anonymous reviewers and to the two series editors for their thorough comments and helpful feedback.

1. Introduction

A longstanding issue in linguistic research lies in determining the psycholinguistic nature of native and non-native grammars and whether adult learners can eventually develop a native-like system as children do (Johnson & Newport 1989; Schwartz & Sprouse 1996; White 2003). In the specific case of heritage language development, previous work has focused on examining the source of heritage speakers' competence outcome to understand where the difficulties lie, and how to best approach them from a pedagogical perspective (Cuza 2012; Cuza & Frank 2011; Montrul 2002, 2011; Montrul & Bowles 2010; Montrul & Perpiñán 2011; O'Grady, Kwak, Lee & Lee 2011; Polinsky 2008; 2011; Rothman 2007, 2008; Valdés 1997). Heritage speakers are second-generation immigrants who acquired their native/minority language at home or in another natural context where a majority language was spoken (Montrul 2008; Valdés 1997).

Montrul (2008), among others, argues that the morpho syntactic difficulties heritage speakers often face are more likely the result of incomplete development during early childhood primarily due to reduced input and use of the heritage language (Montrul 2002, 2004). Other researchers disagree with the notion of incomplete development to account for the source of heritage speakers' competence (Polinsky 2011 Rothman 2007). Rothman (2007), for example, argues that the competence divergence between heritage speakers and monolingual speakers is the result of the complete acquisition of the contact variety to which the speakers are exposed, which may exclude specific linguistic structures from the input (*Missing-input Competence Divergence Hypothesis*). These two proposals contrast with a third possibility in the characterization of heritage speakers' competence, viewing their deficits as the L1 attrition of previously established properties during early childhood and the reanalysis of language over the life span (Cuza & Pérez-Tattam submitted; Polinsky 2011).

The goal of this study is to further examine this issue, with the view of informing the development of Spanish language teaching practices that are suitable for child and adult heritage speakers, particularly with regard the teaching of aspectual distinctions in Spanish. Specifically, we investigate and compare the extent to which simultaneous Spanish-English bilingual children from different age groups and adult heritage speakers show target production of preterite versus imperfect morphology in spontaneous production and, if not, whether their difficulties can be accounted for in terms of child L1 attrition in the life span or incomplete development during early childhood (Montrul 2002, 2004, 2011; Polinsky 2011; Silva-Corvalán 1994, 2003, forthcoming; Zentella 1997). If young Hispanic children show higher levels of target past tense morphology use than adult heritage speakers of similar sociocultural background, then the difficulties heritage speakers have cannot be accounted for in terms of incomplete development during early childhood. Rather, the difficulties might stem from the child L1 attrition of previously established linguistic norms (O'Grady et. al. 2011; Polinsky 2011; Silva-Corvalán 1991). The results of this analysis will allow us to suggest more effective and theoretically grounded classroom interventions in the teaching of tense and aspect morphology to Spanish heritage speakers, as well as advance previous research by disentangling the source of heritage speakers' difficulties (L1 attrition vs. Incomplete acquisition). By understanding the linguistic processes affecting heritage speakers' grammar, and their subsequent impact on their heritage language development, we are in a better position to inform the development of more suitable pedagogical practices for these populations (Bowles 2011).

In section two, we examine the main aspectual differences between English and Spanish. Section three discusses relevant research on the acquisition of tense and aspect morphology in Spanish among bilingual children, L2 learners of Spanish and Spanish heritage speakers. In section four, we present the study, followed by the results, discussion and pedagogical implications for heritage Spanish teaching. Section five presents the conclusions of the study.

2. Aspectual contrasts in English and Spanish

The literature distinguishes three main aspectual descriptions: grammatical aspect (Comrie 1976), lexical aspect (Vendler 1967) and compositional or VP aspect (Schmitt 1996; Verkuyl 1972). Grammatical aspect is represented by verbal inflections and periphrastic expressions, and is the most common aspectual description made in the literature (preterite vs. imperfect distinctions).

In Spanish, there is one specific form for each aspectual value in the past tense. Completed, one-time events are marked with the preterite (*-ó*) (1a), while habitual and repeated events in the past are marked with the imperfect (*-ba, -ía*) (2a). English differs in that completed events in the past with a specific beginning and end-point (punctual eventualities) are marked by the preterite (*-ed*) (1b), while habitual or continuous eventualities with no specific beginning or end-point are marked either by the preterite (2b) or by a periphrastic expression (*used to/would*) (2c):

(1) a. *María comió manzanas.*   (punctual event, preterite)
     b. Mary ate apples.

(2) a. *María comía manzanas.*   (habitual event, imperfect)
     b. Mary ate apples.
     c. Mary used to eat apples.

The imperfect form in Spanish is also used to denote an event that was ongoing in the past when another event happened (3a). This aspectual value can also be represented with the past progressive (3b). In contrast with Spanish, English disallows the use of the preterite in these contexts (3c), and only allows the past progressive (3d):

(3)   a.   *José cocinaba la cena cuando sonó el teléfono.*
     b.   *José **estaba cocinando** la cena cuando sonó el teléfono.*
     c.   *Joseph cooked dinner when the phone rang.
     d.   Joseph *was cooking* dinner when the phone rang.

In contrast with grammatical aspect, and the usual perfective vs. imperfective distinction made in the literature, aspectual meanings are also provided by the lexical properties of the verb, crucially telicity (potential endpoints), durativity (duration of the event) and dynamicity (dynamic vs. non-dynamic events). This is known in the literature as lexical aspect or Aktionsart (Smith 1997; Vendler 1967). Vendler (1967) classifies verb types into four predicate types: *states, activities, accomplishments*, and *achievements*. States (*to be, to love, to feel*), and activities (*to run, to walk, to swim*) are durative as they can endure indefinitely or for a specific length of time. They are also atelic, as they have no intrinsic endpoint or internal structure (i.e., *Ramiro loves to cook*). Statives are also considered non-dynamic, in contrast with activities, which are both dynamic and durative (i.e., *John walked for two hours*). However, accomplishments (*to run a mile, to build a house*) and achievements (*to sink, to die*) are telic, as they have an intrinsic beginning and endpoint. The difference between these two types of predicates is that accomplishments describe a process leading to a result, and are therefore durative (i.e., *Mario built a boat*). Achievements, in contrast, are not durative; their endpoint occurs instantaneously with no time duration (i.e., *The boat sank*) (Labelle, Godard & Lonting 2002; Smith 1997).

Other researchers propose that aspectual descriptions are best determined by the compositional relation between the verb and the other elements within the verbal phrase. This is known as compositional aspect (Schmitt 1996; Verkuyl 1972). For instance, following Vendler's (1967) categorization, the verb *to run* is considered as an activity, as in *John ran for hours* (atelic, no inherent endpoint). However, this aspectual class changes to an accomplishment (telic, inherent endpoint) in cases like *John ran five miles*. The direct object *five miles* switches the aspectual meaning of the clause. Thus, aspectual values do not seem to be determined by the inherent lexical meaning of verbs but by the combination of the verb with other elements in the phrase.

3. The bilingual acquisition of tense and aspect morphology in Spanish

By age 4;0, the production of aspectual morphology in Spanish is relatively stable in normally developing monolingual children (Hernández Pina, 1984; Pérez-Pereira 1989; Pratt, McCurly & Grinstead 2009; Sebastián & Slobin 1994). In a cross-sectional study with 109 monolingual children from Spain (aged 3;0 to 6;0), Pérez-Pereira (1989) found clear patterns of imperfect tense morphology by age 4;0, with a 98% proportion of correct responses with real words for the imperfect and 74% for the preterite. The author argues that the lower proportion of target production with the preterite might stem from the use of verbs with irregular past tense marking such as *anduvo* "walked", *trajo* "brought", *condujo* "drove" and *durmió* "slept". These forms showed a tendency for regularization of the preterite (*andó*, "walked", *trayó*, "brought", *condució*, "drove", *dormió*, "slept"). The author concludes that the learning of irregular past tense forms continues past the age of 6;0, confirming previous research (Hernández Pina 1984).

In a more recent study with 23 monolingual speakers of Spanish aged 2;11 to 4;7, Grinstead, Pratt and McCurly (2009) examined the interpretation of future, present and past events via a picture matching task. Group results show a mean correct answer rate above chance (62%), with higher levels of accuracy of picture and verbal matching with the present tense pictures to present tense sentences, followed by past to past and finally future to future. The authors found that children are more successful matching past telic verbs (*dibujar un barco*, "draw a ship") than they are at matching past atelic verbs (*montar a caballo*, "ride a horse"). Although the children were able to comprehend tense separately from the lexical aspect, they were more successful when aspect and tense were combined.

In contrast to monolingual development, the target interpretation and production of verbal morphology in Spanish has been found to be challenging for bilingual children (Potowski 2005; Sánchez 2004; Silva-Corvalán 1994, 2003, forthcoming), adult L2 learners (Cuza 2008, 2010; Montrul & Slabakova 2002; Pérez-Leroux, Cuza, Majlanova & Sánchez 2008; Salaberry 2002) and adult Spanish heritage speakers (Montrul 2002; Montrul & Perpiñán 2011). In the specific case of Spanish-English bilingual children, Silva-Corvalán (1994) found patterns of aspectual simplification evidenced in an overextension of the preterite form to contexts where the imperfect should be used. This crucially affected stative verbs in the preterite and achievement verbs in the imperfect. As in the case of L2 acquisition, it appears as if bilingual children are using the preterite past tense marking as a default strategy due to cross-linguistic influence from the English simple past (unmarked, default option).

Sánchez (2004) examined two story retelling tasks, one written and one oral, in 38 Spanish-Quechua bilingual children and 10 monolingual Spanish children from Peru. The author shows that transfer occurs cross-linguistically among categories that are present in both languages and that have some functions in common but not others. The categories under examination by Sánchez converge in that, in both languages, they express past tense. However, in Spanish these categories also mark aspect whereas in Quechua they mark evidentiality. Sánchez found strong evidence showing that, when speaking Spanish, Quechua speakers favor the imperfective tense more than monolinguals, which is interpreted as being more reportative. Similarly, the bilinguals used some attested verb forms when retelling stories in Quechua, where all verbs should normally be reportative, due to influence of aspectual marking in Spanish, although this occurred in only 6 instances.

Potowski (2005) tested the *Lexical Aspect Hypothesis* (Andersen 1986; Bardovi-Harlig 1995), which argues for a correlation between inherent lexical aspect and the aspectual inflectional marking on the verb. Preterite forms are argued to appear first with achievements predicates, then with accomplishments and finally with states and activities. Imperfect forms are argued to appear after preterite forms, first with stative verbs, then with activities and finally with accomplishments and achievements (Liskin-Gasparro 2000; Salaberry 1999, 2002; Shirai & Andersen 1995). Using a written retelling task and an oral narrative, Potowski examined the use of preterite vs. imperfect distinctions among L2 learners and simultaneous bilingual children from a dual-immersion school in Chicago. The author did not find support for the Lexical Aspect Hypothesis since there were no group differences in aspectual marking selection across the different types of predicates. However, in general, the L1 Spanish speakers were more accurate than the simultaneous bilinguals who were more accurate than the L2 speakers.

Regarding English-speaking L2 learners of Spanish, previous research shows significant difficulties evidenced in an overextension of the preterite to contexts where the imperfect should be used. Following Giorgi & Pianesi's (1997) morphosyntactic approach, Montrul and colleagues argue that the difficulties with aspectual differences stem from the inability of L2 learners to completely acquire the [±perfective] functional aspectual features of the Spanish aspectual system, not instantiated in English (+perfective only). L2 learners are then unable to successfully associate the corresponding aspectual features with tense/aspect morphemes (Montrul 2002; Slabakova & Montrul 2002).

Other researchers follow de Swart's (1998) selectional view of aspectual differences among English-speaking L2 learners (Cuza 2010; Pérez-Leroux et al. 2008). de Swart's (1998) proposal is based on the notion that aspectual oppositions rely on the semantic-selectional features that tense heads are able to select. Within this theoretical framework, the difficulties L2 learners have are related to their inability to acquire the semantic patterns that tense heads select. This approach is optimal as it accounts for aspectual variation among languages with similar morphosyntactic patterns (i.e. Spanish and Portuguese). L2 learners may activate incorrect aspectual patterns due to the transfer of less complex L1 semantic patterns.

Montrul (2002) examined the interpretation and production of preterite versus imperfect distinctions among Spanish heritage speakers with different ages of onset of bilingualism. The author was particularly interested in whether the loss of aspectual morphology (morpho phonological spell outs) also implied the attrition of the semantic features of functional categories, and how three groups of bilinguals diverged depending on the age of onset of their bilingualism. As predicted, the three groups of bilinguals diverged significantly from the monolingual controls, evidenced in an inaccurate production of aspectual morphology and in the neutralization of preterite vs. imperfect semantic distinctions. Age of onset of bilingualism was the most predictive factor, with the late bilinguals showing fewer deficits in their Spanish L1. The simultaneous bilinguals were less accurate with the use of the preterite with stative verbs (using the imperfect instead) and the early bilinguals overextended the imperfect to telic predicates where the preterite should have been used.

More recently, Montrul and Perpiñán (2011) tested 60 adult heritage speakers of Spanish, 60 adult L2 learners of Spanish and 23 monolinguals to measure knowledge of preterite/imperfect and subjunctive/indicative. The study found that heritage speakers, although more accurate in early-acquired structures like tense and aspect, do not have an advantage over L2 learners in mood, a category acquired later in development. The task type also had significant group effect, giving L2 learners an advantage in tasks that involve more metalinguistic declarative knowledge (i.e., fill in the blank task) and heritage speakers an advantage in more 'intuitive' tasks (i.e., grammaticality judgment task).

3.1 Developmental implications for child and adult heritage Spanish

The acquisition of aspectual morphology among child and adult heritage speakers of Spanish is a challenging process where different linguistic and psycholinguistic dimensions play a role (Silva-Corvalán forthcoming). These include reduced input and use of the first language (coupled with age-related developmental issues) and semantic transfer from the dominant language (English). First, young children from Hispanic backgrounds living in an English dominant context have limited input and use of their mother tongue outside the home environment (Montrul 2008; Pérez-Leroux, Cuza & Thomas 2011). This is particularly the case after immersion in the public school system begins. Immersion in an English-only school system and the related development of English-only peer relationships, make it challenging for young children to continue developing and maintaining their L1 (Jia 1998), specifically age-appropriate lexical categories (verbs and nouns) and their syntactic relations. Second, English differs from Spanish in that the preterite form does not select for any specific aspectual description, but is rather neutral. Within de Swart's (1998) selectional approach, the past tense head in English selects both perfective and imperfective eventualities (*John baked a cake* and *John baked cakes*). This may lead to a higher preference for the use of the preterite tense, compared to monolingual speakers. The preterite may be taken as the preferred aspectual marker due to cross-linguistic influence from English, where there is no imperfect morphology. Bilingual speakers may therefore overextend the preterite to contexts where the imperfect should be used, as documented in previous research with Spanish-English bilingual children and adults (Cuza 2008, 2010; Montrul 2002; Silva-Corvalán 1994). It is also possible that bilingual children and adults may use non-target verbal forms as an avoidance strategy. For instance, they may use the present tense instead of the past tense due to their lack of acquisition or L1 attrition of past tense forms (Laleko 2010). This is particularly so, given that the present tense also selects imperfective eventualities.

We would like to propose that reduced input and use of Spanish during early childhood and L2 lexical transfer may lead to the child L1 attrition or incomplete development of the semantic meaning of verbs, which may cause difficulties in the target selection of past tense aspectual morphology. That is, we view the acquisition of tense/aspect morphology in bilingual children as intrinsically linked to the lexical/semantic development of tense heads. Once a child has acquired verb meaning, and its corresponding argument/event structure, it is easier for the child to select the appropriate aspectual value in the past tense (preterite vs. imperfect). Until then, the bilingual speaker may either select non-target aspectual descriptions (preterite vs. imperfect or vice versa) due to underspecification of the aspectual selectional properties of tense heads or simply show a marked preference for the use of the preterite (default aspectual marker) with a consequent underproduction of imperfect forms. In the specific case of Spanish, bilingual speakers may also overuse the present tense as a type of avoidance strategy for the imperfect tense. Given that the present tense in Spanish (1) can be used to report a past event (reportive speech), (2) describes imperfective eventuality types, and (3) is less marked than imperfective aspectual morphology (Silva-Corvalán forthcoming), its use might become a preferred communicative strategy in child and adult Spanish-English bilinguals together with preterite forms. This bilingual behavior might diverge from monolingual speakers who we predict will show a more balanced production of temporal morphology (preterite, imperfect and present tense).

Finally, we predict cross-linguistic influence from English to increase as Spanish children get older and become more dominant in English (Cuza & Strik 2012; Silva-Corvalán 2003). We propose a bilingual continuum, along the lines of Silva-Corvalán (1994), which starts during early childhood and continues to develop or under-develop during the life span of the bilingual speaker according to the specific input conditions to which the bilingual speaker is exposed. If difficulties with tense and aspect result from child L1 attrition during early childhood and increased L2 dominance (causing a diminished exposure to and contact with the L1 as a result of increased use of the L2), we expect younger children to show better patterns of aspectual production than their older counterparts who are in most scenarios more L2 dominant.

4. The study

4.1   Participants

We discuss semi-spontaneous data from thirty-six (n = 36) participants: 13 simultaneous Spanish-English bilingual children, 11 adult heritage speakers of Spanish, 9 monolingual Spanish children and 3 adult monolinguals. Parents of bilingual children and the adult heritage speakers completed a language history questionnaire which elicited information on place of birth, level of education, linguistic proficiency in each language and patterns of language use at home, school, work and social situations. Parents also completed a child history questionnaire which elicited information on home language practices and child language dominance. The adult heritage speakers also completed an independent proficiency test (adapted version of the *Diploma de Español como Lengua Extranjera*, DELE). Unlike much of the existing research on heritage language learning, this study focuses on child heritage speakers of Spanish as well as adults, allowing a direct comparison between aspectual marking strategies used by children vs. adults, and includes a monolingual baseline to look at the effect of reduced input in Spanish on the patterns of aspectual marking of heritage speakers.

The group of bilingual children (n = 13) was divided into two groups according to their age at time of testing: younger bilingual children (n = 7, age range 5;0–7;4; mean, 6;6) and older bilingual children (n = 6, age range 8;1–9;11; mean, 8;6). All children were born and raised in the United States, except one who immigrated at the age of 3. In terms of language dominance, parents reported 72% (5/7) of the younger children to be *very fluent* or *completely fluent* in Spanish, while the remaining 28% (2/7) were reported to be *somewhat fluent*. Regarding fluency in English, 57% (4/7) were reported to be *very fluent* or *completely fluent* while 43% (3/7) were reported to be *somewhat fluent*. In contrast with the younger children, parents reported 83% (5/6) of the older children to be *somewhat fluent* in Spanish and only 17% (1/6) was considered to be *very fluent*. Regarding their dominance in English, 100% (6/6) of the older children were reported to be *completely fluent* in English. As expected, older children were reported to be more dominant in English than in Spanish in contrast with the younger children. All of the parents were born and raised in Mexico and had resided in the United States for an average of 11 years (range 6–19 years). Their proficiency in English was reported to be basic, and most families came from low socio-economic backgrounds. Spanish was the language of the home and their children were all enrolled in English-only schools in the American Midwest (Indiana).

The adult heritage speakers' group was formed of eleven (n = 11) US born heritage speakers enrolled at a large research university in the American Midwest. Their average age at time of testing was 18 years old (range, 18–23) and 73% (8/11) of them came from families with Mexican heritage. Their language of instruction in primary and high school was English. Six of the participants (55%) reported speaking only Spanish at home in childhood and five (45%) reported speaking both English and Spanish. In terms of language use, participants reported speaking English or mostly English at school and work. At home, 36% reported speaking Spanish or mostly Spanish, 36% reported speaking both, and the rest reported speaking mostly English (18%) or a little more English (9%). In social situations, 64% reported speaking mostly English and 27% reported speaking both.

Following previous research with adult L2 learners and Spanish heritage speakers (Cuza 2012; Montrul & Slabakova 2003), an adapted version of the *Diploma de Español como Lengua Segunda* (DELE) and a multiple choice vocabulary section adapted from an MLA test were used as an independent proficiency measure in Spanish. Four of the participants were classified as advanced learners (mean score, 42/50), six as intermediate learners (mean score, 34/50) and one as a low proficiency learner (score, 28/50).

The monolingual group was comprised of 12 monolingual speakers of Spanish: 9 children and 3 adults. The monolingual child group was divided into two groups according to their age: younger monolingual children (n = 5, mean age 5;00) and older monolingual children (n = 4, mean age 9;00). All the monolinguals were born and raised in Spain in a strictly one-language environment.

4.2   Task and coding

Following previous research (Liskin-Gasparro 2000; Silva-Corvalán 1994, forthcoming), the bilingual children and adult heritage speakers completed a semi-spontaneous oral production task (narrative). Our goal was to analyze the overall patterns of occurrence of preterite versus imperfect forms (i.e., overuse or underuse of forms). This methodology is advantageous as it allows us to focus on the overall patterns of language use, rather than in specific errors, and to observe performance differences between heritage and monolingual grammars that are not necessarily ungrammatical or manifested in production errors. This is particularly relevant to aspectual distinctions, where there is a very fine line between what is ungrammatical or not. Another advantage is that it enables the elicitation of certain forms (preterite, imperfect) within a naturalistic setting (telling a story) without the need of the artificial scenario of an experimental setting. Given that the data collection took place in the United States, we were not able to implement the elicited production task on monolingual Spanish speakers. Instead, we selected 12 narratives by monolingual speakers matched by age from the CHILDES database (Spanish-Sebastián Corpus).

The bilingual children and adult heritage speakers were asked to narrate the fictional story *Little Red Riding Hood* in the past tense on the basis of wordless images from the story. The participants were asked to retell the story using the expression *había una vez* "once upon a time". The narratives were transcribed using the CHAT transcription system. As to the monolingual speakers' narratives, these were elicited using Mercer Mayer's wordless frog story picture book, entitled *Frog, where are you?* The book tells a story without words in 24 pictures (for more information on this work, its rationale, and the various data analysis procedures, see Berman & Slobin 1994). The procedure was similar to ours in that the monolingual children and adults were explicitly oriented to the book as presenting a "story". Specifically, they were asked to look through the entire book, and then to tell the story again, while looking at the pictures. However, the interviewer avoided prompts that would lead to a particular choice of verb tense or aspectual marking.

The aim of this analysis was to compare the levels of preterite and imperfect in bilinguals compared to monolingual speakers of Spanish. All sentences containing inflected and non-inflected verbs were extracted and coded for tense (preterite, imperfect, present, present perfect, past perfect, present progressive, past progressive, future, etc.), and grammatical aspect (perfective or imperfective).[1] We limited our analysis to sentences used in the narratives (*Little Red Riding Hood* in the case of the bilinguals, and *Frog, where are you?* in the case of the monolinguals), excluding any other forms of interaction with the interviewer. We analyzed a total of 1,422 utterances for use of tense and use of perfective vs. imperfective (bilingual children, $N = 264$; bilingual adults, $N = 409$; monolingual children, $N = 465$; monolingual adults, $N = 284$). We compared bilingual children with monolingual children, bilingual adults with monolingual adults, and compared the different age groups (younger children, older children, adults) within the two language groups.

---

1.   A preliminary analysis on the use of the preterite and the imperfect per predicate type showed a preference for the use of the preterite with telic predicates among the bilingual speakers. However, the production of the imperfect was very limited and thus we limit our discussion to the overall proportion of tense (preterite, imperfect, present) and grammatical aspect (perfective, imperfective) found among bilingual and monolingual groups.

4.3   Results

4.3.1   *Tense*

We compared use of tense in child bilinguals (all ages) in relation to child monolinguals. That is, the proportion of preterite, imperfect, present perfect, past perfect, present progressive, past progressive, present and other (i.e., future, conditional, subjunctive forms and non-inflected forms such as the infinitive or the gerund) present in the analyzed utterances. We found that both the child monolinguals and the child bilinguals showed a higher proportion of preterite forms (38.92%, and 40.53% respectively) compared to the imperfect tense (15.48% and 13.26%). Both groups also showed a high proportion of present tense use (30.97%, and 27.27%). These results are represented in Figure 1 and Table 1 below:

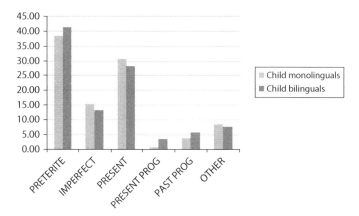

Figure 1. Proportion of grammatical tense produced by monolingual and bilingual children

Table 1. Raw numbers and proportions of grammatical tense produced by monolingual and bilingual children

	CHILD MONOLINGUALS		CHILD BILINGUALS	
	N	%	N	%
PRETERITE	181	38.92	107	40.53
IMPERFECT	72	15.48	35	13.26
PRESENT	144	30.97	73	27.27
PAST PROG	18	3.87	15	5.68
PRES PROG	3	0.65	9	3.41
OTHER	47	10.11	26	9.85
TOTAL	465	100	264	100

The differences in the proportion of preterite, imperfect and present found in the narratives were significant for child bilinguals [$\chi^2(2, N = 214) = 36.35, p = .000$] and child monolinguals [$\chi^2(2, N = 397) = 46.43, p = .000$]. The differences between child bilinguals and child monolinguals were significant for the preterite [$\chi^2(1, N = 288) = 19.01, p = .000$], the imperfect [$\chi^2(1, N = 107) = 12.79, p = .001$] and the present [$\chi^2(1, N = 216) = 24.00, p = .000$].

With regard to the adult speakers, the bilinguals showed much higher production of preterite forms (34.23%), and reduced production of the imperfect (10.51%). This contrasts with the adult monolinguals, who showed a more balanced production of preterite (27.11%) and imperfect (22.89%) forms. These results are represented in Figure 2 and Table 2:

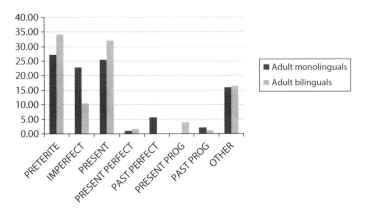

Figure 2. Proportion of grammatical tense produced by monolingual and bilingual adults

Table 2. Raw numbers and proportion of grammatical tense produced by monolingual and bilingual adults

	ADULT MONOLINGUALS		ADULT BILINGUALS	
	N	%	N	%
PRETERITE	77	27.11	140	34.23
IMPERFECT	65	22.89	43	10.51
PRESENT	72	25.35	131	32.03
PAST PROG	6	2.11	5	1.22
PRES PROG	0	0	16	3.91
OTHER	64	22.54	74	18.09
TOTAL	284	100	409	100

The differences in the production of preterite, imperfect and present found in the narratives were significant for adult bilinguals [$\chi^2(2, N = 314) = 54.88, p = .000$], but not for adult monolinguals [$\chi^2(2, N = 214) = 1.02, p = .601$]. The differences between adult bilinguals and adult monolinguals were significant for the preterite [$\chi^2(1, N = 217) = 18.29, p = .000$], the imperfect [$\chi^2(1, N = 108) = 4.48, p = .034$] and the present [$\chi^2(1, N = 230) = 17.15, p = .000$].

Although our monolingual sample for both children and adults were speakers of Peninsular Spanish, which favors the use of the present perfect (*he ido* 'I have gone') over the use of the preterite (*fui* 'I went') in certain contexts, we found very few tokens of present perfect: three tokens in the monolingual adult data (e.g., *ha desaparecido* 'he/she disappeared') and eight tokens in the monolingual child data (e.g., *se ha escapado* 'he/she has escaped'). We also found some use of the present progressive in the data from the bilingual adults (3.91%), but none in the data from the monolingual adults.

We also compared use of tense by age group (younger children, older children, and adults). As expected, we found that the older bilingual children used a higher proportion of preterite forms than the younger bilingual children (48.08% vs. 29.63%), but the use of the imperfect remained relatively stable between the two groups (11.11% and 14.74%). The younger bilingual children used a higher pro-portion of present tense (38.89%) than the older bilingual children (19.23%). These results are represented in Figure 3 and Table 3.

The differences in the production of preterite, imperfect and present found in the narratives were significant for younger bilingual children [$\chi^2(2, N = 86) = 16.28, p = .000$] and older bilingual children [$\chi^2(2, N = 128) = 37.33, p = .000$]. The differences between younger and older bilingual children were significant for the

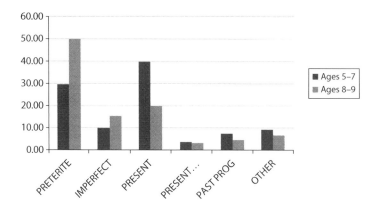

Figure 3. Proportion of grammatical tense use by younger and older bilingual children

Table 3. Raw numbers and proportion of grammatical tense use by younger and older bilingual children

	CHILD BILINGUALS (AGES 5–7)		CHILD BILINGUALS (AGES 8–9)	
	N	%	N	%
PRETERITE	32	29.63	75	48.08
IMPERFECT	12	11.11	23	14.74
PRESENT	42	38.89	30	19.23
PAST PROG	8	7.41	7	4.49
PRES PROG	4	3.70	5	3.21
OTHER	10	9.26	16	10.26
TOTAL	108	100	156	100

preterite $[\chi^2(1, N = 107) = 17.28, p = .000]$ and the imperfect $[\chi^2(1, N = 35) = 6.08, p = .014]$, but not for the present $[\chi^2(1, N = 72) = 2.00, p = .157]$.[2]

Compared to the bilingual children (and particularly the older bilingual children), the proportion of preterite and imperfect decreases for the adult bilinguals (34.23% and 10.51%, respectively), whereas the proportion of present increases (32.03%) (as the use of the preterite decreases). This is represented in Figure 4 and Table 4:

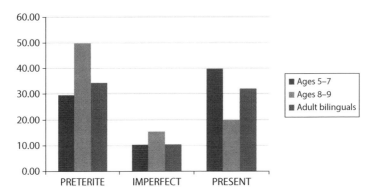

Figure 4. Proportion of preterite, imperfect and present tense use among younger, older and adult bilinguals

2. We conducted a chi-square analysis to compare the production of tense and aspect in the different language and age groups. As a non-parametric test, it tends to overestimate differences and does not correct for type 1 errors. However, it is the appropriate test to examine nominal (categorical) variables and non-balanced/variable data.

Table 4. Raw numbers and proportion of preterite, imperfect and present tense use among younger, older and adult bilinguals

	PRETERITE		IMPERFECT		PRESENT	
	N	%	N	%	N	%
AGES 5–7	32	29.63	12	11.11	42	38.89
AGES 8–9	75	48.08	23	14.74	30	19.23
ADULT BIL	140	34.23	43	10.51	131	32.03

The differences between adult and child bilinguals were significant for the preterite [$\chi^2(2, N = 247) = 71.81, p = .000$], the imperfect [$\chi^2(2, N = 78) = 19.00, p = .000$] and the present [$\chi^2(2, N = 203) = 89.98, p = .000$].

With regard to the monolinguals, we found that the older children use a higher proportion of present tense than the younger children and the adult monolinguals (44.98% vs. 19.53% and 25.35%, respectively). The younger children use a higher proportion of preterite as opposed to the older children and the monolingual adults (44.53% vs. 32.06% and 27.11%, respectively). This is shown in Table 5.

The differences in the production of preterite, imperfect and present in the narratives were significant for younger children [$\chi^2(2, N = 209) = 42.50, p = .000$] and older children [$\chi^2(2, N = 188) = 36.26, p = .000$]. The differences between the younger and older children were significant for the preterite [$\chi^2(1, N = 181) = 12.20, p = .000$], the imperfect [$\chi^2(1, N = 72) = 4.50, p = .034$] and the present [$\chi^2(1, N = 144) = 13.44, p = .000$]. The differences between monolingual children and adults were significant for the preterite [$\chi^2(2, N = 258) = 14.26, p = .001$], the imperfect [$\chi^2(2, N = 137), p = .000$] and the present [$\chi^2(2, N = 216) = 13.44, p = .001$].

Table 5. Proportion of preterite, imperfect and present tense use among younger, older and adult monolinguals

	PRETERITE		IMPERFECT		PRESENT	
	N	%	N	%	N	%
AGES 5–7	114	44.53	45	17.58	50	19.53
AGES 8–9	67	32.06	27	12.92	94	44.98
ADULT MON	77	27.11	65	22.89	72	25.35

4.3.2   *Grammatical aspect*

We compared the use of perfective vs. imperfective forms in bilingual children as opposed to monolingual children (all ages) found in the analyzed utterances. Perfective forms include the preterite and the present perfect. Imperfective forms include the imperfect, the present progressive and the past progressive. Although the present tense is an imperfective form, we analyzed it separately because of the high proportion of present found in the narratives.

Bilingual and monolingual children use roughly the same proportion of perfective forms to imperfective forms (44.96% and 44.76% of perfective forms vs. 24.37% and 21.68% of imperfective forms respectively). In contrast, the use of perfective vs. imperfective forms in monolingual adults is somewhat more balanced than in bilingual adults (40.17% vs. 29.71% as opposed to 42.98% vs. 18.71%). In bilinguals, the proportion of perfective forms and imperfective forms decreases in adults, at the same time as the proportion of present tense increases (38.30% vs. 30.67%). In monolinguals, the proportion of perfective forms decreases in adults (40.17% vs. 44.76%%), as the use of imperfective forms increases (29.71% vs. 21.68%). These results are represented in Table 6.

The differences in the production of perfective vs. imperfective forms used in the narratives were significant for bilingual children [$\chi^2(1, N = 165) = 18.33$, $p = .000$], monolingual children [$\chi^2(1, N = 284) = 35.21, p = .000$], bilingual adults [$\chi^2(1, N = 211) = 32.65, p = .000$] and marginally significant for monolingual adults [$\chi^2(1, N = 167) = 3.74, p = .053$]. The differences between child bilinguals and monolinguals were significant for perfective forms [$\chi^2(1, N = 302) = 22.26, p = .000$] and imperfective forms [$\chi^2(1, N = 147) = 9.31, p = .002$]. The differences between adult bilinguals and monolinguals were also significant for perfective forms [$\chi^2(1, N = 243) = 10.70, p = .001$], but not for imperfective forms [$\chi^2(1, N = 135) = .36, p = .547$].

We also compared the use of perfective vs. imperfective forms by age group (younger children, older children, adults). We observed that the proportion of perfective forms increases in the older bilingual children compared to the younger bilingual children (53.57% vs. 32.65%). This is probably related to the increased use of the preterite in the older children observed previously. The proportion of perfective forms decreases in the adult bilinguals (42.98%). This is probably related to the increased use of the present in the adults compared to the older children

Table 6. Proportion of perfective and imperfective grammatical aspect among all groups

	PERFECTIVE		IMPERFECTIVE		PRESENT	
	N	%	N	%	N	%
CHILD BIL	107	44.96	58	24.37	73	30.67
CHILD MON	192	44.76	93	21.68	144	33.57
ADULT BIL	147	42.98	64	18.71	131	38.30
ADULT MON	96	40.17	71	29.71	72	30.13

observed previously. The proportion of imperfective forms also decreases in the adult bilinguals. These results are represented in Figure 5 and Table 7:

The differences between younger and older bilingual children were significant for perfective forms [$\chi^2(1, N = 110) = 19.24, p = .000$] and not significant for imperfective forms [$\chi^2(1, N = 55) = 1.47, p = .225$]. The differences between older bilingual children and adult bilinguals were also significant for perfective forms [$\chi^2(1, N = 225) = 21.16, p = .000$] and for imperfective forms [$\chi^2(2, N = 257) = 78.22\ p = .000$].

With regard to the monolinguals, the proportion of perfective forms is greatest in the younger children (52.59%), whereas the proportion of imperfective forms is greatest in the adults (29.71%). The older children produce the highest proportion of present tense forms (47.72%). These results are represented in Table 8.

The differences between younger and older monolingual children were significant for perfective forms [$\chi^2(1, N = 192) = 14.08, p = .000$] and imperfective forms [$\chi^2(1, N = 92) = 7.35, p = .007$]. The differences between monolingual children and adult monolinguals were significant for perfective forms [$\chi^2(2, N = 288) = 14.08, p = .001$] and for imperfective forms [$\chi^2(2, N = 163) = 13.89, p = .001$].

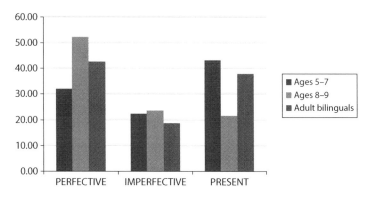

Figure 5. Proportion of perfective and imperfective grammatical aspect among all groups

Table 7. Raw numbers and proportion of perfective and imperfective grammatical aspect among all groups

	PERFECTIVE		IMPERFECTIVE		PRESENT	
	N	%	N	%	N	%
AGES 5–7	32	32.65	23	23.47	43	43.88
AGES 8–9	75	53.57	35	25.00	30	21.43
ADULT BIL	147	42.98	64	18.71	131	38.30

Table 8. Proportion of perfective and imperfective grammatical aspect among younger, older and adult monolinguals

	PRETERITE		IMPERFECT		PRESENT	
	N	%	N	%	N	%
AGES 5–7	122	52.59	60	25.86	50	21.55
AGES 8–9	70	35.53	33	16.75	94	47.72
ADULT MON	96	40.17	71	29.71	72	30.13

4.3.3 Discussion

In terms of grammatical tense, our results demonstrate an increased production of the preterite tense among older bilingual children compared to younger children and adult bilinguals. This confirms our hypotheses. The older bilingual children use more instances of preterite forms than any other tense, followed by the use of present tense forms, which also confirms our expectations. The present tense was used in some occasions in contexts where the preterite or the imperfect tense is normally preferred in monolingual speakers, as shown below:

(5) *Después, el lobo quería meterse en casa de la abuela... para comer el, ... el comida que #tiene (tenía, IMP) caperucita roja y se *vistó (vistió) como el abuela y estaba esperando. El Caperucita Roja #viene (vino, PRET). #Toca (tocó, PRET) el puerta. Después el lobo #dice (dijo), ¿Qué tal? Y el Caperucita Roja #dice (le dijo) qué grande nariz, qué grande ojos, qué grande orejas y qué grande dientes y después el lobo #quiere (quería, IMP) comer comida que #tiene (tenía) El Caperucita Roja.*

"Then the wolf wanted to get inside the grandma's house... to eat the, ... the food that the Little Red Riding Hood *has* and dressed like the grandma and he was waiting. The Little Red Riding Hood *comes*. She *knocks* at the door. Then the wolf says, "How are you? And the Little Red Riding Hood *says* what a big nose, what big eyes, what big ears, what big teeth and then the wolf *wants* to eat the food that the Little Red Riding Hood *has*." (ABA, M, 9;9)

This pattern of preterite and present tense use among the older children differed from the adult bilingual speakers, who use the preterite and the present tense almost equally. We did not find overgeneralization of the preterite form in contexts where the imperfect should have been used, in contrast with previous research (Montrul 2002; Silva-Corvalán 1994). The only errors found were related to incorrect tense conjugation, evidenced in a regularization of irregular past tense forms (e.g., *vinió* vs. *vino* "he/she came"), confirming previous research (Hernández Pina

1984), as well as the use of the present tense in contexts where the imperfect or preterite was preferred.

Regarding grammatical aspect, the older bilingual children show a high proportion of perfective forms, followed by a much lower production of the imperfect and even lower use of present tense forms. The adult bilinguals, on the other hand, showed a much lower production of perfective forms compared to the older children, a low use of imperfect forms, and higher production of present tense forms, forming a U-shaped development.

We argue that the overuse of the preterite among older children stems from transfer of the aspectual selectional properties that tense heads are able to select in English. Given that the English preterite is selectionally neutral, selecting both perfective and imperfective eventualities, Spanish bilingual children and adults tend to select the preterite more often than the imperfective, rather than having a random behavior or selecting the imperfective form, which is not realized morphologically in English. The imperfect is also more semantically marked/complex than the preterite tense given its wider association in terms of temporal points of reference (Silva-Corvalán forthcoming).[3] Thus, it would be expected to be lost first in the bilingual continuum or incompletely acquired (Silva-Corvalán 1991, forthcoming).

Our data also show a higher use of present tense forms among the adult bilinguals, compared to older bilingual children. It is possible that the adult bilinguals are using the present tense considerably more as a type of avoidance strategy. That is, the present tense appears to represent a competing form for the imperfect. This is consistent with previous research with heritage speakers and L2 learners where a less marked form (i.e., imperfect indicative, overt noun phrase) has been found to represent a competing form for more complex/marked options (imperfective subjunctive, object clitic) (Potowski, Jegerski & Morgan-Short 2009; Sánchez & Al-Kasey 1999; Silva-Corvalán 1994). The imperfect subjunctive occurs in subordinate clauses and is thus more complex to process than the simple present (Silva-Corvalán, forthcoming).

The adult bilinguals and the younger child bilinguals showed similar patterns of preterite and imperfect tense use (Figure 4). This suggests a possible regression process among the adult bilinguals back to early stages of bilingual development, corroborating previous research (Silva-Corvalán 2003). In contrast with the bilingual speakers, the monolinguals start out using more preterite and present tense forms but by the time they are adults the use of the preterite, the imperfect and the present becomes more or less balanced.

---

3.   Silva-Corvalán (forthcoming) considers the imperfect to have a level 3 of complexity, compared to the preterite, which has a level 1.

Although a longitudinal study is necessary to confirm a regression trend among the adult bilinguals due to L1 attrition or incomplete acquisition (see Silva-Corvalán 2003 and Potowski et al. 2009 for discussion), our cross-sectional data show that there is an increase in the use of the preterite during the ages of 8–9, compared to the younger children, but eventually the present tense starts to compete with the preterite in adulthood. This is not typical of the full-fledged temporal system characteristic of adult monolingual speakers, as our data also show (Figure 2), which suggests a case of L1 attrition rather than incomplete acquisition in the bilingual grammar of these speakers. This rationale, however, is not supported by the data in the case of the imperfect tense, which remains around the 10% range across all age groups. We found no significant development and later simplification of the imperfect form across the bilingual groups. This suggests incomplete development during early childhood, as has been previously argued by Montrul and colleagues. The end result, though, is a simplified temporal system, stemming from both L1 attrition and incomplete development. Rather than one process versus the other, our data show that both processes (L1 attrition and incomplete acquisition) can occur at the same time depending on the domain of linguistic knowledge.

To sum up, our results show that the process of tense and aspect development in heritage language learners of Spanish does not occur uniformly across the board but rather in a piece-meal fashion. Some properties will undergo L1 attrition (overuse of the preterite) (Polinsky 2011; Silva-Corvalán forthcoming) while more marked properties may indeed undergo incomplete development due to insufficient input to trigger the specification of relevant morpho semantic properties (Montrul 2002, 2004). The development of tense and aspect morphology in the heritage grammar appears to take independent paths. The preterite tense initially assumes both selectional values (perfective and imperfective eventualities), but eventually adult learners start to notice the presence of the imperfect form in the input. This causes them to rely more on the present tense, an imperfective tense by definition, as a type of an avoidance strategy (less marked form). Since the use of the present is pragmatically odd but not ungrammatical, we suspect that no explicit or implicit feedback is provided, and thus this form remains as an integral part of the bilingual aspectual system to denote past events. Laleko (2010) documents comparable patterns (preference for the perfective aspect and overuse of the present tense) in adult heritage speakers of Russian.

4.3.4 Implications for heritage language teaching pedagogy

Our results show differential outcomes in the development of aspectual distinctions in Spanish among young bilingual children and adult bilinguals. Bilingual children seem to prefer the preterite form while adult speakers show a preference for both the preterite and the present tense. In contrast with previous research documenting overextension of the preterite to imperfect contexts (Montrul 2002; Silva-Corvalán 1994), their use of preterite forms was contextually appropriate as represented in (5). Their difficulties were also related to a decreased production of the imperfect, which appears to be substituted by the present tense, especially among the adult heritage speakers.

These results suggest that the pedagogical emphasis should be placed on the teaching of imperfect forms from early on and on target form-meaning connections. This, however, must be conducted in a meaningful and age-appropriate way. In most Spanish heritage language textbooks, it is safe to say that preterite vs. imperfect distinctions are presented explicitly to the students (Marqués 2008). The preterite is often taught as the tense that refers to "completed events in the past" and the imperfect as the tense for "habitual events in the past". This explanation is often followed by written exercises in the form of cloze tests where students must fill in blank spaces using the correct form. This type of pedagogy has proven to be ineffectual for L2 learners who, in most scenarios, fail to achieve native-like knowledge of aspectual distinctions, and is also quite ineffectual for heritage speakers.

Instead, interactive reading aloud practices of stories in Spanish (e.g., fairy tales in the case of child heritage language learners) might be an effective way to reinforce the use of the imperfect and it's meaning both at home and in the school setting. Young children enjoy guided reading activities, and when done in small groups, this could be an effective input and output activity. Children can also be asked to retell the stories so they become aware of the different aspectual uses while they read aloud. Reading aloud practices, although an integral part of most literacy programs (Dreher 2003; Martin 1993) so far have not been consistently integrated into heritage language pedagogy. Some instructors may have the misconception that heritage speakers do not need oral practice in Spanish because they already speak the language or that reading is not a skill that needs to be developed because they can transfer that skill from English. This misguided belief may lead some practitioners to prioritize writing proficiency and put less emphasis in the development of reading accuracy and fluency. Although this cannot be generalized across the board, the development of reading fluency, accuracy and comprehension needs to be integrated more consistently in heritage language curricula, just like it is in elementary literacy instruction (Allington & Johnston 2002).

Consistent and frequent reading lessons and reading aloud practices, together with effective focus-on-form techniques (Doughty & Williams 1998; Montrul & Bowles 2010; Potowski, et al. 2009) might help heritage speakers to draw their attention to the notorious Spanish *imperfecto* and help them perceive and manipulate aspectual distinctions more accurately. Following VanPatten's (2007) methodology, and specifically the *Processing Instruction Approach*, the readings should be structured so that they are exempt of any temporal adverbs (*siempre* "always", *normalmente*, "usually") so that the learners are forced to pay attention to the verbal ending rather than processing the meaning of the sentence via the lexical item or content word (*Lexical Preference Principle*, Lee & VanPatten 2003; VanPatten & Cadierno 1993). This, of course, must take place in a communicative, engaging and meaningful way, which is the challenge many practitioners still have in understanding and integrating reading practice into the heritage language classroom.

5. Conclusions

Finding the linguistic and psycholinguistic sources of heritage speakers' intuitions and discovering whether their difficulties stem from incomplete development or the L1 attrition of previously learned properties is crucial to understanding how heritage speakers comprehend and manipulate their minority-language system (Cuza & Pérez-Tattam submitted; Montrul 2011; Polinsky 2011; Rothman 2007). This issue also has crucial implications for the type of pedagogical intervention heritage language instructors should implement. The process of re-activating previously learned properties is psycholinguistically different from the process of teaching specific form-meaning connections from scratch (Valdés 2005). This is particularly so when the pedagogical intervention is applied to young minority-language children from different linguistic, sociocultural and socioeconomic backgrounds.

The objective of this study was to inform the development of pedagogical interventions in Spanish language for child and adult heritage Spanish speakers by analyzing the development of tense/aspect morphology among young, older and adult Spanish-English bilingual speakers born and raised in the United States. Our research questions were: Do young and adult heritage speakers of Spanish born and raised in the US show accurate and consistent production of past tense aspectual morphology? If not, do their difficulties increase with age as heritage speakers leave the home environment and integrate into the dominant L2 context? Finally, we discussed implications of our results for heritage language pedagogy, and specifically the teaching of preterite vs. imperfect distinctions to Spanish heritage speakers.

The results of this cross-sectional study show difficulties exhibited by child and adult heritage speakers of Spanish in their production of past tense morphology. Older children showed elevated levels of preterite use, in contrast with their younger counterparts, while the adult learners demonstrated almost equal number of preterite and present tense use. These results contrast with adult monolinguals who demonstrated a more balanced production of preterite, imperfect and present tense morphology. Although our data do not show overextension of the preterite to imperfect contexts, we did find use of the present tense among the bilingual speakers in contexts where the imperfect tense was more pragmatically felicitous and the preferred form among monolingual speakers of Spanish.

We have argued that the overproduction of the preterite tense stems from lexical (semantic) transfer from English, where the simple past selects both perfective and imperfective eventualities. There appears to be a morphosemantic restructuring in the child bilingual grammar, where one form assumes two aspectual values. In addition, we have argued that, in the process of heritage language development, both L1 attrition and incomplete development play a fundamental role depending on the type of linguistic knowledge. We have observed an overuse of the preterite among the older children but this pattern decreases in adulthood, when the present tense becomes a competing form. This is, without a doubt, the result of L1 attrition during the life span, confirming recent research (Polinsky 2011; Silva-Corvalán 2003). However, we have also observed that this underdevelopment pattern does not affect the use of the imperfect, which remains in the 10% range across all age groups in the bilingual population. This indicates that the Spanish imperfect tense, and related semantic entailments remain incompletely acquired in the heritage language grammar and eventually yield their place to the competing present tense, also an imperfective form, during adulthood. As indicated by one of the reviewers, preferences in production are not a direct window into the speakers' knowledge of the relevant aspectual distinctions, and the results should be taken with caution. However, production data do give us an insight into developmental trends and differences across ages and language backgrounds.

Finally, we have suggested that, In the case of aspectual marking in Spanish, future pedagogical interventions with child and adult heritage speakers focus on the development of interactive reading aloud and retelling activities to draw the bilinguals' attention to target form-meaning connections, especially in relation to the *imperfecto*, to target decreased production of the imperfect (in children and adults) and substitution of the imperfect by the present (particularly in adults). Reading aloud activities are a crucial component of most L1 literacy programs, and should thus be integrated consistently into heritage language pedagogy at all levels of instruction.

This study adds to previous research by further examining current discussions on the source of heritage speakers' linguistic competence (incomplete acquisition vs. L1 attrition). It also contributes to previous research on the study of temporal morphology in child as well as adult heritage Spanish, an area of research still underexplored in these populations. We have also provided some suggestions based on linguistic research relative to pedagogical applications. This is important given the necessity to implement scientifically sounded curricula at both the elementary and university levels. Future research would benefit from a larger data set per age group, and from a long-term pedagogical intervention to validate the effects of interactive reading aloud activities in the specification of aspectual morphology in heritage Spanish.

References

Allington, R. & Johnston P. (2002). *Reading to learn: Lessons from exemplary fourth-grade classrooms.* London: Guilford Press.

Andersen, J. (1986). El desarrollo de la morfología verbal en el español como sengundo idioma. In J. Meisel (Ed.), *Adquisición de lenguaje* (pp. 115–138). Frankfurt: Vervuert.

Bardovi-Harlig, K. (1995). The interaction of pedagogy and natural sequences in the acquisition of tense and aspect. In F.R. Eckman, D. Highland, P.W. Lee, J. Mileham & R.R. Weber (Eds.), *Second language acquisition theory and pedagogy* (pp. 151–168). Mahwah, NJ: Lawrence Erlbaum Associates.

Berman, R., & Slobin, D. (1994). *Relating events in narrative: A crosslinguistic developmental study.* Hillsdale, NJ: Lawrence Erlbaum Associates.

Bowles, M. (2011). Exploring the role of modality: L2-heritage learner interactions in the Spanish language classroom. *The Heritage Language Journal, 8*, 30–65.

Comrie, B. (1976). *Aspect.* Cambridge, UK: Cambridge University Press.

Cuza, A. (2008). *The L2 acquisition and L1 attrition of the interpretation and use of aspectual properties in Spanish among English-speaking L2 learners and long-term Spanish immigrants.* Unpublished PhD dissertation, University of Toronto.

Cuza, A. (2010). The L2 acquisition of aspectual properties in Spanish. *Canadian Journal of Linguistics, 55*(2), 1001–1028.

Cuza, A. (2012). Cross-linguistic influence at the syntax proper: Interrogative subject-verb inversion in heritage Spanish. *The International Journal of Bilingualism.* , 17(1), 71–96.

Cuza, A., & Frank, J. (2011). Transfer effects at the syntax-semantics interface: The case of double-*que* questions in heritage Spanish. *The Heritage Language Journal, 8*(2), 66–89.

Cuza, A., & Perez-Tattam, R. (Submitted). Grammatical gender selection and phrasal word order in the grammar of Spanish/English bilingual children.

Cuza, A., & Strik, N. (2012). Patterns of morphosyntactic convergence and child L1 attrition: Evidence from subject-verb inversion in Spanish-English bilingual children. Paper presented at the 42 *Linguistic Symposium on Romance Languages (LSRL42).* Southern Utah University, April 20–22, 2012.

de Swart, H. (1998). Aspect shift and coercion. *Natural Languages and Linguistic Theory, 16*, 347–385.

Doughty, C., & Williams, J. (1998). *Focus on form in classroom second language acquisition.* Cambridge: CUP.

Dreher, S. (2003). A novel idea: Reading aloud in a high school English classroom. *English Journal, 93*, 50–53.

Giorgi, A., & Pianesi, F. (1997). *Tense and aspect: From semantics to morphosyntax.* Oxford: OUP.

Grinstead, J., Pratt, T., & McCurley, D. (2009). Comprehension of prototypical tense and aspect combinations in child Spanish. *Studies in Hispanic and Lusophone Linguistics, 2*, 435–450.

Hernández Pina, F. (1984). *Teorías Psicosociolingüísticas y su Aplicación a la Adquisición del Español como Lengua Materna*. Madrid: Siglo XXI.

Jia, G. (1998). *Beyond brain maturation: The critical period hypothesis in second language acquisition revisited*. Unpublished PhD dissertation, New York University.

Johnson, J.S., & Newport, E.L. (1989). Critical period effects in second language learning: The influence of maturational state on the acquisition of English as a second language. *Cognitive Psychology, 21*, 60–99.

Labelle, M., Godard, L., & Lonting, C.M. (2002). Grammatical and situational aspect in French: A developmental study. *Journal of Child Language, 29*(2), 301–326.

Laleko, O. (2010). On covert tense-aspect restructuring in heritage Russian: A case of aspectually transient predicates. In M. Iverson, I. Ivanov, T. Judy, J. Rothman, R. Slabakova, & M. Tryzna (Eds.), *Proceedings of the 2009 Mind/Context Divide Workshop* (pp. 72–83). Somerville, MA: Cascadilla.

Lee, J., & VanPatten, B. (2003). *Making communicative language teaching happen* [2nd edition]. New York, NY: McGraw-Hill.

Liskin-Gasparro, J. (2000). The use of tense-aspect morphology in Spanish oral narratives: Exploring the perceptions of advanced learners. *Hispania, 83*, 830–844.

Martin, P. (1993). Capture silk: Reading aloud together. *English Journal, 82*, 16–24.

Marqués, S. (2008). *La lengua que heredamos* [6th edition]. Hoboken, NJ: John Wiley & Sons.

Montrul, S. (2002). Incomplete acquisition and attrition of Spanish tense/aspect distinctions in adult bilinguals. *Bilingualism: Language and Cognition, 5*, 39–68.

Montrul, S. (2004). Subject and object expression in Spanish heritage speakers: A case of morphosyntactic convergence. *Bilingualism: Language and Cognition, 7*, 125–142.

Montrul, S. (2008). *Incomplete acquisition in bilingualism. Re-examining the age factor*. Amsterdam: John Benjamins.

Montrul, S. (2011). The linguistic competence of heritage speakers. *Studies in Second Language Acquisition, 33*, 155–161.

Montrul, S., & Bowles, M. (2010). Is grammar instruction beneficial for heritage language learners? Dative case marking in Spanish. *The Heritage Language Journal, 7*(1), 47–63.

Montrul, S., & Perpiñán, S. (2011). Assessing differences and similarities between instructed heritage language learners and L2 learners in their knowledge of Spanish tense aspect and mood (TAM) morphology. *Heritage Language Journal, 8*(1), 90–133.

Montrul, S., & Slabakova, R. (2002). The L2 acquisition of morphosyntactic and semantic properties of the aspectual tenses preterite and imperfect. In A.T. Pérez-Leroux & J. Liceras (Eds.), *The acquisition of Spanish morphosyntax* (pp. 113–149). Dordrecht: Kluwer.

Montrul, S. & Slabakova, R. (2003). Competence similarities between native and near-native speakers: An investigation of the preterite/imperfect contrast in Spanish. *Studies in Second Language Acquisition, 25*, 351–398.

O'Grady, W., Kwak, H-Y., Lee, O.S, & Lee., M. (2011). An emergentist perspective on heritage language acquisition. *Studies in Second Language Acquisition, 33*, 223–245.

Pérez-Leroux, A. Cuza, A. Majlanova, M., & Sánchez-Naranjo, J. (2008). Non-native recognition of the iterative and habitual meanings of Spanish preterite and imperfect tenses. In J. Liceras, H. Zobl, & H. Goodluck (Eds.), *The role of formal features in second language acquisition* (pp. 432–451). Mahwah, NJ: Lawrence Erlbaum Associates.

Pérez-Leroux, A., Cuza, A., & Thomas, D. (2011). Clitic placement in Spanish/English bilingual children. *Bilingualism: Language and Cognition, 14*, 221–232.

Pérez-Pereira, M. (1989). The acquisition of morphemes: Some evidence from Spanish. *Journal of Psycholinguistic Research, 18*, 289–312.

Polinsky, M. (2008). Gender under incomplete acquisition: Heritage speakers' knowledge of noun categorization. *Heritage Language Journal, 6*(1), 40–71.

Polinsky, M. (2011). Reanalysis in adult heritage language: A case of attrition. *Studies in Second Language Acquisition, 33*, 305–328.

Potowski, K. (2005). Tense and aspect in the oral and written narratives of dual immersion students. In D. Eddington (Ed.), *Proceedings of the Seventh Hispanic Linguistics* Symposium (pp. 123–136). Somerville, MA: Cascadilla.

Potowski, K., Jegerski, J., & Morgan-Short, K. (2009). The effects of processing instruction on subjunctive development among Spanish heritage language speakers. *Language Learning, 59*, 537–579.

Pratt, T., McCurley, D. Grinstead, J., & Wagner, L. (2009). Child Spanish comprehension of verbal tense morphology. *Proceedings of the Annual Boston University Conference on Language Development, 33*(2), 410–419.

Rothman, J. (2007). Heritage speaker competence differences, language change and input type: Inflected infinitives in heritage Brazilian Portuguese. *International Journal of Bilingualism, 11*(4), 359–389.

Rothman, J. (2008). Aspectual selection in adult L2 Spanish and The Competing Systems Hypothesis: When pedagogical and linguistic rules conflict. *Languages in Contrast, 8*(1), 74–106.

Salaberry, R. (1999). The development of past tense verbal morphology in classroom L2 Spanish. *Applied Linguistics, 20*(2), 151–178.

Salaberry, R. (2002). Tense and aspect in the selection of Spanish past tense verbal morphology. In R. Salaberry & Y. Shirai (Eds.), *The L2 acquisition of tense-aspect morphology* (pp. 397–415). Amsterdam: John Benjamins.

Sánchez, L. (2004). Functional convergence in the tense, evidentiality and aspectual systems of Quechua-Spanish bilinguals. *Bilingualism: Language and Cognition, 7*(2), 147–162.

Sánchez, L., & Al-Kasey, T. (1999). L2 acquisition of Spanish direct objects. *Spanish Applied Linguistics, 3*, 1–32.

Schmitt, C. (1996). *Aspect and the syntax of noun phrases.* Unpublished PhD dissertation, University of Maryland.

Schwartz, B., & Sprouse, R. (1996). L2 cognitive states and the full transfer/full access model. *Second Language Research, 12*, 40–72.

Sebastián, E., & Slobin, D. (1994). Development of linguistic forms: Spanish. In R.A. Berman & D.I. Slobin (Eds.), *Relating events in narrative: A cross-linguistic developmental study* (pp. 239–284). Hillsdale, NJ: Lawrence Erlbaum Associates.

Shirai Y, & Andersen R.W. (1995). The acquisition of tense-aspect morphology: A prototype account. *Language, 71*, 743–762.

Silva-Corvalan, C. (1991). Spanish language attrition in a contact situation with English. In H.W. Seliger & R.M. Vago (Eds.), *First language attrition* (pp. 151–171). Cambridge: CUP.

Silva-Corvalán, C. (1994). *Language contact and change.* Oxford: OUP.

Silva-Corvalán, C. (2003). Linguistic consequences of reduced input in bilingual first language acquisition. In S. Montrul & F. Ordoñez (Eds.), *Linguistic theory and language development in Hispanic languages* (pp. 375–397). Somerville, MA: Cascadilla Press.

Silva-Corvalán, C. (Forthcoming). *Bilingual language acquisition: Spanish and English in the first six years.* Cambridge: CUP.

Slabakova, R., & Montrul, S. (2002). On aspectual shifts in L2 Spanish. In B. Skarabela, S. Fish, & A.H-J. Do (Eds.), *Proceedings of the 26th Boston University Conference on Language Development* (pp. 631–642). Somerville, MA: Cascadilla Press.

Smith, C. (1997). *The parameter of aspect*. Dordrecht: Kluwer.

Valdés, G. (1997). The teaching of Spanish to bilingual Spanish-speaking students: Outstanding issues and unanswered questions. In M.C. Colombi & F.X. Alarcón (Eds.), *La enseñanza del español a hispanohablantes. Praxis y teoría* (pp. 8–44). Boston, MA: Houghton Mifflin.

Valdés, G. (2005). Bilingualism, heritage language learners, and SLA research: Opportunities lost or seized? *Modern Language Journal, 89*, 410–426.

VanPatten, B. 2007. Input processing in adult second language acquisition. In B. VanPatten & J. Williams (Eds.),*Theories in second language acquisition: An introduction* (pp. 115–135). Mahwah, NJ: Lawrence Erlbaum Associates.

VanPatten, B., & Cadierno, T. (1993). Explicit instruction and input processing. *Studies in Second Language Acquisition, 15*(2), 225–243.

Vendler, Z. (1967). Verbs and times. *Philosophical Review, 56*, 143–160.

Verkuyl, H. (1972). *On the compositional nature of the aspects*. Dordrecht: Reidel.

White, L. (2003). *Second language acquisition and Universal Grammar*. Cambridge: CUP.

Zentella, A.C. (1997). *Growing up bilingual: Puerto Rican children in New York*. Malden, MA: Blackwell.

PART II

Cognitive perspectives and implications for L2 pedagogy

CHAPTER 10

Control and representation in bilingualism

Implications for pedagogy

Deanna Friesen and Ellen Bialystok
York University

The bilingual advantage in executive functioning is often contrasted with a disadvantage in lexical access, but the two are based on different processes. The former entails fluid operations used for intentional processing (i.e., cognitive control) and the latter involves crystallized knowledge (i.e., representations). On this view, the processes associated with control and representation are interactive systems responsive to different developmental factors rather than mutually exclusive alternatives. Nonetheless, the majority of research in bilingualism has investigated either control or representation in isolation by minimizing participants' reliance on the other factor. This chapter will review research investigating the interaction between these processes by bilinguals during language processing tasks and discuss how this relationship can provide new insights to pedagogy.

1. Introduction

Much of the research on bilingualism highlights the dichotomy between bilinguals' advantages in executive control abilities and their apparent disadvantages in language abilities compared to monolinguals (Bialystok 2001). Executive control (EC) refers to processes such as monitoring the environment, focusing and shifting attention and ignoring irrelevant information. A possible source for superior bilingual EC is that bilinguals, unlike monolinguals, must constantly utilize EC during language selection. This use of EC to select the target language is required because a large body of research has demonstrated that for bilinguals both languages are concurrently active (e.g., Friesen & Jared 2012; Marian, Spivey & Hirsch 2003). Bilinguals, therefore, recruit attentional processes to prevent interference from the unwanted language (Green 1998). Following extensive practice, the necessity to utilize EC for general language processing results in a more efficient EC system (Bialystok 2001). However, the bilingual experience also necessitates dividing learning between languages (Bialystok, Luk, Peets & Yang 2010; Michael & Gollan 2005). The combination of weaker language abilities and constant competition between languages compromises language processing in bilinguals.

A more general way of conceptualizing this relationship is within the framework of control and representation. Control entails fluid operations used for intentional processing and representation refers to crystallized knowledge (e.g., language knowledge) (Craik & Bialystok 2006). Previous research has investigated these constructs separately such that non-verbal conflict tasks serve as relatively pure measures of control and tasks requiring lexical access measure representation. However, by taking this approach, the literature has often neglected to address how control and representations jointly contribute to behaviour. Similarly, pedagogical practice may unnecessarily isolate language processing from EC. Here, we adopt the perspective that they should be viewed as complementary and interactive systems. Specifically, control systems manipulate and combine representations and in turn the nature of currently-held representations influence what information the control system extracts from the environment (Craik & Bialystok 2006).

This chapter will describe a framework for the interactive nature of control and representation. We will begin by briefly reviewing research demonstrating bilingual EC advantages in non-verbal tasks and lexical access disadvantages in verbal tasks. We then review research combining both domains in order to address how control ability and representations interact and whether language proficiency interacts with EC advantages. Finally, we will outline how adopting the control/representation framework can inform pedagogy.

2.   Executive control

It is a well-established finding that bilinguals exhibit processing advantages in non-verbal tasks that place high demands on executive control ability (see Hilchey & Klein 2011, for a recent meta-analysis). In general, these advantages are observed on non-verbal conflict tasks that require participants to attend to one dimension of a stimulus and to ignore a second dimension that favors a conflicting response, or monitoring tasks that require switching between two rules or two goals. This advantage has been observed across the lifespan with children (e.g., Bialystok 2010; Bialystok, Martin, & Viswanathan 2005; Carlson & Meltzoff 2008; Martin-Rhee & Bialystok 2008), young adults (e.g., Bialystok, Craik & Luk 2008a; Colzato et al. 2008; Costa, Hernández, Costa-Faidella, & Sebastián-Gallés 2009) and older adults (e.g., Bialystok, Craik, Klein & Viswanathan 2004; Salvatierra & Rosselli 2011).

In research with young children, Bialystok and Martin (2004; see also Bialystok 1999) compared bilinguals and monolinguals on the Dimensional Change Card Sorting task (DCCS). In the typical version of this task, children must sort cards with colored shapes printed on them based on one dimension (color or shape). Once they have mastered sorting on that dimension, they are asked to sort based on the other dimension. Typically, 3-year old children perseverate on the first dimension and fail to make the appropriate switch. By 4- or 5-years old, children are able to correctly switch rules (Frye, Zelazo & Palfai 1995). Bialystok and Martin found that 4-year old bilinguals were more likely to correctly switch rules than 4-year old monolingual children, but only when they were required to ignore a perceptually salient and conflicting dimension. The bilingual children were no more successful than monolingual children when the sorting rule was a conceptual category, such as "toys" or "clothing", where there was no salient perceptual feature attracting their attention. Similarly, Bialystok and Shapero (2005) found that 6-year old bilinguals were more successful in identifying the other image in an ambiguous figure (e.g., a picture that could be either a rabbit or a duck) than their monolingual peers. Furthermore, performance on this task was correlated with their ability to successfully perform the DCCS task following the rule change. In both tasks, selective attention is required to isolate the relevant dimension and avoid distraction from the irrelevant dimension. Using a battery of tests, Carlson and Meltzoff (2008) confirmed that bilingual 6-year olds outperformed monolinguals on tasks that required this type of conflict resolution but there was no difference between language groups on tasks that required delay of gratification, such as not acting on the desire to eat a treat or peek at a gift. These results indicate that childhood bilingualism promotes greater cognitive flexibility which enables more effective problem solving in non-verbal conflict tasks.

The majority of work investigating executive control ability in monolingual and bilingual adults has focused on the efficiency of online processing when individuals are presented with conflict in a non-verbal task (although see Barac & Bialystok 2012, for similar methodology with children). Two tasks that have been used extensively are the Simon task and the Attentional Network task (ANT, a type of flanker task); both tasks place little demand on language knowledge but require EC ability. In the Simon task, participants are presented with a square that is one of two colors and they must quickly indicate the color by pressing the response key designated for that color. The response keys are positioned on either side of the computer monitor, creating trials in which the correct response key is either congruent with the position of the stimulus or conflict trials in which the correct response key is incongruent with the position. The additional time needed to respond in the incongruent trials is the Simon effect. In the simplest version of the ANT, target arrows are presented either in isolation or surrounded by flanking arrows. Participants must indicate with a button press the direction of the central target arrow. The flanking arrows can be facing the same direction as the target, creating congruent trials, or pointing in the opposite direction, creating incongruent trials. Participants must ignore the flankers and respond only to the direction of the target arrow. Again, the extra time required for incongruent trials is a reliable cost called the flanker effect.

Evidence for a bilingual processing advantage in young adults in these online non-verbal tasks has been somewhat sporadic (Hilchey & Klein 2011 for a review). Bialystok et al. (2005) failed to observe a reaction time difference between bilingual and monolingual university students in a simple version of the Simon task. However, when Bialystok (2006) increased the cognitive load by increasing the number of switches, a bilingual processing advantage emerged in which bilinguals responded more quickly on the most difficult condition. Similarly, Costa, Hernández and Sebastián-Gallés (2008) compared a large group of bilingual and monolingual university students on the ANT and found reliable but small processing advantages for the bilinguals. Difficulty observing robust group differences in this population may be the result of the fact that at this age both groups are operating at peak executive functioning efficiency (see also Bialystok et al. 2008a). Thus, only when the task necessitates high levels of cognitive control or the design has sufficient power does evidence of the underlying cognitive difference between groups emerge. In older adults, more robust findings are observed. For example, in a simple version of the Simon task, Bialystok et al. (2004) found that older bilingual adults (60 or older) processed the incongruent trials more efficiently than monolingual older adults. This finding suggests that the cognitive decline associated with aging is less steep for bilinguals than for comparable monolinguals. Thus across the lifespan, research has revealed that bilinguals develop more efficient executive control abilities.

3.   Language representation

Concerns that bilinguals' language knowledge may be weaker than that of their monolingual peers are well supported in the literature. On average, bilinguals perform more poorly on measures of formal language knowledge. For example, bilinguals tend to know fewer words in each of their languages than monolinguals know in their single language (Oller, Pearson & Cobo-Lewis 2007), a difference found for both children (Bialystok et al. 2010) and adults (Bialystok & Luk 2011). Importantly, the nature of these formal language tasks requires the use of representational knowledge with little requirement for control processes.

The group differences on language knowledge tasks has been attributed to differences in language learning opportunities rather than to differences in learning ability (Oller et al. 2007). For example, bilinguals may use their native language at home and a second language in school or the community, so the nature of their language exposure differs across contexts. Bialystok et al. (2010) compared a sample of over 1700 bilingual and monolingual children who were 3- to 10-years old on the Peabody Picture Vocabulary Test, a test of receptive English vocabulary knowledge, and found that the monolingual children outperformed the bilinguals at all ages despite scores for both language groups being in the normal range. Importantly, words that were more likely to be learned in a home environment were the locus of the group differences and school-based words were understood similarly by children in the two groups. All the children were being educated in English, but the bilingual children used a different language at home and so were less familiar with the English labels of objects they were more likely to encounter at home.

Words or concepts that are known in only one language are called singlets, whereas words or concepts that can be labeled in both languages are called doublets (Oller et al. 2007). Consistent with the work by Bialystok et al. (2010), Umbel, Pearson, Fernández and Oller (1992) compared first grade Spanish-English bilingual children's receptive vocabulary knowledge in both their languages and found approximately 10% of words known in each language were singlets, whereas 60% there were doublets. Importantly, as bilinguals gained more language experience in each language the number of doublets increased and the number of singlets decreased (Oller et al. 2007). What this indicates is that vocabulary knowledge across languages becomes more comparable as bilinguals gain more experience in both languages. That is, proficient and balanced bilingual adults are likely to know the same words in each of their languages.

Possibly as a result of additional exposure to both languages, research comparing bilingual and monolingual adult language knowledge produces more mixed results than the children's literature. Some research has found that English vocabulary knowledge of bilingual adults (i.e., their L2) is similar to their English monolingual peers (Bahrick, Hall, Goggin, Bahrick & Berger 1994), whereas others have shown a monolingual advantage (Bialystok et al. 2008a; Portocarrero, Burright & Donovick 2007). However, in a large scale study, Bialystok and Luk (2011) confirmed that the vocabulary difference observed in children was also present in adults. Importantly, however, even if bilinguals have a linguistic representation for a concept as revealed in vocabulary tests, their access to this word may not be as well established. Research using picture naming has found that bilingual adults exhibit slower lexical access in both their second (Gollan, Montoya, Fennema-Notestine & Morris 2005) and first language (Ivanova & Costa 2008) relative to monolinguals. These slower response times have been attributed either to "weaker links" between an object's semantic features and its lexical identity (Gollan &

Acenas 2004) or to the competition between languages for selection (Green 1998). Nonetheless, regardless of the mechanism, bilinguals experience more effortful access to language representations.

4.   Executive control and language representations

To this point, the chapter has reviewed research in which executive control and language representation were studied in isolation of each other. The results typically showed a bilingual advantage in EC tasks and a disadvantage on language measures. Language switching paradigms, where bilinguals switch between naming digits or pictures in each of their languages based on a cue, have been used to examine language control in bilinguals. However, these tasks are only appropriate for bilinguals since knowing two languages is a prerequisite for performing the tasks. Here we focus on language conflict tasks because successful performance requires both representation and control and can be performed by both bilinguals and monolinguals. In these language conflict tasks, participants must activate linguistic representations and use executive control to resolve linguistic conflict. Determining whether or not the bilingual advantage in executive control extends to linguistic tasks has important pedagogical implications. Since academic success is predicated both on language proficiency (i.e., representation) and executive functioning ability (i.e., control), understanding this relationship provides a novel basis for informing pedagogy.

Two types of tasks can be employed to examine the role of executive control in language processing: metalinguistic tasks and language conflict tasks. Metalinguistic awareness can be thought of as the need for attention to be actively focused on the explicit properties of language independently of meaning (Bialystok 2001). In metalinguistic tasks, this attention is assessed by asking individuals to manipulate language form and ignore its function, generally considered to be its meaning. For example, in the Wug test (Berko 1958), children must make explicit their implicit understanding of English morphological rules by applying them to novel words, such as pluralizing the nonsense word "wug". These metalinguistic tasks can differ in their relative need to recruit EC functions and language representations. The Wug test is relatively low in control demands and high in representation demands; no conflicting information needs to be ignored but children must know the correct morphological rule. Only if bilingual children possess the same level of English language knowledge as their monolingual peers do they outperform monolinguals on this task (Barac & Bialystok 2012). This metalinguistic advantage has been attributed to an accelerated understanding of the separation of form and meaning because bilinguals learn quite early that objects have a label in each of their languages. This separation of form and meaning in turn may enable them to focus their attention on the form of language (Cummins 1978).

Metalinguistic tasks can also be designed to recruit greater reliance on EC ability. In one version of a grammaticality judgment task, individuals must make grammaticality judgments on three types of sentences: grammatical sentences (e.g., Apples grow on trees), ungrammatical sentences (e.g., Apples growed on trees) and grammatical but semantically anomalous sentences (e.g., Apples grow on noses). In the semantically anomalous condition, participants must ignore the odd meaning of the sentence in order to determine that the grammar is correct. These sentences require the use of EC to ignore the conflicting information. In repeated studies, bilingual children between 5- to 9-years old outperformed monolingual children on the semantically anomalous sentences, but monolingual and bilingual children performed equivalently on the ungrammatical sentences (Bialystok 1986, 1988; Bialystok, Peets & Moreno in press). Cromdal (1999) divided children into more and less proficient bilinguals and compared them to a group of monolinguals. He found that the more proficient bilingual children outperformed the monolinguals on these sentences, whereas the less proficient bilinguals performed equivalently to the monolinguals. He proposed an interaction between language representation and control in which the less proficient bilinguals used their superior EC abilities to compensate for their weaker language abilities (see also Hermanto, Moreno & Bialystok 2012). Taken together, these findings indicate that bilinguals can take advantage of their superior EC ability on a metalinguistic task that requires control. Importantly, EC ability is able to compensate for weaker language knowledge.

As noted above, bilinguals tend to have both fewer words in their vocabulary and slower access to the words that are present in their lexicons. However, less is known about how bilinguals are able to benefit from EC ability to manipulate these language representations particularly when the task is more difficult and requires additional cognitive processing. Verbal fluency is a test used as a neuropsychological assessment instrument to evaluate the integrity of brain functioning. The test usually includes various conditions that differ in the extent to which they recruit language representations and EC (Delis, Kaplan & Kramer 2001). Participants are asked to generate as many words as possible in 60s that belong either to a semantic category (e.g., animals) or that start with a specific letter (e.g., F). Category fluency is the easier of the two tasks because words to be produced are consistent with how concepts are stored in semantic memory. It is a linguistic task rather than a metalinguistic task because participants are not asked to focus on the word form. In contrast, letter fluency is a metalinguistic task because participants must focus on the word form. This task also requires greater control because words are not listed alphabetically in memory and participants must ignore semantic competitors that might be activated in order to focus on words that share the same initial letter. Moreover, more control is also required to comply with a set of restrictions provided to participants. Specifically, proper names, numbers and morphological variants are not accepted responses (Delis et al. 2001).

Studies comparing monolingual and bilingual participants on verbal fluency tasks typically report more words produced by monolinguals, especially for category fluency conditions (Gollan, Montoya & Werner 2002; Rosselli et al. 2002; Sandoval, Gollan, Ferreira & Salmon 2010). A study by Bialystok, Craik and Luk (2008b) controlled for the level of English vocabulary knowledge in the two groups to examine the relative contributions of control and representation. When participants were matched on vocabulary knowledge, differences in category fluency were no longer significant and bilinguals outperformed the monolinguals on letter fluency. Thus, if linguistic knowledge is equivalent, bilinguals are able to use their superior EC ability to better perform this verbal task. Work with children has led to a similar conclusion; Hermanto et al. (2012) found that bilingual children were less impacted by their weaker language ability when the fluency task allowed them to utilize their EC ability. Thus, a metalinguistic task that enables control to be exerted during language processing is performed better by bilinguals.

Luo, Luk and Bialystok (2010) investigated how executive control ability contributes to verbal fluency performance by charting the time course of performance on this task by adults. Typically, participants begin with a spurt of words that declines rapidly over the course of the 60s. As the task progresses, more executive control is required to ignore previously generated items or in the case of letter fluency, semantic distractors that do not belong to the response set. Luo et al. divided the responses into 5s bins in order to investigate the rate of response decline. They predicted that because bilinguals have superior EC, they would generate more responses later in the time course for the letter fluency task, resulting in a less steep response slope than for the monolinguals. This prediction was supported, indicating that both language knowledge and executive control jointly contribute to lexical access in this task. Importantly, executive control enables bilinguals to more efficiently resist interference generated by semantic competitors, an interference that increases as the task unfolds.

Metalinguistic tasks are one means of examining how control and representation jointly contribute to performance in a language task. A second approach is to investigate whether more efficient executive control ability enables bilinguals to more readily select the correct word and ignore lexical competitors during online language processing. Monolinguals, too, constantly need to make lexical choices, as in selecting an appropriate synonym for a concept. However, since bilinguals must ignore lexical competitors from both their languages (e.g., Hermans, Bongaerts, De Bot & Schreuder 1998) they may be more efficient at doing so than monolinguals. Research by Linck, Hoshino, and Kroll (2008) with bilingual adults found a correlation between inhibitory control ability in a non-verbal Simon task and degree of non-target language interference in a picture naming task. Specifically, bilinguals who experienced less impact of the added cognitive load in a Simon task were also less impacted by the lexical competitors from their non-target language in a picture naming task.

The correlation between inhibitory control ability and degree of between-language lexical interference for bilinguals suggests that bilinguals may use executive control during online processing to efficiently inhibit within-language competitors. If so, bilinguals should resolve lexical competition more efficiently than monolinguals. Blumenfeld and Marian (2011) investigated this question by examining the ability of English monolinguals and English-Spanish bilinguals to inhibit the spatial location of a strong lexical competitor during a speech perception task. Participants were presented with a four-picture display and asked to look at one target picture. Distractor pictures were either neutral or shared a phonological onset with the target picture (e.g., "candy" and "candle"). The authors postulated that since the phonological distractor was a strong lexical competitor, it should promote greater use of inhibition and subsequent responses made about that quadrant of the display should be slower than neutral quadrants because more time would be needed to overcome the inhibition. Consistent with this prediction, Blumenfeld and Marian found that the monolingual group was slower to identify the location of a gray asterisk when it was in the same location as the phonological distractor relative to location of a neutral picture, but the bilinguals did not exhibit a difference. The authors interpreted these results to indicate that due to a more efficient control system, bilinguals had already resolved the interference created by the onset distractor. Additionally, for the bilinguals only, the residual inhibition on this linguistic task was correlated with non-linguistic Stroop inhibition, suggesting that there is a link between general inhibitory control ability and language processing and advances the possibility that bilinguals may employ inhibitory control differently during language processing than monolinguals. However, this conclusion is tentative and requires further investigation.

Recent research in our lab has taken two approaches to investigating the ability of monolingual and bilingual adults to resolve competition from lexical items within a language. Participants saw two pictures on a computer screen that were either related phonologically (e.g., beaver and beard), semantically (e.g., beaver and otter) or unrelated (e.g., beaver and table). At the same time, they heard the name of one of the pictures and were asked to indicate with a button press on which side of the screen the named picture appeared. Both bilinguals and monolinguals were slower to respond to the target pictures when they appeared in the presence of the phonological or semantic distractors than when they appeared with the unrelated picture. Importantly, the semantic cost (i.e., semantic distractor RT – unrelated RT) was significantly larger for the monolinguals than for the bilinguals, suggesting that the bilinguals were better able to ignore the competing picture and focus on the correct picture. These results support the interpretation that bilinguals were able to resolve the competition more efficiently than the monolinguals and allow for the possibility that they were able to engage in greater control to ignore these competitors.

A second study addressed this question by employing a priming paradigm to determine whether bilingual adults were more efficient than monolinguals at inhibiting lexical activation from a misleading prime. Participants made living/non-living judgments on a series of words presented individually. Critical words were non-living homophones (e.g., "towed") that had living homophone mates (e.g., "toad") and non-living non-homophonic control words (e.g., "toned"). The trial preceding the critical words were either related (e.g., "frog") or unrelated (e.g., "girl") to the unseen living homophone mates. If participants activate the phonological representation of the homophone as well as the meaning of both the critical homophone and its living homophone mate, then they should be slower and less accurate in deciding that the critical homophones are not living things relative to their control words. Likewise, if the related prime spreads activation to the meaning of the unseen homophone mate, then rejecting the critical homophone should be more difficult in the related condition than in the unrelated condition. However, because participants make a response on the prime and are unaware of its importance to the critical trial, they should make a decision on the prime and refocus for the critical trial, thereby inhibiting the activation from the prime. Although both groups showed sensitivity to the meaning of the homophone mate by making more errors on homophones than on control words, the monolinguals were slower to correctly reject the non-living homophone as a living thing when the previous trial was related to its homophone mate. That is, having "frog" precede "towed", produced significantly more interference for the monolinguals than for the bilinguals. These results suggest that both bilinguals and monolinguals activated lexical competitors, but that the bilinguals were better able to inhibit irrelevant lexical information. Taken together, work examining executive control use in language tasks is beginning to converge on the conclusion that bilinguals can utilize superior executive control ability to more efficiently manipulate language representations and ignore competing representations within a language.

In sum, metalinguistic tasks and language conflict tasks necessitate both language knowledge and the use of executive control ability to attend to the relevant stimuli and ignore competing irrelevant information. Established work has demonstrated that in metalinguistic tasks, bilinguals are able to compensate for poorer language knowledge if the task places high demands on the executive control system. Likewise, an emerging field of research has begun to demonstrate that this executive control system may be employed during online language processing to resolve lexical competition and that bilinguals may benefit from superior executive control to resolve this competition.

5. Implications for pedagogy

The control and representation framework has important implications for education. First, when considering language acquisition and use in both monolingual and bilingual circumstances, there is a tendency to place greater importance on gaining oral language proficiency (i.e., acquiring representations) (Limbos & Geva 2001) than on improving other skills such executive control ability. However, the recognition that both representation and control jointly impact performance on metalinguistic and language processing tasks enables both components to be targeted as areas for possible improvement. Depending on the nature of the academic task, executive control ability may compensate for weaker language knowledge.

Second, the control and representation framework provides insight into two different bilingual circumstances: (1) individuals whose home language is different from the language of the majority and thus their bilingualism arises through interactions in the community and schooling in the majority's language, and (2) individuals whose home language is that of the majority, but whose instruction is in a different language. Since there are a different set of implications for each group, we will address each of these educational circumstances in turn.

The majority of work on bilingualism has focused on bilinguals whose dual language status arises from having a home language that is different from the language of the community. In a North American educational setting, these children are identified as English as a Second Language (ESL) or English Language Learners (ELL) (Geva & Zadeh 2006). For this population of children, the control and representation framework allows us to evaluate how measures of language proficiency (i.e., representation) adequately capture second-language use. Given that language use requires having both representations and the ability to control and manipulate those representations, formal tests of vocabulary and grammar knowledge may underestimate bilingual children's ability to *use* language effectively. Evidence for this comes from work on academic discourse and literacy. For example, Peets and Bialystok (in press) administered standardized tests of language knowledge to bilingual and monolingual kindergarten students and also engaged them in narrative and explanatory talk. Although bilingual children performed more poorly than monolinguals on the formal measures of language knowledge, measures of informal vocabulary knowledge and grammar use as measured by the accuracy of these forms in the narratives were comparable for the two groups. Importantly, the sophistication of the bilingual children's discourse in terms of organization, structure, ideas, and use of language was equivalent to that of their monolingual peers in spite of demonstrating lower language proficiency on formal tests. In essence, these bilingual children were able to use the resources that they had more effectively.

As with discourse, learning to read relies on both cognitive and linguistic processes in order to produce successful performance. When learning to read an alphabetic language, children must utilize both attentional resources and spelling-sound correspondence knowledge to efficiently decode words; once they are able to automatically and quickly recruit these representations from memory, attention can then be allocated to higher order processes such as comprehension (Wolf & Katzir-Cohen 2001). A number of studies comparing reading performance in monolingual and bilingual children have reported that the two groups do not differ significantly on basic word reading skills, despite weaker vocabulary and grammar knowledge in bilinguals, (e.g., Peets, Yim & Bialystok 2010; Geva & Zadeh 2006; Limbos & Geva 2001). Such a finding lends itself to two possibilities; first, that bilinguals are able to use attentional resources to compensate for weaker language ability, or second, that oral language knowledge is not an important variable in early reading acquisition. Although oral language knowledge emerges as a significant predictor of reading skill (e.g., Adams 1990; McBride-Chang & Chang 1995), it may not be as important as other underlying cognitive abilities. When controlling for phonological awareness and naming speed, oral language is no longer a significant predictor of efficient word reading in L2 (e.g., Arab-Moghaddam & Sénéchal 2001; Geva & Siegel 2000).

Despite producing weaker oral language skills, there is some research that reports that bilingualism nonetheless has an advantageous effect on the cognitive and linguistic preliteracy skills necessary for learning to read. Specifically, phonological awareness and naming speed (as measured by Rapid Automatized Naming tests (RAN)) are strong predictors of word reading accuracy and have been found to demonstrate a bilingual advantage. Phonological awareness refers to the understanding of a language's sound structure and naming speed is the fluency with which letters, digits, colors or words are named quickly (National Reading Panel 2000). Some studies have found superior phonological awareness in 5-year old bilingual children that disappears when reading instruction begins (e.g., Bruck & Genesee 1995; Campbell & Sais 1995). Bialystok, Luk and Kwan (2005) reported that bilingual children in first grade whose two language systems were both alphabetic outperformed English monolingual peers on phonological awareness and English decoding tasks. With respect to naming speed performance, Geva and Zadeh (2006) found that despite poorer vocabulary and grammatical knowledge, bilingual grade 1 children named letters and read isolated words more quickly than their monolingual peers. Although there is currently debate in the literature about the exact nature of the skill that RAN assesses (Savage 2004), the need to quickly refocus attention from one item to the next may tap into control processes that are necessary for reading and at which bilinguals excel (Geva & Zadeh 2006). This suggestion is speculative and warrants further investigation.

Importantly for children, therefore, the assessment of language knowledge itself (i.e., vocabulary and grammar) is not a complete predictor of basic word reading skills (i.e., language use) relative to phonological awareness and RAN ability. This finding is crucial for education given the perceived link between basic reading skills and oral language ability may be used as a basis for recommending reading intervention in bilingual children. Specifically, Limbos and Geva (2001) found that despite finding no correlation between objective measures of oral language proficiency and basic word recognition skills, Grade 1 teachers were more likely to identify an ESL child as at risk for reading impairment if they had poor oral language knowledge. Similarly, poorer reading ability may be explained away as a consequence of weaker oral language knowledge. In the former case, ESL students would be unnecessarily recommended for reading intervention and in the latter case, they would not receive the necessary support for reading difficulties. Thus, an important advantage of the control and representation framework is that it provides a basis for understanding why formal measures of language representations do not necessarily capture a bilingual's facility with language and must be interpreted with caution.

An important caveat to these recommendations is that bilingualism research with both children and adults is typically conducted with bilinguals who are highly proficient in both their languages. That is, although on average these bilinguals perform more poorly than monolinguals on standardized language tests, they do perform within the normal range. Thus from an educational perspective, it is unclear at what point an individual is "sufficiently" bilingual to demonstrate advantages in executive control or how much second language knowledge is necessary to take advantage of that control ability in language tasks. The former question may be addressed by research examining individuals who are in the process of becoming bilingual, either as adults or as children enrolled in an immersion program. There is very little research on representation and control in adult second language learners and these issues remain open questions, but work with children learning a second language in immersion programs provides insight.

Children who are becoming bilingual by choice rather than by necessity learn the language of the majority at home and are enrolled in a program where their instruction is in a different language. A widespread example of this educational option is French Immersion in Canada (Genesee 2012). Importantly, French immersion students in grade 6 do not differ on measures of English knowledge relative to students enrolled in an English program indicating that first language educational trajectories are not adversely impacted by second language education (Genesee 2012; Hartley, Hart & Turnbull 2003). Additionally, their performance on French language measures, although not at native-like levels (Lyster 2004), is superior to children who take French classes in an English program (Genesee 2012). Thus with respect to representation, immersion programs provide a basis for maintaining native language knowledge and abilities as well as acquiring a new language, resulting in partial bilinguals. In addition to gaining second language knowledge, there is evidence that Grade 2 and 5 students in immersion programs also demonstrate superior metalinguistic performance on both the Wug test and on semantically anomalous sentences in a grammaticality judgment task compared to their peers in an English program (Bialystok et al. in press).

Only a few studies have investigated whether this emerging bilingualism produces the same advantages in executive control ability as those observed with fluent bilinguals. Bialystok and Majumder (1998) found that although fluent 8-10 year old bilinguals exhibited processing advantages on non-verbal executive control tasks, partial bilinguals did not differ from English monolinguals. Similarly, Carlson and Meltzoff (2008) did not observe executive control advantages for kindergarten students enrolled in an immersion program relative to monolingual children. Bialystok and Barac (2012) took a different approach by investigating which background variables account for executive control performance in emerging bilinguals in immersion programs in Grade 2 and 5. They found that length of time in the immersion program and degree of bilingualism accounted for a unique portion of the explained variance, indicating that as individuals spent more time in a bilingual program and gained a greater degree of bilingualism, their executive control ability improved. Moreover, in contrast to the lack of difference observed with children, Linck et al. (2008) found that adults who participated in an immersion program showed greater executive control ability than adults who were not. However, more research is warranted with adult second language learners. Taken together, both language knowledge and executive control ability is benefited by an additive language environment.

6. Conclusions

This chapter has demonstrated that bilinguals and monolinguals differ in both executive control ability and representational sophistication. However, language use involves using executive control to manipulate representations, so the two abilities inevitably interact in a wide variety of contexts. As a result, in metalinguistic and language processing tasks, bilinguals can take advantage of superior control ability to compensate for weaker language abilities. Thus, the control and representation framework provides important and new insight on why (1) tests and perceptions of oral language knowledge in bilingual children may not be a complete predictor of their ability to accomplish academic tasks, (2) both representation and executive control are modified by experience and can be targeted for improvement, and (3) immersion education provides an opportunity to improve both language knowledge and executive control ability.

References

Adams, M.J. (1990). *Beginning to read: Thinking and learning about print.* Cambridge, MA: The MIT Press.

Arab-Moghaddam, M., & Sénéchal, M. (2001). Orthographic and phonological processing skills in reading and spelling in Persian/English bilinguals. *International Journal of Behavioural Development, 25,* 140–147.

Bahrick, H.P., Hall, L.K., Goggin, J.P., Bahrick, L.E., & Berger, S.A. (1994). Fifty years of language maintenance and language dominance in bilingual Hispanic immigrants. *Journal of Experimental Psychology: Genera, 3,* 264–283.

Barac, R., & Bialystok, E. (2012). Bilingual effects on cognitive and linguistic development: Role of language, cultural background, and education. *Child Development.* Advance online publication. doi: 10.1111/j.1467-8624.2011.01707

Berko, J. (1958). The child's learning of English morphology. *Word, 14,* 150–177.

Bialystok, E. (1986). Factors in the growth of linguistic awareness. *Child Development, 57,* 498–510.

Bialystok, E. (1988). Levels of bilingualism and levels of linguistic awareness. *Developmental Psychology, 24,* 560–567.

Bialystok, E. (1999). Cognitive complexity and attentional control in the bilingual mind. *Child Development, 70,* 636–644.

Bialystok, E. (2001). *Bilingualism in development: Language, literacy and cognition.* Cambridge: CUP.

Bialystok, E. (2006). Effect of bilingualism and computer video game experience on the simon task. *Canadian Journal of Experimental Psychology, 60,* 68–79.

Bialystok, E. (2010). Global-local and trail-making tasks by monolingual and bilingual children: Beyond inhibition. *Developmental Psychology, 46,* 93–105.

Bialystok, E., & Barac, R. (2012). Emerging bilingualism: Dissociating advantages for metalinguistic awareness and executive control. *Cognition, 122,* 67–73.

Bialystok, E., Craik, F.I.M., & Luk, G. (2008a). Cognitive control and lexical access in younger and older bilinguals. *Journal of Experimental Psychology: Learning, Memory and Cognition, 34,* 859–873.

Bialystok, E., Craik, F.I.M., & Luk, G. (2008b). Lexical access in bilinguals: Effects of vocabulary size and executive control. *Journal of Neurolinguistics 21,* 522–538.

Bialystok, E., Craik, F.I.M., Klein, R., & Viswanathan, M. (2004). Bilingualism, aging and cognitive control: Evidence from the Simon task. *Psychology and Aging, 19,* 290–303.

Bialystok, E., & Luk, G. (2011). Receptive vocabulary differences in monolingual and bilingual adults. *Bilingualism, Language and Cognition, 15*, 397–401.

Bialystok, E., Luk, G., & Kwan, E. (2005). Bilingualism, biliteracy, and learning to read: Interactions among languages and writing systems. *Scientific Studies of Reading, 9*, 43–61.

Bialystok, E., Luk, G., Peets, K.F., & Yang, S. (2010). Receptive vocabulary differences in monolingual and bilingual children. *Bilingualism, Language and Cognition, 13*, 525–531.

Bialystok, E., & Martin, M.M. (2004). Attention and inhibition in bilingual children: Evidence from the dimensional change card sort task. *Developmental Science, 7*, 325–339.

Bialystok, E., Martin, M.M., & Viswanathan, M. (2005). Bilingualism across the lifespan: The rise and fall of inhibitory control. *International Journal of Bilingualism, 9*, 103–119.

Bialystok, E., & Majumder, S. (1998). The relationship between bilingualism and the development of cognitive processes in problem solving. *Applied Psycholinguistics, 19*, 69–85.

Bialystok, E., Peets, K., & Moreno, S. (In press). Producing bilinguals through immersion education: Development of metalinguistic awareness. *Applied Psycholinguistics.*

Bialystok, E., & Shapero, D. (2005). Ambiguous benefits: The effect of bilingualism on reversing ambiguous figures. *Developmental Science, 8*, 595–604.

Blumenfeld, H.K., & Marian, V. (2011). Bilingualism influences inhibitory control in auditory comprehension. *Cognition, 118*, 245–257.

Bruck, M., & Genesee, F. (1995). Phonological awareness in young second language learners. *Journal of Child Language, 22*, 307–324.

Campbell, R., & Sais, E. (1995). Accelerated metalinguistic (phonological) awareness in bilingual children. *British Journal of Developmental Psychology, 13*, 61–68.

Carlson, S.M., & Meltzoff, A.N. (2008). Bilingual experience and executive functioning in young children. *Developmental Science, 11*, 282–298.

Colzato, L.S., Bajo, M.T., van den Wildenberg, W., Paolieri, D., Nieuwenhuis, S., La Heij, W., & Hommel, B. (2008). How does bilingualism improve executive control? A comparison of active and reactive inhibition mechanisms. *Journal of Experimental Psychology: Learning, Memory, and Cognition, 34*, 302–312.

Costa, A., Hernández, M., Costa-Faidella, J., & Sebastián-Gallés, N. (2009). On the bilingual advantage in conflict processing: Now you see it, now you don't. *Cognition, 113*, 135–149.

Costa, A., Hernández, M., & Sebastián-Gallés, N. (2008). Bilingualism aids conflict resolution: Evidence from the ANT task. *Cognition, 106*, 59–86.

Craik, F.I.M., & Bialystok, E. (2006). Cognition through the lifespan: Mechanisms of change. *Trends in Cognitive Sciences, 10*, 131–138.

Cromdal, J. (1999). Childhood bilingualism and metalinguistic skills: Analysis and control in young Swedish-English bilinguals. *Applied Psycholinguistics, 20*, 1–20.

Cummins, J. (1978). Bilingualism and the development of metalinguistic awareness. *Journal of Cross-Cultural Psychology, 9*, 131–149.

Delis, D.C., Kaplan, E., & Kramer, J.H. (2001). *Verbal Fluency Subtest of the Delis-Kaplan Executive Function System.* San Antonio, TX: The Psychological Corporation.

Friesen, D.C., & Jared, D. (2012). Cross-language phonological activation of meaning: Evidence from category verification. *Bilingualism: Language and Cognition, 15*, 145–156.

Frye, D., Zelazo, P.D., & Palfai, T. (1995). Theory of mind and rule-based reasoning. *Cognitive Development, 10*, 483–527.

Genesee, F. (2012). Literacy outcomes in French immersion [Rev. edition]. *Encyclopedia of Language and Literacy Development* (pp. 1–8). London, ON: Canadian Language and Literacy

Research Network. <http://www.literacyencyclopedia.ca/pdfs/topic.php?topId=27> (23 March 2012).

Geva, E., & Siegel, L.S. (2000). Orthographic and cognitive factors in the concurrent development of basic reading skills in two languages. *Reading and Writing: An Interdisciplinary Journal, 12*, 1–31.

Geva, E., & Zadeh, Z.Y. (2006). Reading efficiency in native English-speaking and English-as-a-Second language children: The role of oral proficiency and underlying cognitive linguistic processes. *Scientific Studies of Reading, 10*, 31–57.

Gollan, T.H. & Acenas, L.R. (2004). What is a TOT? Cognates and translation effects on tip-of-the-tongue states in Spanish-English and Tagalog-English bilinguals. *Journal of Experimental Psychology: Learning, Memory and Cognition, 30*, 246–269.

Gollan, T.H., Montoya, R.I., Fennema-Notestine, C., & Morris, S.K. (2005). Bilingualism affects picture naming but not picture classification. *Memory & Cognition, 33*, 7220–7234.

Gollan, T.H., Montoya, R.I., & Wener, G. (2002). Semantic and letter fluency in Spanish-English bilinguals. *Neuropsychology, 16*, 562–576.

Green, D.W., 1998. Mental control of the bilingual lexico-semantic system. *Bilingualism: Language and Cognition, 1*, 67–81.

Hartley, B., Hart, D., & Turnbull, M. (2003). Grade 6 French immersion students' performance on large-scale reading, writing, and mathematics tests: Building explanations. *Alberta Journal of Educational Research, 49*, 6–23.

Hermans, D., Bongaerts, T., de Bot, K., & Schreuder, R. (1998). Producing words in a foreign language: Can speakers prevent interference from their first language? *Bilingualism: Language and Cognition, 1*, 213–229.

Hermanto, N., Moreno, S., & Bialystok, E. (2012). Linguistic and metalinguistic outcomes of intense immersion education: How bilingual? *International Journal of Bilingual Education and Bilingualism, 15*, 131–145.

Hilchey, M.D., & Klein, R. M. (2011). Are there bilingual advantages on nonlinguistic interference tasks? Implications for the plasticity of executive control processes. *Psychonomic Bulletin and Review, 18*, 625–658.

Ivanova, I., & Costa, A. (2008). Does bilingualism hamper lexical access in speech production? *Acta Psychologica, 127*, 277–288.

Limbos, M., & Geva, E. (2001). Accuracy of teacher assessments of second-language students at risk for reading disability. *Journal of Learning Disabilities, 34*(2), 136–151.

Linck, J.A., Hoshino, N., & Kroll, J.F. (2008). Cross-language lexical processes and inhibitory control. *The Mental Lexicon, 3*, 349–374.

Luo, L., Luk. G., & Bialystok, E. (2010). Effects of language proficiency and executive control on verbal fluency performance in bilinguals. *Cognition, 114*, 29–41.

Lyster, R. (2004). Research on form-focused instruction in immersion classrooms: Implications for theory and practice. *French Language Studies, 14*, 321–341. doi: 10.1017/S0959269504001826.

Marian, V., Spivey, M., & Hirsch, J. (2003). Shared and separate systems in bilingual language processing: Converging evidence from eyetracking and brain imaging. *Brain and Language, 86*, 70–82.

Martin-Rhee, M.M., & Bialystok, E. (2008). The development of two types of inhibitory control in monolingual and bilingual children. *Bilingualism: Language and Cognition, 11*, 81–93.

McBride-Chang, C., & Chang, L. (1995). Memory, print exposure, and metacognition: Components of reading in Chinese children. *International Journal of Psychology, 30*, 607–616.

Michael, E., & Gollan, T.H. (2005). Being and becoming bilingual: Individual differences and consequences for language production. In J.F. Kroll & A.M.B. de Groot (Eds.), *Handbook of Bilingualism: Psycholinguistic Approaches* (pp. 389–407). Oxford: OUP.

National Reading Panel. (2000). Teaching children to read: An evidence-based assessment of the scientific research literature on reading and its implications for reading instruction (NIH Pub. No. 00-4769). Bethesda, MD: National Institutes of Health, National Institute of Child Health and Human Development.

Oller, D.K., Pearson, B.Z., & Cobo-Lewis, A.B. (2007). Profile effects in early bilingual language and literacy. *Applied Psycholinguistics, 28*, 191–230.

Peets, K.F., & Bialystok, E. (In press). Academic discourse: Dissociating standardized and conversational measures of language proficiency in bilingual kindergarteners. *Applied Psycholinguistics*.

Peets, K.F., Yim, O., & Bialystok, E. (2010). Proficiency, reading and home literacy in bilingual children. Poster presented at the Development 2010 Conference, Ottawa, Ontario.

Portocarrero, J.S., Burright, R.G., & Donovick, P. J. (2007).Vocabulary and verbal fluency of bilingual and monolingual college students. *Archives of Clinical Neuropsychology, 22*, 415–422.

Rosselli, M., Ardila, A., Salvatierra, J., Marquez, M., Matos, L., & Weekes, V.A. (2002). A cross-linguistic comparison of verbal fluency tests. *International Journal of Neuroscience, 112*, 759–776.

Salvatierra, J.L. & Rosselli, M. (2011). The effect of bilingualism and age on inhibitory control. *The International Journal of Bilingualism, 15*, 26–37.

Sandoval, T.C., Gollan, T.H., Ferreira, V.S., & Salmon, D.P. (2010). What causes the bilingual disadvantage in verbal fluency? The dual-task analogy. *Bilingualism: Language and Cognition, 13*, 231–252.

Savage, R. (2004). Motor skills, automaticity and developmental dyslexia: A review of the research literature. *Reading and Writing: An Interdisciplinary Journal, 17*, 301–324.

Umbel, V.M., Pearson, B.Z., Fernández, M.C., & Oller, D.K. (1992). Measuring bilingual children's receptive vocabularies. *Child Development, 63*, 1012–1020.

Wolf, M., & Katzir-Cohen, T. (2001). Reading fluency and its intervention. *Scientific Studies of Reading, 5*, 211–238.

CHAPTER 11

Language selection, control, and conceptual-lexical development in bilinguals and multilinguals*

John W. Schwieter and Aline Ferreira
Wilfrid Laurier University

This chapter presents recent developments in the cognitive underpinnings of bilingual speech production. Upon close observation of the theories explaining how speakers of non-native languages are able to select the language in which to speak and control cross-linguistic interference from non-target words competing for selection, it is apparent that these abilities – and more generally, the cognitive processes of bilingual speech production – take shape in the context of a dynamic conceptual and lexical framework that is adaptable to accommodate various functionalities during non-native language development. This chapter also addresses the effects of language acquisition beyond two languages and highlights the implications for teaching and learning of non-native languages by advocating for immersion experiences and pedagogical considerations that foster conceptual and lexical development.

1. Introduction

Cognitive perspectives of second language (L2) acquisition and bilingualism continue to be a primary research interest among many scholars (for recent comprehensive work, see de Groot 2011; Grosjean & Li 2013). When we stop to think about the efforts that the human mind puts forth in order to create language, we are left amazed. Indeed, the ability to transmit one thought into the mind of another individual through speech is truly remarkable. Yet as speakers, we do this every day when we communicate. While this may be a natural and automatic ability, each word that is uttered has been carefully chosen and accessed by a complex

* A previous version of this paper was presented at the *8th Quebec-Ontario Dialogues on the Acquisition of Spanish* at Université de Montréal. We would also like to thank Panos Athanasopoulos, Annette de Groot, and Eileen Fancher for their comments on this chapter. Their suggestions have without a doubt helped to improve the quality of this chapter.

cognitive procedure. For example, when a monolingual English speaker sees a friend whom he wishes to greet, he might say, *hi*. But he could also say *hello* or *greetings*, two other words which provide satisfactory alternatives. Fortunately or unfortunately for him, simply the intent to greet someone results in the activation of a number of potential word candidates in the speaker's mind, but what regulates this activation? What helps disregard the other word choices that are competing for selection but are not chosen for production? In other words, what is ultimately responsible for selecting the right word?

Let's imagine that the speaker had been a bilingual. This complicates the situation given that the activated greeting words would potentially create even more competition due to the activated translation equivalents (e.g., perhaps for an English-Spanish bilingual, *hola, saludos*, and *buenas*). After posing the same questions as in the monolingual case, we are left with an additional question of how a word is chosen in one language over its translation equivalent. Indeed, once language learners begin acquiring L2 vocabulary, they develop a conceptual system shared by two languages in which each concept is represented by more than one word (e.g., for English learners of Spanish, the concept BOOK would be attached to the words *book* and *libro*)[1]. Under this assumption – and because bilinguals almost always say the right word in the language they wish to speak – this implies that there must be a process that facilitates language selection and a cognitive control procedure that prevents wrong lexical items from being erroneously selected for production.

This chapter will discuss studies and recent developments in research exploring the specific cognitive underpinnings of bilingual speech production. It will investigate how the bilingual mind selects the language in which to speak and overcomes cross-linguistic lexical interference in order to support and execute an accurate and efficient lexical access procedure. In addition to discussing language and concept selection, lexical processing, and cognitive control, special emphasis will be placed on the variability of these procedures, the organization of the conceptual store, the effect of language learning beyond two languages, and the implications for teaching and learning of non-native languages.

2.   Bilingual speech production

In the example above in which a bilingual uttered a greeting, he/she was faced with selecting the right word in the right language, whether he/she was conscious of it

---

1.   Recent studies, however, reveal that in most cases, concepts themselves can be language-specific, and there are very few words, if any, in the bilingual lexicon that are true translation equivalents (Ameel, Storms, Malt, & Sloman 2005; Pavlenko 1999, 2005; Pavlenko & Malt 2011; but see Pavlenko 2011 for an overview).

or not. The fact that there are multiple possible choices gives rise to interference from those belonging to the non-target language. Although some explanations may posit that contextual or social factors may guide this procedure such as Grosjean's (2000) notion of language modes, others emphasize cognitive perspectives. To better understand this phenomenon via the latter line of thought, let's imagine that when a bilingual intends to say the word *table*, the conceptual representation mapping on to the word is activated. However, related concepts and words (chair, plate, etc.) are also activated during this process. If this speaker is an English-Spanish bilingual, for instance, the word *mesa* (along with other related words in Spanish) may also become activated. Under this assumption, at least two lexical representations, namely *table* and *mesa*, are activated and compete for selection. How is the right word in the right language chosen for speech production? This theoretical question became known as *the hard problem* (Finkbeiner, Almeida, Janssen & Caramazza 2006). Figure 1 demonstrates the complex interactions between the concepts and the words they represent and indeed show inconclusive activation flow between the conceptual and lexical systems (as noted by the question mark). When intending to say the word *cat*, the identified concept CAT sends activation to the words mapped on to it in both languages. The notion of the hard problem prompted researchers to investigate and articulate how activation flows through the conceptual and lexical systems and how such activation plays a role in language selection and lexical processing.

Previous research in the last decade has explored this question by probing two main issues: how the target language is selected for production and how nontarget

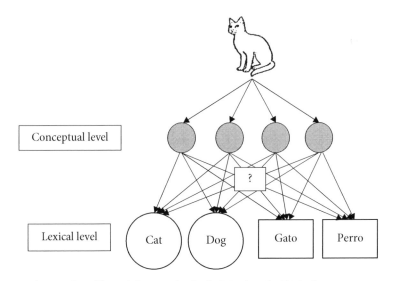

Figure 1. The Hard Problem: Selecting the Right Word in the Right Language

interference is controlled. From these studies emerged two distinct explanations suggesting that bilingual speech production is either a language-selective or non-selective procedure. From Figure 1, we can see that coming to speak a word is a multiple level process in which concepts, words, and their sounds receive activation in a cascaded manner. Once the target concept has been activated, the ability to rely on higher-linguistic information (i.e., language of production, register, etc.) and the ways in which cross-linguistic information is controlled have been the primary motivation for recent studies. The next sections will discuss how activation flows through the conceptual to the lexical systems in either language-selective or non-selective manners.

3. Language selection

As pointed out by La Heij (2005), lexical access is an important part of bilingual speech production that connects nonverbal thought and language. Models of bilingual speech production such as La Heij's Concept Selection Hypothesis (CSH) explain the process of retrieving words during speech production on the basis of higher-linguistic information. While in the conceptual system, nonverbal representations express world knowledge (i.e., the conceptual representations of words), in the lexicon, words are mapped on to these concepts along with their syntactic and phonological components. The CSH model discusses the notion of conceptual mediation, the ability to utilize higher-linguistic cues at the conceptual level in order to facilitate language processing.

An important part of the Concept Selection Hypothesis is that bilinguals are able to make use of a complex set of higher linguistic cues and, in particular, a language cue which specified the language in which to speak (La Heij 2005). The notion of a language cue originates as early as Levelt's (1989) monolingual speech production model which was defined as an abstract cue found within the preverbal message which allows lexicalization to occur and automatically raises activation levels of the target language's lexicon.

La Heij (2005: 290) suggests that with respect to the simple modular account of bilingual lexical access, two explanations can be proposed:

> First, the language in which the bilingual intends to speak is in the form of a "language cue" – part of a complex preverbal message that contains all conceptual, pragmatic, and affective characteristics of the word to be retrieved. Second, the actual selection of a word is a relatively simple process mainly based on the activation levels of the lexical representations.

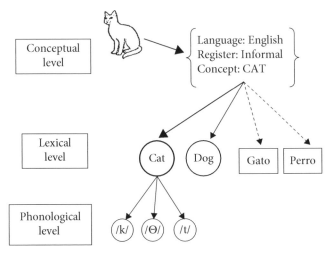

Figure 2. Bilingual Speech Production according to the CSH (La Heij 2005)

This language-specific approach with a language cue at its core can be seen in Figure 2. In the figure, the concept CAT is also accompanied with other high-linguistic information, one of which is the language cue which helps focus activation flow to the target language (as noted by the boldness of the arrows). Because *cat* has received the highest level of activation, it will be chosen for phonological encoding.

Empirical support for the CSH (La Heij 2005) has emerged in several studies (Bloem & La Heij 2003; Bloem, van den Boogaard & La Heij 2004; La Heij, Hooglander, Kerling & Van der Velden 1996; La Heij, Kuipers & Starreveld 2006). In this model of bilingual speech production, emphasis is placed on the ability to rely on higher-linguistic information – and in particular, a language cue which is available at the conceptual level (preverbalization). Under this assumption, when a bilingual is asked to name an object, the visual input of this object activates its conceptual representation along with semantic features that are attached to the word in question and other higher-linguistic information such as language or production, register, etc. This available information will cause additional activation is sent to lexical nodes in the appropriate language, given that the language of production has already been identified. As such, the CSH simplifies the lexicalization process by assuming that when the target stimulus activates the concept, the (unique) corresponding word is directly activated and selected in the lexicon. This line of thought draws on Poulisse and Bongaerts' (1994) view of bilingual lexical access which likewise assumes that preverbalization will contain higher-linguistic cues that ensure higher activation levels of target words.

4.   Language control

Under the assumptions of the CSH (La Heij 2005) in which a language cue assists subsequent stages of speech production by regulating the amount of activation that is sent to target and non-target words, little is needed to explain how the right word in the right language is chosen for production: this has already been specified from pre-verbalization. However, an explanation for a non-selective account is needed if bilinguals cannot rely on a language cue to point them to the right word in the right language. Costa (2005) assumes that the level of the activation is not regulated by a language cue and thus, when activation from the conceptual level is dispersed to the corresponding lexical nodes, it creates a competitive lexical selection process that requires language selection. This non-selective line of thought suggests that selecting the language of production is a competitive process that is not readily available throughout speech planning. Costa further examines both language se-lective and non-selective views and the extent to which both accounts make dif-ferential predictions regarding the flow of activation from conceptual to lexical stages and language selection processes. Although Costa's review of the literature overall suggested that activation flow is language nonspecific, he argued that lan-guage selection, on the other hand, may or may not be language specific. Indeed, because of this, bilingual speech production may need to rely on further assistance at the lexical level where words in both languages compete for selection.

This competitive process that is hypothesized to take place at the lexical level is argued to be assisted by reliance on inhibitory control (IC). One widely-accept-ed explanation for this is Green's (1986, 1998) Inhibitory Control (IC) Model which argues that the language production system has multiple levels of control and that lexical nodes are marked with language tags which designate them to a specific language. When words in both languages are active and competing to con-trol output, successful selection requires the suppression of competing non-target words. The primary assumption of the IC Model is that language production is a product of inhibition, control schemas, and a supervisory attentional system. Al-though the model further argues multiple levels of control in the bilingual mind with each level corresponding to a specific schema, IC operates exclusively at the lemma level. Figure 3 illustrates both Costa's (2005) and Green's (IC) theories. The figure assumes that when bilinguals speak, the language selection and control pro-cedures entail a conceptualizer which builds conceptual representations that are driven by the communicative goal. These both are mediated by the SAS together with components of the language system (i.e., language task schemas). The bilin-gual mind will turn to language tags to help determine which non-target words (i.e., those competing for selection) will need to be inhibited and subsequently ap-ply IC to those competitors.

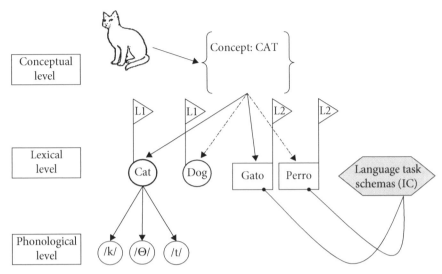

Figure 3. Bilingual Speech Production according to the ICM (Green 1986, 1998)

The IC Model (Green 1986, 1998) is supported by speech production patterns observed in language switching experiments. For instance, Meuter (1994) and Meuter and Allport (1999) observed that the time needed to switch from an L2 to an L1 was longer than vice versa, providing the first evidence that bilingual speech is facilitated by IC. These asymmetrical reaction times were not surprising given that the IC Model predicted that it will take longer to reactivate from inhibition a more dominant language (e.g., L1) compared to a weaker language (e.g., L2). Following Meuter and Allport's pioneering study, other researchers have accepted that support for IC can be validated through switch costs that differ when bilinguals switch from L1 to L2 or vice versa (Costa & Santesteban 2004; Schwieter 2008, 2010; Schwieter & Sunderman 2008, 2011 but see Finkbeiner et al. 2006 and Koch, Gade, Schuch & Philipp 2010 for criticism of this assumption). Theoretically speaking, when bilinguals switch into their more dominant language (L1), they suffer a larger switching cost than if they switch into their weaker language (L2). According to the IC Model, this is expected because it will take more time to reactive the larger L1 from suppression. Although the ICM posits that the size of the language may determine the magnitude of inhibition effect, it goes without saying that this is theoretically confounded with the relative strength of L1 representations due to its higher frequency of usage (Schwieter & Sunderman 2008).

Interestingly, upon closer examination, recent studies have discovered that asymmetrical switch costs may not be observed for highly-proficient bilinguals (Costa & Santesteban 2004; Costa, Santesteban, & Ivanova 2006; Schwieter 2010).

Costa (2005) further proposed that speech production may potentially be achieved without reliance on IC if conceptual representations are language-specific. Following this account, the language of production would be specified as early as preverbalization, as elaborated in the CSH (La Heij 2005), and language tags at the lexical level would be checked to ensure that the target word matched the intended concept. Empirical evidence for the notion of concept mediation has emerged in many studies which have discussed the functionality of a language-specific selection mechanism as an alternative to IC (Costa & Santesteban 2004; Costa et al. 2006; Finkbeiner et al. 2006; Schwieter & Sunderman 2008, 2009). These studies sparked by theories put forth by La Heij and Costa were the first to question the variability of the processes which accompany language selection and lexical control.

5.   The variable nature of language selection and control

Costa and Santesteban (2004) demonstrated that not all speakers of two languages will display asymmetrical switch costs and thus fail to support reliance on IC. In this study, the researchers conducted a series of five picture-naming experiments among less- and more-proficient bilinguals following the language switching experimental paradigm (Meuter & Allport 1999). Although switch costs were reported for all participants, asymmetrical switch costs only emerged for less-proficient bilinguals but not for highly-proficient bilinguals. To further explore this, Costa et al. (2006) investigated the potential effects of language similarity (e.g., Catalan and Spanish) and L2 age of acquisition on reliance on IC. Even though the researchers failed to find significant effects for these variables, their experiments investigating the performance of highly- proficient Spanish-Catalan bilinguals who switched between two weak languages (L3 and L4) showed a number of interesting results. The switch costs were larger for the L3 than for the L4 which led the researchers to hypothesize that if the switching task does not involve at least one of the dominant languages, a language-specific selection mechanism cannot be engaged. Costa et al. concluded that if the language-switching task involves the L1 and a weak language, bilinguals will demonstrate asymmetrical switch costs because lexical representations of the weak language are not integrated to a lexicon. Under this assumption, cross-linguistic interference must be dealt with by mechanisms of IC. In all, Costa et al.'s study suggested that less- and more-proficient bilinguals can exhibit similar patterns with regard to the cognitive underpinnings of the functionality of speech regardless of language similarity or age of L2 acquisition (see also Schwieter, 2008 for additional evidence that discounted the effects of language backgrounds such as heritage speakers vs. language learners). The researchers speculated that there may be two possibilities that reconcile the variability of reliance on IC: (1) the robustness of L2 lexical representations determines the functionality of a language-specific selection mechanism and (2) the L1 mediates lexical access when less-proficient bilinguals need to access the meaning of the L2 word.

Schwieter and Sunderman (2008) furthered defined lexical robustness as an important construct in estimating global proficiency or fluency in a specific language given that it measures the greater automaticity of word retrieval that arises from the familiarity with and frequency of its access. In essence, lexical robustness is a numerical way of estimating the size and strength of the lexicon. From a theoretical standpoint, lexical robustness refers to the relationship that exists between words and the concepts that they represent. As such, when language learners interact in their L2, and in turn engage in lexical access – and more importantly when they regularly do so – they began to strengthen the relationship between non-native words and their concepts. In the simplest terms, lexical robustness incorporates vocabulary knowledge and fluency and effectively provides a way in which to operationalize the dynamic nature of the development and strengthening of word-to-concept relationship.

To probe the effects of lexical robustness, Schwieter and Sunderman (2008) carried out a verbal fluency task (Gollan, Montoya & Werner 2002) that specifically set out to measure the L2 lexical robustness. In this task, typically a total of ten semantic categories (or a combination of semantic categories and first-letter categories) are individually verbalized to each participant. For each category, the participants are given a specific amount of time (usually 30 or 60 seconds) to verbally produce as many items within that category as s/he can in the requested language. The verbal fluency task, thus, taps into the lexicalization process in the form of speeded lexical retrieval and has consistently correlated with participants' self-ratings of proficiency in previous studies (Schwieter & Sunderman 2008, 2009, 2011). In Schwieter and Sunderman (2008), a total lexical robustness score was calculated by adding all responses from each of the ten semantic categories. This was then used in regression analyses along with data from a picture-naming task with language switches (Costa & Santesteban 2004) and suggested that the cost of switching to the L1 was larger than the cost of switching to the L2 but only for bilinguals with relatively weak L2 lexical robustness. A linear visualization of the switch cost with increased L2 lexical robustness demonstrated that the switch cost gradually became zero at approximately a lexical robustness score of 110 (a number which is completely arbitrary for the purposes of this chapter). For this particular sample of bilinguals, a threshold effect suggested that when the strength of L2 lexical robustness was above 110, bilinguals were able to engage a language-specific selection mechanism (i.e., rely on higher-linguistic cues during pre-verbalization) and subsequently avoided the need for mechanisms of IC. The

Selection by Proficiency Model (SbP) (Schwieter & Sunderman 2008, 2009), a bilingual speech production model that visualizes developmental effects on IC and the language-specific selection mechanism was put forth to bring to light the impact of L2 lexical robustness on speech production. In the next section, we return to discuss the SbP Model after outlining the Modified Hierarchical Model (Pavlenko 2009) which illustrates the lexical and conceptual architecture of the developing bilingual system.

6.   The dynamic conceptual-lexical system

A pioneering study that demonstrated the interaction between the lexical and conceptual systems and the developmental effects of L2 acquisition is that of Kroll and Stewart (1994). The Revised Hierarchical Model (RHM) argues that as learners become more proficient in their L2, the strength of word-to-concept connections for L2 increases and the need for lexical processing via the L1 decreases. Although many subsequent studies over the last few decades have generally provided support for the claims put forth by the RHM (Kroll & De Groot 1997; Kroll, Michael & Sankaranarayanan 1998; Kroll & Tokowicz 2001; Schwieter & Sunderman 2009; Sholl, Sankaranarayanan & Kroll 1995), others have reported mixed findings (Bloem & La Heij 2003; Bloem, van den Boogaard & La Heij 2004; De Groot & Poot 1997; La Heij, Hooglander, Kerling & Van der Velden 1996; but see Brysbaert & Duyck 2010 for a full discussion of criticism of the RHM and a rebuttal by Kroll, Van Hell, Tokowicz & Green 2010).

The notion of a dynamic system containing multiple levels of interaction and activation has been posited in a number of models such as the Bilingual Interactive Activation Model (Dijkstra, Van Heuven & Grainger 1998), Shared Asymmetrical Model (Dong, Cui & MacWhinney 2005), and the Distributed Feature Model (De Groot 1992, 1993, 1995; De Groot, Dannenburg & Van Hell 1994; Van Hell 1998; Van Hell & De Groot 1998). These bilingual models have had a tremendous impact on recent work that has made extensions to their predictions, both on what is known about bilingual speech comprehension and production. Two recent developmental models are the Modified Hierarchical Model (MHM) (Pavlenko 2009) and the aforementioned SbP Model (Schwieter & Sunderman 2008, 2009). While the former illustrates the lexical and conceptual architecture of the developing bilingual system, the latter describes the cognitive mechanisms that are utilized during lexical and conceptual selection. Together, these two models help to present a clear overview of the make-up and functionality of the dynamic nature of language selection and lexical processing in bilingual speech.

6.1   The architecture: The modified hierarchical model

A number of studies have suggested that words in the L1 and L2 share a common conceptual store (Costa, Miozzo & Caramazza 1999; Hermans 2000; Hermans, Bongaerts, De Bot & Schreuder 1998, but see Heredia 2008 for a summary). Building on this assumption, Pavlenko (2009) advocates that research should verify what exact elements are shared and what are not shared between conceptual representations and words. Pavlenko argues that naming, categorization, sorting and narrative elicitation tasks are more effective at evoking the ways in which bilinguals connect the words and their real-world referents, since they maintain ecological validity and they can be proposed in any culture without losing the sensitive differences (see Schwieter 2011 for a review).

Pavlenko (2009) also discusses the cross-cultural nature of conceptual equivalence, arguing that linguistic categories differ among cultures. If the bilingual wishes to use both languages accurately and appropriately, he or she will develop different categories, according to the target language. The researcher also discussed the possibility that not all translation equivalents are conceptual equivalents implying that although some words may be in a relationship of conceptual equivalence, other words may only be partially (non)equivalent, or entirely conceptually non-equivalent. In the case of conceptual equivalence, linguistic categories in both functional languages share categorical structure and boundaries.

Pavlenko (2009) argues that when bilinguals are acquiring new L2 words, a process of conceptual restructuring occurs to accommodate this new learning (see also Athanasopoulos 2011; Athanasopoulos & Kasai 2008; Cook, Bassetti, Kasai, Sasaki & Takahashi 2006 for a more detailed account). Under this assumption, the learner readapts the structure of the categories according to the specificities of the new language and also develops a new multimodal representation in order to connect the new words to its real-world referents (Ameel et al. 2005; Athanasopoulos 2009). The ideas put forth by Pavlenko can be visualized through the MHM (see Figure 4) which incorporates into the conceptual-lexical architecture the notion of degrees of relationships of conceptual equivalence (conceptual equivalent, partially equivalent, or non-equivalent).

The MHM (Pavlenko 2009) depicts a dynamic account of conceptual and lexical processing which builds on the strengths and refines the weaknesses of the RHM and other widely-accepted models such as the Distributed Feature model (De Groot 1992, 1993, 1995) and the Shared Asymmetrical Model (Dong, Cui, & MacWhinney 2005). As seen in the figure, the MHM retains the developmental progression from lexical to conceptual mediation to account for L2 acquisition. However, it diverges from previous models by hypothesizing an organization of the conceptual store which includes concepts that may be fully shared, partially

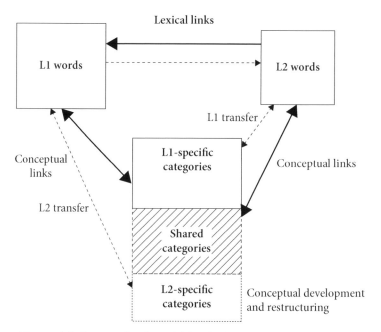

Figure 4. The Modified Hierarchical Model (Pavlenko 2009)

overlapping, or entirely language-specific. Another distinguishing feature is Pavlenko's inclusion of conceptual and semantic transfer (see also Jarvis & Pavlenko 2008) and perhaps more importantly, her general view that one of the primary objectives in L2 acquisition is centered around conceptual restructuring and target-like development of linguistic categories.

6.2   The functionality: The selection by proficiency model

While the MHM (Pavlenko 2009) describes a blueprint for conceptual and lexical structure, the functionality of such a dynamic system can be illustrated through the SbP Model (Schwieter & Sunderman 2008, 2009). Although the SbP Model was originally developed on claims put forth by the RHM (Kroll & Stewart 1994), it can easily adapt the claims of the MHM.

According to SbP Model (Schwieter & Sunderman 2008, 2009), L2 lexical robustness helps determine which cognitive abilities are functional during language selection and lexical access. Essentially, the model argues that when L2 lexical robustness is weak, language learners will rely on IC due to the inability to directly access the conceptual store without consulting the L1. As they develop stronger L2 lexical robustness, they establish stronger L2 conceptual links and develop the

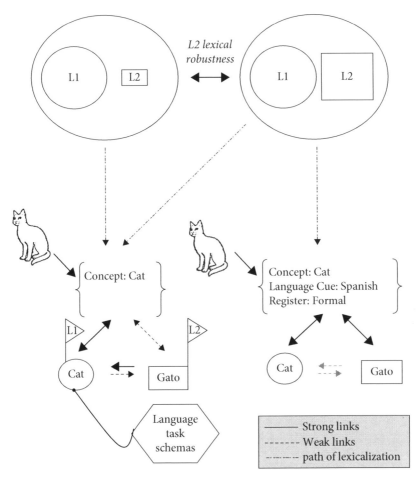

Figure 5. Selection by Proficiency Model (Schwieter & Sunderman 2008, 2009)

ability to engage a language-specific selection mechanism subsumed in the ability to rely on higher-linguistic cues at the conceptual level. Figure 5 shows the effects of lexical robustness development from very weak (left) to very strong (right). In the figure, the differential strengths of association between the conceptual links and lexical links are illustrated by the thickness of the arrows in the model (darker arrows represent stronger links and the dashed arrows represent either weaker links or, as in the right portion of the model, those which may be present but not necessarily called upon). The situation on the left – when differences between L1 and L2 dominance are greatest – suggests that the language of production is not determined until the lexical level where IC will be called upon to assist lexical access. Similar to the CSH (La Heij 2005), the right portion of the model depicts a bilingual who is highly proficient in both languages and is able to rely on higher-linguistic cues at the conceptual level allowing for the target language to be established from the first stages of speech production. The model assumes that in certain situations, even the most proficient bilingual may need to revert back to IC (e.g., as did the highly proficient bilinguals in Costa et al. 2006 when switching between the weaker L3 and L4). The reverse is not true for less-proficient bilinguals whose ability to engage a language-specific selection mechanism has not been fully developed.

Before proceeding to discuss some of these issues in speakers of more than two languages, it is important to point out that the notion of a dynamic conceptual-lexical system that is constantly developing in terms of its cognitive architecture and functionality can be appreciated in both the MHM (Pavlenko 2009) and the SbP Model (Schwieter & Sunderman 2008, 2009). In all, these models attempt to build on the strengths of previous work discussed above which not only differ from one another in the type of conceptual representations that they assume (i.e., unitary or distributed), but also in their assumptions of either language-specific or non-specific elements in the conceptual representations. Additionally, the MHM and SbP display the intricacies of how the form and conceptual representations are connected while explicating how these representations and the links between them change with development.

7.   Beyond two languages

It may not be surprising that with the notion that dynamic changes occur to the conceptual and lexical systems, came studies that sought to test the effects of language development by including participants with relatively weak proficiency in a third language (Costa et al. 2006; Linck, Schwieter & Sunderman 2012, in preparation; Schwieter & Sunderman 2011). For instance, following Schwieter and Sunderman (2009), Schwieter and Ferreira (under review) carried out a Stroop-word translation task with English language learners of a relatively weak L3 Spanish. In two separate Stroop word-translation experiments, the participants orally translated target words from L1 to L3 and L3 to L1 in the context of semantically-related or unrelated distracter words or line drawings (Snodgrass & Vanderwart 1980). For example, in the L1 to L3 translation block, participants may have seen the English word *dog* accompanied by a word distracter such as *gato* (cat, a related item) or *mesa* (table, an unrelated item) or by a picture distracter of a cat or table. The task at hand in this example would be for participants to verbalize into a microphone the translation of the word *dog* (*perro*). The results in Schwieter and Ferreira provided additional support for the notion that language learners with weak L3 proficiency must rely more on L1 lexical links and thus are unable to conceptually mediate in the L3 without consulting the L1 (Kroll & Stewart 1994; Pavlenko 2009). The study also uncovered interesting results suggesting that when restricting the semantic category of the target words, a differential semantic relatedness effect (Bloem & La Heij 2003) emerges demonstrating that the relatedness of word and picture distracters has differential effects depending on the direction of translation. The researchers explain these findings in the context of Pavlenko's work.

In the language switching paradigm, trilingual studies are also gaining momentum. Following Costa et al. (2006), Philipp, Gade, and Koch (2007) conducted separate numeral-naming tasks in which German language learners of English and French switched between their L1 and L2; L2 and L3; and L1 and L3. Although the results revealed asymmetrical switch costs within each of the language pairs, these effects did not significantly differ between the pairs (i.e., the magnitude of switch cost was no longer for L1–L2 than for L2–L3 or L1–L3). The researchers conducted an additional experiment exploring n-2 repetition costs (the performance impairment of language A in sequences of ABA sequences compared to CBA) to further investigate the dominance-related inhibition account (Green 1998; Meuter & Allport 1999). The researchers argued that an n-2 repetition cost can be observed in language switching tasks involving three languages such that the focus is on language A when it is found in the task sequence ABA compared to when it is found in the task sequence CBA. The increased processing time and decreased accuracy of ABA is attributed to persisting inhibition of a task that was recently switched away from (see Mayr & Keele 2000). The study also revealed that while the n-2 repetition cost was significantly greater when n was L1, L3 repetition costs were larger than L2 repetition costs. In a subsequent study, Philipp and Koch (2009) provided further evidence for n-2 language repetitions conditions compared to the n-2 language nonrepetitions. The researchers argued for persisting inhibition of abandoned languages. Together, their results suggest that there is a global inhibitory process effect during speech production tasks that affects the mental representation of competing languages, including the mental lexicon and phonological aspects.

In order to discuss the effects of lexical robustness on the variability of reliance on IC in trilinguals as was suggested in the bilingualism literature (Costa et al. 2006; Schwieter & Sunderman 2008, 2009), Schwieter and Sunderman (2011) conducted a trilingual adaptation of the picture-naming experiment among English (L1) language learners of French (L2) and Spanish (L3). By looking at the extent to which L2 and L3 lexical robustness modulate switch costs, the findings suggested evidence for reliance on IC for all three languages. However, interesting interactions with non-native lexical robustness were uncovered: the strength of L2 lexical robustness affected performance in all languages whereas L3 lexical robustness only affected L3 performance. The results suggest that in the context of having to switch between three languages within a single experiment, trilingual speakers rely on IC. The researchers argued that in terms of the ability to rely on a language-specific selection mechanism, L2 and L3 lexical robustness was not strong enough to conceptually mediate in weak languages. Similar findings were reported in a replication study of a different population of trilinguals by Schwieter (2013a) which again employed a trilingual picture-naming task to examine whether the magnitude of IC for each language would be proportionate to lexical robustness scores. Although IC was again associated with all three languages, there was only a correlation between L3 lexical robustness and L3 switch costs. This provided additional support for the notion that although IC was modulated by L3 lexical robustness, such effect was restricted to the L3. This may not be surprising given that Schwieter and Sunderman (2008) had argued that in bilingual speech production, lexical robustness in the least dominant language would modulate reliance on IC. The results from Schwieter and Sunderman (2011) and Schwieter (forthcoming) shed light on the familiar story as bilingual studies such as Costa and Santesteban (2004) and Costa et al. (2006) that the proficiency level of the least dominant language affects reliance on IC. Although we are far from fully understanding the role of IC and the functionality of a language-specific selection mechanism in trilingual speech production, research in trilingual language switching seems to suggest that each language may produce differential effects on the cognitive control of language.

7.1   Executive functions and a (multi)lingual advantage

A growing area of research has demonstrated the cognitive benefits of bilingualism (see work done by Bialystok and colleagues) and its effects on domain-general executive functions (i.e., those cognitive processes involved in things such as memory, planning, reasoning, and conflict resolution). Indeed, a lifetime of experience being a bilingual has shown cognitive benefits. Bilinguals (both children and aging adults) outperform their age-matched monolingual counterparts on a variety of tasks including the Simon task (Bialystok, Craik, Klein & Viswanathan 2004), ambiguous figures (Bialystok & Shapero 2005), and a modified antisaccade task (Bialystok, Craik & Ryan 2006) (see Bialystok 2009 for a review). In a recent examination of individual differences in language control, Festman, Rodríguez-Fornells and Münte (2010) compared two groups of late bilinguals and found that the group with better language control abilities had a cognitive advantage on tasks measuring executive functions (EFs) such as IC.

Bialystok (2009) compared two groups of bilinguals (less- and more-proficient) and one group of monolinguals and found that the more-proficient bilingual group produced more correct responses in a letter fluency task in spite of longer mean latencies, a finding that potentially emerged because the task demands for controlled processing, such as maintaining a novel retrieval strategy, monitoring, and switching. While other studies have looked at EFs and phonological processing (Hugdahl et al. 2009; Soveri, Laine, Hämäläinen & Hugdahl 2011), Prior and Macwhinney (2010) investigated whether bilingualism may lead to an increased ability to control processes that reconfigure mental resources for a change of mental set (task). In their comparison of bilingual and monolingual groups, their results suggested that bilinguals suffered significantly smaller switch costs in task switching compared to monolinguals. The researchers argued that a lifelong experience in bilingualism, and in particular switching back and forth between languages, may contribute to increased efficiency in shifting between mental sets. The benefits of bilingualism on EFs have been similarity uncovered in several other studies (Costa, Hernández & Sebastián-Gallés 2008; Hernández et al. 2010; La Heij & Boelens 2011; Meiran, Chorev & Sapir 2000; Philipp et al. 2007).

Not surprisingly, this vein of research pointing to a bilingual advantage has consequently sparked studies in trilingualism. Following the findings from Festman et al. (2010) and Schwieter and Sunderman (2011), Linck et al. (2012) questioned whether or not there is a domain-general IC mechanism (e.g., Green 1998) facilitating speech production in trilinguals. The researchers used a Simon task (Bialystok et al. 2004; Simon & Rudell 1967) to estimate IC abilities and whether or not they are related to language switching performance in a picture-naming experiment. The Simon task, unlike the picture-naming task with language switches, provides a way to avoid inhibitory control tasks involving linguistic interference to better examine the role of domain-general rather than language-oriented inhibitory control. In this task, a series of red and blue boxes are presented in one of three locations on a computer screen: central, left of center, or right of center). Participants are instructed to respond with a left or right button press based on the color of the stimulus while ignoring the stimulus location. Congruent trials are when the locations of the stimulus and the correct response match while incongruent trials refer to when the stimulus and response locations mismatch (i.e., the stimulus is presented on the opposite side of the screen from the location of the correct response). Response times are typically longer on incongruent trials than on congruent trials and by calculating the difference between incongruent and congruent trials, we can by a Simon effect which serves as an index of an individual's ability to inhibit the prepotent tendency to respond based on the (task-irrelevant) location of the stimulus (Linck et al.).

Linck et al. (2012) confirmed their assumption that better IC (i.e., smaller Simon effects) predicted smaller switch costs, and that the non-target language is inhibited independently. Furthermore, the results showed that when naming the pictures in the L3 (Spanish), the L1 was strongly inhibited, but they did not find a relationship when switching into L2, showing that the abilities related to the domain-general IC may be related to the level of proficiency in the language and that different EFs may contribute to the cognitive control of language production. Given this finding, Linck, Schwieter, and Sunderman (in preparation) explored individual differences in three EFs (working memory, IC, and task switching) and their relationship with performance on a trilingual language switching task for a group of trilinguals. Analyses indicated complex interactions between EFs and language switching. Better IC was only related to smaller L3 switch costs and whereas better working memory was related to larger switch costs in the L1 as well as the L2 and L3, the latter two effects only emerged when switching from the L1. The researchers argue unique contributions of each EF to cognitive control during language switching. Together, Linck et al. (2012) and Linck et al. (in preparation) suggest that IC mechanisms may functionally operate both proactively and reactively (see also Colzato et al. 2008).

The findings of the studies mentioned thus far have applicable implications for how languages are taught and learned. With a better understanding of the conceptual-lexical structure and its cognitive functionality, we can now turn to discussing how these issues relate to second language teaching and learning.

8.   Implications for language teaching and learning

Many would argue that an ideal environment for L2 learning is one in which learners are immersed in the target language full of meaningful interactions. In the context of what has been discussed in this chapter, a study abroad experience allows the language learner to practice actively suppressing the L1, a larger system which arguably requires more inhibition (and more practice inhibiting) due to its larger system size (Green 1998; Linck et al. 2012). As such, in a perfect world, L2 educators in non-L2-speaking environments would take their students abroad (or to other areas within their country, if possible). Not only have many studies reported significant L2 acquisition during study abroad experiences (see Davidson 2010 for a review) and even during the shortest of study abroad experiences (Allen and Herron 2003; Schwieter 2013b), but the study abroad context provides a way in which L2 learners have the opportunity to potentially develop the ability to conceptually mediate in two languages more quickly. While this benefit may be a payoff on its own, it might also come with a price. Linck, Kroll, and Sunderman (2009) investigated the effects of L2 immersion learning on the L1. In particular, they tested the hypothesis that immersion benefits L2 learning due to attenuated influence and inhibition of the more dominant L1. Participants were English learners of Spanish who were either studying Spanish abroad in Spain or in a traditional classroom in their home country. Performance on both comprehension and production tasks showed that immersed learners outperformed their classroom counterparts with respect to L2 proficiency. However, the results also revealed reduced L1 access for the immersed learners. The researchers explained that this could be explained by an inhibitory account. Specifically, they speculated that increased L1 inhibition during an immersion experience fostered a situation in which stronger lexical-conceptual links developed, "making learners more resistant to L1 lexical competition at multiple levels during translation recognition upon returning home to the L1-dominant environment" (2009: 1513).

Although it may be a challenge from an administrative perspective, L2 educators should consider investing in faculty-led initiatives in which students would travel abroad under the supervision of a professor from the home institution. Under these circumstances, the traditional classroom experience transforms into an environment which provides constant opportunities for meaningful interaction in the target language. In addition to Linck et al. (2009), recent studies reporting on faculty-led initiatives have shown significant benefits for second language identity and socialization (Schwieter & Kunert 2012) and lexical robustness development (Schwieter 2013b).

In Schwieter and Kunert (2012), the researchers implemented pre-departure cultural sessions in the L1 to provide an overview of cultural and historical information that students subsequently contextualized and learned more about during the immersion experience. From the open-ended interviews exploring issues of language development, identity, and socialization, the researchers argued that the cultural sessions created a foundation on which L2 learning in context could grow and increased interaction with L2 community members (Kruse & Brubaker 2007). In another recent study, Schwieter (2013b) discusses non-native lexical development (and attrition) during an L3 short-term study abroad experience among language learners who spoke English as their L1, French as their L2, and Spanish as their L3. Their self-ratings of language abilities and lexical robustness in all three languages were tested on three different occasions (one day before departure, 12 days after arrival, and 18 days after arrival) using a language history questionnaire and verbal fluency measure, respectively. In terms of lexical robustness, the results revealed significant growth only in the L3 but further analyses demonstrated that learners with lower pre-departure L3 lexical robustness realized a significantly larger growth in L3 lexical robustness than those who began the experience with higher L3 lexical robustness. Not surprising is the fact that these findings also emerged when analyzing the self-ratings (i.e., in terms of overall language abilities, learners felt as though their L1 stayed the same but that their L3 significantly improved). However, as for the L2 while immersed in an L3, participants felt as though their overall L2 abilities significantly deteriorated as their L3 abilities gained momentum.

Needless to say, while advocating for immersion experiences has good intention, it is a far cry from representing the typical context in which adults acquire language. Knowing this reality, applied linguists and language educators should also consider exploring and/or implementing pedagogical approaches that accomplish similar goals. Activities would be valuable that emphasize the meaningful development of connections between concepts (e.g., pictures) and the words they represent (Pavlenko, 2009). Potentially, activities could target the effective use of language production in mixed-language environments either by induced language switching and working on activities equally in both languages. Ideally, these pedagogical considerations will take into account previous theoretical findings and the importance of developing both conceptual-lexical architecture and functionality.

A final point to consider in light of this chapter's discussions (particularly regarding language control) is that language educators should be aware that it is not detrimental to L2 acquisition to use the L1 on rare occasions in L2 classrooms. This is not to say that language educators should begin to regularly speak in the L1 in L2 classes. On the contrary, the research that this chapter has reviewed would arguably suggest that incorporating language switching, perhaps in 5–10% of the language input, would not only strengthen a language learner's ability to control his/her languages (a skill that is fortified with gains in native-like competence) but it would also provide instances in which the language switch would perk attention as it would require more cognitive effort on the part of the language learner. Indeed, the cognitive ability to switch back and forth between languages and to control and restrict language input and output to current language demands is an intricate and important skill that can be practiced alongside language learning activities or simply in the input given by the instructor.

9.   Conclusion

This chapter has examined and discussed recent research exploring cognitive perspectives of speech production among multilinguals. We began the chapter by introducing how bilingual speech is manifested – with particular focus on the ability to select the language of production and to control activated, irrelevant items from interfering in successful speech production. Upon closer observation of the stages involved in this mental procedure, we were presented with what was once referred to as *the hard problem* in bilingual speech production (Finkbeiner et al. 2006) which demonstrated that the activation of words in both languages poses a particular theoretical problem when trying to explain at what point the target language is selected and whether or not IC is involved in the procedure. Prominent theories proposed by La Heij (2005) and Costa (2005) were discussed and subsequent studies that tested and expanded on their frameworks were presented.

From the studies discussed, we can clearly see that language selection and lexical control – and the cognitive processes involved in speech production in general – appear to be executed in the context of a dynamic system which is continuously shaped and modulated by a number of individual factors (e.g., lexical robustness, EF abilities, learning environment such as immersion, etc.). Given these vibrant characteristics, we then discussed two theoretical models, the MHM (Pavlenko 2009) and the SbP Model (Schwieter & Sunderman 2008, 2009) which encompass developmental effects that help explain the architecture and functionality of this procedure while keeping at their core the theoretical flexibility to account for dynamic changes.

Following this, we turned to discuss studies that have begun to investigate these issues in the context of language learning beyond two languages. Within this discussion, we became aware of the rapid spread of studies employing a variety of empirical measures looking at effects of individual differences among L2 and L3 language learners. While further studies are certainly needed, some of these studies (Linck et al. 2012; Schwieter & Sunderman 2011) have suggested a more restrictive L3 influence and a continued global L2 influence and that distinct EFs may contribute differently to language selection and lexical control. Additional studies are also needed to investigate whether the cognitive benefits associated with trilingualism are any more significant than those linked to bilingualism (i.e., do additional cognitive benefits beyond bilingualism continue to emerge with learning of each additional language?)

In the last section of the chapter, we addressed how the findings of these issues can inform language teaching and learning by focusing on the benefits of immersion learning. In addition to many other benefits beyond of the scope of this chapter, the immersion environment allows learners to constantly practice the important skill of inhibiting a more dominant language. In turn, this provides learners with the opportunity to develop the ability to engage and rely on a language-specific selection mechanism and to conceptually mediate in languages other than the L1. It was suggested that educators of non-native languages should consider creating and participating in faculty-led study abroad experiences to effectively put these theories into practice.

The limitations and contributions of the frameworks and models discussed in this chapter are important for both theory and practice. From a theoretical perspective, they help to better understand the conceptual and lexical architecture and functionality of such structure during speech production among multilinguals. From an applied perspective, they have implications for how educators view and approach the teaching and learning of non-native languages. If the ability to

262 John W. Schwieter and Aline Ferreira

conceptually mediate – which involves selecting the target language of production before considering lexical candidates that map onto the activated concepts – is harder for weak languages, applied linguists may wish to begin searching for the best pedagogical means the developmental theories discussed in this chapter. While one suggestion advocated for immersion experiences, more feasible, class-room-based activities should be designed that put these theories into practice. Further studies are also needed to better inform the complexity of the dynamic nature of the language selection and lexical control processes that accompany non-native language learning.

References

Allen, H., & Herron, C. (2003). A mixed methodology investigation of the linguistic and affective outcomes of summer study abroad. *Foreign Language Annals, 36*, 370–384.

Ameel, E., Storms, G., Malt, B., & Sloman, S. (2005). How bilinguals solve the naming problem. *Journal of Memory and Language, 52*, 309–329.

Athanasopoulos, P. (2009). Cognitive representation of color in bilinguals: The case of Greek blues. *Bilingualism: Language and Cognition, 12*, 83–95.

Athanasopoulos, P. (2011). Cognitive restructuring in bilingualism. In A. Pavlenko (Ed.), *Thinking and speaking in two languages* (pp. 29–65). Bristol: Multilingual Matters.

Athanasopoulos, P., & Kasai, C. (2008). Language and thought in bilinguals: The case of grammatical number and nonverbal classification preferences. *Applied Psycholinguistics, 29*, 105–121.

Bialystok, E. (2009). Bilingualism: The good, the bad, and the indifferent. *Bilingualism: Language and Cognition, 12*, 3–11.

Bialystok, E., Craik, F., Klein, R., & Viswanathan, M. (2004). Bilingualism, aging, and cognitive control: Evidence from the Simon task. *Psychology and Aging, 19*, 290–303.

Bialystok, E., Craik, F., & Ryan, J. (2006). Executive control in a modified anti-saccade task: Effects of aging and bilingualism. *Journal of Experimental Psychology: Learning, Memory, and Cognition, 32*, 1341–1354.

Bialystok, E., & Shapero, D. (2005). Ambiguous benefits: The effect of bilingualism on reversing ambiguous figures. *Developmental Science, 8*, 595–604.

Bloem, I., & La Heij, W. (2003). Semantic facilitation and semantic interference in word translation: Implications for models of lexical access in language production. *Journal of Memory and Language, 48*, 468–488.

Bloem, I., van den Boogaard, S., & La Heij, W. (2004). Semantic facilitation and semantic interference in language production: Further evidence for the conceptual selection model of lexical access. *Journal of Memory and Language, 51*, 307–323.

Brysbaert, M., & Duyck, W. (2010). Is it time to leave behind the Revised Hierarchical Model of bilingual language processing after fifteen years of service? *Bilingualism: Language and Cognition, 13*, 359–371.

Colzato, L., Bajo, M., van den Wildenberg, W., Paolieri, D., Nieuwenhuis, S., La Heij, W., & Hommel, B. (2008). How does bilingualism improve executive control? A comparison of active and reactive inhibition mechanisms. *Journal of Experimental Psychology: Learning, Memory, & Cognition, 34,* 302–312.

Cook, V., Bassetti, B., Kasai, C., Sasaki, M., & Takahashi, J. (2006). Do bilinguals have different concepts? The case of shape and material in Japanese L2 users of English. *International Journal of Bilingualism, 10,* 137–152.

Costa, A. (2005). Lexical access in bilingual production. In *Handbook of bilingualism: Psycholinguistic approaches,* J.F. Kroll & A.M.B. de Groot (eds), 308–325. Oxford: OUP.

Costa, A., Hernández, M., & Sebastián-Gallés, N. (2008). Bilingualism aids conflict resolution: Evidence from the ANT task. *Cognition, 106,* 59–86.

Costa, A., Miozzo, M., & Caramazza, A. (1999). Lexical selection in bilinguals: Do words in the bilinguals' two lexicons compete for selection? *Journal of Memory and Language, 41,* 365–397.

Costa, A., & Santesteban, M. (2004). Lexical access in bilingual speech production: Evidence from language switching in highly proficient bilinguals and L2 learners. *Journal of Memory and Language, 50,* 491–511.

Costa, A., Santesteban, M., & Ivanova, I. (2006). How do highly proficient bilinguals control their lexicalization process? Inhibitory and language-specific selection mechanisms are both functional. *Journal of Experimental Psychology: Learning, Memory, and Cognition, 32,* 1057–1074.

Davidson, D. (2010). Study abroad: When, how long, and with what results? New data from the Russian front. *Foreign Language Annals, 43,* 6–25.

De Groot, A. (1992). Determinants of word translation. *Journal of Experimental Psychology: Learning, Memory, and Cognition, 18,* 1001–1018.

De Groot, A. 1993. Word-type effects in bilinguals processing tasks: Support for a mixed representational system. In R. Schreuder & B. Weltens (Eds.), *The bilingual lexicon* (pp. 27–51). Amsterdam: John Benjamins.

De Groot, A. (1995). Determinants of bilingual lexicosemantic organization. *Computer Assisted Language Learning, 8,* 151–180.

De Groot, A. (2011). *Language and cognition in bilinguals and multilinguals: An introduction.* Hove, UK: Psychology Press.

De Groot, A., Dannenburg, L., & Van Hell, J. (1994). Forward and backward word translation by bilinguals. *Journal of Memory and Language, 33,* 600–629.

De Groot, A., & Poot, R. (1997). Word translation at three levels of proficiency in a second language: The ubiquitous involvement of conceptual memory. *Language Learning, 47,* 215–264.

Dijkstra, A., Van Heuven, W., & Grainger, J. (1998). Simulating competitor effects with the Bilingual Interactive Activation model. *Psychologica Belgica, 38,* 177–196.

Dong, Y., Cui, S., & MacWhinney, B. (2005). Shared and separate meanings in the bilingual mental lexicon. *Bilingualism: Language and Cognition, 8,* 221–238.

Festman, J., Rodríguez-Fornells, A., & Münte, T. (2010). Individual differences in control of language interference in late bilinguals are mainly related to general executive abilities. *Behavioral and Brain Functions, 6,* 1–12.

Finkbeiner, M., Almeida, J., Janssen, N., & Caramazza, A. (2006). Lexical selection in bilingual speech production does not involve language suppression. *Journal of Experimental Psychology: Learning, Memory, and Cognition, 32,* 1075–1089.

Gollan, T., Montoya, R., & Werner, G. (2002). Semantic and letter fluency in Spanish-English bilinguals. *Neuropsychology, 16,* 562–576.

Green, D. (1986). Control, activation, and resource: A framework and a model for the control of speech in bilinguals. *Brain and Language, 27,* 210–223.

Green, D. (1998). Mental control of the bilingual lexico-semantic system. *Bilingualism: Language and Cognition, 1*, 67–81.

Grosjean, F. (2000). The bilingual's language modes. In J. Nicol (Ed.), *One Mind, Two Languages: Bilingual Language Processing* (pp. 1–22). Oxford: Blackwell.

Grosjean, F., & Li, P. (2013). *The Psycholinguistics of Bilingualism.* Hoboken, NJ: Wiley-Blackwell.

Heredia, R. (2008). Mental models of bilingual memory. In J. Altarriba & R. Heredia (Eds.), *An introduction to bilingualism: Principles and processes* (pp. 39–67). New York, NY: Lawrence Erlbaum Associates.

Hermans, D. (2000). *Word production in a foreign language.* Unpublished PhD dissertation, University of Nijmegen.

Hermans, D., Bongaerts, T., de Bot, K. & Schreuder, R. (1998). Producing words in a foreign language: Can speakers prevent interference from their first language? *Bilingualism: Language and Cognition, 1*, 213–229.

Hernández, M., Costa, A., Fuentes, L., Vivas, A., & Sebastián-Gallés, N. (2010). The impact of bilingualism on the executive control and orienting networks of attention. *Bilingualism: Language and Cognition, 13*, 315–325.

Hugdahl, K., Westerhausen, R., Alho, K., Medvedev, S., Laine, M., & Hämäläinen, H. (2009). Attention and cognitive control: Unfolding the dichotic listening story. *Scandinavian Journal of Psychology, 50*, 11–22.

Jarvis. S. & Pavlenko, A. (Eds.) (2008). *Crosslinguistic influence in language and cognition.* New York, NY: Routledge.

Koch, I., Gade, M., Schuch, S., & Philipp, A. (2010). The role of inhibition in task switching: An overview. *Psychonomic Bulletin & Review, 17*, 1–14.

Kroll, J. & de Groot, A.M.B. 1997. Lexical and conceptual memory in the bilingual. In A.M.B. de Groot & J. Kroll (Eds.), *Tutorials in bilingualism: Psycholinguistic perspectives* (pp. 169–199). Mahwah, NJ: Lawrence Erlbaum Associates.

Kroll, J., Michael, E., & Sankaranarayanan, A. (1998). A model of bilingual representation and its implications for second language acquisition. In *Foreign language learning: Psycholinguistic experiments on training and retention,* A. Healy & L. Bourne (Eds.), 365–395. Mahway, NJ: Lawrence Erlbaum Associates.

Kroll, J., & Stewart, E. (1994). Category interference in translation and picture naming: Evidence for asymmetric connections between bilingual memory representations. *Journal of Memory and Language, 33*, 149–174.

Kroll, J., & Tokowicz, N. (2001). The development of conceptual representation for words in a second language. In J. Nicol (Ed.), *One mind, two languages: Bilingual language processing* (pp. 49–71). Malden, MA: Blackwell.

Kroll, J., Van Hell, J., Tokowicz, N., & Green, D. (2010). The Revised Hierarchical Model: A critical review and assessment. *Bilingualism: Language and Cognition, 13*, 373–381.

Kruse, J., & Brubaker, C. (2007). Successful study abroad: Tips for student preparation, immersion, and postprocessing. *Die Unterrichtspraxis/Teaching German, 40*, 147–152.

La Heij, W. (2005). Selection processes in monolingual and bilingual lexical access. In J.F. Kroll & A.M.B. de Groot (Eds.), *Handbook of bilingualism: Psycholinguistic approaches* (pp. 289–307). Oxford: OUP.

La Heij, W., & Boelens, H. (2011). Color-object interference: Further tests of an executive-control account. *Journal of Experimental Child Psychology, 108*, 156–169.

La Heij, W., Hooglander, A., Kerling, R., & Van der Velden, E. (1996). Nonverbal context effects in forward and backward word translation: Evidence for concept mediation. *Journal of Memory and Language, 35*, 648–665.

La Heij, W., Kuipers, J., & Starreveld, P. (2006). In defense of the lexical-competition account of picture-word interference: A comment on Finkbeiner and Caramazza (2006). *Cortex, 42*, 1028–1031.

Levelt, W. (1989). *Speaking: From intention to articulation.* Cambridge, MA: The MIT Press.

Linck J.A., Kroll, J., & Sunderman, G. (2009). Losing access to the native language while immersed in a second language: Evidence for the role of inhibition in second language learning. *Psychological Science, 20*, 1507–1515.

Linck, J.A., Schwieter, J.W., & Sunderman, G. (2012). Inhibitory control predicts language switching performance in trilingual speech production. *Bilingualism: Language and Cognition, 15*, 651–662.

Linck, J.A., Schwieter, J.W., & Sunderman, G. (In preparation). The differential role of executive functions in trilingual language switching.

Mayr, U., & Keele, S. (2000). Changing internal constraints on action: The role of backward inhibition. *Journal of Experimental Psychology: General, 129*, 4–26.

Meiran, N., Chorev, Z., & Sapir, A. (2000). Component processes in task switching. *Cognitive Psychology, 41*, 211–253.

Meuter, R. (1994). *Language switching in naming tasks.* Unpublished PhD dissertation, Oxford University.

Meuter, R., & Allport, A. (1999). Bilingual language switching in naming: Asymmetrical costs of language selection. *Journal of Memory and Language, 40*, 25–40.

Pavlenko, A. (1999). New approaches to concepts in bilingual memory. *Bilingualism: Language and Cognition, 2*, 209–230.

Pavlenko, A. (2005). Bilingualism and thought. In A.M.B. de Groot & J. Kroll (Eds.), *Handbook of bilingualism: Psycholinguistic approaches* (pp. 433–453). Oxford: OUP.

Pavlenko, A. (2009). Conceptual representation in the bilingual lexicon and second language vocabulary learning. In A. Pavlenko (ed), *The bilingual mental lexicon: Interdisciplinary approaches* (pp. 125–160). Bristol: Multilingual Matters.

Pavlenko, A. (Ed.). (2011). *Thinking and speaking in two languages.* Bristol: Multilingual Matters.

Pavlenko, A., & Malt, B. (2011). Kitchen Russian: Cross-linguistic differences and first language object naming by Russian-English bilinguals. *Bilingualism: Language and Cognition, 14*, 19–45.

Philipp, A., Gade, M., & Koch, I. (2007). Inhibitory processes in language switching: Evidence from switching language-defined response sets. *European Journal of Cognitive Psychology, 19*, 395–416.

Philipp, A., & Koch, I. (2009). Inhibition in language switching: What is inhibited when switching between languages in naming tasks? *Journal of Experimental Psychology: Learning, Memory, and Cognition, 35*, 1187–1195.

Poulisse, N., & Bongaerts, T. (1994). First language use in second language production. *Applied Linguistics, 15*, 36–57.

Prior, A., & MacWhinney, B. (2010). A bilingual advantage in task switching. *Bilingualism: Language and Cognition, 13*, 253–262.

Schwieter, J.W. (2008). The effects of bilingual type on language selectivity. In M. Mantero, P. Chamness Miller, & J. Watze (Eds.), *Readings in language studies, Vol. 1: Language across disciplinary boundaries* (pp. 417–431). New York, NY: International Society for Language Studies.

Schwieter, J.W. (2010). *Cognition and bilingual speech: Psycholinguistic aspects of language production, processing, and inhibitory control*. Saarbrücken, Germany: Lambert Academic Publishing.

Schwieter, J.W. (2011). [Review of A. Pavlenko's *Bilingual Mental Lexicon: Interdisciplinary Approaches*. Bristol, UK: Multilingual Matters]. *The International Journal of Bilingual Education and Bilingualism, 14*(3), 361–364.

Schwieter, J.W. (2013a). Lexical inhibition in trilingual speakers. In E. Anttikoski & J. Tirkkonen (Eds.), *Proceedings of The 24th Conference of Scandinavian Linguistics. Publications from the University of Eastern Finland: Reports and Studies in Education, Humanities, and Theology*. (pp. 249–260). Joensuu, Finland: University of Eastern Finland Press.

Schwieter, J.W. (2013b). Study abroad: Implications for L2 and lexical development. In J. Schwieter (Ed.), *Studies and global perspectives of second language teaching and learning*. (pp. 165–185) Charlotte, NC: Information Age Publishing.

Schwieter, J.W., & Ferreira, A. (under review). Word-level translation and developmental functionalities of language processes.

Schwieter, J.W., & Kunert, S. (2012). Short-term study abroad and cultural sessions: Issues of L2 development, identity, and socialization. In P. Chamness Miller, J. Watze, & M. Mantero (Eds.), *Readings in language studies, Vol. 3: Critical language studies: Focusing on identity*. (pp. 587–604). New York: International Society for Language Studies.

Schwieter, J.W., & Sunderman, G. (2008). Language switching in bilingual speech production: In search of the language-specific selection mechanism. *The Mental Lexicon, 3*, 214–238.

Schwieter, J.W., & Sunderman, G. (2009). Concept selection and developmental effects in bilingual speech production. *Language Learning, 59*, 897–927.

Schwieter, J.W., & Sunderman, G. (2011). Inhibitory control processes and lexical access in trilingual speech production. *Linguistic Approaches to Bilingualism, 1*, 391–412.

Sholl, A., Sankaranarayanan, A., & Kroll, J. (1995). Transfer between picture naming and translation: A test of asymmetries in bilingual memory. *Psychological Science, 6*, 45–49.

Simon, J., & Rudell, A. (1967). Auditory S-R compatibility: The effect of an irrelevant cue on information processing. *Journal of Applied Psychology, 51*, 300–304.

Soveri, A. Laine, M, Hämäläinen, J., & Hugdahl, K. (2011). Bilingual Advantage in Attentional control: Evidence from the forced-attention dichotic listening paradigm. *Bilingualism: Language and Cognition, 14*, 371–378.

Snodgrass, J., & Vanderwart, M. (1980). A standardized set of 260 pictures: Norms for name agreement, image agreement, familiarity, and visual complexity. *Journal of Experimental Psychology: Human Learning and Memory, 6*, 174–215.

Van Hell, J. (1998). *Cross-language processing and bilingual memory organization*. Unpublished PhD dissertation, University of Amsterdam.

Van Hell, J. & de Groot, A. (1998). Conceptual representation in bilingual memory: Effects of concreteness and cognate status in word association. *Bilingualism: Language and Cognition, 1*, 193–211.

CHAPTER 12

Lexical access in bilinguals and second language learners

Gretchen Sunderman and Eileen Fancher
Florida State University

In this chapter, a theoretical account of non-selectivity effects in word recognition with a particular emphasis on the second language (L2) learner is described. Non-selectivity is the idea that lexical items from both languages are activated simultaneously. The focus is on how L2 learners and bilinguals retrieve words in isolation and in a broader contexts (e.g., sentence contexts) that can constrain or facilitate word recognition, thereby leading to selective lexical access. This chapter also addresses how research on L2 word recognition can inform L2 teachers about the underlying mechanisms involved in lexical processing, specifically describing the types of vocabulary errors students make and offering some pedagogical principles that can guide the teaching of L2 vocabulary.

1. Introduction

The observation that words from two languages are active and compete to be selected while a bilingual is reading is now commonplace in the psycholinguistic literature (e.g., Van Heuven, Dijkstra & Grainger 1998; Dijkstra, Timmermans & Schriefers 2000). This evidence has been found for bilinguals (Van Hell & de Groot 2008) and second language (L2) learners alike (Schwartz & Kroll 2006; Sunderman & Kroll 2006). But what does this mean in terms of L2 learning? What are the implications of this research for the teaching of second languages?

In this chapter, a tutorial approach of sorts is taken. The process of lexical access and a model of word recognition are first described. It is important to be aware of the underlying psycholinguistic mechanisms involved in lexical processing to better understand the challenges facing learners. Some of the empirical evidence investigating lexical processing, highlighting how certain types of form similarity across languages (i.e., cognates, homographs, neighbors) have been used as a tool to investigate lexical access, is then discussed. The discussion of the research serves as an introduction to issues and methods of investigating the bilingual lexicon. In the second part of the chapter, a discussion of how the lexical retrieval process might be more constrained in order to facilitate retrieval of words, especially for L2 learners is presented. In this section the role of sentence structure and semantics is discussed. Finally, the chapter ends with some potential pedagogical implications based on current knowledge of word recognition and lexical access in bilinguals and L2 learners. For the purpose of this chapter a bilingual is defined as those individuals with a high level of proficiency in two languages, while L2 learners are those who are less proficient in their L2. In fact, in this chapter and in many studies, individuals are referred to as more and less proficient bilinguals, terms that reflect the relative skill in each language.

2.   Lexical access and word recognition

For decades, psycholinguists have investigated how monolingual readers visually process individual words (e.g. McClelland & Rumelhart 1981). Seeing a word on a page and then connecting it to a meaningful lexical representation is quite a complex process. This comprehension process is called lexical access or word recognition. As one reads the letters "mea," for example, words such as "meat," "meal," and "mead" are all activated in the mind since these words share the first same three letters. However, the competing lexical items are not activated equally; those with higher frequency are activated more quickly. For instance, "meat" may be activated faster than "mead" because it is heard or read more frequently. Once a reader sees that the final letter of the word is "t" (from the example above), the word can be matched with the lexical representation "meat," thus shutting off the activation of the other competing items.

Examining word processing has been the key to understanding how lexical items are stored in the mind and how readers retrieve these lexical representations. Lexical access is more complex for bilinguals because they have two (or more) languages in their mind. Since there is competition when choosing a lexical item while reading, researchers have investigated how the mind eventually chooses the correct lexical item and what types of obstacles may be faced during this process (see De Groot 2011 for a thorough overview of word recognition in bilinguals). A central question related to lexical processing in bilinguals is whether a bilingual activates one lexicon at a time (known as language-selective lexical access) or whether lexical items from both languages are activated simultaneously (known as language non-selective lexical access) (see Dijkstra 2005 for a more in depth treatment of the topic). This chapter begins by reviewing a model of word recognition that describes how lexical access proceeds in bilinguals.

3. A model of word recognition

A well-known psycholinguistic model of the bilingual lexicon is the bilingual in-teractive activation (BIA) model (Dijkstra & Van Heuven 1998; Dijkstra, Van Jaarsveld & Ten Brinke 1998; Van Heuven et al. 1998). The BIA model, as seen in Figure 1, captures how the process of visual word recognition unfolds in bilinguals.

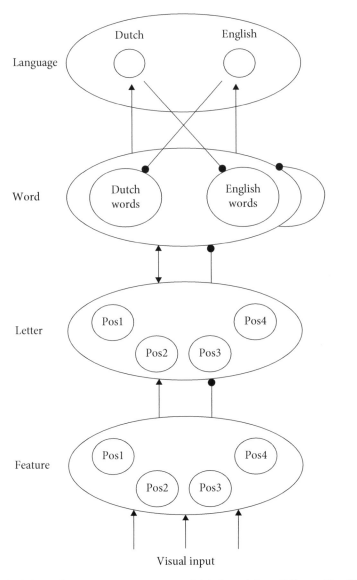

Figure 1. The bilingual interactive activation model (adapted from Dijkstra, Van Heuven & Grainger 1998)

This model was based on the monolingual Interactive Activation model (McClelland & Rumelhart 1981), but created in order to account for lexical processing in more than one language. The model is based on the notion of *competition*. Upon reading a string of letters, a number of words in the reader's mind become activated and then compete to be the best match for what has been seen. What is important about the BIA model is the assumption that this competition takes place at the feature, letter, and word level of *both* a bilingual's languages. The model depicts one single lexicon which holds word forms for both languages. In other words, the model posits non-selective access to an integrated lexicon. According to the model, it is only after activation and the subsequent competition has progressed rather far into the process that language-specific criteria become engaged in the process. The model contains Language-level nodes that specify language membership and have the ability to suppress all of the activated words belonging to the other language.

Illustrating with a concrete example, one can assume that when a proficient English-Spanish bilingual is visually presented with an input letter string ("gate" for example), activation within the lexicon spreads in a bottom-up manner based on the form characteristics of the input, specifically orthographic similarity. As depicted in the model, the activation flows to features and letters in specific position. The arrows in the model depict activation and the filled circles depict inhibition. Thus, the Spanish word *gato*, meaning 'cat' may also be activated. Indeed, several lexical candidates, regardless of language, are activated and compete with each other for selection; other candidates are not activated. If the English-Spanish bilingual above is reading in English, then once a match between the letter string "gate" and the word "gate" is made, the word sends activation to the English language node. The language node then exerts a top-down inhibitory effect on the words of Spanish and word recognition is complete. The predictions of the BIA model have come from an extensive body of psycholinguistic studies that take advantage of certain cross-language features to test the relative activation of the other language. By using lexical neighbors, homographs, and cognates, past studies have shown that words from both languages are activated in parallel and one language is never really "shut off." In the next section, several exemplary studies are reviewed that use these cross-language form similarities to test the notion of non-selective access that occurs despite efforts to control the competition and despite level of proficiency in the second language.

3.1   Neighbors

An orthographic neighbor is any word differing by a single letter from the target word, respecting length and letter position (Coltheart, Davelaar, Jonasson & Besner 1977). An English-Spanish bilingual can have neighbors in English, in

Spanish, and across both languages. For example, in English, the word "gate" would have neighbors such as "mate," "date," "late," "game," "gave," etc. All of those words differ from the word "gate" by one letter, respecting position. In Spanish, the word *gato* would have neighbors such as *pato* 'duck,' *gano* 'I win,' *mato* 'I kill,' etc. However, cross-linguistically, the word *gato* in Spanish is also a neighbor to English "gate." Why would it matter if a word in another language had a neighbor relation to it? The logic is quite clear. When a bilingual is asked to perform a task in one language, then only the words from that language should play a role during word recognition if the bilingual is indeed able to "shut off" one language or the other. Indeed, selective models of word recognition would suggest that cross-language neighbors should have no effect. Non-selective models however suggest that words from both languages will be activated simultaneously and therefore would predict that neighbors from other languages would be active too.

Van Heuven et al. (1998) examined the influence of orthographic neighborhoods within and across languages using a lexical decision task (LDT) with Dutch-English bilingual adults. In lexical decision, a participant is presented with a string of letters and is asked if that string is a word or not. LDTs require an individual to search their lexicon for a meaning-form mapping. Researchers will instruct the participants to search in one language or the other. In this particular study, the participants were asked to determine if the letter string was a word in English or a word in Dutch. What Van Heuven et al. found was that when the bilinguals were identifying English target words, the presence of both Dutch (L1) and English (L2) neighbors affected processing. In other words, the bilinguals could not just complete the task in English, their L2; their L1 was also activated. However, when the bilinguals were identifying Dutch (L1) target words, the amount of interference from the English (L2) was related to their proficiency. The more proficient the bilingual, the more interference the English words caused. The level of interference was linked to the relative strength of the level of activation. Because the participants were affected by the presence of neighbors in the other language, this study provides support for the BIA model and the notion of non-selective access in the bilingual lexicon.

3.2   Homographs and cognates

Further evidence for non-selective access comes from experiments using interlingual homographs, or words that share orthographic features but do not share meaning. For example, in English the words "pan," "soy," and "red" are identical to the Spanish words *pan*, *soy* and *red*. However in Spanish these words mean 'bread,' 'I am,' and 'net' respectively. Thus, for an English-Spanish bilingual, seeing the input string "pan," may activate both meaning representations. In an attempt to understand the nature of the information that is activated, Dijkstra, Grainger and Van Heuven (1999) tested Dutch-English bilinguals using a LDT and progressive demasking task (a task in which the target word is obscured by a mask that degrades over time and participants indicate at which point they can identify the word). The critical materials were English (L2) words that varied in their degree of orthographic, phonological, and semantic overlap with Dutch words. The list also contained cognates, which share both form and meaning. The word "piano" is an example of an English-Spanish cognate. Past studies (Cristoffanini, Kirsner & Milech 1986; Gerard & Scarborough 1989) show a cognate prime "piano" makes the reading time for the target word "piano" faster than for a non-cognate target word. This facilitation is called the cognate priming effect and suggests that words in both languages are being activated in a bilingual's mind. This effect has been found for both bilinguals (Van Hell & de Groot 2008) and L2 learners (Schwartz & Kroll 2006).

The results of Dijkstra et al. (1999), which were later replicated in Lemhöfer and Dijkstra (2004) and Haigh and Jared (2007), showed that the bilinguals' performance in the two experiments was facilitated by cross-linguistic orthographic and semantic overlap, but inhibited by phonological overlap as compared to control words. Overall, the pattern of results suggested, at least in the case of proficient bilinguals, all representations (orthographic, phonologic and semantic) of a word, irrespective of the target language, were activated and competed with each other. Essentially, the proficient bilinguals were not able to inhibit their L1 during these tasks. These experiments provide strong evidence that in bilingual word recognition, lexical access for proficient bilinguals is non-selective in nature, across spelling, sound and meaning.

In another experiment, Dijkstra et al. (1998) found that interlingual homographs could be recognized faster than, slower than, or just as fast as within-language control words, depending on the constraints of the experiment. Dijkstra et al. conducted a set of lexical decision experiments with highly proficient Dutch-English bilinguals. In the first experiment, the participants were asked to make lexical decisions in English, their L2. The stimulus list consisted of English words and non-words. In this experiment, the interlingual homographs had no effect on performance. In the second experiment, the activation of the L1 was increased by including real Dutch words in the stimulus list. Participants again had to decide whether a string of letters were real English words. However, in addition to non-words, the participants had to reject real Dutch words as non-English words. Under these conditions, the interlingual homographs produced interference relative to the unrelated controls. This result suggests that the presence of words in the non-target language were enough to activate the other language and produce interference when the words were interlingual homographs. Language activation thus seems to be bottom-up in nature and driven by the input. In fact, as you will see, in the next two studies presented, it does not seem to matter what you tell participants about the language tasks, the presence of words from another language may affect lexical processing.

3.3 Controlling the competition

In a study to investigate whether expectations could affect lexical processing, Dijkstra, De Bruijn, Schriefers, and Ten Brinke (2000) examined whether instructions could induce activation of the non-target language. Dijkstra et al. examined whether telling the participant that both languages are present in the experiment would activate both languages and increase cross-language activation. In the experiment, they instructed Dutch-English bilinguals to respond to English words and interlingual homographs with "yes" and to English non-words and Dutch words as "no." In the first part of the experiment, the list did not contain any Dutch words, whereas in the second part of the experiment, the list did contain Dutch words. If the instruction to respond to both Dutch and English activated words in both languages, then the homographs would cause interference relative to the controls. However, this only occurred in the second part of the experiment when the actual stimulus list contained Dutch items. The authors suggest that it is not the top-down instructions that drove language activation, but rather the language intermixing that drives the bilinguals' performance (although see de Groot, Delmaar & Lupker 2000; Jared & Szucs 2002 for evidence on non-selectivity in a single language task with homographs).

Along a similar vein, Van Hell and Dijkstra (2002) investigated expectations about an experiment and lexical activation. In their study, Van Hell and Dijkstra instructed the participants that they were interested in examining their performance in Dutch. Van Hell and Dijkstra cleverly recruited trilinguals for this study, with Dutch as their dominant and native L1, English as their L2, and French as their third language. The tasks performed in this study were all completed in Dutch (L1) and the participants were unaware that the study was interested in their other languages. The materials in the tasks were either Dutch words that were cognates in English, cognates in French or were Dutch words that were non-cognates. Again, the logic of using this type of form manipulation is to see whether the presence of certain stimuli in the experiment will affect processing. If the participants were able to complete the task in Dutch with no effects from cross-linguistics items, then it would suggest they were able to shut off their L2 and L3 lexicons. Van Hell and Dijkstra showed that, in a LDT, the Dutch-English bilinguals were faster to recognize Dutch words that were cognates with English. Again, cognates are typically recognized more quickly in a lexical decision task utilizing both languages.

In this task the participants had no instruction to use the other language, but all showed effects of their L2, English. In terms of the cognates with French, only those participants with higher French proficiency were affected. The participants with lower French proficiency did not show a difference in response times between cognates with French and other cognates, thus suggesting again that the strength of the L2 representation is critical in its activation level. In the end however, the results of this experiment suggest that language activation is driven by the nature of the material presented to the bilingual, not by instructions to perform a task in a certain language, which is informative, given that many second language classrooms strive to be purely in the L2.

3.4   L2 proficiency

While most of the previous research investigated highly proficient bilinguals, the same question about non-selective access could also be asked of beginning bilinguals, or L2 learners. In fact, for a L2 learner whose L1 is quite dominant, one might imagine the competition from that dominant language is even more fierce. One of the first tests of the BIA model with second language learners came from Sunderman and Kroll (2006). Sunderman and Kroll used a translation recognition task to test whether the same type of interference from lexical form neighbors would hold for less proficient bilinguals. A translation recognition task asks participants to judge whether two words presented sequentially are translation equivalents. On the critical trials the pair were not translation equivalents, but looked like form neighbors in the other language (*gato*-"gate" for example). The logic was that if word recognition proceeded according to the BIA model described above and could be applied to less proficient bilinguals, then a pair like *gato*-"gate" would be processed with more difficulty compared to an unrelated control pair. In fact, Sunderman and Kroll found that less proficient bilinguals were as sensitive to bottom-up orthographic features as more proficient bilinguals, thus confirming a non-selective access view of the developing lexicon and supporting and extending the predictions of the BIA to less proficient bilinguals. More recently, researchers have found evidence of non-selectivity for bilingual children during word-naming (Jared, Cormier, Levy & Wade-Woolley 2012).

4.   A more detailed model of word recognition

As the research described above suggests and as predicted by the BIA model, the overwhelming evidence suggests that access to the lexicon is non-selective, mostly driven by the input, and occurs for highly proficient bilinguals and language learners alike to varying degrees. Yet, word recognition can be affected by other factors than just orthography, such as phonology and semantics, and even certain demands of the linguistic task. The Bilingual Interactive Activation Plus (BIA+) model (Dijkstra & Van Heuven 2002) is an updated version of the BIA model. For the purposes here, the focus will be on just a few of the ways the BIA+ differs in from the BIA model. First, the BIA+ model contains both phonology and semantics within the word identification system. This distinction is important, as much of the previous research had focused on orthographic non-selectivity in lexical processing (although see Jared & Kroll, 2001 for non-selectivity effects in phonology). Indeed, recent research (Sunderman & Priya 2011) explicitly tested the predictions of BIA+ and found support for phonological non-selectivity using Hindi-English bilinguals, with Hindi and English being two languages that do not share script (see Gollan, Forster & Frost 1997 and Hoshino & Kroll 2008 for additional evidence of phonological non-selectivity in languages that do not share orthography). Other research (Friesen & Jared 2012) has found cross-language phonological activation of meaning as well.

While the findings of non-selectivity supporting the BIA and BIA+ model are important, they simply cannot be the end of the story. There must be situations where the lexicon can be more constrained to help guide lexical access. Thus, the second distinction between BIA and BIA+ is the task schema. The task schema accounts for nonlinguistic processing, such as task demands, instruction, or participant expectations and thus, is an important part in the overall word recognition process. Specifically, the BIA+ model predicts that linguistic context can affect which lexical candidates become activated. Dijkstra and Van Heuven define linguistic context effects as effects resulting from information from the lexical, syntactic, or semantic sources or, in other words, the sentence context. The authors propose that these differing contexts can affect word recognition by constraining the degree of language selectivity. While non-selective access seems to be the default for lexical processing, the question has now turned to investigating the contexts in which lexical processing is selective, or in what contexts bilinguals or L2 learners can shut off one of their languages. In the next section, how the semantic and syntactic constraints of a sentence context can affect word recognition is discussed.

5. Bilingual word recognition in sentence contexts

One avenue that has been productive in examining the contexts when selectivity occurs is the investigation of sentence contexts. Past studies have created sentence contexts that vary in constraint, such as semantic constraint (Schwartz & Kroll 2006; van Hell & de Groot 2008) and syntactic constraint (Gullifer, Dussias & Kroll

2010). Schwartz and Kroll had Spanish-English bilinguals name cognate and non-cognate target words within a sentence context that varied in semantics (e.g., meaning) by having high semantic constraint sentences, which help narrow down the possible target words, and low semantic constraint sentences, which would allow a much larger number of possible items to be the target word. Consider the following sentences from Schwartz and Kroll:

(1)   Before playing, the composer first wiped the keys of the _____ at the beginning of the concert.

This sentence is highly constrained semantically because the context greatly restricts what target word could fill the space. A sentence with low semantic constraint is shown in example (2):

(2)   When we entered the dining hall we saw the _____ in the corner of the room.

This sentence does not restrict which word is possible nearly as much as the high constraint sentences, as many things could be seen in the corner of the room. The results from this study showed that the highly constrained sentences led to selective access, while the low constraint sentence still showed non-selective access. In other words, the target word was read just as fast when it was a cognate as it was when it was a non-cognate (although cognates are expected to be read faster outside of any context due to the overlap of orthographic, phonological, and semantic information) in the highly constrained semantic sentences. The cognates were read faster than non-cognates in the low semantic sentences, showing that a sentence context itself was not enough to make lexical access non-selective. The results from this study show that perhaps certain contexts may facilitate lexical access for the L2 learner who is attempting to overcome strong levels of activation from the dominant L1.

Van Hell and de Groot (2008) found similar results in an experiment where highly proficient Dutch-English bilinguals completed a LDT with cognate target words after reading sentences with high or low semantic constraint. As in Schwartz and Kroll (2006), van Hell and de Groot found that the cognate effect disappeared for the high semantic constraint sentences, but remained with low semantic constraint. These results support the idea that not all sentence contexts are equal, and that some contexts may not constrain non-selectivity. These findings show that sentence contexts can affect word recognition because the degree of semantic restriction determines whether the cognate effect remained or disappeared.

Libben and Titone (2009) further investigated how sentence context may affect word recognition by monitoring the eye movements of French-English bilinguals reading sentences in English (L2). Once again, the target words were cognates and matched controls. The sentence contexts also had two conditions: low and high semantic constraint, and each sentence consisted of two clauses. The first clause biased for high or low semantic constraint for the target word, and the second clause contained the target word. Example (3) gives an example of one high semantic constraint sentence and one low semantic constraint sentence:

(3) a. Because of the bitter custody battle over the kids, the expensive *divorce* was a disaster. (high semantic constraint)
     b. Because they owned a lot of property around the world, the expensive *divorce* was a disaster. (low semantic constraint)

The researchers recorded the reading times for the cognate target word "divorce" in both conditions and compared them to the reading times of non-cognates.

In order to investigate lexical activation initially and further along in the processing of sentences, Libben and Titone used an eye-tracking methodology to examine early-stage comprehension measures and late-stage comprehension measures. In an eye-tracking study, researchers measure the time that the eyes fixate on a specific word while reading. Longer fixation times suggest that there was more difficulty processing, while shorter times imply less difficulty. The early-stage comprehension measures examined initial fixations on the target word, while late-state comprehension measures focused on the total reading time of the targets. The results from the early-stage comprehension measures, which on average measured the time from the initial fixation on the target word until 350ms later, revealed that cognate words were read faster than non-cognate words for both high and low semantic constraint sentences. This finding suggests that lexical access was non-selective at the early stages of reading for both sentence conditions, and word access was not sensitive to sentence context. The late-stage comprehension measures, on average from 350ms to 600ms after first fixating on the target word, showed that the cognate effect was only found for the low semantic constraint condition, not the high semantic condition. Thus, in the later stages of lexical access, the French-English bilinguals were sensitive to sentence context condition, and this sensitivity caused the cognate effect to disappear for the high semantic constraint sentences. The findings from Libben and Titone help specify when in the time course of lexical access that biasing sentence contexts affect word recognition.

Like Libben and Titone (2009), Schwartz and Kroll (2006) and van Hell and de Groot (2008), further findings from Duyck, Van Assche, Drieghe, and Hartsuiker (2007) revealed that Dutch-English bilinguals processed cognate target words faster than non-targets when reading low semantic constraint sentences in their L2. Thus, the L1 was active even when reading entirely in the L2. In a follow-up study, Van Assche, Duyck, Hartsuiker, and Van Diependaele (2009) investigated what happened when Dutch-English bilinguals processed target words while reading sentences entirely in their L1. Although the bilinguals were highly proficient in both of their languages, they wondered if it would be easier to "shut off" their slightly less dominant L2. They found a cognate effect even when reading low semantic constraint sentences in the L1, providing more evidence for non-selectivity and suggesting that even the slightly weaker L2 can affect native language processing.

While it appears the semantic context of a sentence constrains selectivity, an often-overlooked dimension that could potentially affect selectivity is syntax. Indeed, the syntactic frame of a sentence may provide a strong cue toward lexical retrieval (i.e., select the Spanish word since the syntax of the sentence is language specific to Spanish). To date however, there is very little work examining the influence of syntax on lexical processing. One study (Gullifer, Dussias & Kroll 2010) suggests that syntactic constraints can function like semantic constraints and supersede bottom-up processing. Gullifer et al. used a word-naming task for Spanish-English bilinguals and cognate/non-cognate target words. High and low syntactic constraint sentences were created. In the high constraint sentences, the features of the syntax were Spanish-specific. For instance, the high syntactic constraint sentences all had a clitic marker (le 'to him/her') and a null subject (pro) in the relative clause. English syntax does not have an object clitic marker before the verb and always requires an overt subject, so the sentences were clearly constrained for Spanish. The low syntactic constraint sentences had syntactic features shared by both languages. With these sentences, therefore, syntax alone could not be a cue to disambiguate language. The authors found that the cognate effect disappeared when the participants read high syntactic constraint sentences, but remained for the low syntactic constraint sentences. Thus, syntax seemed to act as a cue to constrain selectivity. Since the amount of semantic and syntactic information in sentence contexts differs, more research needs to be done to investigate how these sentential factors may affect processing.

Based on the previous research, it is becoming clearer that reading sentences in only one language is not enough to prevent non-selectivity. While reading low constraint sentences in the L2, bilinguals still show evidence of having a cognate effect. The question remains what other ways one can facilitate L2 word recognition while reading in sentence contexts. Since it is not always possible to use cognates, what can help L2 learners deactivate their stronger L1 while reading in their L2? By creating ways to minimize the activation levels of the L1, and thus by decreasing the competition between languages, L2 word recognition may be facilitated. Based on the past research, the language of the sentence is not enough to "shut off" the L1. The Features restriction hypothesis will now be presented to illustrate in further detail how sentence contexts can restrain selectivity.

5.1   Features restriction hypothesis

The feature restrictions hypothesis (Kellas, Paul, Martin & Simpson 1991; Schwanenflugel & LaCount 1988) makes predictions on how sentence contexts may affect lexical processing. Based on findings from monolingual eye-tracking studies (Balota, Pollatsek, & Rayner 1985; Ehrlich & Rayner 1981; Rayner & Well 1996) which found that more predictable words yield shorter reading times or are skipped entirely, the hypothesis predicts that monolinguals generate semantic, syntactic, and lexical feature restrictions as they read for the word that best fits the sentence. For example, consider example (4):

(4)   John took a bite out of the fresh green _____.

The word that can fit in the blank must have the features [can be bitten], [fresh], and [green]. The semantics of the sentence, therefore, constrains which word can logically fit in the blank. Thus, sentences that are highly constrained will generate more restrictions for target words compared to sentences that are less constrained. When there are less target words to inhibit, word recognition becomes faster. The feature restrictions hypothesis begins to explain why a high semantic constraint sentence yields non-selective access for bilingual word recognition for both cognate and non-cognate target words, while a low semantic constraint sentence cannot. The semantic features restrict cognates and non-cognates equally, so the absence of the cognate priming effect shows that the semantic features override what is being activated. However, the proficiency of the individual will certainly affect the ability to generate certain feature restrictions. For instance, a less proficient learner has a limited L2 lexicon, which will result in fewer activated lexical items compared to a more proficient L2 learner. A sentence with less semantic constraint, thus, may still eliminate the cognate priming effect for less proficient L2 learners, as their limited L2 lexicon already restricts what is being activated. Alternatively, given the limited L2 lexicon of the less proficient learner, the cognate relationship may be even more salient (Brenders, van Hell & Dijkstra 2011).

While the Features restriction hypothesis has been used to explain how sentences with high semantic constraint may constrain non-selectivity, future work needs to further investigate sentence contexts and ask how the cues of semantics and syntax interact and jointly affect lexical processing. Could the semantics of a sentence override the effects of the syntax? Or does syntax provide a stronger cue to bilinguals than semantics? The answers to these questions will certainly inform models such as the BIA+ model (Dijkstra & Van Heuven 2002). A future study could take the next step by investigating how both L2 learners and more proficient bilinguals process words in sentences manipulated for both semantics and syntax in order to examine the relative strength of semantic and syntactic cues.

In the previous sections, the process of word recognition as well some of the research investigating non-selectivity was described. In the next section, how language teachers might be able to apply this knowledge when teaching in the classroom is addressed.

6.   Implications for L2 learning and teaching

Both researchers and L2 teachers alike can benefit from knowing the past research done on L2 word recognition. While researchers have created models to reflect the underlying processes during L2 word recognition, L2 teachers should be mindful of what these models propose, and apply this knowledge to their interactions with L2 learners. There are at least three important factors for language teachers to consider. First, there is the notion that the default setting for L2 learners is non-selectivity. Teachers should expect that students will be unable to turn off their L1, even if they are explicitly told to do so or if they are reading solely in their L2. Results from Arêas Da Luz Fuentes and Schwartz (2010) found that Spanish was still active for Spanish-English bilinguals when processing partial cognates in an all-English context. The researchers concluded that L2 teachers need to be aware of the co-activation of two languages and how this co-activation can affect L2 processing. It only takes one L1 word or an L2 word that shares a similar form to an L1 word (e.g., lexical neighbors, homographs, cognates) to heighten the activation of the L1. Due to the strong overlap between languages (especially between languages such as English and Spanish, for example), it may be impossible to avoid similar cross-linguistic forms. Thus, it is not recommended that L2 teachers should attempt to completely deactivate the L1. Rather, acknowledging that the L1 is present and active while learning an L2 is an important observation for teachers. Indeed, having the L1 active may be beneficial for students. Results from Nagy, Garcia, Durgunoglu, and Hancin-Bhatt (1993) found that Spanish-English elementary school children were facilitated in their English reading because of their knowledge of Spanish vocabulary. These students were able to apply their use of Spanish when reading English-Spanish cognates. Thus, in some cases an active L1 may serve to help L2 readers.

The second key factor for L2 teachers to consider is the nature of student errors. It is common for teachers to become frustrated when their students mix up seemingly distinct words in the L2 (e.g., the verbs *poner* 'to put,' *poder* 'can,' *pedir* 'to order,' in Spanish or word pairs such as *mujer* 'woman' and *mejor* 'best'). Teachers may think that their students did not learn these words well or perhaps believe that they did not effectively teach them well. Without understanding both L1 and L2 word recognition, L2 teachers may not realize that the overlap in word form made it difficult for the L2 learners to retrieve the correct lexical item, due to the highly competitive activation process. By understanding word recognition, L2 teachers realize that their students are doing exactly what their minds should be doing during reading, and neither student nor teacher is at fault.

The third important factor for teachers to take away from this chapter is how to try and prevent these types of errors from occurring in the first place. Taking the example of confusing *mejor/mujer* above, L2 teachers should emphasize the features associated with form-related words, in order to facilitate retrieval. When teaching the word *mujer*, 'woman,' L2 teachers should try and highlight the various features typically associated with women (e.g., certain clothing, activities, and occupational choices). Presenting the vocabulary words in sentences that are manipulated such that the features of the target word are greater emphasized may help facilitate word recognition (as was found in the high constraint sentences from Schwartz & Kroll 2006 and Van Hell & de Groot 2008). Instead of presenting L2 vocabulary in isolation, which is often the case in the L2 classroom, teachers could use semantically rich sentences, such as "The woman wears a dress with high heels," (or whatever description they feel their students will relate with the most) in order to connect the vocabulary word with its features. The next time L2 Spanish learners encounter the word *mujer*, these features will be more strongly activated, which will also help deactivate the form-related items, such as *mejor* 'best.' When teaching the word *mejor* 'best,' L2 teachers can present it in a context that uses a familiar chunk, such as *mejor amigo* 'best friend,' giving more meaning to the lexical item *mejor*. By providing richer input that activates meaningful associations with the form-related words, perhaps word recognition will be facilitated. Future work in L2 vocabulary acquisition will certainly need to investigate this area.

In the area of second language acquisition, the model of input processing (VanPatten 1996, 2004, 2007) proposes principles of strategies L2 learners use when they unravel meaning from the input. While most of these principles address how L2 learners process grammatical features, there is one that focuses on the processing of lexical words in a sentence: The Primacy of Content Words Principle. This principle states that L2 learners will process content words before grammatical features or anything else in the input. For example, L2 learners will process an adverb of time (e.g., "yesterday") before processing a past-tense morphological verb marker (e.g., "-ed") because the adverb is a content word, while the past-tense marker is a grammatical feature.

Based on the past research on form-related lexical items, it becomes clear that not all content words are processed in the same way. Lexical neighbors, partial cognates, and semantically ambiguous words are more difficult for L2 learners to recognize due to competition during lexical processing. In order to reflect what occurs during word recognition, we propose three novel subprinciples that specify how certain types of content words cause processing difficulties for learners. We develop these innovative subprinciples based on the psycholinguistic evidence on word recognition discussed earlier in the chapter. The first subprinciple is the Lexical Neighborhood Principle. This subprinciple states that content words that share lexical neighbors (either within one language or between languages) will generate more competition compared to content words that do not share lexical neighbors. Thus, the Spanish word *cara* 'face' may interfere within the language with the Spanish word *casa* 'house' or cross-language with a word like "card."

The second subprinciple we have proposed is the Partial Cognate Principle: L2 learners may encounter difficulties processing partial cognates. Due to the overlap of orthography, meaning, and phonology of a pair of words between languages, bilinguals process cognates faster than non-cognates. Partial cognates, like the English and Spanish word "grave," however, only share one similar meaning ("grave" meaning "'serious'") in both languages but not a second meaning (in English, "grave" also means "'burial place,'" but this meaning is not encoded in the Spanish word) and may be more difficult to process. Indeed, Sunderman and Schwartz (2008) found that Spanish-English bilinguals processed partial cognates more slowly and less accurately due to the imperfect overlap in meaning. Partial cognates, therefore, belong to a special class of content words that may be more difficult for L2 learners and bilinguals to retrieve during comprehension.

Finally, our third subprinciple is the Ambiguous Words Principle. L2 learners may encounter difficulties processing homographs and words with semantic ambiguity across languages (see Degani & Tokowicz 2010b for a review). Similar to partial cognates, homographs are words whose form is identical (again, either between or across languages), but whose meaning differs; homographs are not partial cognates because the word pair shares no meaning across languages. Consider the famous example of the English word "bug." The meaning of this word specifies an insect, a computer glitch, or even a method of spying on someone. Swinney (1979) examined whether English-speaking participants activated the multiple meanings associated with homographs at different points during processing. Swinney found that participants initially activated the multiple meanings of ambiguous words. Eventually the target meaning was disambiguated, by processing the homograph within the sentence context. Another study, Tokowicz and Kroll (2007) examined the processing of semantically ambiguous words across languages (e.g., the Spanish word *cielo* can be translated as 'heaven' or 'sky'). The results obtained showed that bilinguals were slower to process words with more than one translation than they were with words with only one translation. These semantically ambiguous words are more difficult for L2 learners to retrieve during word recognition. Further studies (Degani & Tokowicz 2010a; Prior, MacWhinney & Kroll 2007) confirmed difficulties with lexical ambiguity for L2 learners.

The BIA+ model predicts that bilinguals will not process all content words in the same way because of the differing orthography, phonology, and semantics of words between and across languages. While some words (e.g., full cognates) are processed more quickly for bilinguals, a large number will be more difficult to process. It is important for L2 teachers to keep in mind that, while L2 learners may have a preference to process content words over grammatical information, the learners may still have trouble retrieving correct lexical items for words that share similar forms or have ambiguous meanings. L2 instructors could employ semantically rich sentence contexts as a teaching strategy. By presenting new vocabulary words, especially homographs and lexical neighbors, in constraining contexts, the features associated with the words would be strengthened and the other lexical items with overlapping form will be eliminated (see Prior, Wintner, MacWhinney & Lavie 2011), helping facilitate L2 word recognition for L2 learners.

7. Conclusion

The purpose of this chapter was to provide an overview of bilingual word recognition, specifically focusing on the models and methods of testing lexical access. An understanding of the underlying processing involved in lexical access is useful to languages teachers and researchers alike. As discussed in this chapter, although both languages are typically active and competing when a bilingual or second language learner is reading, there are ways in which the language selection processes can be more constrained at the sentence level, by semantic and syntactic information. Future research on L2 vocabulary learning and instruction will hopefully garner insights from psycholinguistic models of bilingual lexical processing and apply those insights to pedagogy. Moreover, the three lexical subprinciples proposed in this chapter offer a rich area for future research at the intersection of pyscholinguistics and L2 pedagogy.

References

Arêas Da Luz Fontes, A.B., & Schwartz, A.I. (2010). On a different plane: Cross-language effects on the conceptual representations of within-language homonyms. *Language and Cognitive Processes, 25*, 508–532.

Balota, D. A., Pollatsek, A., & Rayner, K. (1985). The interaction of contextual constraints and parafoveal visual information in reading. *Cognitive Psychology, 17*, 364–390.

Brenders, P., Van Hell, J. G. & Dijkstra, T. (2011). Word recognition in child second language learners: Evidence from cognates and false friends. *Journal of Experimental Child Psychology, 109,* 383–396.

Coltheart, M., Davelaar, E., Jonasson, J.T., & Besner, D. (1977). Access to the internal lexicon. In S. Dornic (Ed.), *Attention and Performance, VI* (pp. 535–555). New York, NY: Academic Press.

Cristoffanini, P.M., Kirsner, K., & Milech, D. (1986). Bilingual lexical representation: The status of Spanish-English cognates. *The Quarterly Journal of Experimental Psychology, 38,* 367–393.

De Groot, A.M.B. (2011). *Language and cognition in bilinguals and multilinguals: An introduction.* Hove,UK: Psychology Press.

De Groot, A.M.B., Delmaar, P., & Lupker, S.L. (2000).The processing of interlexical homographs in translation recognition and lexical decision: Support for nonselective access to bilingual memory. *Quarterly Journal of Experimental Psychology, 52a,* 397–428.

Degani, T., & Tokowicz, N. (2010a). Ambiguous words are harder to learn. *Bilingualism: Language and Cognition, 13,* 299–314.

Degani, T., & Tokowicz, N. (2010b). Semantic ambiguity within and across languages: An integrative review. *The Quarterly Journal of Experimental Psychology, 63,* 1266–1303.

Dijkstra, A. (2005). Bilingual visual word recognition and lexical access. In J.F. Kroll & A.M.B. de Groot (Eds.), *Handbook of bilingualism: Psycholinguistic* approaches (pp. 178–201). Oxford: OUP.

Dijkstra, A., De Bruijn, E., Schriefers, H., & Ten Brinke, S. (2000). More on interlingual homograph recognition: Language intermixing versus explicitness of instruction. *Bilingualism: Language and Cognition, 3,* 69–78.

Dijkstra, A., Grainger, J., & Van Heuven, W.J.B. (1999). Recognizing cognates and interlingual homographs: The neglected role of phonology. *Journal of Memory and Language, 41,* 496–518.

Dijkstra, A., Timmermans, M., & Schriefers, H. (2000). Cross-language effects on bilingual homograph recognition. *Journal of Memory and Language, 42,* 445–464.

Dijkstra, A., & Van Heuven, W.J.B. (1998). The BIA-model and bilingual word recognition. In J. Grainger and A. Jacobs (Eds.), *Localist Connectionist Approaches to Human Cognition* (pp. 189–225). Hillsdale, NJ: Lawrence Erlbaum Associates.

Dijkstra, A., Van Heuven, W.J.B., & Grainger, J. (1998). Simulating cross-language competition with the bilingual interactive activation model. Psychological Belgica, 38, 177–197.

Dijkstra, A., & Van Heuven, W.J.B. (2002). The architecture of the bilingual word recognition system: From identification to decision. *Bilingualism: Language and Cognition, 5*(3), 175–197.

Dijkstra, A., Van Jaarsveld, H., & Ten Brinke, S. (1998). Interlingual homograph recognition: Effects of task demands and language intermixing. *Bilingualism: Language and Cognition, 1,* 51–66.

Duyck, W., Van Assche, E., Drieghe, D., & Hartsuiker, R. J. (2007). Visual word recognition by bilinguals in a sentence context: Evidence for nonselective lexical access. *Journal of experimental Psychology: Learning, Memory, and Cognition, 33,* 663–679.

Ehrlich, S.F., & Rayner, K. (1981). Contextual effects on word perception and eye-movements during reading. *Journal of Verbal Learning and Verbal Behavior, 20,* 641–655.

Friesen, D.C., & Jared, D. (2012). Cross-language phonological activation of meaning: Evidence from category verification. *Bilingualism: Language and Cognition, 15,* 145 – 156.

Gerard, L.D., & Scarborough, D.L. (1989). Language-specific lexical access of homographs by bilinguals. *Journal of Experimental Psychology: Learning, Memory and Cognition, 15,* 305–315.

Gollan, T.H., Forster, K.I., & Frost, R. (1997). Translation priming with different scripts: Masked priming with cognates and noncognates in Hebrew-English bilinguals. *Journal of Experimental Psychology: Learning, Memory, and Cognition, 23*, 1122–1139.

Gullifer, J., Dussias, P., & Kroll, J.F. (2010). Bilingual sentence processing: The role of syntactic constraints in modulating cross-language lexical activity. Poster presented at the 23rd Annual CUNY conference on Human sentence processing, March 18–20. New York, NY.

Haigh, C.A., & Jared, D. (2007). The activation of phonological representations by bilinguals while reading silently: Evidence from interlingual homophones. *Journal of Experimental Psychology: Learning, Memory & Cognition, 33*, 623–644.

Hoshino, N., & Kroll, J.F. (2008). Cognate effects in picture naming: Does cross-language activation survive a change of script? *Cognition, 106*, 501–511.

Jared, D., Cormier, P., Levy, B.A., & Wade-Woolley, L. (2012). Cross-language activation of phonology in young bilingual readers. *Reading and Writing, 25*, 1327–1343.

Jared, D., & Kroll, J.F. (2001). Do bilinguals activate phonological representations in one or both of their languages when naming words? *Journal of Memory and Language, 44*, 2–31.

Jared, D., & Szucs, C. (2002). Phonological activation in bilinguals: Evidence from interlingual homograph naming. *Bilingualism: Language and Cognition, 5*, 225–239.

Kellas, G., Paul, S.T., Martin, M., & Simpson, G.B. (1991). Contextual feature activation and meaning access. In G.B. Simpson (ed.), *Understanding word and sentence* (pp. 47–71). Amsterdam: North-Holland.

Lemhöfer, K., & Dijkstra, A. (2004). Recognizing cognates and interlingual homographs: Effects of code similarity in language specific and generalized lexical decision. *Memory & Cognition, 32*, 533–550.

Libben, M., & Titone, D. (2009). Bilingual lexical access in context: Evidence from eye movements during reading. *Journal of Experimental Psychology: Learning, Memory, and Cognition, 35*(2), 281–390.

McClelland, J.L., & Rumelhart, D.E. (1981). An interactive activation model of context effects in letter perception, Part 1: An account of basic findings. *Psychological Review, 88*, 375–407.

Nagy, W.E., García, G.E., Durgunoglu, A.Y., & Hancin-Bhatt, B. (1993). Spanish-English bilingual students' use of cognates in English reading. *Journal of Reading Behavior, 25*(3), 241–259.

Prior, A., MacWhinney, B., & Kroll, J.F. (2007). Translation norms for English and Spanish: The role of lexical variables, word class, and L2 proficiency in negotiating translation ambiguity. *Behavior Research Methods, 39*, 1029–1038.

Prior, A., Wintner, S., MacWhinney, B., & Lavie, A. (2011). Translation ambiguity in and out of context. *Applied Psycholinguistics, 32*, 93–111.

Rayner, K., & Well, A.D. (1996). Effects of contextual constraint on eye movements in reading: A further examination. *Psychonomic Bulletin & Review, 3*, 504–509.

Schwanenflugel, P.J., & La Count, K. (1988). Semantic relatedness and the scope of facilitation for upcoming words in sentences. *Journal of Experimental Research: Learning, Memory, and Cognition, 14*, 344–354.

Schwartz, A.I., & Kroll, J.F. (2006). Bilingual lexical activation in sentence context. *Journal of Memory and Language, 55*, 197–212.

Sunderman, G., & Kroll, J.F. (2006). First language activation during second language lexical processing: An investigation of lexical form, meaning and grammatical class. *Studies in Second Language Acquisition 28*: 387–422.

Sunderman, G., & Schwartz, A.I. (2008). Using cognates to investigate cross-language competition in second language processing. *TESOL Quarterly, 42*, 19–33.

Sunderman, G., & Priya, K. (2011). Translation recognition in highly proficient Hindi-English bilinguals: The influence of different scripts but connectable phonologies. *Language and Cognitive Processes*. Advance online publication. doi: 10.1080/01690965.2011.596420.

Swinney, D.A. (1979). Lexical access during sentence comprehension: (Re)consideration of context effects. *Journal of Verbal Learning and Verbal Behavior, 18*, 645–659.

Tokowicz, N., & Kroll, J.F. (2007). Number of meanings and concreteness: Consequences of ambiguity within and across languages. *Language and Cognitive Processes, 22*, 727–779.

Van Assche, E., Duyck, W., Hartsuiker, R., & Diependaele, K. (2009). Does bilingualism change native-language reading? Cognate effects in a sentence context. *Psychological Science, 20*, 923–927.

Van Hell, J.G., & de Groot, A.M.B. 2008. Sentence context modulates visual word recognition and translation in bilinguals. *Acta Psychologica, 128,* 431–451.

Van Hell, J.G., & Dijkstra, A. (2002). Foreign language knowledge can influence native language performance. Psychonomic Bulletin & Review, 9(4), 780–789.

Van Heuven, W.J.B., Dijkstra, A., & Grainger, J. (1998). Orthographic neighborhood effects in bilingual word recognition. *Journal of Memory and Language, 39,* 458–483.

VanPatten, B. (1996). *Input processing and grammar instruction.* Westport, CT: Ablex.

VanPatten, B. (2004). Input processing in second language acquisition. In B. VanPatten (Ed.), *Processing instruction: Theory, research, and commentary* (pp. 5–31). Mahwah, NJ: Lawrence Erlbaum Associates.

VanPatten, B. (2007). Input processing in adult second language acquisition. In B. VanPatten & J. Williams (Eds.), *Theories in second language* acquisition (pp. 115–135). Mahwah, NJ: Lawrence Erlbaum Associates.

CHAPTER 13

Cognitive foundations of crosslinguistic influence

Scott Jarvis, Michelle O'Malley, Linye Jing, Jing Zhang, Jessica Hill, Curtis Chan and Nadezhda Sevostyanova
Ohio University

Most previous research on crosslinguistic influence (CLI) has focused on the linguistic consequences of CLI, but researchers have also begun to investigate the cognitive processes through which it occurs. This chapter is a state-of-the-art review of empirical research that has examined the cognitive and conceptual factors that account for performance differences between individuals who differ in terms of the specific combinations of languages they know. The chapter is divided into three main sections. The first deals with the cognitive consequences of acquiring languages beyond the first, the second with the relationship between crosslinguistic similarity, executive control, and memory, and the final section deals with how the conceptual structures acquired through one language can affect a person's use of another language.

1. Introduction

Crosslinguistic influence (CLI) – or the influence of a person's knowledge of one language on the person's knowledge or use of another language – has been one of the central concerns of the fields of second language acquisition (SLA) and bilingualism since their very early days (e.g., Corder 1967; Lado 1957; Weinreich 1953). Most of the research on CLI has been product-oriented, focused either on the linguistic outcomes of this phenomenon in individuals' language production or on the knowledge structures (e.g., crosslinguistic associations stored in long-term memory) that the linguistic outcomes entail (see, e.g., Jarvis & Pavlenko 2008; Odlin 1989; Ringbom 1987). The fields of SLA, bilingualism, and multilingualism are nevertheless rapidly adopting process-oriented perspectives, with a particular focus on the effects of cognitive processes and capacities on language acquisition and use. Although models and measures of cognition – including models and measures of attentional control, working memory, and conceptualization – have already been applied to the investigation of numerous facets of language acquisition and use (e.g., Goo 2010; Rai et al. 2011), they have just recently begun finding their way into research on CLI. The preliminary work that has been conducted to date in this area suggests that this will indeed be an exciting and very fruitful avenue for future research. The purpose of this chapter is to describe some of these models and measures and to discuss how they have begun to be applied to the investigation of CLI.

2.   Cognitive consequences of bilingualism and multilingualism

The cognitive effects of crosslinguistic influence overlap to some degree with the effects of simply knowing more than one language, and it is useful to begin with an understanding of what those latter effects are. Historically, the question has often been framed in terms of whether bilingualism and multilingualism have cognitive benefits, or whether it would be better for people to remain monolingual. Prior to 1960, most research suggested that bilingualism was an impediment to cognitive development (e.g., Saer 1923), but a good deal of research since then has emphasized its positive consequences for cognition (e.g., Peal & Lambert 1962). Researchers today try to maintain a balanced view, recognizing the advantages and disadvantages of bilingualism and multilingualism in narrowly defined types of tasks and contexts (e.g., Costa et al. 2009; Ricciardelli 1992; Ransdell & Fischler 1987).

One of the narrowly defined areas of investigation involves memory tasks. Until Ransdell and Fischler (1987), most studies had shown that bilinguals tend to perform more poorly (i.e., more slowly and less accurately) than monolinguals on tasks such as those that require participants to recall the names of objects, remember series of digits, and follow sequences of directions (e.g., Magiste 1980). However, as pointed out by Ransdell and Fischler, the research design of many of those studies had created artificial disadvantages for bilinguals. For example, bilinguals were often tested in a nonnative, less dominant language while monolinguals were (of course) tested in their native language. Bilinguals in such studies were also often required to use both languages during the testing session while monolinguals used only one. To address these potential confounds, Ransdell and Fischler compared native English-speaking monolinguals and bilinguals in their native language on four verbal memory tasks: list recognition, lexical decision, object naming, and free recall. The first two tasks were referred to as data-driven because they involved the use of verbal prompts. The latter two tasks were referred to as conceptually driven because words were the expected response rather than being part of the prompt. The results showed no significant differences between the bilinguals and monolinguals in terms of recall accuracy on any of the four tasks, but did show a significant advantage for monolinguals in terms of speed of recall on the two data-driven tasks. The researchers (1987: 392) interpreted the results as showing that a monolingual advantage occurs only "where language-specific, data-driven processing predominates".

Even though this and many other studies have shown that bilinguals tend to perform more slowly than monolinguals on verbal memory tasks (e.g., Magiste, 1980), phoneme detection (e.g., Blair & Harris 1981), and lexical judgment tasks (e.g., Altenberg & Cairns 1983; Nas 1983; Soares & Grosjean 1984), bilinguals and multilinguals have been found to have clear and significant advantages in other areas. In the recent literature, the two most frequently noted cognitive advantages of bilingualism and multilingualism involve enhanced language awareness and improved attentional control. Regarding the first of these, Jessner (2006) points to past research showing that language awareness increases with each new language a person acquires, and that this in turn accelerates the rate at which a person is able to acquire any subsequent language. Some of the more specific consequences of increased language awareness, according to Jessner, are (a) the ability to recognize and make use of similarities between the languages a person already knows and the one that is currently being acquired, (b) enhanced creative thinking due to having gained an expanded repertoire of perspectives that the different languages represent, and (c) improved communicative flexibility and awareness of nuanced communicative requirements.

The second general advantage of bilingualism and multilingualism is improved attentional control – or what Bialystok (2005: 425) alternatively refers to as selectivity of attention and cognitive control of attention. Although attention is thought to comprise multiple components – i.e., selective attention, inhibitory control, and planning – Bialystok suggests that "bilingualism exerts its effect primarily on the inhibition component of attention". This component of attention – inhibitory control – is the ability to inhibit (or suppress) distracting, interfering, or misleading information while performing a task, and this is one area where bilinguals show a fairly consistent advantage over monolinguals. By way of illustration, studies cited by Bialystok have investigated monolingual and bilingual children's ability to perform a task that requires them to sort a set of cards according to a simple rule (e.g., color), and then to re-sort the same cards using a different rule (e.g., shape). The results of the relevant research have shown that bilinguals have much less difficulty in switching their mode of thought from one rule to the other. According to Bialystok, this is because bilingual children are better able to inhibit the original values of the cards while shifting their attention to the new values.

Bialystok's explanation for bilinguals' superior inhibitory control is consistent with the tenets of Green's (1998) bilingual inhibitory control model, which rests on evidence that both of the languages of a bilingual are simultaneously activated in the mind when either of them is in use (for a review of such evidence, see, e.g., Marian & Spivey 2003). According to Green's model, in order for bilinguals to keep their two languages functionally distinct, they must suppress one while using the other. "If the inhibitory control model of Green is correct, then bilingualism by its very nature results in greater use of inhibitory control because it is invoked every time language is used" (Bialystok 2005: 427). Crucially, the mastery bilinguals gain over their ability to inhibit task-irrelevant information carries over into a variety of cognitive domains, both within and outside of language.

Inhibitory control by itself might not adequately account for the bilingual advantage, however. Inhibitory control is an executive function of cognition that a person relies on to ignore distracting and conflicting information, but Costa et al. (2008) show that bilinguals often exhibit an advantage even when the context is neither distracting nor conflicting. They demonstrated this through the use of a flanker task in which participants were shown a central arrow surrounded by four flanker arrows (e.g., →→→→→). The participants were asked to indicate as quickly as possible what the direction of the central arrow was. In some trials, the direction of the central arrow was congruent with the direction of the flanker arrows (e.g., →→→→→), and in other trials the direction of the central arrow was incongruent with the flanker arrows (e.g., →→←→→). This latter condition created a conflict that presumably required the participants to inhibit potential interference from the flanker arrows while attending to the direction of the central arrow. Not surprisingly, the bilinguals were significantly faster than the monolinguals in the incongruent condition. However, the bilinguals were also significantly faster in the congruent condition. The latter advantage is difficult to account for on the basis of inhibitory control, and the authors interpret it as a consequence of bilinguals' heightened alertness and ability to monitor changes in the stimuli. Thus, if Costa et al. are correct, it appears that bilingualism produces positive benefits in two independent components of a person's attentional control: monitoring processes and inhibitory control.

One of the interesting characteristics of the results of Costa et al. is that they suggest that the bilingual advantage is concentrated primarily in just one brain network. According to Posner and Petersen (1990), there are three general types of brain networks, and attentional processes can be divided into three separate categories in accordance with the brain networks that subserve them. The three types of attentional processes include alerting (achieving and maintaining a state of alertness), orienting (selecting information in the sensory input), and executive control (monitoring and resolving conflict). It is this last category of attentional processes – i.e., executive control – that is believed to govern both monitoring processes and inhibitory control. Accordingly, bilinguals' cognitive advantages appear to lie primarily in their enhanced executive control. The following sections describe the relationship between CLI, executive control, and related domains of cognition.

3. CLI, executive control, and memory

3.1 Effects of crosslinguistic relationships on executive control

Although Bialystok (2005), Costa et al. (2008), and others tend to characterize the positive consequences of bi- and multilingualism as general effects that occur regardless of the specific combination of languages that a person knows and/or is learning, it is relevant to ask whether the degree to which bi- and multilingualism enhance a person's executive control might vary in accordance with the types and magnitudes of similarity found in the specific combination of languages in question (cf. Emmorey, Luk, Pyers & Bialystok, 2008). It is not possible at present to give a definitive answer to this question, but the existing evidence does suggest that crosslinguistic similarity is likely to modulate the effects of bilingualism on executive control. This seems particularly clear with respect to the inhibition component of executive control. Evidence for this can be found in the fact that learners of a target language that is closely related to one that they have already mastered often find it difficult to avoid formal and structural interference from the related language. Such interference manifests itself in the form of crosslinguistic slips of the tongue (Poulisse 1999), unintentional switches into the related language (Ringbom 1987; Williams & Hammarberg 1998), lexical blends and hybrids (Cenoz 2001; Dewaele 1998; Ringbom 1987), and various forms of phonological, morphological, and syntactic interference (see Jarvis & Pavlenko 2008; Odlin 1989; Ringbom 2007). The prevalence of interference from closely related languages suggests that language learners, bilinguals, and multilinguals might exert less executive control (including especially inhibitory control) over a language that is closely related to the one they are presently using.

Evidence from brain-imaging research supports this notion. Studies by Jeong et al. (2007a, 2007b) used fMRI imaging to monitor blood flow in the brains of Korean-speaking and Chinese-speaking learners with approximately equal levels of proficiency in both English and Japanese. Their levels of proficiency were determined with the level 2 Japanese Language Proficiency Test (JLPT) and the level 2 Society for Testing English Proficiency (STEP) test, both of which are widely used language proficiency tests in Japan. In separate trials, the participants were asked to listen to sentences recorded in English, Japanese, and their L1. Crucially, the word order of the target sentences was congruent between Korean and Japanese, as well as between Chinese and English, but incongruent between Korean and English, as well as between Chinese and Japanese, as shown in the following examples from Jeong et al. (2007b: 177):

(1) *English*   John met the teacher at school.

(2) *Japanese*
     Tarou-wa   gakkou-de   sensei-to   a-tta.
     Tarou-TOPIC   school-at   teacher-with   meet-PAST

(3) *Korean*
     Chelswu-nun   hakkyo-eyse
     Chelswu-TOPIC   school-at
     sensayngnimkwa   manna-ss-ta
     teacher-with   meet-PAST

(4) *Chinese*
     Zhāngsān   zài xuéxiào   jiàn-le   lǎoshī.
     Zhāngsān   at-school   meet-PERFECT   teacher

The results of the study showed that, despite the fact that the participants were equally proficient in both English and Japanese, their patterns of blood flow showed that more areas of their brains were activated while listening to the incongruent language (English for Korean speakers, Japanese for Chinese speakers) than when listening to the congruent language. Importantly, some of the areas of the brain that showed increased activation with the incongruent language are areas known to be related to executive control, including but perhaps not limited to inhibitory control (see, e.g., Krivitsky et al. 2011; Rubia et al. 2007). Though other interpretations are possible, these results are consistent with the notion that learners exert less inhibitory control while processing and producing languages that are very similar to a language they have already acquired.

The degree of involvement of executive control and other attentional processes is not determined solely by crosslinguistic similarity, however, but there does seem to be a consistent effect of the nature of the relationship between the target language and languages already acquired. Some of the most interesting effects involve cases where one language lacks a form, feature, or structure that another one has. Ringbom (2007) refers to this condition as a zero relationship, whereas Tokowicz and MacWhinney (2005) describe it as a condition of uniqueness. The important point is that there are multiple types of zero relationships between languages, and each type may have its own consequences for the degree to which a learner deploys executive and attentional functions. For example, when the L1 has a structure that the L2 lacks, the learner is likely to exert a fair amount of inhibitory control over the L1 form while producing the L2, but is likely to rely less on the inhibitory function while receptively processing the L2. When the L1 lacks a structure that the L2 has, the learner will probably need to deploy attentional and executive functions other than inhibitory control (such as performance-monitoring functions) while both producing and interpreting the L2 (cf. Trofimovich, Gatbonton & Segalowitz 2007). The picture becomes even more nuanced when focusing more narrowly on learners' sensitivity to errors in the input of an L2 that has a feature that the L1 lacks. Psycholinguistic and neuroimaging studies show that even early learners develop a sensitivity to errors involving the use of the wrong form (e.g., grammatical gender, see Tokowicz & MacWhinney 2005), whereas not even advanced learners develop a sensitivity to errors involving the omission of a form that does not have a counterpart in the L1 (e.g., plural markers, see Jiang et al. 2011). Given that sensitivity measured in the form of reaction times and electrical activity in the brain presumably reflects attentional and executive activity, it seems clear that crosslinguistic relationships combined with specific task demands have important consequences for the types and levels of executive control a learner will deploy at any given moment.

3.2   Effects of executive control on CLI

While it seems likely that crosslinguistic relationships affect learners' use and development of their executive control, it is also worthwhile to consider the potential for effects in the opposite direction. That is, do learners who already have more developed executive control differ from learners with weaker executive control in relation to the types and amounts of CLI they exhibit in their use of an L2? To our knowledge, there has so far been only one study that has addressed this question empirically. The study, conducted by Trude and Tokowicz (2011), was designed primarily to test one of the corollaries of Green's (1998) inhibitory control model, which, again, assumes that (1) a bilingual's two languages are simultaneously active in the mind regardless of which language the person is using at the moment, and (2) the bilingual must therefore inhibit one language while using the other. The corollary of these assumptions that Trude and Tokowicz set out to test is whether language learners with stronger inhibitory control abilities would be better able than learners with weaker inhibitory control abilities to suppress the effects of the L1 while performing a task in an L2 or L3. To measure language learners' inhibitory control abilities, the researchers used an operation span task, which is a commonly used test of executive control by researchers who view executive control as a component of working memory (cf., Baddeley 2003; Kane & Engle 2003).

The participants in the study were native English speakers enrolled in the University of Pittsburgh. Approximately half of the participants had no prior instruction in a Romance language, and the other half had completed the equivalent of at least four semesters of university-level Spanish. The experiment began with a computer-based pronunciation tutorial that provided the participants with instruction and practice in Portuguese sound-letter correspondences. This was followed by an operation span task, which consisted of a series of trials involving math problems and words to remember. Each trial began with a math problem the participants had to solve, after which they were shown an L1 English word they were asked to remember. After a sequence of between two and six trials, participants were asked to write down as many words from that series of trials as they could remember. Each participant performed three series of trials at each length (e.g., two words to remember from a series of two trials, three words to remember from a series of three trials, …six words to remember from a series of six trials). The number of words they could remember across all series and trials was used as an index of the effectiveness of their executive control, which, among other functions, is used to maintain viable levels of activation for information (e.g., words) stored in working memory while the person is performing other cognitive operations (e.g., solving math problems) (Baddeley 2003). After the operation span task, the participants were tested to see how well they could remember and pronounce the Portuguese sound-letter correspondences they had learned earlier.

The results of the study showed that learners with higher levels of executive control are indeed significantly more successful in inhibiting negative interference from the L1. The results were not altogether in line with expectations, however. For example, those participants who had studied Spanish as a foreign language showed a positive correlation between their working memory capacities (or inhibitory control) and the number of Spanish-like errors they made in their Portuguese pronunciation. The researchers interpreted this result as showing that learners exert more inhibitory control over their L1 than over an L2 when performing a task in an L3. Exactly why this would be the case is not clear, and one might prefer an interpretation that considers the close similarities between Spanish and Portuguese. As discussed in the preceding subsection, learners appear to exert less inhibitory control over a previously acquired language that is very similar to the language they are currently producing. A full account of this phenomenon would need to explain why learners appear to exhibit less inhibitory control over closely related languages. Perhaps one reason is the difficulty of keeping two closely related languages distinct in the mind: A prerequisite for being able to inhibit task-irrelevant information is the ability to recognize it as such and to isolate task-irrelevant information from information that is relevant. This might be an overwhelming task in some cases involving closely related languages.

3.3   Effects of CLI and executive control on memory

As mentioned, Trude and Tokowicz (2011) examined the effects of executive control as a component of working memory (WM). WM is generally modeled as consisting of both a storage and a processing component. The storage component corresponds roughly with what has traditionally been regarded as short-term memory (STM), whereas the processing component is generally defined as executive control (e.g., Baddeley 2003; Cowan 1999; Kane & Engle 2003). Among other functions, executive control regulates the information stored in STM and keeps it in a viable state of activation. A number of memory tasks, such as the traditional digit-span task, are believed to tax STM but not executive control, whereas other tasks, such as those that involve multi-tasking or the reordering of information, are believed to tax both the executive system as well as STM. This combination of simultaneous storage and processing is the essence of WM and the functional core of a cognitive construct that supports complex, online mental operations like language processing, mental arithmetic, and verbal reasoning (Baddeley & Hitch 1994; Gathercole, Pickering, Ambridge & Wearing 2004; Jarrold, Baddeley, Hewes, Leeke & Phillips 2004). The processing efficiency and storage capacity of a person's WM are collectively referred to as the person's working memory capacity (WMC), and this appears to play a central role in both L1 (Alloway, Gathercole, Willis & Adams 2004; Baddeley, Gathercole & Papagano 1998) and L2 acquisition (Atkins & Baddeley 1998; Brooks, Kempe & Sionov 2006; French 2004; Hummel 2009; Papagano & Vallar 1995), particularly in relation to how efficiently learners are able to recognize, integrate, and comprehend the incoming input, how much of the input they can retain, and how accurately they can retain it (e.g., Andersson 2010; Dufva & Voeten 1999; Rai et al. 2011; Service & Kohonen 1995).

Intriguingly, the effects of WMC on learners' ability to process and retain L2 input appear to overlap with similar effects arising from crosslinguistic similarity. Some evidence for this can be seen in a study by Fender (2003), which compares Arabic- and Japanese-speaking learners of English in relation to their word-recognition and word-integration abilities. Word recognition was measured through a lexical-decision task that required participants to decide, as quickly as possible, whether a series of words shown to them individually on a computer screen were real words or pseudo-words. Word integration, in turn, was measured through a moving-window self-paced reading task in which participants read sentences that were shown to them, but only one word at a time. The participants controlled the pace of reading themselves by pushing a button on the keyboard to move to the next word. They were asked to read as quickly as they could and then answer a comprehension question after each sentence. Word integration was defined by Fender as the learners' ability to combine words into larger units of meaning in their minds.

Their performance on this task was measured in relation to both their speed of processing and the accuracy of their answers to the comprehension questions.

The results of Fender's study show that the Japanese speakers recognized words significantly faster and more accurately than the Arabic speakers, but that the Arabic speakers were significantly more accurate than Japanese speakers at "integrating English words into larger phrase and clause units of meaning" (2003: 289). As discussed by Fender, these results can be accounted for largely in terms of relationships between English and the learners' L1s. That is, regarding word recognition, the writing system of Japanese makes speakers of this language sensitive to exact graphemic representations, which assists them in the recognition of real words in an L2. Concerning word integration, the word order of the target sentences in English was far more congruent with Arabic word order than with Japanese word order, and this seems to have given the Arabic speakers an advantage in combining the words they saw in the moving-window task into an accurate representation of the sentence's meaning. Fender did not specifically test for the potential effects of his participants' WMCs, but he did point out that word recognition and word integration involve processes of WM, and that speakers of different L1s rely on and become skilled in the use of differing processes.

The authors of the present chapter have begun an investigation into possible interactions between CLI and WMC in relation to how efficiently learners are able to process L2 input for comprehension, how much of the input they can retain, and how accurately they can retain it. Similar to Fender (2003), the authors have been using a moving-window self-paced reading task to measure learners' abilities to integrate (or process for comprehension) words in a sentence into a meaningful whole. However, the present research design differs from Fender's in multiple ways. First, the current participants are Chinese-speaking learners of English enrolled in either an intensive English program or full-time academic studies at a medium-sized university in the US Midwest. Second, instead of investigating CLI through a comparison of speakers from different L1 backgrounds, the present investigation uses target L2 sentences that represent three levels of word-order congruence between Chinese and English: (1) sentences involving coordination that are fully congruent between the two languages, (2) sentences involving possessive prepositional phrases (e.g., "mother of the child") that are less congruent with Chinese, and (3) sentences involving relative clauses that are very incongruent with Chinese.

Other differences between the current study and Fender's include the fact that the current study uses L1 and L2 digit-span tests (i.e., measures of the storage component of WMC) and an operation span test (a measure of the executive control function of WMC) as independent variables. The present study does not use a lexical-decision task, as Fender did, but it does use a second language task that was not included in Fender's study: an elicited imitation task. Whereas the use of a self-paced timed reading task helps to gauge the difficulty participants face while processing the target structures (i.e., coordinate clauses, prepositional phrases, and relative clauses), the elicited imitation task allows for the more direct examination of how well the target structures are integrated into and retained in participants' STM. The data collection and analysis are ongoing, but the preliminary results reported in Jarvis et al. (2012) show that the learners perform significantly worse in both language tasks with the structures (i.e., relative clauses) that are the most incongruent with their L1. This is true across the entire range of the learners' L2 proficiency levels, but is not found in the performance of native English speakers. Regarding the effects of WMC, the preliminary results show that L1 digit-span performance (i.e., storage capacity) is a fairly good predictor of how quickly the learners are acquiring English, whereas performance on the operation span task (i.e., processing efficiency) is a better predictor of their levels of ultimate attainment. Neither measure of WMC correlated significantly with performance on the self-paced timed reading or elicited imitation tasks for learners still in the intensive English program, but both measures correlated significantly, though moderately, with performance on these two language tasks among learners who were enrolled in full-time study and whose L2 proficiency was at or near their presumed level of ultimate attainment.

The relationship between CLI and WMC thus appears to be quite complicated, and it will clearly take a good deal more work to sort out how these two factors complement versus overlap with each other in learners' processing, comprehension, retention, and recall of L2 input. In the meantime, it is useful to consider how CLI interacts not just with WM, but also with long-term memory (LTM). In fact, the effects of CLI on learners' abilities to retain and recall L2 input appears to blur the distinction between WM and LTM. Some models of WM, such as that of Baddeley (2003), assume that WM and LTM are independent constructs that are nevertheless linked through a mutual interface. Other models, such as that of Cowan (2005), view WM as being embedded within LTM in the sense that WM representations are LTM representations that have been activated. Cowan's model is intriguing from the perspective of CLI in that it seems to predict that learners of an L2 that is very similar to their L1 will find it much easier to create WM representations of the L2 input because the relevant representations (or ones very similar to them) are already part of their WM-LTM systems. Likewise, if the relevant representations already have a more or less permanent status in the learners' memory systems, Cowan's model seems to account for how learners of a similar language might be able to retain L2 input more accurately and for longer periods of time.

The results of a study by Odlin (2009) seem to confirm these predictions. In this study, Odlin examined data originally collected by Jarvis (2000) from native

Finnish-speaking and native Swedish-speaking learners of English enrolled in grades 5, 7, and 9 in public schools in Finland. The Finnish speakers all spoke Finnish at home and attended schools where Finnish was the language of instruction, and the Swedish speakers all spoke Swedish at home and attended schools where Swedish was the language of instruction. The data used in Odlin's analysis included written narrative descriptions of an eight-minute segment of a Charlie Chaplin film (i.e., *Modern Times*) that was shown to the participants. The film was a silent film (with a music soundtrack), but the film segment in question included nine intermittent titles that showed what the characters were saying to one another. One of the titles, which occurs just one minute and 10 seconds into the film segment, says "It was the girl – not the man." This appeared in the context of a scene where a poor woman steals a loaf of bread from the back of a bakery truck and accidentally collides with Chaplin while she is running away. During the mix-up, Chaplin ends up with the loaf of bread and gets arrested, but a woman who witnessed the theft then goes up to the baker and points out that "it was the girl – not the man" who stole the bread.

The results of Odlin's analysis show that Swedish speakers use exact wording from the titles far more than Finnish speakers do. This is true even among the Swedish speakers who have had only two years of English instruction, in comparison with Finnish speakers who have had up to six years. While interpreting these results, it is important to keep in mind that the learners did not begin writing anything down until after they had finished viewing the film, which means that several minutes had passed between the time that they saw the titles and began describing the relevant scenes. Except in cases of constant rehearsal, the contents of WM are assumed to degrade after only a few seconds (e.g., Baddeley 2003), so the fact that the Swedish speakers were able to recall a good deal of the exact wording of the titles suggests that the close crosslinguistic similarity between Swedish and English not only allows them to retain L2 input far longer and more accurately than the Finnish speakers, but also allows them to retain L2 input far longer and more accurately than traditional models of STM and WM would predict. In certain critical respects, the effects of crosslinguistic similarity on memory performance resemble the effects of what Ericsson and Kintsch (1995) call long-term working memory, retrieval structures, and retrieval schemas. These are memory structures that result from substantial amounts of practice in the relevant domain, and which have the potential to support exceptional memory performance. As described in the following section, such memory structures have implications not just for retention and recall, but also for the conceptualizations that underlie the language production of learners from different L1 backgrounds.

4. Conceptualization

Conceptualization involves the process of forming a complex, temporary mental representation of something a person experiences directly (e.g., sees, hears, feels), remembers, learns about through communication with others, or imagines. Because it involves temporary mental representations, conceptualization by definition takes place in working memory (see Jarvis 2011). Conceptualization is essentially synonymous with thinking (i.e., "What are you thinking about?" = "What are you conceptualizing?"), and it underlies any meaningful use of language – both overt language use and inner speech (e.g., Pavlenko 2011). During language comprehension and other forms of receptive language processing, conceptualization can be understood in terms of what Fender (2003) calls word integration – or the process of extracting meaning from words and phrases and combining them into larger units of meaning that reflect the semantics of full clauses, sentences, and beyond. Presumably, this involves activating the relevant concepts in LTM (which renders them part of WM, cf. Cowan 2005) and configuring those activated concepts vis-à-vis one another in a way that approximates the intended meaning.

Most of the relevant literature on conceptualization focuses on the nature of thinking that leads to or occurs simultaneously with language production. Slobin's (1993, 1996) notion of *thinking for speaking* assumes that meaningful language production begins with an intended message (e.g., a conceptualization of an event) that must be modified through a series of mental processes that render the message compatible with and directly mappable to the lexical, morphological, syntactic, and discursive inventories and requirements of the language being used. It is at this level and only at this level, according to Slobin, that thinking is language-specific. It is also at this level where Slobin (1993) points out that the patterns of conceptualization (or thinking for speaking) that have been acquired through one's L1 are likely to be carried over into the person's production of an L2.

Levelt (1989) has proposed similar ideas about the role of conceptualization in language production and about the degree to which it is language-specific. Levelt describes two stages of communication-oriented conceptualization (or what Slobin would call thinking for speaking). The first involves macro-planning, or determining which conceptual elements within the conceptualized message should be communicated and at what degree of granularity. The second stage involves micro-planning, or organizing and ordering the selected conceptual elements into a mental representation that can be more or less linearly encoded into language. Levelt claims that micro-planning but not macro-planning is language-specific.

An even more elaborate model of communication-oriented conceptualization can be found in von Stutterheim and Nüse (2003), who distinguish between multiple levels of macro- and micro-planning, and provide empirical evidence that language-specific effects can be found at each level. One of the main areas of focus in the work of von Stutterheim and her colleagues is the relationship between grammatical aspect and event construal – the main finding being that speakers of languages that lack a grammaticalized progressive/imperfective aspect (e.g., German, Swedish) tend to produce real-time descriptions of witnessed events that depict those events as being bounded – i.e., viewed as a whole event with a beginning and an endpoint. Speakers of languages that have a grammaticalized progressive/imperfective (e.g., English, Spanish), on the other hand, tend to describe those same events in a way that depicts them as unbounded – i.e., zooming in on the action without alluding to the end of the action. Crucially, whether a person conceptualizes an event as being bounded or unbounded is demonstrated not just in their use of verbal morphology, but also by whether the person mentions the endpoint of the event. The endpoint of a bounded motion event is usually a location – the final destination (e.g., "walk to the house") – whereas the endpoint of other types of bounded, resultative events is the product of the action (e.g., "bake a cake"). Von Stutterheim (2003) found that L1 German speakers have a significantly stronger predilection for referring to endpoints than L1 English speakers do, and this pattern also carries over into their use of an L2. Other studies conducted by von Stutterheim and colleagues have found similar results in a wide variety of L1s and L2s (see, e.g., Schmiedtová, von Stutterheim & Carroll 2011).

At first glance, crosslinguistic differences among speakers of different L1s and corresponding patterns of CLI in L2 learners' reference to endpoints may seem like a semantic or possibly even a discursive or pragmatic phenomenon that has little bearing on the types of cognitive processes described in the preceding sections of this paper. However, there is some evidence that suggests that CLI involving patterns of conceptualization is closely tied to CLI involving attentional control, processing efficiency, and memory. Some of the most interesting evidence comes from Flecken (2010), whose data include not just real-time event descriptions, but also eye-tracking data indicating what the participants spent the most time looking at while describing the events, as well as memory performance data that show which elements of the events the participants were best able to remember. Participants in the study included native speakers of Standard Arabic, Czech, Dutch, English, German, Russian, and Spanish. Even though the participants were tested only in their native languages, which means that the study does not provide direct evidence of CLI, the crucial point is that the researcher demonstrated that speakers of languages that are more likely to refer to event endpoints also direct their attention more to (i.e., spend more time looking at) endpoints, and are also better able to remember those endpoints later. Corroborating evidence involving CLI in the attentional patterns of L2 learners can be found in Schmiedtová et al. (2011).

The results of these studies, again, show that differing patterns of conceptualization can and do transfer into a person's use of another language, and that these differing patterns of language use are directly linked to patterns of attention and recall. These findings of course beg the question of what it is within a person's cognitive system that underlies these patterns of crosslinguistic difference and CLI in people's attention and recall. Von Stutterheim and Nüse (2003: 870) claim that "the structural feature [+/−aspect] induces a specific pattern of event construal". However, this claim is questionable in light of Flecken's (2010) finding that Czech speakers, whose language has grammaticalized imperfective and progressive aspect, perform very similarly to German speakers, whose language does not have a grammaticalized progressive or imperfective aspect. Evidently, long-term, intensive language contact between Czech and German has resulted in a good deal of borrowing of German discourse patterns into Czech. This has not caused Czech to lose its grammaticalized progressive or imperfective aspect, but it has resulted in new discourse conventions in Czech that mirror German speakers' predilection for depicting events as bounded. In other words, the existence of progressive and imperfective aspect in Czech does not seem to determine how Czech speakers conceptualize events nearly to the same degree that their discourse conventions do.

According to Bylund and Jarvis (2011), the more frequently a person is exposed in discourse to certain ways of construing a particular type of event, the more likely she is of construing it that way in her own language use. The cognitive explanation that these researchers advocate draws from Langacker's (2008) theory of cognitive grammar, which holds that grammatical constructions and conceptual representations are bound together through elaborate mental schemas. The theory also holds that the frequent activation of any given schema leads to its progressive entrenchment in the person's mind. This is an outcome that is very similar to what Ericsson and Kintsch (1995) refer to as retrieval structures, or well-worn, easily activated neural pathways that serve as the basis for what Ericsson and Kintsch call long-term working memory.

The findings reported in the preceding section suggest that when a person's L1 and L2 rely on the same (or very similar) form-meaning schemas, and when the L1 has led to the entrenchment of those schemas, the recognition, processing, comprehension, retention, and recall of the relevant L2 input is greatly enhanced. These findings relate mainly to the receptive processing of linguistic form, but one can ask corresponding questions dealing with meaning. In the receptive domain, one can ask whether conceptual schemas entrenched through extensive use of one language will have an effect on how sentences are comprehended in another language (cf. Fender 2003), and in the productive domain, one can ask whether conceptual schemas entrenched through extensive exposure to one language will affect which meanings a person expresses while describing events in another language (e.g., Pavlenko 2003). The study by Bylund and Jarvis (2011) addresses both questions.

The participants in the study by Bylund and Jarvis included 40 native speakers of Spanish (all from South America, mainly from Chile) who had emigrated to Sweden at various ages, had lived in Sweden for at least 12 years, and were all deemed to be native-like speakers of Swedish by at least three judges on a panel of 10 native Swedish-speaking listeners. Although the participants were all native Spanish speakers who had maintained high levels of proficiency in their L1, the researchers hypothesized that their intensive and extensive use of Swedish may have resulted in the entrenchment of Swedish-like schemas relating to the conceptualization of motion events as bounded versus unbounded. Spanish has progressive and imperfective aspect, and Spanish speakers have been found to tend toward real-time depictions of events as unbounded with no mention of an endpoint (e.g., Bylund 2008; Flecken 2010); Swedish, on the other hand, has no grammaticalized progressive/imperfective aspect, and Swedish speakers tend toward bounded depictions of events, and specifically tend to mention an endpoint (Bylund 2008). The participants were given two tasks: an L1 Spanish grammaticality judgment test, and an L1 Spanish film-description task where participants described brief goal-oriented motion events while they were watching them on a computer screen. In some of the events, the trajectory of the action was shown all the way to the endpoint (e.g., a dog going into a greenhouse), whereas in others the endpoint could only be inferred or imagined (e.g., a person driving a jeep in the middle of a desert).

The results of the event-description task showed that the Spanish-Swedish bilinguals referred to event endpoints significantly more frequently than a comparable group of monolingual L1 Spanish controls. The results of the grammaticality judgment task, in turn, showed that the participants received high scores on the test overall, and that there was no significant correlation between their overall score on this test and the frequency with which they referred to event endpoints in the event-description task. However, a different pattern emerged when the researchers looked more specifically at the participants' scores on just those items of the grammaticality judgment test that dealt with aspectual distinctions. The less sensitive the participants were to errors involving ungrammatical uses of imperfective aspect (e.g., *cuando su padre era joven, tenía un accidente muy grave = "when his father was young, he was having a serious accident"), the more likely they were to refer to endpoints in the event-description task. The researchers interpreted these results as reflecting the effects of L2 Swedish-based schema entrenchment on the participants' use of L1 Spanish. The schema in question is one that represents events as perfective and bounded – a schema that is frequently activated in Swedish discourse. Interestingly, according to the researchers, schema entrenchment leads to conceptualization-related effects in both reception and production: Regarding reception, it appears to have caused the participants to overlook imperfective morphology in the sentences presented to them and to resort instead to a default, bounded-event interpretation regardless of the morphology. In production, it likewise appears to have increased their likelihood for describing events as bounded, and correspondingly for referring to the endpoints of those events. These results and interpretations are by no means definitive, but they do suggest some intriguing connections between linguistic and conceptual processing and offer a possible explanation for the mechanisms underlying CLI in these areas of cognition.

5. Conclusion

Although traditional, linguistic analyses of learners' patterns of language use will always play a central role in the investigation of CLI, recent advances in the modeling and measurement of attention, executive control, WM, LTM, schemas and retrieval structures add clarity to the field's understanding of the sources and causes of CLI, as well as of the mechanisms and processes through which it occurs. The relevance of such models and measures to the investigation of CLI has only recently been recognized, but it seems likely that the exploration of the cognitive foundations of CLI will become increasingly refined and will increasingly define this area of investigation.

References

Alloway, T., Gathercole, S., Willis, C., & Adams, A. (2004). A structural analysis of working memory and related cognitive skills in young children. *Journal of Experimental Child Psychology, 87*, 85–106.

Altenberg, E., & Cairns, H. (1983). The effects of phonotactic constraints on lexical processing in bilingual and monolingual subjects. *Journal of Verbal Learning and Verbal Behavior, 22*, 174–188.

Andersson, U. (2010). The contribution of working memory capacity to foreign language comprehension in children. *Memory, 18*(4), 458–72.

Atkins, P.W.B., & Baddeley, A. (1998). Working memory and distributed vocabulary learning. *Applied Psycholinguistics, 19*, 537–552.

Baddeley, A. (2003). Working memory and language: An overview. *Journal of Communication Disorders, 36*, 189–208.

Baddeley, A., Gathercole, S., & Papagano, C. (1998). The phonological loop as a language learning device. *Psychological Review, 105*, 158–173.

Baddeley, A., & Hitch, G. (1994). Developments in the concept of working memory. *Neuropsychology, 8,* 485–493.

Bialystok, E. (2005). Consequences of bilingualism for cognitive development. In J.F. Kroll & A.M.B. de Groot (Eds.), *Handbook of bilingualism: Psycholinguistic* approaches (pp. 417–432). Oxford: OUP.

Blair, D., & Harris, R. (1981). A test of interlingual interaction in comprehension by bilinguals. *Journal of Psycholinguistic Research, 10,* 457–467.

Brooks, P., Kempe, V., & Sionov, A. (2006). The role of learner and input variables in learning inflectional morphology. *Applied Psycholinguistics, 27,* 185–209.

Bylund, E. (2008). Procesos de conceptualización de eventos en español y en sueco: Diferencias translingüísticas [Event conceptualization processes in Spanish and Swedish: Crosslinguistic differences]. *Revue Romane, 43,* 1–24.

Bylund, E., & Jarvis, S. (2011). L2 effects on L1 event conceptualization. *Bilingualism: Language and Cognition, 14*(1), 47–59.

Cenoz, J. (2001). The effect of linguistic distance, L2 status and age on cross-linguistic influence in third language acquisition. In J. Cenoz, B. Hufeisen, & U. Jessner (Eds.),*Cross-linguistic influence in third language acquisition: Psycholinguistic perspectives* (pp. 8–20). Clevedon: Multilingual Matters.

Corder, S.P. (1967). The significance of learner's errors. *IRAL – International Review of Applied Linguistics in Language Teaching, 5*(4), 161–170.

Costa, A., Hernández, M., & Sebastián-Gallés, N. (2008). Bilingualism aids conflict resolution: Evidence from the ANT task. *Cognition, 106*(1), 59–86.

Costa, A., Hernández, M., Costa-Faidella, J., & Sebastián-Gallés, N. (2009). On the bilingual advantage in conflict processing: Now you see it, now you don't. *Cognition, 113*(2), 135–49.

Cowan, N. (1999). An embedded-processes model of working memory. In A. Miyake & P. Shah (Eds.), *Models of working memory: Mechanisms of active maintenance and executive control* (pp. 62–101). Cambridge: CUP.

Cowan, N. (2005). *Working memory capacity: Essays in cognitive psychology.* New York, NY: Psychology Press.

Dewaele, J.-M. (1998). Lexical inventions: French interlanguage as L2 versus L3. *Applied Linguistics, 19,* 471–490.

Dufva, M., & Voeten, M.J. (1999). Native language literacy and phonological memory as prerequisites for learning English as a foreign language. *Applied Psycholinguistics, 20,* 392–348.

Emmorey, K., Luk, G., Pyers, J.E., & Bialystok, E. (2008). The source of enhanced cognitive control in bilinguals: Evidence from bimodal bilinguals. *Psychological Science, 19*(12), 1201–1206.

Ericsson, K.A., & Kintsch, W. (1995). Long-term working memory. *Psychological Review, 102*(2), 211–245.

Fender, M. (2003). English word recognition and word integration skills of native Arabic- and Japanese-speaking learners of English as a second language. *Applied Psycholinguistics, 24*(02), 289–315.

Flecken, M. (2010). *Event conceptualization in language production of early bilinguals.* Nijmegen: Netherlands Graduate School of Linguistics, Radboud University.

French, L.M. (2004). Phonological working memory and L2 acquisition: A developmental study of Quebec Francophone children learning English. *Dissertation Abstracts International, 65*(2-A), 487.

Gathercole, S., Pickering, S., Ambridge, B., & Wearing, H. (2004). The structure of working memory from 4 to 15 years of age. *Developmental Psychology, 40*(2), 177–190.

Goo, J. (2010). Working memory and reactivity. *Language Learning, 60*(4), 712–752.

Green, D. (1998). Mental control of the bilingual lexico-semantic system. *Bilingualism: Language and Cognition, 1,* 67–81.

Hummel, K. (2009). Aptitude, phonological memory, and second language proficiency in non-novice adult learners. *Applied Psycholinguistics, 30,* 225–249.

Jarrold, C., Baddeley, A., Hewes, A., Leeke, T., & Phillips, C. (2004). What links verbal short-term memory performance and vocabulary levels? Evidence of changing relationships among individuals with learning disability. *Journal of Memory and Language, 50,* 134–148.

Jarvis, S. (2000). Methodological rigor in the study of transfer: Identifying L1 influence in the interlanguage lexicon. *Language Learning, 50*(2), 245–309.

Jarvis, S. (2011). Conceptual transfer: Crosslinguistic effects in categorization and construal. *Bilingualism: Language and Cognition, 14*(1), 1–8.

Jarvis, S., O'Malley, M., Mitchell, A.E., Correnti, C., Hilterbran, A., Jing, L., & Cao, L. (2012). From input to intake: Effects of and interactions between prior knowledge and working memory capacity. Paper presented at the 65th annual Kentucky Foreign Language Conference. Lexington, KY, April 19–21, 2012.

Jarvis, S., & Pavlenko, A. (2008). *Crosslinguistic influence in language and cognition.* London: Routledge.

Jeong, H., Sugiura, M., Sassa, Y., Haji, T., Usui, N., Taira, M., Horie, K., Sato, S., & Kawashima, R. (2007a). Effect of syntactic similarity on cortical activation during second language processing: A comparison of English and Japanese among native Korean trilinguals. *Human Brain Mapping, 28*(3), 194–204.

Jeong, H., Sugiura, M., Sassa, Y., Yokoyama, S., Horie, K., Sato, S., Taira, M., & Kawashima, R. (2007b). Cross-linguistic influence on brain activation during second language processing: An fMRI study. *Bilingualism: Language and Cognition, 10*(2), 175–187.

Jessner, U. (2006). *Linguistic awareness in multilinguals: English as a third language.* Edinburgh: EUP.

Jiang, N., Novokshanova, E., Masuda, K., & Wang, X. (2011). Morphological congruency and the acquisition of L2 morphemes. *Language Learning, 61*(3), 940–967.

Kane, M., & Engle, R. (2003). Working memory capacity and the control of attention: The contributions of goal neglect, response competition, and task set to Stroop interference. *Journal of Experimental Psychology: General, 132*(1), 47–70.

Krivitzky, L.S., Roebuck-Spencer, T.M., Roth, R.M., Blackstone, K., Johnson, C.P., & Gioia, G. (2011). Functional magnetic resonance imaging of working memory and response inhibition in children with mild traumatic brain injury. *Journal of the International Neuropsychological Society: JINS, 17*(6), 1143–1152.

Lado, R. (1957). *Linguistics across cultures.* Ann Arbor, MI: University of Michigan Press.

Langacker, R.W. (2008). *Cognitive Grammar.* Oxford: OUP.

Levelt, W. (1989). *Speaking: From intention to articulation.* Cambridge, MA: The MIT Press.

Magiste, E. (1980). Arithmetical calculations in monolinguals and bilinguals. *Psychological Research, 42,* 363–373.

Marian, V., & Spivey, M. (2003). Competing activation in bilingual language processing: Within- and between-language competition. *Bilingualism: Language and Cognition, 6*(2), 97–115.

Nas, G. (1983). Visual word recognition in bilinguals: Evidence for a cooperation between visual and sound-based codes during access to a common lexical store. *Journal of Verbal Learning and Verbal Behavior, 22,* 526–534.

Odlin, T. (1989). *Language transfer: Cross-linguistic influence in language learning.* Cambridge: CUP.

Odlin, T. (2009). *Language transfer and the link between comprehension and production.* Keynote paper presented at the International Symposium on Language Transfer in Second Language Acquisition. Shanghai, China, March 21, 2009.

Papagano, C., & Vallar, G. (1995). Verbal short-term memory and vocabulary learning in polyglots. *Quarterly Journal of Experimental Psychology, 48,* 98–107.

Pavlenko, A. (2003). Eyewitness memory in late bilinguals: Evidence for discursive relativity. *International Journal of Bilingualism, 7,* 257–281.

Pavlenko, A. (Ed.). (2011). *Thinking and speaking in two languages.* Bristol: Multilingual Matters.

Peal, E., & Lambert, W.E. (1962). The relation of bilingualism to intelligence. *Psychological Monographs, 76.*

Posner, M.I., & Petersen, S.E. (1990). The attention systems of the human brain. *Annual Review of Neuroscience, 13,* 25–42.

Poulisse, N. (1999). *Slips of the Tongue: Speech errors in first and second language production.* Amsterdam: Benjamins.

Rai, M.K., Loschky, L.C., Harris, R.J., Peck, N.R., & Cook, L.G. (2011). Effects of stress and working memory capacity on foreign language readers' inferential processing during comprehension. *Language Learning, 61*(1), 187–218.

Ransdell, S.E., & Fischler, I. (1987). Memory in a monolingual mode: When are bilinguals at a disadvantage? *Journal of Memory and Language, 26,* 392–405.

Ricciardelli, L.A. (1992). Bilingualism and cognitive development in relation to threshold theory. *Journal of Psycholinguistic Research, 21*(4), 301–316.

Ringbom, H. (1987). *The role of the first language in foreign language learning.* Clevedon: Multilingual Matters.

Ringbom, H. (2007). *Cross-linguistic similarity in foreign language learning.* Bristol: Multilingual Matters.

Rubia, K., Smith, A.B., Taylor, E., & Brammer, M. (2007). Linear age-correlated functional development of right inferior fronto-striato-cerebellar networks during response inhibition and anterior cingulate during error-related processes. *Human Brain Mapping, 28*(11), 1163–1177.

Saer, D.J. (1923). The effects of bilingualism on intelligence. *British Journal of Psychology, 14,* 25–38.

Schmiedtová, B., von Stutterheim, C., & Carroll, M. (2011). Language-specific patterns in event construal of advanced second language speakers. In A. Pavlenko (Ed.), *Thinking and speaking in two languages* (pp. 66–107). Bristol: Multilingual Matters.

Service, E., & Kohonen, V. (1995). Is the relation between phonological memory and foreign language learning accounted for by vocabulary acquisition? *Applied Psycholinguistics, 16,* 155–172.

Slobin, D. (1993). Adult language acquisition: A view from child language study. In C. Perdue (Ed.), *Adult language acquisition: Cross-linguistic perspectives* (pp. 239–252). Cambridge: CUP.

Slobin, D. (1996). From "thought and language" to "thinking for speaking." In J. Gumperz & S. Levinson (Eds.),*Rethinking linguistic relativity* (pp. 70–96). Cambridge: CUP.

Soares, C. & Grosjean, F. (1984). Bilinguals in a monolingual and a bilingual speech mode: The effect on lexical access. *Memory and Cognition, 12*(4), 380–386.

Tokowicz, N., & MacWhinney, B. (2005). Implicit and explicit measures of sensitivity to violations in second language grammar: An event-related potential investigation. *Studies in Second Language Acquisition, 27*: 173–204.

Trofimovich, P., Gatbonton, E., & Segalowitz, N. (2007). A dynamic look at L2 phonological learning: Seeking processing explanations for implicational phenomena. *Studies in Second Language Acquisition, 29*, 407–448.

Trude, A.M., & Tokowicz, N. (2011). Negative transfer from Spanish and English to Portuguese pronunciation: The roles of inhibition and working wemory. *Language Learning, 61*(1).

von Stutterheim, C. (2003). Linguistic structure and information organization: The case of very advanced learners. EUROSLA Yearbook, 3, 183–206.

von Stutterheim, C., & Nüse, R. (2003). Processes of conceptalization in language production: Language-specific perspectives and event construal. *Linguistics, 41*, 851–881.

Weinreich, U. (1953). *Languages in contact*. The Hague: Mouton.

Williams, S., & Hammarberg, B. 1998. Language switches in L3 production: Implications for a polyglot speaking model. *Applied Linguistics, 19*, 295–333.

PART III

Concluding remarks

CHAPTER 14

Ideas for the practice of instructed SLA and their rationale

A summary and commentary

James F. Lee
University of New South Wales

In developing this summary and commentary, I have chosen to highlight the connections the authors make to the practice of instructed second language acquisition and their rationale. To that end, I have classified the pedagogical applications, implications and extrapolations offered by the authors into three categories. First, we find suggestions for particular types of instructional materials, activity sequences, and/or approaches to instruction. Second, we find recommendations for curricular changes and language programs in terms of the timing, sequencing and/or the content of instruction. Lastly, we find calls for teacher education and/or awareness of the processes and products of second language acquisition. I will summarize and comment on each chapter as it relates to these categories.

The works presented in this volume share a philosophy that Lee & VanPatten (2003: 23; emphasis original) expressed as follows. We

> cannot force or cause the creation of the learner's implicit system. We may not be able to force or cause the acquisition of speech-making procedures that are essential to skill development. ...we can only provide opportunities in the classroom for acquisition to happen, but that these opportunities must be informed by what we know about acquisition. ...we [must] explore ways in which instruction can work *in unison with* acquisitional processes rather than *against* them.

By understanding learning, we can approach teaching. The works collected in this volume, *Innovative research and practices in second language acquisition and bilingualism*, have at heart the position that by first understanding learning, we can then approach teaching. Teaching minimally involves instructional materials, curriculum, teacher education and teacher awareness.

I have classified the pedagogical applications, implications and extrapolations offered by the authors into three categories. First, we find suggestions for particular types of instructional materials, activity sequences, and/or approaches to instruction. Second, we find recommendations for curricular changesand language programs in terms of the timing, sequencing and/or the content of instruction. Lastly, we find calls for teacher education and/or awareness of the processes and products of second language acquisition. I will summarize and comment on each chapter as it relates to these categories.

1.   Instructional materials

Wong, in *Input and output in SLA: From theory and research to the classroom* (Chapter 2), addresses the gap between research and classroom practice by offering language instructors examples and explanations of pedagogical activities that are grounded in SLA research. She, and others in this volume, are concerned that little SLA research on the roles of input and output are reflected in pedagogical materials and that many SLA researchers are not as concerned about the pedagogical relevance of their work as might have been the case some 40 years ago. She agrees with VanPatten's position on mental representation and skill and so provides examples of input-rich activities that promote the development of mental representation and output-based activities to promote fluency and accuracy (i.e., language skill).

VanPatten stated (in Chapter 1) that supplying learners information about the language will not affect mental representation, but, because input is a crucial factor in the development of mental representation, manipulating input in order to push acquisition is. Processing instruction, for example, provides structured input (a type of manipulated input) so that the processors are forced to process data in ways they might not under naturalistic conditions. The point of manipulating input is to alter the data used by the processors and by Universal Grammar (UG) in the development of a mental representation. Wong provides different examples of activities that have learners working with input. In the structured input activity learners hear sentence fragments and must complete them based on having processed correctly the mood of the verb. She provides the examples of a scrambled dialogue for which learners must process discourse to unscramble conversation and a film clip-based dictogloss activity in which learners reconstruct the text. Wong explains the role of input in SLA (i.e., mental representation) as the rationale why a teacher would use such input-based activities.

Wong views output practices as a way to get more input. Learners' speech, misunderstandings and communicative breakdowns encourage an interlocutor, particularly one of higher proficiency, to generate more speech in which learners can attend to forms in the input and their meanings. She therefore ties output practice to the expression of meaning in order to promote fluency and accuracy needed in skill development. She provides three sample output activities. The first of these is a structured output activity that provides learners meaningful grammar practice. The second activity combines input and output practice as learners re-write a scene. The original scene is, of course, the principle source of input. The final activity is a film making project for which learners write a script and film a 2–3 minute scene. Wong explains the role of output in SLA (i.e., skill development) as the rationale why a teacher would use such activities.

Long & Rothman, in *Generative approaches and the competing systems hypothesis: Formal acquisition to pedagogical application* (Chapter 4), account for why very advanced instructed learners perform differently than equivalent naturalistic L2 learners of the same proficiency. They appeal to Rothman's Competing Systems Hypothesis (CSH) and the research that supports it to demonstrate that instructed learners uniquely possess an explicit pedagogically-designed metalinguistic knowledge that competes with a naturally acquired L2 grammar (i.e., mental representation). Rothman's claim is that oversimplification of the grammar in classroom instruction leads to the formation of a system of learned rules that are imprecise in their description of how the L2 grammar actually operates. As VanPatten stated in his chapter, textbook-type rules are a short hand way to describe a particular consequence of more abstract principles of the grammar. Rothman hypothesizes that the pedagogical linguistic system competes for primacy with the naturally acquired one especially in contexts that favor the application of metalinguistic knowledge. Therefore, the CSH predicts differences in performance between instructed and naturalistic learners traceable to pedagogical oversimplifications.

Long & Rothman then present the findings from Rothman's previous research on Spanish aspect. Aspect refers to the speaker's perspective on the boundedness in time of an event: bounded [+perfective] and unbounded [−perfective]. This distinction in Spanish is encoded morphologically in two distinct paradigms: preterite [+perfective] and imperfect [−perfective]. The [+perfective] aspect is not realized morphologically in English. The simple past in English can convey either an episodic [+perfective] or iterative [−perfective] reading. In Spanish, only the imperfect can convey two readings: progressive or iterative. The preterite can only convey an episodic reading.

Preterite and imperfect and the preterite/imperfect contrast appear early in Spanish textbooks, usually being covered in the first semester of language instruction. Textbook descriptions of preterite/imperfect generally present the two as discrete semantic entities. They are often associated with particular adverbials (e.g., *siempre* 'always' for imperfect) and via English translation equivalents (e.g., *saber* means 'to know' in the imperfect and 'to find out' in the preterite) rather than as the linguistic consequence of aspectual distinctions. The results of the study they present are based on the performance of three groups: very advanced instructed learners (university-level instructors of Spanish), very advanced naturalistic learners, and native speakers. They performed two tasks. The first was a multiple (binary) choice cloze paragraph based on a fairy tale for which the appropriate responses coincided with typical pedagogical explanations of preterite/imperfect. The second was a fill-in-the-blank sentence-level production task. Some of the appropriate (grammatically correct) responses contradicted typical pedagogical explanations.

The results indicated that the three groups performed equally well on the cloze paragraph. The instructed learners performed quite differently than the naturalistic learners and native speakers on the production task. The instructed learners performed differently from the native speakers 25% of the time; the range of deviation was from 0% to 58%. The naturalistic learners performed differently from the native speakers only 2.27% of the time; the range of deviation was from 0% to 8%. Long and Rothman point out that 25% of the instructed learners performed into the native speaker range demonstrating that some instructed learners are not held back by their pedagogical metalinguistic system. The instructed learners performed differently from naturalistic learners and native speakers in 3 contexts that can be attributed to imprecise pedagogical rules: commonly used stative verbs; preterite/imperfect contrasts that are taught via English equivalents; and, after adverbials that are taught as triggers for one or the other of the past tenses.

On the basis of these findings Long & Rothman recommend that the imprecision of explicit grammatical rules in textbooks be done away with. They do not suggest that grammar rules should not be taught explicitly, only accurately. They believe that teacher education is essential in two areas. First, they recommend that teachers need to be educated about language as a cognitive system and about second language acquisition. Second, they would provide teachers with precise rules of the target grammar via a descriptive grammar. In order to do so, teachers would need to be educated in the basics of linguistic theory. The descriptive grammar they envision would describe what can be observed in the speech of native speakers and what native speakers intuit (judge) as possible and impossible sentences in their language. They would minimize references and comparisons to the L1 as these will always fall short. They place the burden on linguists to create accessible descriptive grammars.

Barcroft, in *Input-based incremental vocabulary instruction for the L2 classroom* (Chapter 6), presents a model he developed, Types of Processing Resource Allocation (TOPRA), to account for different types of processing producing different types of learning outcomes. The term 'processing resource allocation' refers to how learners distribute their limited cognitive resources toward one or more of three key components of word learning: word form, word meaning, and/or form-meaning mapping. Different tasks and methods of presenting new words can cause learners to differentially allocate processing resources toward one or more of these key components of word learning. His review of the literature on lexical input processing yielded five generalizations that form the basis of his proposed approach to vocabulary instruction: (1) repeated exposure benefits new word learning; (2) presentation factors such as multiple talkers, varied speaking styles, or speaking rates enhance word learnability; (3) semantically elaborate tasks exhaust processing resources in initial stages of word learning and should be avoided; (4) producing output without access to meaning (e.g., copying words) during initial learning, negatively affects learning; and, (5) after initial input processing, opportunities to retrieve a word (i.e., produce output) positively affects learning.

From these findings, Barcoft has developed over the years the ten principles of input-based incremental (IBI) vocabulary instruction, which he then presents in this chapter. The principles are accompanied by a seven item checklist for designing IBI vocabulary lessons. Finally, Barcroft presents and comments on a fully elaborated sample IBI lesson. The lesson begins with how to select target words and then, in steps, Barcroft describes a series of activities to conduct across two days of instruction. His commentary demonstrates how the lesson embodies the ten principles of IBI. The input-based aspects of the lesson are the use of a picture file and providing definitions. The incremental aspect of the lesson is how the later activities are more demanding: charades, writing original topical sentences, a topical discussion and writing an original story.

Presson, Davy & MacWhinney, in *Experimentalized CALL for adult second language learners* (Chapter 7), describe various empirical studies and projects that use experimentalized CALL (eCALL). Their perspective is that eCALL can inform as well as be informed by SLA research. First, eCALL training programs can be created based on pedagogical principles based in SLA research. In turn, the eCALL programs can refine and test those principles and then improve the eCALL methods. Presson et al. present research findings that explore the role of four instructional factors: immediate feedback, modeling of learner knowledge, repeated practice and explicit instruction.

Presson et al. discuss the positive effect of targeting a specific aspect of performance in immediate feedback, thus yielding immediate targeted feedback for learners. The feedback to learners is beyond the binary correct/incorrect response. The eCALL program they refer to is the Pinyin Tutor for which learners produce pinyin (i.e., romanized spelling for transliterating Chinese) corresponding to a speech signal of single and multi-syllabic words. A simple feedback response of 'incorrect' would not alert the learner to the source of the error for there are many error types: the letter sequence, the initial or final sound of either syllable, the number of syllables, the tone of one or both syllables. In the Pinyin Tutor the feedback is targeted to indicate the type of error made and the feedback is provided immediately after the student types an answer.

Modeling learner knowledge and responding with individualized feedback is possible in eCALL contexts because information can be gathered and integrated for individuals. The example provided is an eCALL tutor for the English article system. The developer created a list of cues for selecting an article and differentiated rule-based and feature-based cues. She found that rule-based cues were easily acquired without explicit instruction but that feature-based rules required explicit instruction.

The role of explicit information is much discussed and researched in SLA. Presson et al. describe an eCALL tutor for grammatical gender in French that varied the level of explicitness in feedback. Learners selected the gender of nouns and received immediate corrective feedback under three conditions: no additional information, explicit orthographic cue statements, or highlighting the relevant ending. Findings indicate that explicit feedback led to better learning and retention with and without time pressure constraints.

Presson et al. also take up the issue of repeated practice and highlight the results of several studies involving eCALL contexts. eCALL tutors can be used to determine the most effective practice schedule for learning vocabulary, to practice and improve pronunciation, to fluency and phonological accuracy on sentences and to increase fluency and accuracy with a discourse-level speaking task, not just during the practice sessions but on tests where the speaking activities were unrelated to the practice sessions and on novel topics.

Presson et al. are aware of the limitations of eCALL. They first point to speech recognition technology that has improved dramatically in the last ten years but still is not reliable enough to be used alone as a feedback mechanism. Users must anticipate a certain rate of failure with speech recognition. Second, they acknowledge that the social, interpersonal aspect of classroom language acquisition and NS-NNS interactions would be difficult to replicate on a computer. Third, they acknowledge the initial cost of programming and equipment and then the cost of implementation of computerized training facilities as a limitation to the use of eCALL. Yet, the findings of the many studies they review present a very promising picture.

Cuza, Pérez-Tattum, Barajas, Miller and Sadowski, in *The development of tense and aspect morphology in child and adult heritage speakers* (Chapter 9), examine speakers' use of preterite, imperfect and present tenses in oral narratives. Their participants are simultaneous Spanish-English bilingual children divided into two age groups, adult US-born Spanish heritage speakers, Spanish monolingual children divided into two age groups, and adult Spanish monolingual speakers. The oral narratives were elicited using wordless picture books. They analyzed the proportion of use of preterite, imperfect and present tenses among the different groups of speakers. They found significant differences in proportionate use of the three tenses for child monolinguals, child bilinguals, adult bilinguals but not adult monolinguals, and for younger and older bilingual children.

Use of the preterite is significantly higher among child bilinguals than child monolinguals, bilingual adults than monolingual adults, older bilingual children than younger bilingual children, older bilingual children than adult bilinguals and younger monolingual children than older monolingual children. Use of the imperfect is significantly higher among child monolinguals than child bilinguals, adult monolinguals than adult bilinguals, older bilingual children than younger bilingual children, older bilingual children than adult bilinguals, and, although they indicate a significant difference between older and younger monolingual children's use of the imperfect, they do not indicate the direction. Use of the present tense is significantly higher for child monolinguals than child bilinguals, adults bilinguals than adult monolinguals, adult bilinguals than older bilingual children, older monolingual children than younger monolingual children. There were no significant differences in present tense use between younger and older bilingual children.

Cuza et al. argue that these results indicate that the adult heritage speaker possesses a simplified temporal system stemming from both L1 attrition and incomplete development. Monolingual development shows that children start out using more preterite and present tense forms but that adults use preterite, imperfect and the present tense in a more balanced way. The bilingual route of development is different. As younger bilingual children become older, they increase their production of preterite and imperfect as they decrease their production of the present tense. The bilingual adults, in contrast, produce fewer preterites and imperfects and more present tense. Cuza et al. argue that the acquisition of preterite tense amongst bilinguals represents L1 attrition rather than incomplete acquisition. They argue that the pattern of performance for the imperfect represents incomplete acquisition rather than attrition. The adult bilingual's use of the present tense in imperfective contexts is seen as an avoidance strategy for the imperfect tense.

Cuza et al. recommend that pedagogical interventions come early for heritage speakers with an emphasis on imperfect form-meaning connections so that adult learners do not replace it with the present tense. The traditional approach to teaching preterite/imperfect contrasts does not reflect the divergent acquisition paths for preterite and imperfect. The challenge is not the preterite, but the imperfect. Moreover, they recommend the use of interactive reading practices so that heritage speakers are exposed to appropriate input, especially with the imperfect because the language in their environment is unlikely to have many exemplars of the imperfect. They also see benefits to the use of structured input activities (see Wong, this volume for an example) for heritage speakers.

2.   Curricular changes and language programs

Bruhn de Garavito, in *Why theory and research are important for the practice of teaching: The case of Spanish relative clauses* (Chapter 5), asserts that research findings lead us to an understanding of the magnitude of the task learners face and an appreciation of learners' developmental readiness to acquire a structure. She addresses a particular structure in Spanish, although common to Romance languages: mood selection in relative clauses. This structure is quite complex. On the one hand, mood selection is the result of lexical selection in cases where there is no mood alternation possible. That is, the selection of the incorrect mood results in ungrammaticality. On the other hand, mood selection is the result of polarity in cases where the presence of negation or interrogation in a sentence with a verb that normally selects indicative. Both moods alternate with no ungrammaticality; it is a question of interpretation. A [+specific] antecedent yields the indicative whereas a [–specific] antecedent the subjunctive. As Bruhn de Garavito indicates, there are four tasks the learner must face to acquire the subjunctive: the morphology of subjunctive and indicative; the syntax of relative clause formation; the semantics of subjunctive/indicative contrasts; and, the pragmatics to understand the subtle differences conveyed.

The basis for Bruhn de Garavito's pedagogical recommendations are the results of research she and her colleagues have undertaken. Native speakers, an intermediate and an advanced group of learners of Spanish were given a truth value judgment task in which they first read a short scenario in English, their L1, that established the specificity of the head noun phrase. They were then given two minimal pair sentences (subjunctive/indicative) and asked to rate the appropriateness of each on a scale from +2 to –2. The results showed that the learners deal more easily with [+specific] contexts in which the appropriate use of the indicative is strong. Their rejection of the subjunctive in these contexts reflects native speaker performance. The [–specific] contexts are more challenging. Learners generally prefer the subjunctive but they reject the indicative less frequently than do native speakers and respond to different contexts differently. To appreciate the learners' performance we must keep in mind that the intermediate learners had studied Spanish for two years and were, at the time of the study, studying in Mexico. The advanced learners had ten years experience with Spanish; other researchers might refer to them as very advanced learners.

Bruhn de Garavito then examined two introductory and one advanced text-book. The tendency is to introduce the subjunctive with complement clauses first and then with relative clauses. She underscores that the treatment of embedded clauses, indicative or subjunctive, only begins with the introduction of the subjunctive. The textbooks include an explicit explanation, some provide contextualized dialogue or sentences, but all provide exercises (fill in the blanks, sentence completion, semi-controlled production). Then they move to a different grammar point. Bruhn de Garavito expresses her concern with this approach by stating that mood selection is reduced to a grammar point that is placed, like a brick in a wall that is under construction in the learners' minds, to then move on to some other brick (grammar point) to place.

To address the issue of learnability or developmental readiness, Bruhn de Garavito suggests that learners first be given practice with embedded clauses using known tenses before being introduced to the subjunctive. Her second suggestion is to delay the introduction of the subjunctive until the intermediate level and to introduce it in limited contexts. Finally, Bruhn de Garavito recommends that mood selection in relative clauses should be taught within a context, providing learners a great deal of contextualized input and perhaps the opportunity to produce contextualized output. The input is essential to interpret the concept of ±specific.

Perpiñán, in *Accounting for variability in L2 data: Type of knowledge, task effects and linguistic structure* (Chapter 8), compares the performance of native speakers of Spanish to that of two groups of L2 learners of equivalent intermediate level proficiency in Spanish: native speakers of English and native speakers of Arabic. The participants performed two tasks: a two-picture description task that elicited an oral response and a sentence combining task that elicited a written response. The tasks elicited two types of relative clauses, direct object and oblique (object of a preposition). The results of the statistical analyses indicate that the native speakers and L1 Arabic learners performed significantly better on the written task than on the oral one whereas there was no task effect for the L1 English learners. Both groups of L2 learners performed significantly better on direct object relative clauses than on oblique relative clauses whereas the native speakers performed equally well with both types. The effect of linguistic structured does not interact with the effect for modality. Finally, the performance of the L1 English group in both modalities is highly correlated with proficiency whereas the correlation is weak for the L1 Arabic speakers. Performance on oblique relative clauses is moderately correlated with proficiency in both modalities for both groups of L2 learners.

Why are the native speakers, half of whom are monolingual, showing variability in their oral and written performance? Perpiñán's argument is that their variability cannot be due to a mismatch between competence and performance, especially since the L1 English learners showed no variability across modality. Acknowledging that oral tasks come with processing costs, she looks to type of knowledge used in the tasks as an explanation. Relative clauses are late acquired syntactic structures. Children only start producing them at around age 3 and do so in keeping with the Noun Phrase Accessibility Hierarchy. Oblique relative clauses are low in the hierarchy and native speakers would, therefore, learn them in a school setting. That is, native speakers would learn oblique relative clauses as an explicit rule, so to use an oblique relative clause accurately, the native speaker would need to be form focused as in the written sentence completion task. Perpiñán asserts that in L2 settings, learners would benefit from an explicit focus on form approach to learning oblique relative clauses and that the order of introduction of relative clause types follow the Noun Phrase Accessibility Hierarchy.

Friesen & Bialystock, in *Control and representation in bilingualism: Implications for pedagogy* (Chapter 10), first explain the constructs of executive control and representation. Control entails the fluid operations used for intentional processing whereas representation refers to crystalized knowledge such as language abilities. As the authors point out, the research has consistently found that bilinguals have an advantage over monolinguals in executive control abilities but are disadvantaged in language abilities. The bilingual experience privileges executive control in that one language is being selected over another, that is, as bilinguals attend to one they must ignore or supress the other. Bilinguals have more experience than monolinguals using the control system and it becomes quite efficient. But, because learning is divided between two languages, language abilities are weaker. Indeed, bilinguals' access to both their languages is slower than monolinguals'. Friesen and Bialystock are concerned with the interplay of executive control and representation as they jointly contribute to behavior.

They focus their review of literature on studies that have examined both control and representation in a single study. Their rationale is that control systems manipulate and combine representations while at the same time these representations influence what information the control systems have to extract from the environment. These studies use metalinguistic tasks and language conflict tasks. The findings related to grammaticality judgment tasks reveal that bilinguals can outperform monolinguals on metalinguistic tasks that require control and that one interaction between control and representation is that less proficient bilinguals use executive control abilities to compensate for weaker language abilities. The findings related to verbal fluency indicate that if bilinguals and monolinguals are matched for linguistic knowledge, then the bilinguals are able to use their superior executive control to outperform monolinguals. Superior executive control abilities allow bilinguals to have less decline in their response rates over the time course of a lexical access task. Metalinguistic tasks and language conflict tasks require both language knowledge and the use of executive control to attend to relevant information and ignore competing irrelevant information. Bilinguals can utilize superior executive control abilities to efficiently manipulate language representation and ignore competing representations within a language.

From these findings and others that they present in the final section of the chapter, Friesen & Bialystok extrapolate the following pedagogical implications. Oral language knowledge in bilingual children, either as tested for or perceived by teachers, is an incomplete indicator of the children's ability to accomplish academic tasks. While representation is typically targeted in instruction, executive control, because it is important in language processing and benefits from experience, should also be targeted in the instructional context. They recommend immersion education because it provides the learners the opportunity to improve both language knowledge and executive control ability.

3.   Teacher education and awareness

VanPatten, in *Mental representation and skill in instructed SLA* (Chapter 1), adopts the position that by understanding second language acquisition processes teachers and curriculum developers alike will be better informed consumers of new developments in and proposals for language teaching. Important to his consideration of instructed SLA, VanPatten explains how mental representation develops as a result of three factors working together: (1) input, (2) Universal Grammar (UG), and (3) the parsing/processing mechanisms that mediate between the first two factors mentioned. He then addresses the question, Is the development of mental representation amenable to instruction?, which he answers in the negative. Because UG operates only on processed data from the input instruction does not and cannot directly cause mental representation to develop. Instruction cannot operate on information about the language, for example, grammar rules, explanations and other explicit information given during instruction. Moreover, mental representation does not result from drilling, correction, and any other external manipulation we find in many instructional formats. These attempt to induce or cause learning to happen do not influence mental representation.

VanPatten offers the example of yes/no questions in English. The structure of a sentence such as "Do you understand UG?" is often presented with a shorthand grammar rule such as "insert do before the verb and then switch the position of do and the subject". The UG account of the structure of this sentence has to do with whether the Comp that heads the Complementizer Phrase has the feature +Strong, which would force the movement of 'do' out of the Inflectional Phrase where it was generated and where it picked up tense features, as English is also +Strong for Tense.

Supplying learners information about the language will not affect mental representation, but, because input is a crucial factor in the development of mental representation, manipulating input in order to push acquisition is theoretically possible. Processing instruction, for example, provides structured input (a type of manipulated input) so that the processors are forced to process data in ways they might not under naturalistic conditions. See Wong (this volume) for examples of structured input activities. The point of manipulating input is to alter the data used by the processors and by UG in the development of a mental representation. Instructional settings need to supply learners with opportunities to process input, to maximize instructed learners' exposure to language data to construct a mental representation of the L2 grammar. This idea is echoed in several chapters of this volume.

VanPatten then examines the concept of skill as taken from the literature on cognitive psychology. Skill refers to the speed and accuracy with which people can perform certain actions or behaviors; speed and accuracy are key constructs in skill acquisition theory. As applied to language, skill refers to communication in all of its manifestations: interpretation (reading, listening), expression (writing, speaking) and negotiation (conversational interaction, turn taking). Skills develop with task and context-appropriate behavior. That is, people become skilled in doing something by engaging in the very behavior or activity in which they would like to become skilled. We learn to write by writing, read by reading, speak by speaking. If skills develop because of engagement with the very behaviors that people would like to develop, that is, with practice, then skills really cannot be taught. Rather, teachers and materials can only provide opportunities for skills to develop. VanPatten also addresses the popular idea of grammar as skill that has emerged from the position that declarative knowledge of grammar rules gets proceduralized and then automated. Thus we develop an ability to speak the L2. His position is that grammar, as the formal properties of language, is not a skill to be acquired. Grammar is abstract implicit knowledge that is tapped during linguistic performance. And so, VanPatten concludes that explicit instruction will affect neither language as mental representation nor language as skill. His position is that teachers should be aware that both mental representation and skill will evolve in learners based on their experiences with the L2 and it is teachers who provide the classroom experiences.

Behney & Gass, in *Interaction and the noun phrase accessibility hierarchy: A study using syntactic priming* (Chapter 3), address the relationship between input (the linguistic environment) and form selection by second language learners. The Accessibility Hierarchy accounts for differences among languages and attempts to predict the types of relative clauses a given language will have based on the hierarchy. The hierarchy is based on the grammatical role of the head noun phrase and its relative clause (RC) modification: subject (SU) > direct object (DO) > indirect object (IO) > oblique (OBL) > genitive (GEN) > object of comparison (OCOMP). If we know that a language has, for example, oblique relative clauses then we can predict that it has all the relative clause types higher in the hierarchy. Some research on second language acquisition has demonstrated that learners follow the orderings of the hierarchy; relative clause types higher in the hierarchy (SU and DO) are generally learned before those lower in the hierarchy. When learners are directed to produce RC types lower in the hierarchy, they produce RC types higher in the hierarchy but not vice versa. When instructed on direct object RC but not subject RC, learners generalize the instruction to subject RC but not vice versa. In fact, past research suggests that early stage learners produce few direct object relative clauses.

Behney & Gass conducted an experiment to determine if they could prime direct object relative clauses as opposed to subject relative clauses. Syntactic priming refers to the tendency to repeat previously uttered or comprehended syntactic structures when an alternate is available. Syntactic priming is a way to manipulate the input to which learners are exposed. The experimental context is a way of controlling the input and the interaction between interlocutors. Behney and Gass's experimental task required a learner to interact with a more proficient speaker of Italian. The task was a picture description task in which the researcher and learner took turns describing to each other cards on which appeared a single colored object and finding the card that matched the other's description. Unbeknownst to the learner, the researcher's cards were scripted so as to prime subject and direct object relative clauses equally. The learner's cards contained a prompt for a relative clause. Both researcher and learner had a box of description cards and a set of matching cards spread out before them. For each description they heard, they had to find the matching card and remove it.

Behney & Gass found a significant effect for prime type. More direct object RC targets are primed by direct object RC primes than by subject RC primes. Likewise, more subject RC targets are primed by subject RC primes than by direct object RC primes. The effects are greater with subject RC primes in that they yielded 81% subject RC targets whereas the direct object RC primes yielded 33% direct object RC targets. Behney and Gass conclude that priming, or extensive input, supplied in a conversational context can aid learning a complex structure. In a sense, syntactic priming can be likened to input flood, but the key element Behney and Gass would have educators consider is the interactional context to support flooding the input with a particular form. There is a relationship between input and form selection by learners that teachers should be aware of; the structure of their speech matters.

Schwieter & Ferreira, in *Language selection, control and conceptual-lexical development in bilinguals and multilinguals* (Chapter 11), review research on bilingual speech production, how the bilingual mind selects the language to produce and overcomes cross-linguistic lexical interference. They treat the areas of language and concept selection, language and lexical control, the variable nature of language selection and lexical control, before turning to the architecture of the system. Schwieter & Ferreira present several different (competing) explanations of what happens when going from the conceptual system to the lexicon such as the Concept Selection Hypothesis and Inhibitory Control Model, among the differences being that the former posits a language-specific selection mechanism at the conceptual level. They then present the results of research that demonstrate the variable nature of language selection and lexical control. These results argue against the Inhibitory Control Model because inhibitory control is variable.

The conceptual-lexical system of bilinguals is dynamic (as is all of L2 acquisition). General consensus supports the notion that bilinguals possess a dynamic system containing multiple levels of interactions and activation and several models have been developed. Schwieter & Ferreira refer to two models, the Modified Hierarchical Model and the Selection by Proficiency Model, to help explain the make-up and functionality of the dynamic nature of language selection and lexical processing in bilingual speech production. The Modified Hierarchical Model provides the blueprint for conceptual and lexical structure. The Selection by Proficiency Model illustrates the functionality of such a dynamic system. This model proposes that language learners with a weak L2 lexicon will rely on inhibitory control because they are unable to directly access the conceptual store without going through the L1. As learners develop a stronger L2 lexicon, they develop stronger L2 conceptual links. Consequently, they develop the ability to engage a L2-specific selection mechanism. The authors then present the bilingual advantage in executive control functions (see also Friesen & Bialystock, this chapter).

The implications of research on bilingual speech production for language teaching and learning are clear to the authors. They advocate immersion via a study abroad experience. The interesting perspective they have on the study abroad experience is that it provides learners the opportunity to practice suppressing (inhibiting) their L1's thus developing more efficient executive control. Also, they argue that the study abroad context provides learners the opportunity to develop the ability to conceptually mediate in two languages more quickly. Finally, the immersion experience would foster stronger L2 lexical-conceptual links.

Sunderman & Fancher, in *Lexical access in bilinguals and second language learners* (Chapter 12), describe the underlying mechanisms of L2 lexical processing. They review a selection of studies that examine lexical access/word recognition in isolation and then in sentence contexts. They present the results of studies that manipulated the relationship between target words: neighbors, homographs and cognates. An orthographic neighbor is a word that maintains length and letter position but differs by a single letter "gate/mate" in English, "gato/mato" in Spanish, and "gate/gato" and "mate/mato" crosslinguistically. Research findings indicate that when identifying L2 words both L1 and L2 neighbors affect processing. When identifying L1 words the amount of interference from L2 neighbors is related to the learners' L2 proficiency such that the more proficient the learner the greater the effect of L2 neighbors. Homographs are words that share orthographic features (i.e., form) but not meaning. Crosslinguistically in Spanish and English, the orthographic strings "pan", "soy" and "red" are homographs. Cognates are words that share both form and meaning across languages such as the exact Spanish-English cognate "piano" and the high degree cognate such as "cognate" and "cognado". The purpose in creating such word sets is to determine whether bilinguals activate one or both languages during lexical access. Research has clearly demonstrated a cognate priming effect for bilinguals and second language learners such that reading times are faster for cognate words than non-cognate words. Research with neighbors, homographs and cognates has also demonstrated that proficient bilinguals are unable to inhibit (i.e., shut off) their L1 during L2 lexical processing meaning that lexical processing is non-selective. That is, one language is not selected for activation over the other. A non-selective view of lexical access for less proficient bilinguals (i.e., second language learners) was found by asking L2 learners if form neighbors were translation equivalents. These were processed more slowly than non-neighbors.

Whereas non-selective access appears to be the default for lexical processing, research is emerging on the effect of sentence contexts that show when lexical processing is selective (i.e., bilinguals shut off one of their languages). Research shows that highly constrained sentences that greatly restrict the semantic context lead to selective access while low constraint sentences still show non-selective access. Other research has demonstrated that high semantic constraint in sentences supersedes the cognate priming effect. Low semantic constraint sentences still show the priming effect. Syntax may also be a cue to limit selectivity. Research has shown that the cognate priming effect disappears in sentences with high syntactic constraints (i.e., the syntax of the sentences is unique to the L2) compared to its presence in sentences with low syntactic constraints (i.e., the L1 and L2 share the syntactic pattern).

Sunderman & Fancher extrapolate three factors from the research findings that language teachers should consider. First, because lexical access is non-selective, teachers should be aware that learners are unable to turn off their L1. It is too easily activated by an L1 word, neighbors, homographs and cognates. Second, because L2 neighbors activate each other, teachers should be aware that L2 learners may make errors in word retrieval, and, importantly, that these errors do not reflect incomplete learning but are a natural outcome of lexical processing in bilinguals and learners. Third, they recommend that teaching semantic features that are strongly associated with a lexical item will help lower the activation level of form-related items. This recommendation is for richer input in the classroom environment.

Jarvis, O'Malley, Jing, Zhang, Hill, Chan & Sevostyanova, in *Cognitive foundations of crosslinguistic influence* (Chapter 13), present selected research findings on the cognitive consequences of SLA, bilingualism and multilingualism. The cognitive advantages of bilingualism and multilingualism involve enhanced language awareness and improved attentional control. In particular, enhanced language awareness is seen to provide bi/multilinguals the ability to recognize and make use of crosslinguistic similarities to help in language acquisition, enhanced creative thinking as a result of exposure to L2 perspectives, and greater communicative flexibility. Improved attentional control is related to the selectivity of attention and cognitive control of attention. The component of attention most affected appears to be inhibitory control (executive control), the ability to supress distracting, interfering or misleading information while performing a task. It also appears that bi/monolinguals have an advantage with another aspect of attentional control, i.e., monitoring processes. Research has emerged from a crosslinguistic influence perspective that provides a more nuanced account of the effect of inhibitory control. Bilinguals demonstrate less inhibitory control for languages that are very similar to each other. We can scale learners' inhibitory control abilities from weak to strong. Learners with stronger inhibitory control abilities are more successful in inhibiting negative interference from their L1 while performing L2/L3 tasks.

Perhaps the most intriguing findings of which language teachers could be aware, for their students and themselves, are those related to conceptualization. Conceptualization is thinking. It is the process of forming a temporary, mental representation of something a person experiences, remembers, learns about through communication with others or learns. For language processing, conceptualization can be seen as the process of making meaning from words and phrases and building them into full clauses, sentences, and paragraphs. Learners' L1 patterns of conceptualization influence their L2 production. For example, there is a relationship between grammatical aspect and event construal. Languages such as German and Swedish lack grammaticalized progressive/imperfective aspect and so speakers of these languages produce descriptions of witnessed events depicting those events as bounded and mention the endpoint of the event. By way of contrast, language such as English and Spanish do have grammaticalized progressive/imperfective aspect and speakers of these languages produce descriptions of the same witnessed events depicting them as unbounded. Research has shown that L1 German speakers refer to endpoints more often than L1 English speakers and the pattern carried over to their L2 production. Eye tracking data suggest that speakers of languages that mention endpoints direct more of their attention to endpoints in their L1 and L2. Research on very advanced Spanish-Swedish bilinguals (near native in Swedish) showed L2 influence on L1 conceptualization. A group of native Spanish speakers who had lived at least 12 years in Sweden performed an event description task and mentioned endpoints more often than a group of monolingual Spanish speakers. The less sensitive the Spanish speakers were to errors involving ungrammatical uses of imperfective aspect on a grammaticality judgment task, the more likely they were to mention endpoints in their descriptions. Although Jarvis et al. do not mention instruction, it does seem that teachers could be aware that the L2 acquisition of aspect is not merely a question of acquiring the right morphemes in Spanish or English, but it may entail acquiring the L2 perspective on event boundedness.

4.   Conclusion

L2 acquisition is opportunistic in that the right conditions must exist for it to take place. The quote I began this chapter with is worth repeating.

> [W]e can only provide opportunities in the classroom for acquisition to happen, but that these opportunities must be informed by what we know about acquisition. ...we [must] explore ways in which instruction can work *in unison with* acquisitional processes rather than *against* them" (Lee & VanPatten 2003: 23; emphasis original).

The works gathered in this volume have suggested ways in which instruction could work in unison with acquisitional processes:

1. We must understand acquisitional processes in order to work in unison with them (Behney & Gass; Jarvis et al.; VanPatten; Wong).
2. Instructional materials and practices can reflect empirical findings (Barcroft; Cuza et al.; Long & Rothman; Presson et al.).
3. Instructional sequencing might reflect acquisitional sequencing (Bruhn de Garavito; Perpiñán).
4. Opportunities to develop executive control for successful bilingual processing are important for long term success (Friesen & Bialystock; Schwieter & Ferreira; Sunderman & Fancher).

In conclusion, the works collected in this volume add much to the practice of instructed second language acquisition.

References

Lee, J.F., & VanPatten, B. (2003). *Making communicative language teaching happen* [2nd edition]. New York, NY: McGraw-Hill.

About the editor

Dr. John W. Schwieter holds a Bachelor of Arts (BA) in Spanish and a Master of Science in Language, Culture, and Education (MSEd) from Western Illinois University and a Doctor of Philosophy (PhD) in Spanish Language and Linguistics from the Florida State University. He has been an instructor of Spanish at Western Illinois University and Spoon River College in Macomb, Illinois and at Tallahassee Community College and Florida State University in Tallassee, Florida. In 2007, Schwieter joined Wilfrid Laurier University in Waterloo, Ontario, Canada as an assistant professor of Spanish and linguistics and as an associate professor of Spanish and linguistics in 2011. At this institution, he was recently named Faculty of Arts Teaching Scholar and his teaching, both in Spanish and English, spans from language courses to theoretical and applied linguistics. Outside of Canada and the United States, Schwieter also has extensive study abroad and international teaching experience in Latin America and Spain and has visited nearly 50 countries.

Dr. Schwieter's research interests include psycholinguistics, bilingualism, second language acquisition, the development of translation competence, and language teaching and learning. At Wilfrid Laurier University, he is the director of the Psycholinguistics and Language Acquisition Laboratory where research is conducted to explore the cognitive processes that support the acquisition and use of non-native languages. He has edited or authored *The development of translation competence: Theories and methodologies from cognitive science* (forthcoming, Cambridge Scholars Publishing); *Studies and global perspectives of second language teaching and learning* (Information Age Publishing); and *Cognition and bilingual speech: Psycholinguistic aspects of language production, processing, and inhibitory control* (Lambert Academic Publishing) and is currently working on The *Cambridge handbook of bilingual processing* (under contract with Cambridge University Press). Some of his other research has appeared in *Bilingualism: Language and Cognition*; *Diaspora, Indigenous, and Minority Education: An International Journal*; *Language Learning*; *Linguistic Approaches to Bilingualism*; *The Mental Lexicon*; and *Readings in Language Studies*.

About the contributors

Elizabeth Barajas
Purdue University
barajase@purdue.edu

Joe Barcroft
Washington University
barcroft@artsci.wustl.edu

Ellen Bialystok
York University
ellenb@yorku.ca

Jennifer Behney
Youngstown State University
behneyje@msu.edu

Joyce Bruhn de Garavito
Western University
joycebg@uwo.ca

Curtis Chan
Ohio University
curtismchan@gmail.com

Alejandro Cuza
Purdue University
acuza@purdue.edu

Colleen Davy
Carnegie Mellon University
cdavy1@andrew.cmu.edu

Eileen Fancher
Florida State University
ell09@my.fsu.edu

Aline Ferreira
Wilfrid Laurier University
ferr9730@mylaurier.ca

Deanna Friesen
York University
friesen@yorku.ca

Susan Gass
Michigan State University
gass@msu.edu

Jessica Hill
Ohio University
hill.jessicamarie@gmail.com

Scott Jarvis
Ohio University
jarvis@ohio.edu

Linye Jing
Ohio University
lj114910@ohio.edu

Gabrielle Klassen
University of Toronto
klas1590@mylaurier.ca

James F. Lee
University of New South Wales
james.lee@unsw.edu.au

Drew Long
University of Florida
long.andrew.b@gmail.com

Brian MacWhinney
Carnegie Mellon University
macw@cmu.edu

Lauren Miller
Purdue University
larzie314@yahoo.com

Michelle O'Malley
Ohio University
haugh@ohio.edu

Rocio Pérez-Tattam
Swansea University
r.s.perez-tattam@swansea.ac.uk

Silvia Perpiñán
Western University
sperpina@uwo.ca

Nora Presson
Carnegie Mellon University
presson@cmu.edu

Jason Rothman
University of Reading
jrothman@ufl.edu

Claudia Sadowski
Purdue University
claudiasadowski@gmail.com

John W. Schwieter
Wilfrid Laurier University
jschwieter@wlu.ca

Nadezhda Sevostyanova
Ohio University
nadine.sevost@gmail.com

Gretchen Sunderman
Florida State University
gsunderman@fsu.edu

Wynne Wong
Ohio State University
wong.240@osu.edu

Bill VanPatten
Michigan State University
bvp@msu.edu

Jing Zhang
Ohio University
jz164511@ohio.edu

Index